Ted Poston

Pioneer American Journalist

KATHLEEN A. HAUKE

UNIVERSITY OF GEORGIA PRESS *Athens & London*

© 1998 by the University of Georgia Press

Athens, Georgia 30602

All rights reserved

Designed by Walton Harris

Set in 10/13 Sabon by G & S Typesetters, Inc.

Printed and bound by Maple-Vail

The paper in this book meets the guidelines for
permanence and durability of the Committee on
Production Guidelines for Book Longevity of the
Council of Library Resources

Printed in the United States of America

02 01 00 99 98 C 5 4 3 2 1

Library of Congress Cataloging in Publication Data

Hauke, Kathleen A.

Ted Poston : pioneer American journalist /
Kathleen A. Hauke.

  p.   cm.

Includes bibliographical references and index.

ISBN 0-8203-2020-X (alk. paper)

1. Poston, Ted, 1906–1974.   2. Afro-American
journalists—20th century—Biography.   3. United
States—Race relations.   I. Title.

PN4874.P595H38   1998

070'.92—dc21

[b]   98-23104

                                          CIP

British Library Cataloging in Publication Data available

Excerpts from "The Dream Keeper" (page 1), "Mother to
Son" (page 11), and "Sylvester's Dying Bed" (page 187)
reprinted by permission of Harold Ober Associates, Inc.
© by the Estate of Langston Hughes.

For my husband, Richard; our children, Katy, Nellie, Andrew, Hank; my sister, Nellie Ann; and the memory of my mother, Katherine Emma Gall Armstrong

"Herein lie buried many things which if read with patience may show the strange meaning of being black here at the dawning of the Twentieth Century."

—W. E. B. DU BOIS, *The Souls of Black Folk*

Contents

Preface

Ted Poston played a pivotal role in opening up
a new field for blacks, but did so without
surrendering his madcap character.
—BILL ARTIS

Ted Poston infused an African American perspective into mainstream journalism as the first black to spend his career on a major metropolitan daily
newspaper. He softened readers with humor. But the humor masked bitterness and deflected personal sadness.

The mandate for this biography came from Ted Poston's best friend and
the executor of his estate, Henry Lee Moon, onetime public relations director for the National Association for the Advancement of Colored People
(NAACP). When I was working on an essay about Poston for the *Dictionary
of Literary Biography,* Moon showed me Poston's childhood short stories,
and I tried to get them published. The result was *The Dark Side of Hopkinsville* in 1991. Soon I told Moon, "Ted Poston had such an interesting life.
Someone should write his full biography." Moon said, "Why don't *you?*"
Thus, for ten years, I read, did research in archives, and collected oral histories of his childhood friends in Hopkinsville, Kentucky; of the World
War II Black Cabinet; of reporters from the "golden age" of the *New York
Post;* and of other colleagues in order to compile and document the history
of a man through whose eyes many white and black Americans witnessed
history in the making.

Ted Poston's parents were Kentucky educators at the turn of the century,
and his older brothers became right-hand men to black nationalist Marcus
Garvey during the 1920s. Ted put himself through college as a railroad porter
and dining car waiter. He went to Russia in 1932 with a group of twenty-
one other blacks to make a film on American racism. As city editor of the
black *Amsterdam News* and a labor sympathizer, he helped Heywood
Broun found the American Newspaper Guild in 1935. After being fired for
union organizing, he joined the Federal Writers' Project of the New Deal's

Works Progress Administration. Then, through his colorful writing, he gained a foothold on the white *New York Post.*

Robert C. Weaver and Mary McLeod Bethune of President Franklin D. Roosevelt's Black Cabinet lured him to Washington for the five years of World War II. He then returned to New York and, under the liberal publisher Dorothy Schiff and editor James A. Wechsler, developed into an ace reporter for the *Post.*

Through his long friendships with Henry Lee Moon and Thurgood Marshall he had imbibed the details of and insight into the endeavors of the National Association for the Advancement of Colored People and its quest to eliminate segregation's legal status. While reporting the Scottsboro trial in Jim Crow–infested Alabama in 1932, he used trickster techniques to save his neck. He covered Martin Luther King, Jr., during the Montgomery, Alabama, bus boycott and in 1957–59 reported on the desegregation of Little Rock Central High, in Arkansas, living in one bedroom at "headquarters," the home of Little Rock's NAACP head, Daisy Bates, and her husband, L. C., who published the *Arkansas State Press.* He was on the scene of riots in Harlem and in Cicero, Illinois, and for the trials for the murderers of Emmett Till and Medgar Evers.

A coterie of young black journalists who followed in his steps—Robert Maynard, editor and publisher of the *Oakland Tribune,* was one—regarded him as the "dean of black journalists." Poston wore that mantle with a charming, gregarious self-confidence, Fern Eckman says: "He was breezy, accomplished, sophisticated. . . . Ted Poston would have made it in any society . . . one of that unquenchable unconquerable elite." His history parallels the nation's; his viewpoint on race relations is an insider's.

It was a research problem that I had not known Ted Poston personally. I wanted to ask him to relate his Russia stories and those that he called "The Little Red Cars," about working on the railroad. I wondered about his sister Lillian and why she went to the mental hospital; what his relationship was with his sisters after their mother died; and whether and how his surviving siblings had provided emotional support for each other.

Following interviews and perusal of archives, I have had to make judgments about whose version of Ted Poston is reliable. His publisher, Dorothy Schiff, declined to be interviewed. In many instances, unverifiable information is all one has to go on. Few Poston letters and no diaries have surfaced. All but a smattering of Poston papers—those in Moon's possession—have vanished. The source of the *New York Post* on microfilm was the New York Public Library Annex, and that archive did not lend. A National Endowment for the Humanities Summer Stipend enabled me to go to New York to locate and photocopy all of Poston's extant journalistic work. Photographs of Poston's forebears were described to me, but none turned up. His second wife, Marie, could be seen only in grainy reproductions in *Ebony* and *Jet*. No picture of his first wife, Miriam Rivers, has surfaced. And where did the death mask of brother Robert go, which Robert's wife, Augusta Savage, had sculpted before his burial in Hopkinsville in 1924?

Ted Poston's problem as a black journalist was American racism and where and how he could fit into the scheme for resistance. He dealt with discrimination by means of joviality and amusing stories, but this covered a sadness and loneliness he seemed to have carried since he was ten years old, when his mother died. In some ways, even the grown Ted Poston was like a terminally ill child whom Elisabeth Kubler-Ross described; she could face her end if she knew the ambulance would come and blow its siren and flash its red light for her. Poston held listeners with his stories as he, too, fought mortality. He was here, and he mattered. This biography aims to be a small Ted Poston light that flashes out Horace's words, "I am not altogether dead."

The little that Poston penned of his forebears appears in *The Dark Side of Hopkinsville*. It proves that once there was the Poston family and once it was happy. The public record certifies that three Poston sons—Robert, Ulysses, and Ted—amounted to something.

Ted Poston was a human being with flaws but also a gifted writer who loved America and carved opportunities to use journalism as a vehicle to improve the country. His family in Hopkinsville in the early twentieth century had sparked a fire in him that propelled him through the intense years when American blacks were struggling to be considered valued American citizens.

Joel Dreyfuss wrote on his death, "For long periods of time, Poston was the only black reporter on any major white-owned newspaper in the country" and that being the first black at something is "one experience many members of my generation have been spared." That is why Dreyfuss "was not particularly impressed by the disheveled old man" who "limped over to my desk in the cramped city room of the *New York Post* to shake my hand the first day I worked there." But that was before Dreyfuss had learned the man's story and how Poston had breached barriers.

Acknowledgments

Ersa Poston gave me my start when she set me on the road to Henry Lee Moon and Allison Williams; Williams led the way to Rat Joiner and Mary Duncan Wilson; Fern Eckman made the connection with Paul Sann and George Trow; Ruth Banks knew how to contact Diana Bonnor Lewis, who said, "Talk to Kenneth Clark." Clark said, "Nancy Hicks Maynard feels indebted to Ted." Guts made me dial Ellen Tarry. Joe Kahn sent me to the *Post* archives. All the associations led to others. Sadly, Henry Lee Moon, Allison Williams, Rat Joiner, Mary Duncan, Bill Trent, Robert C. Weaver, Paul Sann, Diana Bonnor Lewis, and Bob Maynard did not live to see that the end was reached.

Interviewees took time out of crowded schedules to honor Ted Poston. Nancy Hicks Maynard was in law school, helping her husband run the *Oakland Tribune,* and raising young children, yet she met me for our interview on Tressider Plaza at Stanford University one afternoon before she headed home. When I thanked her, she said, "For anyone but Ted, I would have been in Guam. For Ted, yeah!"

I am grateful to the inventor of instant photocopying—the technological replacement for time-consuming note-taking. During the winter of 1943, Arna Bontemps and Langston Hughes had excitedly written to each other of postwar planning and that Negro papers might be photographed and put on something called microfilm so that they would not be lost to history.[1] That speculation came to pass, and the technique assisted me in this project. I am also grateful to Hulda Wilson of Woodruff Library, Atlanta University Center, for the use of a carrel for two years while I was putting this manuscript together.

Finally, thanks to Richard L. Hauke, who did not resist when I envisioned this book. He cared for our children the summer I was in New York, and he held our home together when I taught one autumn in Hopkinsville so I could poke around in Poston's native place. When I had to leave teaching to keep the research going, he supplied tape recorders, film, computer. He patiently, stoically accepted it when my anticipated two-year project ran to fifteen years. In the end, he served as first reader.

Editorial Note

Unacknowledged quotations in the text have come either from letters or interviews with the source named. Poston's articles which I found only in the *Post* clipping files had no page numbers on them, only the date of publication. Apparently they appeared in editions of the paper other than the one that was microfilmed for the historical record.

Readers who want more information than is in the text should consult the notes, which contain some incidental information or amplification.

The many years of my reading, interviewing, and researching archives for traces of Ted Poston led to the acquisition of much material on him. Those documents have been placed in the archives of the Auburn Avenue Research Library on African American History and Culture, Atlanta, Georgia. Print-out copies of all Poston's extant writings have been given to the Schomburg Center for Research in Black Culture of the New York Public Library.

1

· ·

Childhood

· ·

1906–1917

Bring me all your dreams,
You dreamers . . .
That I may wrap them . . .
Away from the too-rough fingers
Of the world.
—LANGSTON HUGHES, "The Dream Keeper"

Ted Poston was born on the fourth of July 1906 in Hopkinsville, Kentucky. He joked that all of America celebrated his birthday. Small-town life seemed salubrious, but Ted learned to tread a fine line between the black and white worlds. Subtly, consistently, observation of his small border-state town would indoctrinate him in the idea that subordinated groups have a way of getting around oppression even as the dominant class operates according to its unconscious agenda. Like many blacks, Ted Poston would try to disprove white attitudes that everything black was hideous. In W. E. B. Du Bois's words, "If they fought for freedom, they were beasts; if they did not fight, they were born slaves. If they cowered on the plantations, they loved slavery; if they ran away, they were lazy loafers." [1]

With his claim that the whole nation celebrated his birthday, Poston not only included himself on the American scene but made himself the star of the Fourth of July, countering Frederick Douglass's assertion that to the black, the Fourth of July "reveals to him . . . the gross injustice and cruelty to which he is the constant victim." [2] Throughout his life, Poston aggressively declared himself a true American and ridiculed those who would refuse him admittance to the national banquet.

Ted Poston's father, Ephraim (called Eph, pronounced Eeph), was born the same decade as Du Bois, on October 15, 1863, in Clarksville, Tennessee, twenty-five miles south of Hopkinsville.[3] Situated on the bank of the Cumberland River, Clarksville was a flourishing tobacco and commercial receiving and shipping center.[4] Dozens of steamboats plied the river.[5] The 1860 census listed twenty-two white Postons in Clarksville as heads of households. Ephraim's parents, Ephraim and Louisa Rivers Poston, doubtless were named for one of them. Ted's peer, white newspaper editor and publisher Elizabeth Poston McHarry, says Ted told her that the Postons of Clarksville had been Quakers. Probably Eph's parents' "owner" had been John Hamill Poston, a merchant who sold "almost every article to be found in a store in the western country."[6] From the white Postons, Eph's people would have learned contemporary "delicacy of sentiment and refined manners," for in a typical colored home, one would find "not barren walls and carpetless floors, but rooms neatly furnished, prints, chromos, engravings gracing the walls, and a stand of books—modern and ancient history—the novelists, Scott, Thackeray, Dickens, some of the poets, Longfellow, Moore and Shakespeare."[7] Idealistic white teachers came from the North to teach at mission schools such as those in which the elder Postons were educated. They laid the foundation of the institutions that became colleges[8]—the centers of a "training in leadership and ideals for the whole Negro race."[9] College then meant a school that taught all subjects at every grade level—starting with basic literacy. That education became "the salvation of the South and the Negro." Ted Poston's parents were part of the "little group of trained leadership which grew by leaps and bounds" from those early efforts.[10] Young people such as Eph Poston attended the mission schools for a few months, then went out to teach as best they could, returning for additional study until a course was finished.

Ted's mother, Mollie Cox, grew up at a train stop on the Nashville and Hopkinsville road, Bell's Station, three miles north of the Kentucky-Tennessee state line. Her mother, Hettie Peay Cox, was raised on the Peay plantation, which one hundred years later would be encompassed by the Fort Campbell military complex.[11] Before passenger trains provided employment, black males toiled on the plantations where they had once been slaves. On their own, the most that black farmers could hope for was to sharecrop, and the introduction of machinery foreclosed even that opportunity. "No blacks owned farms in our neighborhood," says Brooks Major of Hopkinsville Community College.

Ephraim Poston and Mollie Cox met at Nashville's Roger Williams University, the teacher-training college from which Ephraim graduated in 1886.[12]

Kentucky's state superintendent of public instruction then "viewed blacks as 'a non-conformable element,' who at best could acquire only the basics of education." [13] It was in this unhelpful Kentucky-Tennessee environment that Ephraim Poston and Mollie Cox committed their lives to the education of their children and their people.

Both were acutely aware of racial discrimination. After the Fifteenth Amendment in 1870 guaranteed black males the right to vote, terrorist groups such as the Ku Klux Klan prevented them from exercising the right. On March 1, 1875, a Civil Rights Act was passed designed to protect Negroes against discrimination in hotels, railroads, steamboats, theaters, and other places of amusement, but conflict ensued. After hearing several cases of violation of that Civil Rights Act, the Supreme Court decided in 1883 that the act was unconstitutional, and segregation gripped the country for the next several generations.

The Postons were married on December 22, 1887, at Mollie's home. Mollie was fifteen years old, Eph twenty-three. [14] Expecting their first child in 1888, the hopeful pair went north along a bit of the Cherokee Indians' Trail of Tears to the promising town of Hopkinsville, where they established their family.

Hopkinsville was a "tranquil backwater," unknown outside the state except to a "few visiting tobacco-buyers." Horses and buggies were common personal transportation until 1909, when automobiles began to appear on the dirt roads. Life moved with "such sublime peacefulness" that when the city fathers decided to prohibit hogs and cows from walking the streets unattended, the community was "thrown into an uproar." [15] In 1892 native son Adlai Stevenson had been elected vice-president of the United States when the honest Democrat Grover Cleveland was elected president for the second time. Hopkinsville celebrated with torchlights and flags, and whiskey "flowed as easily as talk." [16] Cleveland made moderate use of the patronage system of doling out government jobs. Patronage was the avenue to a public job before there was civil service. [17]

Hopkinsville's town hangout was the Louisville and Nashville railroad station, where black hack driver Uncle Billy Evans was the friendly local interface between the races. [18] When the Postons arrived, the main newspaper was the *South Kentuckian,* which claimed, "We're Democratic to the backbone." The Democrats' most recent president, Grover Cleveland, had been the "clean government" candidate who pursued a conscientious, independent course. The *South Kentuckian* promoted "excursion trips by train to such places as Niagara Falls, California, Chicago, and the World's Fairs." [19] The excursions were "considered the thing to do by [white] Hopkinsville society." Citizens of what Ted called "the dark side of Hopkinsville," however, were permitted along only as waiters and porters.

Literate households, both black and white, subscribed to the *Ladies' Home Journal*. That periodical united the citizens in a vision of domesticity to which both groups aspired. Because they were mere adjuncts to whites' comfortable living, however, few blacks had much opportunity to seek their own comfort. Most worked in white households, as "part of the family," but blacks' personal lives were little known by whites. They recognized their "place" and accepted it on the surface, but their minds roiled over how to make changes. Ted's boyhood friend J. T. Lynch says "We didn't have any black leaders beyond everyone requiring us to behave. No black person had influence in town government because the town was so deeply segregated. No one from the black community had any power."

By 1892, Mollie Poston had given birth to three boys—Frederick Douglass (1888), Robert Lincoln (1890), and Ulysses Simpson (1892), their names a testament to the racially proud yet patriotic tendencies of the family. As they grew, the boys noticed the white neighborhood where streets were shaded by trees that sat back "behind long shrub-studded lawns." Everything had "an air of security, and the church spires seemed genuine symbols of eternity." But an experience common to both black and white neighborhoods was the fragrance of seasons. "In autumn, when the tobacco was being fired . . . smoke rose to the eaves. . . . In the smokehouse, a smudge fire of hickory and sassafras chips sent incense drifting up to the bacon, the sausage, and the shoulders of ham. . . . The woods were full of dogwood, redbud . . . and May apples . . . the mandrake of the Bible, with a blossom in May and a fruit that is ready to eat in late June." [20] Boys learned to hunt quail and rabbits in the woods. Brooks and ponds teemed with fish, inviting the children with fishing poles to their banks. [21]

Downtown, Hopper Brothers' bookstore employed a clairvoyant teenager, Edgar Cayce, to unlock the door each morning, raise the summer shades, and let the awning down. [22] Cayce's shop sold textbooks used in the local schools and at the colleges for whites—South Kentucky College, Baptist Girls' College, and Ferrell's School for Boys, the principal seats of learning.

In their separate world, blacks at "M. and F. College" (Male and Female) used books handed down from whites. At M. and F., Mollie Cox Poston completed the education she had interrupted when she married. Subsequently, all of Eph and Mollie's children would study at M. and F., except for Ted, because a public high school was erected "for colored" in 1917. The eldest Poston sons and Eph—"Professor Poston"—himself, would teach at M. and F. at various times. [23]

Ephraim, Jr., was born in 1893 and daughters Roberta in 1895 and Lillian in 1903. In 1906, when their last child was born, they named him Theodore Roosevelt Augustus Major Poston (which became TRAMP as acronym). Ulysses Poston would one day note that under President Theodore Roosevelt, his baby brother's namesake, "the Negro race of this country received the largest amount of patronage and recognition ever accorded it since Reconstruction Days." Ulysses would also laud that Roosevelt for his courage in inviting black educator Booker T. Washington to the White House as a dinner guest.[24]

From 1904 to 1909, Christian County, including Hopkinsville, suffered unrest and organized lawlessness because of problems with the source of the local livelihood, tobacco.[25] When Ted was barely walking, on December 7, 1907, the night riders—tobacco farmers irate over low tobacco prices—raided the city.[26] The governor had to send troops to quell the disturbance.

Grandparents were key parts of both black and white worlds. They were potent forces who passed their time gossiping, dipping snuff, and admonishing the young.[27] Ted would describe family relationships in his story "The Werewolf of Woolworth's," in which he told of how Grandma Hettie scared his sister Lillian with ghost stories at night. Once Grandma Hettie remembered that the wash was still hanging on the line and told Lillian to go get it. Ted says, "Lillian didn't dare to disobey. . . . She knew perfectly well the old lady would just tell her, 'I don't take no back-sass from no grandchildren nohow. Even if they is growing up girls. Get on out there fore I go up side your head.' So, shaking in every bone and sinew, poor Lillian went out there to get that wash."[28]

When Lillian fell and scraped her elbows to the bone on that occasion, Dr. Bankie Moore tended her. Tall, heavyset Dr. Moore was a quiet and unassuming physician who had built a hospital for blacks because the community hospital was segregated. He and his wife, a nurse, were very religious members of the Postons' own Virginia Street Baptist Church.

The church played a central role in black life. Two Poston cousins, Johnella Braxton Palmer and Lydia Braxton Moten, maintain, "We were *all* taught black pride there. We enjoyed going to church."[29] There Ted imbibed the beliefs that would remain constant in his value system. Johnella Braxton Palmer suggests an opportunistic motivation for the family's church attendance as well: "Every family here who wants to be a desirable, respected family comes up in the church. Ted came from a Christian and professional family. To be looked upon as stable citizens, you grew up in the church."[30]

Poston's stories hint at conflict underneath the surface harmony of Hopkinsville's whites and blacks. When the Ku Klux Klan ceased using terror to prevent black men from exercising their right to vote, Dan Massie's picnic grove would be enlisted for the enjoyment of three thousand Negroes on election day. White political operatives paid Massie to give the blacks food and alcohol to keep them from the polls.

Racial hierarchies were subtly instilled in black children even by their schoolteachers. Ted's sweetheart, Mary Duncan, for example, came from the prominent family of dark-skinned Dr. James Duncan. But because of Mary's light skin, inherited from her mulatto mother, she was considered especially beautiful and was cast by the fifth and sixth grade teacher H. Belle LaPrade as Sleeping Beauty in the school play, as told in Ted's story "The Revolt of the Evil Fairies." But because Ted's skin was so dark, LaPrade would never let the effervescent boy play Prince Charming to his beloved Sleeping Beauty. LaPrade was merely following the hidden transcript of the dominant culture that white and light were desirable; blacks should keep back.

Dark Ted pondered this discrimination, but he was a free spirit and developed "a way of looking out for himself," says Allison Williams. Williams, light-skinned and handsome, was always cast as one of the "good fairies" in the "annual dramatic offering." [31]

Light-skinned Fannie Bronston Postell was principal of Ted's Booker T. Washington Colored Grammar School and a founder of Crispus Attucks High School. [32] She taught and spoke Latin and French, her students remember. She had graduated from Kentucky's Berea College and "had class about her. They taught 'em to be ladies up there," says Williams. [33] Postell, too, contributed to the notion that light-skinned Negroes were superior to dark-skinned. She taught piano in her home after school and required her dark-skinned students to use the side door, as if they were servants, a former student, Alberta Holloway, remembers. Postell recognized that the "blue veins," the light-skinned Negroes, did not have the power of whites, yet they asserted dominance among the "quality colored folks" in town.

The Postells were most prominent of the blue veins, but the smartly dressed mortician, Ed W. Glass, was another fair-skinned Negro who was well respected locally. His ad called him "The Old Reliable, Funeral Director and Embalmer." [34] Charles Bronaugh says, "We had a lot of very, very good Negro businessmen" of all racial hues. "It made you feel proud to be a Negro in Hopkinsville because we had something on the ball." [35] The "quality colored folks" achieved in ways that countered the dominant culture's image of all blacks as inferior.

In his memoir, Ted denigrates the light-skinned members of the "blue-veined society" but otherwise describes both races by perceived character—"quality colored folks" and "quality white folks." The family of Ted's friend

Jennie Knight was light and "quality." Jennie's father, Will Knight, had one of the best jobs held by any black person—railway mail clerk. His steady government employ provided a secure income that made others in the community regard the Knights as prosperous.[36] Jennie recalls that when her father's train passed through Hopkinsville "we'd take his meals to him—a big basket with hot coffee, steak and potatoes." His job was dangerous: "He had to carry a gun on the train because there were so many mail robberies." People whom Ted did not describe as "quality" would be "the ones who didn't try," according to Jennie. "It wasn't just financial success. None of us had much money although some had more than others." For Ted, Jennie's lovely home on Fourth Street was a friendly place with good conversation. "People would stop by and whatever Mama was doing, she'd stop and talk to them," Jennie says. "Ted always had a lot to talk about, and he was always a topic of conversation."

The hub of Ted Poston's child life was Hayes Street. His gray two-story frame house with white trim contained indoor plumbing, several bedrooms, and a library.[37] Across from the Postons lived Dr. James S. May, who was cause for excitement in town when he was gunned down one afternoon by J. B. Pettus, a tailor.[38] Rumor had it that Pettus was having an affair with Dr. May's wife. Another neighbor, Emma Bacon, remembers good times: "All the neighbor children would go to the Little River to swim" or to the dam just below the waterworks because it had a solid rock bottom. "These were all fun places." Black and white children used the same swimming holes but consecutively.[39] Besides swimming, Ted was most fond of fishing.[40] For both black and white residents, "The days were long and hot. . . . Women stayed indoors, canning fruits and vegetables. . . . [One] was glad to get away for long hours beside the water, dreaming as he waited for a fish to come and take the worm he offered."[41] Ted would combine fishing with reading.[42]

Both racial groups took pride in acquiring personal libraries although Hopkinsville's public library, built through Andrew Carnegie's philanthropy, was off-limits to colored people. To compensate, Mary Duncan's father "bought all the books, magazines, music we needed." The "quality" white and colored folks read the *Louisville Courier-Journal* with its syndicated cartoon "Hambone's Meditations," featuring a wise old pipe-smoking Negro man who dispensed a homespun philosophy.[43] Hambone illustrated for Ted that the world was attracted to blacks who were witty and amusing. Henry Lee Moon culled from Ted's later tall tales that Hopkinsville was full of incipient wise and witty Hambones such as Ted's pal Rat Joiner, who "routed the Klan in a classic maneuver worthy of a great tactician." Of course, the "town intellectual and arbiter of all community disputes [was] Professor Eph Poston," Moon relates, tongue-in-cheek. "There were, to be sure, some white folk around—minor characters like the mayor, the banker, the judge, the newspaper editor and the owner of the Rex Theatre, the town's movie house. But these served mainly as background and props for the Black cast."[44]

Discipline of the black Hopkinsville children was imposed by the whole neighborhood, for the honor of the race was at stake. One was "as much raised by the neighbors as by your parents. If you done somethin' wrong at somebody else's house, they'd whup you for it. Your parent would say, 'Thank you,' and then whup you hisself."[45] The nature of community discipline was apparent in one of Ted Poston's 1930s book reviews when he wrote of *The Battle of the Bloods:* "In case the depression has you in its grip . . . and you can't afford the price, you can still read the book by just closing your eyes and remembering every one of the old orations you heard in your childhood about 'The Progress of the Negro Race.'"[46] Ted thought that the white writer of that book exaggerated, however, in being certain that "the Negro is the backbone of American civilization," with the greatest moral fiber, the greatest strength of character, the economic agricultural nucleus, the staunchest patriotism, and the only true religion. Ted would eventually try to show black virtues himself but he did not go overboard about it.

Ted dealt throughout his life with discrimination in a way that he learned in Hopkinsville. He ignored it. Williams says:

> There was nothing you could do about it. If you vented your anger on some white who had mistreated you, and you had some influential white friends, that was all right. But you couldn't continue that. Most Negroes built up a defense, like in going the other way.
>
> Or, certain things they accepted and laughed it off. [In history] Denmark Vesey was militant, but look what it got him, death. When the Ninth Cavalry resented being sent to Brownsville, Texas, they took the situation into their own hands and look what happened. The government hung thirteen of them in one day. That shows you there wasn't nothin' you could do about it.

As a dark-skinned black, Ted was less likely to be given the leeway a light-skinned black would get from whites. For Ted, the injustice of America to her black citizens became a subject of derisive humor.[47]

The realities of life beyond their local world struck all the Poston family by 1912 when Ted was an observant six-year-old. Grandma Hettie had died;

mother Mollie was supervisor of domestic science for colored in Christian and Trigg Counties; and Ted started school. Brother Robert Poston—whom Ted referred to in his stories as "B'Rob"—was twenty-two and leaving straitlaced Walden College in Nashville for Washington and Boston.[48] En route, he stopped home with the family in Hopkinsville and told Ted that he should regard himself as "as good as anybody" and that he must always respect himself whether or not society respected him in return.

Robert had lived with undeserved disrespect and would tell of it in the *Negro World*. He went to the Emerson School in Boston to sharpen his oratorical skills and experienced intraracial disloyalty there that embittered him even toward mulattoes. Robert entered a restaurant with a light-skinned friend who was "imbued with the same racial feeling as I was . . . a burning desire to do something to help this race of ours." The friend was allowed in; dark-skinned Robert was ejected. Robert expected to see his friend immediately come out, but he "remained at his meal." While dining, the "friend" decided to "pass" into the white world. When he exited the restaurant, he said to the furious Robert, "What is the need of my being colored?" Robert excoriated him: "I presume you realize . . . the great denial you are making. . . . The man who abused your mother did not stop to see whether you were a boy or a girl . . . you secured your education from the sweat and toil of that mother who brought you into being almost at the doors of death. If you pass over, you know that if that mother came to visit you in Boston, you must deny her." Robert concluded, "That was my answer." He admonished the friend, "If you wish to go over, go ahead and God bless you: good-bye." Then Robert "shook the dust off my feet from that day" so far as that friend was concerned.[49] None of the Postons, "salt-water Negroes" as Ted called them, had the option to "pass over."

Ted spent the years 1912 to 1917, ages six to ten, happily conscious mostly that he was his family's cherished youngest child. In wonderment he observed the death in March 1914 of artistically talented Ephraim, Jr., his fourth oldest brother, of a sarcoma on the neck and what that passage took from his family's zeal.

As an adult, Ted never referred to unhappy events of his youth. Instead, he turned his past into oral comic anecdote for the pleasure of listeners, but the reality of Poston's family life was grimmer than he let on. His oldest sister, Roberta, born in 1895, graduated from Kentucky Normal and Industrial Institute in Frankfort in 1916, trained to teach in a rural black Kentucky school, like the one described in the *Biennial Report of the Superintendent of Public Instruction:* "a little house on a little ground, with a little equipment and a little attendance from a little district having little ideals of education, where a teacher . . . for a little period of her life, for a little term during the year, at a little salary, taught little children little things in a little way." [50]

On the side, Roberta helped keep her working parents' home going and followed the family avocation of writing poetry. The male Postons all hankered to wield a journalistic influence in America but assumed that it probably would occur within a black milieu, although Eph had published *Pastoral Poems* in 1906 and from 1908 to 1912 a series of "Political Satires" in Hopkinsville's white *Kentucky New Era*. [51]

Ted told Henry Lee Moon that his father may have been an intellectual leader, but financial acumen eluded him. The Postons lost their property on Hayes Street early in 1917. [52] Eph might have forfeited his assets when he sold made-to-measure suits as Ted claims in his story "Cousin Blind Mary"; surviving cohorts of the Postons did not know. [53] Eph and his eldest sons operated a tiny grocery in 1907; it failed. Perhaps Eph's dips into political journalism and literature ruined the family financially.

Losing their home was not the worst event of 1917. On May 11, Ted's forty-three-year-old mother took to her bed with Bright's disease, inflammation of the kidneys. [54] Dr. May was summoned, and Ted, now ten, watched his mother's quick decline. Mollie Poston had given birth eight times, starting at age sixteen. She had kept the family larder filled with canned goods and the smokehouse full of hams and bacon; she had corrected Ted's grammar and assured him that his color was a beautiful chocolate brown. She had also gone around Christian and Trigg Counties in horse and buggy boosting the morale of teachers in one-room schools and instructing black homemakers how to preserve fruits and vegetables through canning. Her death at 4:30 A.M. on May 31 robbed Ted of his feeling of being unconditionally loved.

Psychologically, Ted's childhood was now over, and loneliness enveloped him, although he usually succeeded in hiding it. Eventually he would deal with his bewilderment, but during the summer of 1917 he clung to his equally bereft "Papa," Eph, and cogitated on survival strategies. Because he could not anticipate when caring people might again be taken from him, it was safer to keep his dreams to himself. More tragedies soon followed, but the loss of his mother marked the end for Ted of Hopkinsville as Eden. About his life after this juncture, Ted would tell no comical personal stories.

2

End of Innocence

1917–1924

> . . . all the time
> I'se been a'climbin' on. . . .
> So, boy, don't you turn back. . . .
> Don't you fall now—. . . .
> —LANGSTON HUGHES, "Mother to Son"

Mollie Poston had instilled in Ted the traits needed to keep climbing—a belief in himself, good English, native intelligence, and curiosity. He was essentially on his own from sixth grade through high school and college. His petite sister Roberta, age twenty, became the "mama figure" in the household, as Allison Williams remembers, but Ted was a headache for Roberta and a nuisance to Lillian, who was just two days shy of her fourteenth birthday when her mother died. "Roberta tried to make Ted behave, but trying to make Ted do anything was an outlandish job because he had a mind of his own." Much of the time there was no woman in the house. Robert was teaching at M. and F., reading all the newspapers he could get his hands on, and preoccupied with discussing politics with Eph.

His cousin Mary Belle Braxton, Ted's favorite fishing companion, lived in the neighborhood, but Ted mostly hung out with such age-mates as Rat Joiner of Billy Goat Hill and Reuben "Tack-Haired" Baker.[1] Theodore Roosevelt Joiner, called "Rat" by blacks and "Theodore" by whites, was tiny, but Ted portrayed him as so tough as to rival the first black heavyweight champion, Jack Johnson. Reuben was a light-brown friend of Ted's whose hair kinks were so tight they looked like tacks on his head.

At Crispus Attucks High School, Ted learned chemistry from Claybron W. Merriweather, a part-time lawyer who also published bucolic verse. Merriweather was known as one who "reads, thinks, analyzes, discriminates, writes. . . . [He] has observed and studied the Negro, his persistent smile, his loud laughter and sunny disposition under conditions that would have discouraged most men." [2] Ted imitated those characteristics. Classmates recall his appealing personality. Frances Wagner Knight, another top scholar in Ted's graduating class, who also attended Sunday school with Ted and Lillian, says he was "jolly and humorous, talking funny in all he would say or do." She surmises, "I don't think Ted went in for winning; he didn't *strive* to be at the head of the class. From way back, he was interested in people, a *good listener.*" Jasper Brown says, "Ted was popular, period. He could talk to anybody. It didn't matter about a person's background. He was never stuck up, never hostile."

Ted's romance with Mary Duncan was an important part of his high school years. Mary was three years younger than he, a member of a clique called the "Big Six." [3] Ted composed love letters to her and cut paper dolls out of the *Ladies' Home Journal* for her. He would walk by Mary's house after school to listen to her practicing the piano. Getting close to Mary, however, was difficult because of her parents' strictures.

Sometimes they met at the home of Jennie Knight, one of the "Big Six." Jennie's parents provided a gathering place for black teenagers that the community did not. She says, "People came to my house after the basketball games or for any excuse. We had parties with a three-piece orchestra— piano, bass fiddle, and horn. We rolled up the rugs, pushed the furniture back and danced all around four rooms." Of dancing with Ted, Mary Duncan remembered that "being in his arms was always thrilling."

Getting to and from the parties was a part of the pleasure that was denied Mary, however. The boys would walk to collect the girls. By the time they arrived at the party, fifteen or twenty of them would be there. At the end they would all "leave together and drop kids off." But Mary was excluded because "my father would take me and say, 'You telephone me when it's time to come home.'" Dr. Duncan never wanted Mary to walk home with her group because he was afraid she would "get into mischief." When she went to Sunday school, he would say, "I will pick you up after church"; otherwise she could not go. One of the things she wanted to do most was "to walk home in the dark with my friends."

Going to the movies was the Saturday pastime for the youth of Hopkinsville; Negroes were confined to the balcony. [4] The best part of going to church and the movies for Ted was being with Mary. At the movies, the couple's desire for friendly intimacy was not thwarted, for there Mary and Ted would "sit up in the segregated Rex Theatre, watch Clara Bow, and hold hands," she says. Ted would come up the stairs, "look around to see where I was sitting, then slide into the seat beside me and we would steal kisses. We were unconcerned that we couldn't sit with the white people. We had all the fun we wanted upstairs in the balcony."

Mary feels that she and Ted had "a beautiful friendship" because "the love was mutual." She resented the fact that they could not go to the public library and were barred from some of the parks, but "we didn't go into deep discussions about it. We were too young, and I was too protected. My father tried in every way to keep me from being hurt by [racial] slights. We just went on our merry way." To the end of her life, Mary shuffled cards the way Ted had taught her sixty years earlier. She says, "I will never forget Ted even though I was age fifteen when we were in love." Jennie Baker confirms that "Ted was just wild about Mary. She *was* a darling girl and Ted adored her. I think it had a more lasting effect on him than it did on Mary because Ted married several times."

As a teenager, Ted needed to earn his own way. Every June morning from 1916 to 1924, for example, he and his friends would run the eight miles to Pembroke to pick strawberries for the Christian County Strawberry Growers' Association.[5] Sometimes Ted's uncle John Braxton, "the barbecue king" of Hopkinsville, hired Ted and a few other boys to help him with a big shindig.[6] And fortunate Christian County Negro youths found work at the Latham hotel.[7]

When Ted tended the fireplaces at the home of Dr. Amos H. Tunks, a dentist,[8] he was introduced to sexual intercourse. He reiterated the details to Allison Williams many times through the years, whether from pride or because it traumatized him Williams did not know. At Dr. Tunks's house, Williams says, Ted was hired to bring in the wood for all the fireplaces and to carry out the ashes. This was "a typical job for a colored kid. He would earn maybe fifty cents a week." In one room on Ted's job, Williams says,

> was a grown young lady. She was layin' in the bed. . . . But she kept looking at Ted, and one morning she said, "Come here, Ted." He walked over and she put her hand on the front of his pants and said, "Well! You're quite a young *man!*" Ted was maybe thirteen years old. And the word he said she used, she said, "Are you *diddling* with the little nigger gals?" Ted was so frightened he didn't know what to say, and she repeated, "Well, are ya?" He wanted to *be* a big man, so he said, "Yessum, yessum!"

She said, "Well, if you can do it to them, you can do it to me." She throwed the cover back and she was lyin' there just as naked as a jay bird.

He told me, "Oh, that pussy was so pretty."

She pulled him down on her. He said he wasn't really big enough to do anything, but it got to be an every-morning occurrence. He was *scared* to tell anybody. Back then, they did all kinds of things to Negroes if they caught 'em with white girls. Ted finally told the lady he was going to quit his job. She said, "If you quit, I'm going to tell the doctor you raped me." That scared him even more. Ted stuck it out there for two or three years and every morning she called on him, and he was scared enough to perform. But he said he was *glad* when that was over with.[9]

"Sin" was not new to Hopkinsville. Sometimes "drunks at the Latham would ask a bellboy to get them a woman." The bellboys did procure white women, but "we had an aversion to getting a black woman for a white man," Williams says. "If the white man wanted a black woman, he had to make his own arrangements. And some of them did." There *were* black women for hire in Hopkinsville, at the Tin Top, on Fifth Street between Virginia and Main, "an old rattle-trap building that used to be a stable," Williams says. On a rainy day, one fellow might say, "Let's go down and play with the whores," then they would go there and listen to the rain pattering on the tin roof. Williams, who had left school at age fourteen to see the world, recalled "Sally Moriah, a big, pretty, brownskin girl," who "turned tricks for never over fifty cents." Moriah went away, then one day came back in a Cadillac. The guys asked her if she had found a man with a thousand dollars. She told them, "No, but I found a thousand niggers with a dollar a piece."

Williams does not remember that Ted frequented the Tin Top. Ted and Allison discussed these things, however, for through the years when the two got together, "we'd have a few drinks, get to lying, and away we'd go."

Absorbed in his baffling sexual life, Ted was probably only partially aware of the directions his remaining siblings were taking—Lillian isolated in bereavement and in her own adolescence; his older brothers in military service, then with Marcus Garvey; and the quick death of Roberta.

At age twenty-four, Roberta had completed her third year of teaching, most recently at Oak Grove School. On April 14, 1919, she developed a severe stomachache, saw the doctor, and the next day died of acute peritonitis.[10] In a shaky hand, Eph Poston filled out and signed her death certificate. Roberta was buried in a public cemetery with no markers, which is now "covered with weeds and crawling with snakes," Williams says. There is no record of what happened to eldest brother, Frederick Douglass Poston, after the census for 1910 said he had gone to sea.[11]

Until 1918, Ulysses—who had graduated in 1914 from Kentucky Normal and Industrial Institute where Eph was an instructor in the preparatory department—taught in the Kentucky hinterlands and Robert at M. and F. College. In June, at the height of World War I, both Robert and Ulysses were inducted into the army.[12] Ted read about the war in the *Louisville Courier-Journal* and saw a reference to Theodore Roosevelt's sons who were wounded (Quentin died) in the world war as "scions" of their family. Ted liked the word "scion" and, thinking that his own family was as distinguished as his namesake's, he considered himself the Poston family's scion.[13] Being a scion, then, laid on him a responsibility whose promise he must fulfill.

On June 20, 1918, Robert and Ulysses had been sent to Camp Zachary Taylor, near Louisville, which was geared up for such recruits as they. All men taller than sixty inches who weighed at least 110 pounds were eligible for induction.[14] Ted later wrote:

> Negro troops were herded into Jim Crow camps, into drudgery divisions, even into the trenches, with solemn promises that "things are going to be made much better for you back home." Negro children were urged to buy Thrift Stamps, their mothers to make Red Cross bandages, their fathers to purchase Liberty Bonds in the heroic battle against the horrible Huns. Yet, during the first fourteen months of our participation in the World War, 259 Negroes were lynched in the United States of America. And no Hun atrocity was half as revolting.[15]

Du Bois had said that Negroes were "disliked and feared almost in exact proportion to their manifestation of intelligence and capacity."[16] The Postons' acuity, indeed, blocked their "learning their role in relation to white officers."[17] They started basic training as privates but were quickly made sergeants and assigned to the 159th Depot Brigade at Camp Taylor. Three months later, however, they were demoted back to privates and assigned to the base hospital.[18] The *Negro World* has the only record of what caused the demotion, and Garvey's paper took the brothers' side.

A story on Robert says he had been "inspired with a high sense of justice and fair play" but soon "found himself in serious difficulty with a white sergeant with southern tendency of a rank below himself." To keep from being sent to Leavenworth, the federal military prison, "Mr. Poston had to wage one of the greatest legal battles undertaken by any colored person during the whole period of the war." His company commander, a Lieutenant Taylor, was

> demoted and confined to camp, because of his part in the matter. Major Luedke, who was head of the battalion, committed suicide a few days after the case was disposed of. Another captain who was sent to take Lt. Taylor's place as commander, had a nervous breakdown and was committed to the base hospital for the insane. Mr. Poston himself was reduced in rank and made a clerk in the discharge department of Camp Taylor. Eleven months afterwards he was honorably discharged without having had the privilege of engaging in the activities across the sea.

The *Negro World* claimed that Robert was "not at all embittered . . . but made more determined to fight for fair play." [19]

After the war, the Poston brothers chose the venue of the black press as their battleground even though it presented dangers. When such radical Negro publications as *Challenge,* the *Crusader, Emancipator,* and A. Philip Randolph's *Messenger* spoke out against racial discrimination in the military, U.S. attorney general A. Mitchell Palmer tried to suppress those periodicals. All of the Postons had habitually perused the black press and valued its role in informing readers and "stir[ring] the race into action" while simultaneously instilling "desirable qualities in the race." [20] Black politicians, too, acknowledged journalism's power, for the black press reflected the diversity of Negro readers and interests; the white press saw the group as a kind of backward monolith. From the time of the Civil War, when blacks were "left to shift for themselves in a hostile community," their press worked to "combat mounting anti-Negro sentiment" and to unify the black population "for aggressive counter-action." Beyond that, the black press was simply a source of "fresh, accurate and important information." [21]

In 1919, Robert, Ulysses, and Eph Poston launched a paper of their own, the *Hopkinsville Contender,* and used Ted, now fourteen, as copy boy.[22] The Poston brothers' interests expanded in 1920 to theater, when they staged *Tallaboo,* a "race drama," written by a black Louisville attorney, N. R. Harper. They enlisted the talents of a multitude of Hopkinsville citizens, including Lillian Poston, in the cast.[23] But the brothers' local activity was cut short when Christian County celebrated the return of all soldiers and consigned those from the "colored regiment" to march at the end of the parade. Robert protested this discrimination in the *Contender,* and his words aroused the town's ire. Subsequently the Postons were "not permitted to print" their paper in Hopkinsville.[24] Robert "boarded a train and went to

Nashville" and engaged the National Baptist Publishing Board to publish the paper. This long-distance method of publication and the paltry financial returns on their four-page sheet returned no profit, so in September 1920, as Ted started high school, Robert and Ulysses moved the *Contender* to Detroit, a city fast becoming a locale of "opportunity for ambitious colored young men." [25]

In their Detroit paper's right-hand top corner, the brothers placed a biblical verse: "And if a man strive for mastery, yet he is not crowned except he strives lawfully" (2 Tim. 2:5). Robert and Ulysses filled the *Detroit Contender* with church, club, and local news. They met Claude Barnett, founder of the Associated Negro Press news syndicate, and used many articles from Barnett's shoestring enterprise. Thus through the journalistic medium, the Poston brothers had embarked on challenging American racial discrimination and black pessimism. [26]

Simultaneously exploiting distress at racial attitudes, a short, dark-hued Jamaican printer, Marcus Aurelius Garvey, promoted an independent black economy within white capitalism. Garvey's Universal Negro Improvement Association (UNIA) had infiltrated the African diaspora by 1919 and seemed "on the verge of sweeping aside conservative civil rights organizations." Marxists, black nationalists, and such socialists as A. Philip Randolph at first "publicly applauded Garvey's program." [27] The *Detroit Free Press* mentions no Garvey visit to Detroit in 1920; yet Robert and Ulysses covered his activities at Utopia Hall. Then, intrigued by Garvey, they closed down the *Detroit Contender* in 1921 and followed the UNIA's president-general to Harlem, where Robert became Garvey's "right-hand man, his right-arm," according to Marcus Quarles. Garvey had attracted the Postons with the perquisite of his weekly, internationally distributed *Negro World*. Garvey recognized that the UNIA would benefit if he could get the aggressive Postons on his team.

At the 1921 UNIA convention, Ulysses Poston was elected minister of industries, to oversee the building and operating of "factories in the industrial centres of the United States, Central America, the West Indies and Africa, to manufacture every marketable commodity." [28] J. Raymond Jones, Ulysses' assistant, described him as "a powerful man in the movement" for controlling those business ventures. Ulysses stressed commerce with black farmers in the South who wanted to sell products directly in the New York and New Jersey markets and "bypass the white middlemen who cheated them with impunity." Ulysses and Jones would buy shipments of Caribbean limes and Florida oranges and grapefruit, sell them at a profit for the producer, and retain a small fee for the UNIA. Once, however, when Ulysses was out of town, after disposing of two tank cars of cane molasses from Georgia and getting a check from the purchaser, Jones showed the check to Garvey, and Garvey pocketed it all. Jones could not retrieve the money to pay the growers. That persuaded Jones that Garvey was naive regarding the principles of commerce.[29] Yet Jones credited Garvey with stirring the imagination of his listeners. The UNIA "raised more money in a few years than any other Negro organization ever dreamed of." Garvey's difficulty was that his "deficiencies as a leader outweighed his abilities."[30]

In 1922 the Postons contributed to New York's cultural life by bringing the race drama *Tallaboo* to a UNIA audience. Ulysses found a wife in the New York star Sybil Bryant, the Indian princess in the play. The *Negro World* critic described Bryant as "perfect, putting her whole soul in the part," and said that "Mr. U. S. Poston, as Chapman Smithford, in love with Tallaboo, knows how to love. He 'says' it with his eyes. . . . In the villain scene, however, he should have gripped his revolver more firmly, showing more fight, in defence of the girl he loved."[31] Ulysses and Sybil Bryant married five months later, on May 30, 1922. That summer, Ulysses was named managing editor, under T. Thomas Fortune, of a new UNIA publication, the *Daily Negro Times,* a more frequent version of the weekly *Negro World,* although Garvey held the title of executive editor.[32]

Fortune had reigned as American dean of black journalists for years. But he had also written editorials at the turn of the century for the white, "chatty little" *New York Sun* and contributed essays to other white periodicals.[33] Thus Fortune was the first black to work, though part-time, in the white press. Fortune's and Ulysses Poston's *Daily Negro Times* lasted only twenty-six issues.

In Hopkinsville, Ted took pride in his brothers' important work. He did not hear of detrimental machinations within the UNIA, being aware only of what he read in the copies of the *Negro World* and *Daily Negro Times* which they sent him. Ted paid particular attention to a *Negro World* campaign to "interest young men in . . . taking up the study of journalism as a learned profession." It preached that Negro schools and colleges should offer courses in economics, sociology, history, politics, and diplomacy, plus "journalistic art for the training of such young men who shall be the future leaders of the race."[34] Ted, at a pivotal point in plotting his own future, followed his brothers' lead.

In July 1922, Robert Poston and Garvey had an altercation. Garvey ordered seats for nine UNIA delegates at the upcoming League of Nations meeting in Switzerland, and Robert wanted to go. Garvey nominated others, appeasing Robert that "there must be sufficient men of ability left behind" to complete the work of the August convention.[35] The critically thinking Poston brothers were beginning to regard Garvey as a demagogue. By August, the UNIA finances were in disarray. Garvey could no longer pay his officers or finance his incipient Black Star shipping line. Robert felt disillusioned, but he kept up appearances with Garvey, whereas Ulysses differed with the president-general in public. Garvey told the UNIA delegates that "he had been beset throughout the year" with "a number of incompetent, disloyal, dishonest and characterless individuals" who were unable to perform their functions but instead carried on "intrigues, plots and other evil designs against the welfare of the organization." Ulysses considered this a personal slur against such executive officers as himself. Ulysses' own manner seemed pompous to Ted's friends—his childhood nickname had been "General." But given the proud nature of both Garvey and Ulysses, his humiliation by the president-general disaffected him. Thus by the end of the 1922 UNIA convention, the "Hon. U. S. Poston" had resigned as minister of labor and industry as a result of being "not in harmony with the administration."[36]

The following New Year's Day, 1923, Rev. James W. H. Eason, the UNIA's American provisional president, who, like Ulysses, had disagreed publicly with Garvey, was murdered in New Orleans. Robert was privy to internal UNIA conversations surrounding the assassination. Just as blacks needed to dissemble in the strategic use of hegemonic values with the white race, Robert used such strategies with Garvey.[37] He may have felt that if Garvey became disenchanted with him as he had with the murdered Eason, Robert's life, too, might be in danger. Robert spoke unknowingly with a Bureau of Investigation undercover informant after which the agent reported to J. Edgar Hoover that he had "talked to Mr. R. L. Poston, one of the [*Negro World*] editors, who said that Garvey hadn't been in his office for the last three days because he was dodging his creditors. . . . Poston also said it was too bad that Garvey had Eason killed and that if he finds that Garvey ever threatens him, he will take his gun, go to his [Garvey's] office and get him first."[38]

In mid-1923 Garvey was jailed for three months in New York's federal prison, the Tombs, for mail fraud—selling stock in his bankrupt shipping line. His wife, Amy Jacques Garvey, and Robert Poston attempted to hold the UNIA together. The non-UNIA press had been mocking Garvey and, by association, Robert, in describing UNIA activities. For example, Robert had accompanied Garvey to Raleigh, North Carolina, in October 1922. A local newspaper made fun of his aristocratic mien, saying, "With 'his excellency' was 'Sir' Robert Poston . . . the very picture of dignity with a swallow tail

coat and a chivalrous grace." Robert "made a five minute speech to introduce Garvey, then 'Sir Robert' lent enthusiasm to the crowd by constantly
chiming a string of approving 'all right's.'"[39]

By helping Garvey save face despite his own qualms about him, Robert
Poston had put himself in the crossfire between Garvey and his detractors,
but the assassination of Eason "cast a pall over the UNIA movement."[40] It
stifled further "open revolt and sent his opponents underground for a
while."[41] Robert Poston defended Garvey's movement in a *Negro World* essay, saying that the UNIA must focus on its goals for the race and not be distracted by the president-general's legal troubles. He reminded readers what
the world war had taught them by citing a poem of racial resolve that he had
written for the army newspaper. Ironically, Robert's poem seemed to fore-
shadow his own imminent fate:

> I'll be back when matters stand to suit me. . . .
> When it's clear the bully holds no quarter here. . . .
> I'll be back when Belgium's wrongs have been atoned for,
> When poor Serbia—bleeding Serbia—is intact;
> When we get the things for years the world has groaned for.
>
> . . . So prepare your heart to wait for this great dawning,
> Ask the God of love to make you strong withal;
> I'll be back when all that's dark has turned to morning;
> Otherwise, my dear, I'll not be back at all.[42]

W. E. B. Du Bois had coined the term "the talented tenth" to predict that
"the Negro race like all races is going to be saved by its exceptional men."[43]
The Poston brothers seemed to be such exceptional people. Because Garvey
had disappointed Robert when he failed to send him to the League of Nations
meeting in Switzerland, he appointed Robert leader of a UNIA mission to
Liberia, West Africa. Robert, "Lady Henrietta Vinton Davis" (fourth assistant president-general of the UNIA), and Milton Van Lowe, a Detroit attorney born in the British West Indies, were designated to make arrangements
with the Liberian government for resettlement there of descendants of former American slaves. In a reciprocal arrangement, UNIA migrants wanting
relief from American racism would assist Liberians with industrialization.
The little group led by Robert reached Liberia in February 1924. Robert carried a letter from Garvey to President C. D. B. King.[44] According to Lady
Davis, the group was "so elated after our interview with the president" that
Robert Poston at once "cabled the Hon. Marcus Garvey the one word,

'Success.'" President King had assured them that they would be given "all the land that they will desire." On Sunday, March 16, the day of the delegation's expected arrival back in New York, Garvey was addressing a UNIA rally in Madison Square Garden when he received a radiogram announcing Robert Poston's death of pneumonia that morning aboard the S.S. *Roosevelt*. The UNIA resettlement scheme came to naught; all Liberia got from the UNIA was a tractor.

Floyd Calvin's eulogy in the *Pittsburgh Courier* said that Robert Poston had been herald of "an honored and respected family in Kentucky" and that although the *Courier* differed widely from Garvey's views, "we freely admit" that Robert was "one of the most brilliant men Marcus Garvey had at his command."[45]

The people on "the dark side of Hopkinsville" remember that Robert's pregnant wife, Augusta Savage, brought his body home. "The train had a special car for him," Allison Williams recalls. "Flowers? I had never *seen* so many flowers." The UNIA and Hopkinsville's blacks arranged the funeral. The black schools let out "so we could go," said Francis Eugene Whitney. "Here was one of us who had come into a national movement, been to Africa, and was going through the process of trying to liberate the people. A great wreath made in the shape of a floral clock showed the hour at which he passed. It was a historical event for us." For Mary Duncan, this was "the time I saw Ted the most sad, when they brought his brother's body back from Africa. Ted was broken-hearted." He was probably grieving, finally, for all the losses of his adolescent years. In July 1924, Robert's wife gave birth to a daughter whom she named Roberta. The baby died a few days later, the only descendant the Poston family of Hopkinsville would ever have.[46]

Ted Poston made few references to Garvey when he became a professional reporter. He developed a cynical aversion to any cults that were dependent on leaders' personalities. In reviewing C. Eric Lincoln's *Black Muslims in America* years later, Ted would mention Garvey's movement only fleetingly, saying that many "Negro and white leaders tend to dismiss this [Muslims'] mushrooming hate movement with deprecating comparison to the Marcus Garvey 'Back to Africa' phenomenon and other flamboyant cults of the past."[47] With hindsight and information from Ulysses, Ted saw that his brothers had been in a no-win situation with the UNIA. Government hostility and Garvey's drawbacks as a leader precluded the UNIA from enjoying long-term success. The movement did reveal to all American blacks, however, that the race could wield power and that it was time to emerge from behind the "veil." Ted himself would henceforth act warily toward any "ism" that claimed to represent blacks—Communism in the 1930s, Black Power advocates in the

1960s. The only racial organizations he would consistently support through the years would be the National Association for the Advancement of Colored People, the Brotherhood of Sleeping Car Porters, and the National Urban League.

Two months after Robert was buried, on June 6, 1924, Ted graduated from Crispus Attucks High School with few family members left to celebrate. One of his teachers recalled him as "the most outstanding student that the Attucks High School ever turned out; Poston was straight morally and mentally; his mother was dead and his father did not give him any money to spend and he often came to school in rags because he did not have good clothes to wear. Poston was a good athlete and a good public speaker while in high school; he was respected by all who knew him." [48]

The class motto was "We build the ladder by which we climb." All of Ted's family had helped build the ladder by which he climbed, having given him an impetus that later black journalists could envy. But he had to climb most of the rest of the way alone.

3

. . . .

College

. . . .

1924–1928

Man is made of clay and like a meerschaum pipe
is more valuable when highly colored.
—PHIL H. BROWN [1]

The youngest Postons, Lillian and Ted, felt like peripheral characters in the
maelstrom of family change. Two months after Robert's death, Ephraim
married Susie Forrest and left Hopkinsville for Paducah, Kentucky, where
he became head of the English department at West Kentucky Industrial College
and Susie taught sewing in the home economics department.[2] A Hayes
Street neighbor, Emma Bacon, recollects that for a while the "household
consisted of Lillian, Ted, and two cousins. The father came home once or
twice a month."[3] The young people "did a good job of running the house,
one of the nicest in the community. But being without a mother at that age
when you need a lot of love and care, and having the responsibility for the
home was too much for Lillian. It caused stress that no one recognized."

Puzzling out her future, Lillian Poston, three years Ted's elder, had no desire to become someone's washerwoman, the alternative to teaching as a career for black women.[4] She tried to follow Roberta at Kentucky Normal and
Industrial Institute, strove to be top student in her class, and broke down,
Mary Duncan heard. There was talk of distressing conflicts between Lillian
and her stepmother, raising doubts about Lillian's sanity in her own mind.
Lillian had survived the flu epidemic of 1918 but with a weakened constitution: "There was a history of bad lungs in Ted's family and in that one case,
if not more, there was the history of insanity," says Mary Duncan. "We were

of the opinion that there was a weak strain in the family. I didn't know Lillian intimately, but she had a reputation for being a bookworm."

Madness was the local diagnosis for most signs of extraordinary mental activity. Mary Duncan's father had warned her against Ted, pointing to the reputed connection between genius and madness. Throughout the state the town of Hopkinsville was known as the location of a mental asylum. To "go to Hopkinsville" is still used as an allusion to the state mental hospital there. Modern black feminist Gloria Watkins (pseudonym bell hooks) came out of the same milieu as Ted and Lillian Poston but forty years later. Watkins/hooks has articulated how a black Hopkinsville girl was indoctrinated through "the way we talked to one another, our words thickly accented black southern speech. . . . I realized (and it was a painful and potentially devastating realization) that I did not understand fully what it meant to be a black woman in the United States." Watkins, too, worried about going mad: "From slavery to the present, education has been revered . . . yet it has also been suspect. . . . Too much book learning could lead to madness," and madness was "deemed to be any loss of one's ability to communicate effectively with others, one's ability to cope with practical affairs." [5]

Lillian Poston could not cope, was judged mentally ill, and was committed to Western State Mental Hospital on August 24, 1924. She died there on October 10, 1927. Her death certificate lists the cause as "pulmonary tuberculosis," and she was buried in an unmarked grave in the colored Cave Spring Cemetery.

The September after his high school graduation, Ted, figuring that education was "his best bet," according to Allison Williams, started his freshman year at Tennessee Agricultural and Industrial College (A. and I.). Eph had relatives in nearby Clarksville, Tennessee, who let Ted use their address, making him eligible for in-state tuition. And Tennessee A. and I. had an excellent journalism department. Many of Ted's friends from Hopkinsville attended either Tennessee A. and I. or Nashville's black elite Fisk University. His neighbor Alex Lee Hopson from Hayes Street was at A. and I. Marcus Quarles and the precocious James T. Whitney, who had edited a black newspaper, the *New Age,* in Hopkinsville while in high school, were at Fisk.[6] Ted planned with Mary Duncan that when she graduated from high school in two years, she would follow him to Nashville and that she and Jennie Knight would enroll at Fisk as well.

Getting ready for college, Ted packed "fifty-two pieces of luggage," Allison Williams claims, "a deck of cards." Williams, in an interview at age seventy, took a cigarette from between his lips and chuckled as he related how he helped Ted prepare for his higher education: "We went down to

Franklin's—a typical bargain store like Jews used to have.[7] Ted put a suit on and his old clothes over it, then walked out. Next we went to Abe Arkovitch's second-hand shoe store, up where the black pool rooms are. All you had to do was go in and take off your old shoes. You found a good second-hand pair and put them on.[8] That's how Ted got his wardrobe to go to college."

Why did Ted steal clothes for college? Williams laughed as he replied: "Colored folks didn't consider that stealing. Hell, they weren't paid nothin'."[9] The idea came out of slavery. Pilfering was a technique subordinates used against the dominant culture, James C. Scott says in *Domination and the Art of Resistance*. They do it in retribution for the psychological taxes that whites required in the form of "deference, demeanor, posture, verbal formulas, and acts of humility."[10] There is "abundant evidence that bondsmen stole from their masters on a widespread basis," according to historian Peter Kolchin. They regarded such "appropriation as 'taking' or 'using' what was rightfully theirs."[11]

What did this exploitation of "the system" in the form of Hopkinsville's Jewish merchants show about Ted? He had nothing against Arkovitch. Williams declared, "Abe Arkovitch was a nice old guy. We used to tease with him." But Ted was destitute and proud. He wanted to be dressed suitably when he set off for college.[12] Psychologist Kenneth B. Clark thinks that it shows Ted took care of himself, that "he took risks." Sociologist Hylan Lewis adds, "Ted was not above venture. If it were Dickens, it would be a loaf of bread. This is Kentucky Dickens."

Ted left for Nashville on foot, old-time Tennessee State alumni and retired faculty told the school's archivist, Georgianna Cumberbatch-Lavender. She heard that "no one in the admissions office knew he was coming. He had hitchhiked and walked. He had nothing but the clothes on his back and the shoes on his feet. A lady helped him get employment in the dining hall and doing yard work."[13] Ted at age eighteen reached Nashville on September 22, 1924, and registered as a freshman.[14] He found a mentor in the dynamic George William Gore, Jr., professor of English and journalism, who became dean of the college during Ted's stay. Gore was the only faculty member with a Ph.D. Educated at Fisk and DePauw, Harvard and Columbia, Gore knew professional techniques of journalism and took a humanitarian interest in his students.[15]

In 1927 the streetcar line was extended as far as the college.[16] Ted would take the streetcar downtown to the Bijou to "date up" the Brownskin Models ("who were neither brownskin nor model," he later confessed).[17] Sedate Alex Lee Hopson persuaded Ted to try out for basketball with him. Ted stands in his basketball uniform in photographs in the yearbooks of 1926 through 1928 with his bony legs and knobby knees protruding, arms folded across his chest. In spite of this awkward pictorial frozen moment in time, as an adult he would insist, over a few rounds of the Jack Daniels which he could finally afford, that he had been Tennessee A. and I.'s Beau Brummell.[18] He had tried to replicate the English dandy and wit in his fastidious appearance and confident manner. This demeanor is evident in another yearbook picture, for the Eight Links Club, where Ted with serious mien, the tallest of the group, points his feet slightly outward, arms behind his back.[19] Here he wears a suit and bow tie, more truly resembling Beau Brummell.

Ted contributed an imagistic piece, his first extant writing, to one of the school yearbooks. He artistically described a mother who concocted costumes for her sons from black crepe paper for the "annual dramatic offering" at the Booker T. Washington Colored Grammar School each year.[20] In Ted's story, the narrator compared the rhetoric of Mother's Day—"the first to understand; the quickest to forgive; the most anxious to sacrifice"—with the reality. The speaker thought back to "Home:—a stooped little woman— shrivelled, work-worn hands. . . . A wry smile . . . a slightly twitching underlip—a suspicious moisture in her eyes—'Pa, Sue's been elected hostess of her club; she must have a new dress'—a hard swallow—'Sho' we can manage it; I really don't need no new shoes.'"[21] This story probably reflected Poston's memories of his own mother. Its sentimental tone contrasts with the comical tone of his later childhood stories in *The Dark Side of Hopkinsville*.

The happiest, most stable part of Poston's young manhood was his continuing romance with Mary Duncan. She says he wrote "beautiful letters, each like a poem in the way it was worded, his expressions. At an early age he acquired those cultural things that set him apart." During the summers from 1924 to 1927, Ted would see Mary in Hopkinsville when he stayed with his cousins or with Allison Williams. He and Mary would talk then about "our careers, our plans for the future." Mary had thought Ted might become a politician like his father and brothers. "Everyone in Ted's family was educated. They really loved learning."

Mary encouraged Ted's plan that one day they would make it together in life, even though her parents cautioned her against Ted because of the genius-insanity syndrome. "With my family it was a matter of choosing someone whom they thought would be morally acceptable and would not get me in trouble."[22] Mary remembers that in January 1926, when she graduated from high school, her father bought her a fur coat. She walked down the street in it and found "Ted sitting on the curb. He told me how nice I looked. He reached in his pocket and pulled out a quarter and a dime. He said, 'I only have thirty-five cents, but someday I'm going to have enough money to buy you something pretty like that.' "

Ted was in his sophomore year at A. and I. in Nashville when Dr. Duncan pressured Mary to enroll at Butler University in Indianapolis, rather than at Fisk, mainly to get her away from Ted. An obedient daughter, Mary turned her sights from Ted and Nashville. In Indianapolis, she acquired more suitors. Tall, dark, and handsome Clifford Wilson, a science student and athlete who was then enrolled at the University of Michigan, fell in love with her and proposed. Dr. Duncan approved of the clean-cut and healthy Wilson. "Health was high on his list of requirements," Mary said. "He expected me someday to have children and he didn't want them to inherit anything that wouldn't keep them alive a long, long time."

Then in 1928 Dr. Duncan suddenly died. In the confusion of the moment but knowing she had her father's blessing, Mary accepted Wilson's proposal, and Mary's mother and brothers moved to Indianapolis to be near her. That ended Ted and Mary's childhood expectation of a life united.

Others who would participate in Ted Poston's drama were evolving elsewhere. Will Alexander, the man who would in 1940 recommend that the New Deal bring Ted to Washington as an adviser on racial affairs, had studied theology at Vanderbilt University in Nashville as a "reticent, unsophisticated youth who had never [before] seen an elevator or registered at a hotel." [23] In that city, Alexander had initiated several humanitarian activities, foreshadowing his later efforts to benefit the whole South—black and white.

In Cleveland, Ohio, Ted's future best friend, Henry Lee Moon, was, like him, training for a career in journalism. Moon had edited both the *University Journal* and the yearbook as an undergraduate at Howard University. He then earned his master's degree in journalism at integrated Ohio State University. He aspired one day to cross the color line in journalism. He early told himself, "I'm going to try to break through. I'm not going to let the road be closed by default, without an effort." First, in 1925 Moon would take a job at Tuskegee Institute in the office of the principal, Robert Russa Moton (successor to Booker T. Washington), and "get into public relations." Moon was stoking a journalistic philosophy which he would share with Ted: "I was working not alone for myself but for all of us. . . . Black folk in the pursuit of parity. . . . [For] what's good for us is good for the nation and for all humanity."

While Moon and Poston trained separately for journalism, on the banks of the James River at Rock Castle, in Powhatan, Virginia, two fair-skinned young Negro women who would figure in Ted's future—one as colleague, one as wife—were being indoctrinated in the culture of virtuous Catholic womanhood at St. Francis de Sales High School. Ellen Tarry, who entered the school as a Protestant from Birmingham, Alabama, finished in 1923, transformed into a devout Catholic. Tall and beautiful but prickly Marie Byrd, already a devout Catholic, would remain so. She entered the boarding school in 1926 and left in 1928.[24] St. Francis de Sales was a mission effort of the millionaire Philadelphia Drexel family. A girl paid sixty dollars per year for room, board, and tuition.[25] Called "the castle on the James," the school became known for the "high caliber of its training in producing the true Christian woman and scholar with a practical realization of first principles, a well trained power of reasoning, and an appreciation of all that is true and good and beautiful." The ideal of the nuns who ran the school was realized in the cases of Marie Byrd and Ellen Tarry. They were disciplined and refined to the point that Allison Williams described Marie as "a perfect lady. She goes to church every day. She lives for church." And Ellen Tarry, as a senior citizen, would be as respected in Harlem nearly as highly as the school's founder, the saintly Mother Katharine Drexel herself, or as Haitian–New Yorker Pierre Toussaint, about both of whom Tarry would later write biographies. The "private school" had prepared these young black women to believe in themselves and to live independent lives.

Ted Poston was independent by default; his only rein was self-imposed discipline. He received moral but not financial support from his father, who was paid his salary only intermittently from the impoverished West Kentucky Industrial College.[26] When he finished high school, Ted had answered an ad in Hopkinsville's *New Age:* "WANTED—Colored men to qualify for sleeping car and train porters. Experience unnecessary."[27] That was how, during his college years, Ted got summer jobs on the Louisville and Nashville, Illinois Central, New York Central, and Pennsylvania Railroads. "Perhaps the best benefit . . . was the opportunity to travel and visit many different cities."[28] The premier porters and waiters practiced what they called "brownskin service," serving someone "the best it can be done," says Williams.[29] David Perata claims that the railroad passenger car workers "transformed" cold pieces of steel "into a warm inviting atmosphere and did more than simply provide a service: in their hands, passenger cars were a kind of theater. . . . It was the African American men who worked these cars who brought them to life."[30] Ted mastered the art of brownskin service.

Laughter salved the porter's feelings concerning the deference required from black men who needed tips from whites. Between jobs, railroad workers got together and pondered their lot. Pittsburgh was a layover town on the

Pennsylvania line, where a "dull-gray street of grocery and fruit shops and South-European children" led to "long, uphill" Wiley Avenue, called "niggers' run." [31] In the poolroom on Wylie Avenue, Ted picked up all the current Negro publications—the *Pittsburgh Courier,* the *Baltimore Afro-American,* and the *Chicago Defender.* These complemented the leading white papers, which he procured in other cities. He would later say, "I was reared from my earliest days on the *Louisville Courier-Journal.* As a college student, Pullman porter, and dining-car waiter, I received a valuable adjunct to my education through the *Tennessean* [Nashville], the *Atlanta Constitution,* the *St. Louis Post-Dispatch,* and other pillars of liberal journalism in the South." [32] Though his intellectual life flourished, the railroad did not make Ted affluent. When the Depression hit, Ted says, "tips became non-existent."

Through the rest of his life, Poston's railroad stories would enhance his oral repertoire. Fern Marja Eckman of the *New York Post* started hearing them when Ted returned from his World War II service in Washington. "Two anecdotes have always stuck in my memory," she says. In one, the train stopped to take on water and all the stewards took a breather. So did the rats from the dining car. When the whistle blew to start the train again, the stewards and the rats got back on. The other story is that there was one steward who was always swiping things—linen, dishes, silver—and when the chief steward was invited to that waiter's home—Ted was there—the chief steward walked in, looked around, saw all these familiar items, and said, "All aboard?"

Ted Poston's railroad work was a milestone in his life. It led to his subsequent commitment to the fight for unions. He had read carefully the writings of socialists A. Philip Randolph and Chandler Owen in their periodical, the *Messenger,* rallying support for the formation of the Brotherhood of Sleeping Car Porters. The socialists were the main white political group to care about black interests during the 1920s. The *Messenger* articles told that the average monthly income for a full-time Pullman porter was $110—salary and tips combined. "Any who claim to be making [more] must either be stealing, bootlegging or gambling on the job and probably all three." [33] The Brotherhood of Sleeping Car Porters asked the Pullman company for "a wage of $150 a month so that the degrading practices of tipping" and having to "leave on another trip right after arriving from one" could be ended. [34] It took Randolph ten long concentrated years to get the Pullman company to recognize the Brotherhood.

Ted studied the lay of the journalistic landscape while completing his studies, making his train trips around the country, and noting the necessity for unions. He had seen that the only white newsman who consistently heeded the concerns of black workers was Heywood Broun, columnist for the popular *New York World*. But only the black press concentrated full-time on the racial fight. Ted's goal was to join that struggle. He would aim to work in black journalism immediately and ultimately to garner a spot on a mainstream paper where he could influence white readers as well, while plugging unions for all working people.

Other black journalists in 1928 attacked the "Negro problem" in other ways. Vinegar-tongued George Schuyler in the *Pittsburgh Courier* assailed middle-class black fraternal organizations for their insensitivity to the needs of the masses. Schuyler was depressed to see "unsanitary, congested shacks . . . bursting with Negroes when a block or so away stands a large office building erected by a [Negro] fraternal society." In 1928, the *Courier*'s publisher, Robert Vann, tried to attack racism by supporting the Democratic candidate for president, New York governor Alfred E. Smith, who should have been alert to discrimination since he, as a Roman Catholic, was also maligned by the Ku Klux Klan.[35]

The *Courier* published analytical essays by Ulysses Poston as part of its election year coverage. One of them castigated Negroes for not being more like Jews. Still stung by the failures of the UNIA, Ulysses scolded readers for not informing themselves on efficient business methods such as the Jews practiced and as he and J. Raymond Jones had taught themselves while organizing their UNIA business ventures.[36] The Jews were a group whose methods, virtues, and shortcomings the elder Poston brothers noticed and discussed, and Ted paid attention.

He read the philosophies of A. Philip Randolph, Norman Thomas, and Frank Crosswaith in a range of black periodicals. Crosswaith, for example, had warned that without action on his own behalf the Negro was destined "for all time to do no more than hew wood and draw water," for white trade unionists believed that because of "certain physiological and psychological distinctions" blacks would never "fit in" to the "complicated industrial system."[37] Ted Poston knew of all this turmoil while he was completing college.

In 1927, Ulysses and Sybil Poston had moved into the modern, Rockefeller-financed Dunbar cooperative apartments in Harlem at 2588 Seventh Avenue, considered the "most glamourous apartment building Negroes had in New York."[38] The Dunbar was stocked with intellectual neighbors. Randolph lived there, and he and his cohorts "revelled in the cut and thrust of argument" in "drawing room forensics" on Sunday mornings. Theophilus Lewis compared their discussions to "Samuel Johnson's arguments in the coffeehouse." Schuyler described the gatherings as "Athenian conclaves." Nothing, Schuyler said, "escaped the group's probing minds and witty shafts." [39] Randolph, who had lauded Marcus Garvey when he first came to Harlem, had turned against him in the pages of the *Messenger* as the UNIA waxed and waned. When Ulysses broke with Garvey, Randolph invited him to write for the *Messenger*.

On his railroad layovers in New York, Ted stayed with his brother and sister-in-law. They assured him he would have a home with them when he graduated and that Ulysses needed his help on the Democratic campaign sheet he was putting out for the November election, the *New York Contender*.[40] Thus through Ulysses' network of connections, Ted would become an ally of New York's intellectuals.

Ted itched to relocate to Harlem. His teachers at Tennessee A. and I. sent him off knowing that he was "more intelligent than his grades indicated," a person "who did not study unless he was interested in the subject." Ted graduated on June 5, 1928, "with a slightly above average record and a B.S. degree." [41] By train and cattle boat, Ted Poston left the South to make New York his permanent home.[42]

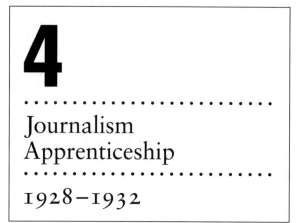

4

Journalism
Apprenticeship

1928–1932

One of the glories of New York [is] that here—
more than anywhere else in America—a Negro
can, at times, forget that he is a Negro. It is one
of the tragedies of New York—and America—
that no Negro, at all times, can forget
completely.

—TED POSTON, "The Negro in New York"

Immigrants had streamed into New York City for decades seeking "some greater or lesser grail." The city had been so safe that one could walk across the Brooklyn Bridge at night. E. B. White did it and heard the *Queen Mary*'s whistle blow, carrying "the whole history of departure and longing and loss."[1]

Uptown, Harlem, in its metamorphosis from a white to a black community, had become a place of gaiety, good feeling, and jazz. "Laughter was easy, loud."[2] In 1928 the Harlem Renaissance still beckoned to multitudes of the talented tenth. Ted Poston discovered not only a field of excitement in Harlem but a sense of mission in all of New York City. One editor declared that the city "should be the paradise of the newspaper man. Nowhere is the performance louder, funnier, or with more provocative, mysterious overtones."[3] That atmosphere challenged Ted.

Ulysses had become active in black political clubs and was writing on current events for both the *Pittsburgh Courier* and *Inter-State Tattler,* so he hired Ted to take care of the *Contender,* paying him $30 a week.[4] Ted laid out the *Contender*'s pages, wrote headlines, then cut and pasted the sheet together, working in a bedroom in Ulysses and Sybil's apartment. In this way, Ted learned to navigate in the city in as prosperous times as black Harlem would ever see. When lean times arrived, he already knew his way around.

Sybil Poston took a big-sisterly interest in Ted and encouraged him to assert himself in a way that would have been unthinkable in the South. He would write of it years later, as he tried to remember how much time had passed before he was reminded he had the taboo black skin. For example, in 1928 he had gone to the theater to buy a ticket "for a pleasure forbidden in the South, an orchestra seat." When he tried to use his ticket, two "husky white ushers" told him he would have to sit upstairs, despite his main floor ticket. The same summer, at Far Rockaway beach, a white woman started to drown and Ted swam out to rescue her. A white man intervened, barking at Ted, "Get your goddam black hands off this white woman; she don't need no help from you." Just then, a wave knocked the white man unconscious, and Ted kept both victims above water until a life guard arrived. When he came to, on the beach, the white man apologized, and Ted wondered how he could "hate the first white man who had ever apologized" to him for anything.[5]

Poston ran elevators, waited tables at the Cotton Club, and kept up his railroad runs while he wondered whether he would ever be able to break into big-league journalism. For one thing, white papers were disappearing. A would-be press baron, Frank A. Munsey, had bought and killed four newspapers in the first quarter of the century.[6] The *Herald-Tribune* would not hire a Negro, but it allowed one to ghost stories about Harlem that would then appear under the names of its regular writers.[7]

The shining light of New York newspapers was the *New York World,* owned by a Hungarian-born Jew, Joseph Pulitzer.[8] If Ted were able to cross the color line, the *World* would be a perfect medium for him because his own kind of "cheerfulness, breeziness, enterprise" pervaded it.[9]

The *World* had pierced the color line briefly when executive editor Herbert Bayard Swope hired Lester A. Walton, who would influence the *World* to capitalize the word *Negro.*[10] Walton had been Swope's classmate back in St. Louis. He had come to New York in 1917 as managing editor of the black *New York Age,* then Swope commissioned him to write first a series on southern blacks who had migrated north, then a Sunday column on news of blacks in New York. The *Dunbar News* commented that Swope's hiring of Walton "may be taken to mark the beginning of a new day in American journalism." The circulation of the *World* shot up in Harlem, but its business executives complained that other papers were "underhandedly telling advertisers that the *World* was excessively partial to Negroes and was read *only* in Harlem." Pulitzer "refused to be swayed" when his advertising department requested that he "countermand Swope's recognition of a colored society." [11] Anyway, Walton "didn't have flair," St. Clair Bourne says. And the *World* itself would not survive the economic crash of 1929.

The *World*'s Heywood Broun was one of Ted Poston's heroes, as Broun was to most New York newspeople. E. B. White "burned with a low steady fever just because I was on the same island" as Broun. African Americans appreciated Broun's championing of their cause. As early as 1922, Broun had responded when the NAACP wanted "an open and authoritative investigation of charges of segregation, discrimination, inefficiency and mismanagement" lodged against the administration of Harlem Hospital; then Broun revealed his findings at a "monster mass meeting" at the Abyssinian Baptist Church. [12] At an NAACP *Crisis* dinner, Broun declared that America needed to change, for "as it exists today, [the United States] is not a good place for the Negro." [13] The circulation of the *World*, with its many ethnic readers, rose by sixty thousand the day after the first installment of its series on the Ku Klux Klan. [14] Editor Swope's crusade against Florida's slave-labor peonage system also aroused high reader interest. But in January 1925, the *World* had raised its price from two cents to three while the *Times* and *Herald-Tribune* remained at two cents. Circulation sank immediately; the price returned to two cents in 1927, but not all of the readers returned. Swope resigned in 1928. The *World* without Swope was particularly vulnerable, then, to the Depression. On February 27, 1931, the paper died. *World* reporters wept and the black press mourned. [15] The *Chicago Defender* said, "No stouter, no firmer friend to freedom and justice ever labored against the brutality of American race prejudice than the *New York World*."

And while Ted Poston's new column, "Harlem Shadows," ran on one page of the *Pittsburgh Courier,* that paper was editorializing on another page, "There are millions of people who will miss the *New York World*," for in the *World*, "nearly every man, regardless of his social, economic or political strata, could find a brief in his behalf." [16]

Ted Poston had been particularly attuned to Heywood Broun's championing of unions as necessary for all America's workers, even intellectual workers, which newspeople were. Ben Hecht and Charles MacArthur's hit play *The Front Page* had dramatized the working conditions of reporters. [17]

Newsmen suffered burnout from their long, irregular hours and low pay.[18] They thought of forming a trade union and needed an advocate, which Broun would become. Such was the situation in New York's newspaper world when Ted Poston entered the Harlem milieu, made acquaintances, and sought a reportorial foothold.

Leaving his ultimate dreams in abeyance, Ted got on with life and made friends. Ellen Tarry came to town in 1929 bringing a desire to earn enough of a living to attend the "Pulitzer school," as Columbia's School of Journalism was called. Instead, after the stock market crash, she counted herself lucky to have a job running an elevator. All around her, tenants were being evicted.[19] The Pennsylvania Railroad sold more tickets to southbound black passengers than at any other period.[20] A. Philip Randolph was evicted from Sleeping Car Porter headquarters because union members could not pay their dues; therefore, the union could not pay its rent.[21]

Claude McKay wrote that to avoid worrying over the economic plight, "happy or unhappy, Harlem dances abundantly."[22] Everybody was "angry with poor old [President] Herbert Hoover. . . . except people in the entertainment world," added band leader Cab Calloway.[23] At the Savoy Ballroom the Lindy Hop originated, a "flying dance done by couples in which a girl is thrown away in the midst of a lightning two-step, then rudely snatched back to be subjected to a series of twists, jerks, dips and scrambles."[24] Ted Poston wrote: "To the thrill-seeking whites of the Roaring Twenties, [Harlem] was the place to go—the home of happy feet, Connie's Inn, the Cotton Club and other late hour oases where gangster owners saw to it that the high-stepping entertainment was all Negro and the paying customers all white."[25] At the Savoy ballroom, however, the paying customers were black. Here, with the rest of the Harlem community and their "shared culture of adversities and humiliations," Ted stepped out on his own happy feet.[26] Mollie Lewis Moon, who would become a Harlem socialite and social activist, told her husband later that Ted was the best dancing partner she had ever encountered.

Ted strolled down Seventh Avenue regularly. James Weldon Johnson captured that street's pleasures: "One saunters along, hails this one, exchanges a word or two with that one, stops for a short chat with the other one."[27] And in a similar manner, Ted Poston picked up the news. Wanting to sharpen his skills in the concise New York style, during the academic year of 1928–29 he enrolled in three noncredit courses at New York University—short story writing, editorial writing, and feature writing. Using his new skills, he worked his way into nonpolitical journalism. In 1931 his chatty, lightweight "Harlem Shadows" column, by "T. R. Poston," had begun in the *Pittsburgh Courier,* headed by a verse reflecting his newly jaded attitudes. For example, in the first column he tossed off an encomium to Pauli Murray, who also aspired to an adventurous life.

> I, who am aged, met Youth tonite—
> Youth—in a stripling girl;
> Youth—with Ambition, Hope, and Fight—
> Youth—with Illusions unfurled. . . .
>
> When she told me her dreams, I thought of my own
> Which were shattered in ages long past;
> When she spoke of her hopes, I stifled a groan—
> To think that I'd lost mine so fast. . . .
>
> But now I'm so old . . . and she is so young—
> She's hardly twenty—no more. . . .
> While I, from whom Hope and Ambition are flung,
> Am decrepit and old . . . twenty-four.

Murray says that because Poston was "so chained to deadlines," they had developed "a lunch counter friendship. If he saw me in the Monterey Luncheonette, he would whiz in for a cup of coffee between assignments and we would twirl on our stools, chatting for a few minutes." She described Ted in this period as a young man whose eyes "smiled but hinted sadness." Ted "never pitied himself," but he sometimes "betrayed his sorrow when telling an uproariously funny tale . . . in a voice that ran the scale from high-pitched laughter to a whisper that was half sob." [28]

Ted was angry rather than sad that he had to write "puff pieces" to get "ten or fifteen dollars" from the subject of the puff.[29] For his "Harlem Shadows" column, he often went unreimbursed when advertisers could not pay the *Courier*.[30] Still, Ted was becoming Harlem's rising journalistic star. The *Courier* had four editions—local, northern, eastern, and southern— and a circulation of fifty thousand. Furthermore, each issue of any black newspaper went through multiple readers. Noted for its "sparkling society, entertainment, and sports pages," the *Courier* was promoted as a "national urban newspaper." [31] Sometimes Ted's column bordered on silly in style while he conversationally related misfortune. For example,

We had just received a letter from the pater down in Paducah. (Yes, stupid, your humble correspondent is a scion of the deah ol' Bluegrass state, suh). The letter disclosed . . . that the sire had suffered . . . heavily when his local bank closed its doors suddenly. . . . Feeling badly about it, I relayed the information to the sister-in-law. . . .

"That's terrible!" ejaculated the shocked Mrs. Poston, but with the characteristic patriotism of a Harlemite who thinks that everything South of the Ferry is wilderness, she added, "But what can one expect of those Southern Banks? I'm surprised that you should allow your father to keep his money down there. Write him immediately and tell him that as soon as he gets on his feet again, he should send it to you and let you bank it up here—for New York is the only safe place in the world to bank money."

And the next morning—less than twenty-four hours after her little speech—sixty-two separate banks, all branches of the Bank of the United States, located in New York City, closed their doors . . . to set a record for the biggest banking crash in history.[32]

Ted's last "Harlem Shadows" column appeared in the *Courier* on April 25, 1931. It detailed a reporter's daily anxiety in thinking up ideas.[33] The column was only four months old when a headline announced, "Harlem Agog over Newspaper 'War,' " and that "T. R. Poston" had been stolen away by the *Amsterdam News* to counteract Ulysses Poston's rage over the *Amsterdam's* politics.[34] The article explained that Ted, after three years as managing editor of his brother's *Contender,* was hired by the *Amsterdam News* because at the *Contender* he and Ulysses had berated the *Amsterdam* for appearing to favor the Democratic party and taking money from it, then, at the last minute, bitterly attacking the Democrats and publishing a full-page Republican party ad. Other newspaper people claimed that the *Amsterdam* "grabbed young Poston to head off his brother" so that Ulysses would cease attacking the paper and Ted would be too busy to assist Ulysses with the sporadically published *Contender.*[35]

Ted's journalistic style tended to human interest whereas Ulysses was a polemicist. Now that he was working full-time on a regular newspaper, Ted's responsibilities increased and silliness disappeared, although bathos remained in his subject matter when the foibles connected with the human condition were the topic. His 1931–32 series "Garland Patton, Gigolo" described a clever Harlemite who lived off his girlfriend's relationship with a wealthy white man. That series was snapped up by readers who were voracious for juicy tales of whites bluffed by blacks. Some of Poston's best pieces simply described a 1930s summer, such as "Harlem Gasps for Cool Breath of Air on Hot Nights After Weather Prophet Orders Worse: Those with Money Go to Beaches, but the Poor and Lowly Creep to Piers and Parks to Await Morning" or "Depression Brings Harlem Better Food by 'Eat All You Want for 35 Cents' Plan: Customer Benefits by Keen Competition in Community."

At the *Amsterdam News,* Ted finally met the bespectacled, dignified, and friendly Henry Lee Moon, his best pal for the rest of his life.[36] Moon resembled Ulysses in his proper decorum, but he was only four years older than Ted, not a gaping fourteen years, the spread between Ted and his big brother. Moon's parents had been stalwarts of the NAACP back in Cleveland. He had loved doing public relations at Tuskegee from 1926 to 1931 amid the idyllic surroundings of rural, though segregated, Alabama, when he had received a letter from William M. Kelly, editor of the *Amsterdam News,* offering him a job "at the magnificent sum of twenty-five dollars a week."[37] The *Amsterdam News* was the most widely read Negro newspaper in New York then, according to novelist Ann Petry, because "it reports the births and deaths, the defeats and victories, the sins and virtues of the Negro. . . . It headlines the ripest scandals and the goriest murders. . . . By contrast, its editorials are . . . sedately written and . . . innocuous."[38]

The *Amsterdam* called itself "One of America's Greatest Newspapers— We Only Print the News—We Do Not Make It." The *Amsterdam* was the black paper in New York most like the defunct white *World.* Moon viewed Poston as "a promising young man from a semi-benighted land." Moon, who "could not then perceive the full blossoming of that promise," soon realized that he was being paternalistic and that Poston "didn't *need* my guidance."[39] Moon would soon be awed by the able Ted, "one of the most glamorous and productive newsmen in the New York area. He had a talent of enlivening dead copy," Moon said. It was "a magic touch, and he was eagerly read by the readers of the *Amsterdam News.*"[40]

When they covered the same story, the basic facts in Poston's and Moon's articles would be the same, but otherwise they "differed vastly," Moon says. "His would be full of detail which escaped me." Perhaps the "enlivening aspects" were produced by a "highly animated imagination." But Moon felt unable to disentangle himself from his "rigid training. Happily," Moon says, "Ted never had to contend with such inhibitions. Nothing . . . could throttle the Poston fancy. . . . That has been his genius."[41] An objective friend of both men, Robert C. Weaver, says that in temperament, Poston and Moon contrasted "like Mutt and Jeff. Henry was conservative, introverted, middle-class, from a background of intellect, reading, education. Ted was energetic, all over the place, an extrovert. They complemented each other."

Poston and Moon worked together battling poverty and deadlines at the *Amsterdam.* Poston's stories were streetwise and sensationalistic. Moon marveled how he got hold of the reports of a private investigator, the basis of the "Garland Patton, Gigolo" series, "so popular that people eagerly waited for it to come off the presses."[42] Moon did ruminative essays and countless book reviews. In June 1931, they collaborated on a series on capital crimes. For one aspect of the stories, Ted was to cover the execution of the criminal, while Moon did background. The *Amsterdam* also mounted a campaign against lynching, and Ted penned a series, "Judge Lynch Presides," relating the practice's atrocities.[43]

In one article, he told of having stood on a street corner in Indiana in 1930 when a snickering white youth came up and asked if he would like to buy a picture. Poston said no, but the youth pushed "a large photograph into the writer's hand and scurried up the street." The *Amsterdam* printed the picture, and Poston described "the swinging, mutilated bodies" that had been dragged from an Indiana county jail, "beaten and clawed to death," and strung up on the courthouse lawn. Cut down later, the bodies were "further mutilated by bloodthirsty white women who drove their sharp heels into the eye sockets and faces of the victims." Poston sarcastically commented that the picture demonstrated "the high level of culture in the 'advanced' Northern states."[44] For the next forty years, Moon and Poston would recall images of gleeful and barbaric expressions on the white faces of people brutalizing blacks.

Once he had a permanent professional job, Ted moved out of Ulysses and Sybil's place and rented a basement apartment at 363 Edgecombe Avenue, sharing it with Moon and dapper Thurston Lewis, a social worker from Greenville, Mississippi, by way of the University of Chicago.[45] With his two roommates Ted had Depression experiences that he made light of in later years, adding the adventures to his ever-enlarging stock of oral narratives. During the lean period, Ted later told Diana Bonnor Lewis, "Nobody had a job except Ted. He was making thirteen dollars a week. The rest of them were broke. Ted said that *some*body would have to register for relief and get some money. They drew lots and Henry lost. But Henry had a fit; no Moon had ever been on relief; there was no way he was going to do this. But up they all went to the relief office and threw Henry in the door while the rest of them waited outside. Henry finally emerged, grinning. He said, 'I signed Ted Poston's name and it was perfectly all right.'"

Another tale of Ted's from their impoverished period was that one housemate, a doorman at the Metropolitan Opera, occasionally drank to excess and was not in condition to work. Only Moon fit his uniform; Moon would have to substitute. Being a doorman, too, was against the Moon ethic. A man could wash dishes for survival but not wait tables because that required subservience and accepting tips. Moon says, "My parents felt tipping was another way whites put us in debt to them." But the housemates needed his income so Henry was sent out in the housemate's uniform to act as doorman. One woman tipped him five dollars. Ted told the "lie" ever after that Henry was so grateful he followed the woman forty blocks to Park Avenue repeating, "Thank you, ma'am; thank you, ma'am; thank you ma'am." Gentleman Henry himself testifies to the truth of another Poston narrative, that Moon went into a certain restaurant and was told, "Nigger, get the hell out of here before I blow you out," at which Moon left, "with as much dignity as I could muster."[46]

Ted got obsessed with New York's civil rights laws, which were frequently broken but never challenged by blacks. Poston himself lived within the prevailing system, but he bucked it when he legally could. For example, he took Moon and Lewis with him to visit friends from home at Columbia University. Riled when an elevator operator refused to transport them, the three chose to "test the Civil Rights law which had been amended to make possible the arrest as well as civil action against any person who discriminated because of race, creed, or color." Ted later recounted the incident in a *New York Post* piece, projecting familiarity by writing in second person: "You order the arrest—much to the indignation of an Irish desk-lieutenant—of a Negro elevator operator at a Claremont Av. apartment house. . . . 'We don't allow Nigras in this house,' said the Negro elevator man, speaking for the insurance company which owned the building. (The girls you wished to visit, summer students at Columbia, were both colored, but apparently their fair complexions had fooled the management. Thurston, who was fair also, had visited them earlier with no difficulty.)"

After the offending elevator man had been booked and jailed, Poston called an NAACP lawyer in triumph to boast that he had "forced an arrest under the amended law." The lawyer listened, then informed him, "Ted, the amended law covers apartment hotels, but not apartment houses. You've locked that man up illegally. He's got a good case of false arrest against you if he ever finds out." The magistrate who heard the case was also "ignorant of the fine distinction in the law." The magistrate called Moon, Poston, and Lewis behind the bench and whispered, "motioning at the disheveled defendant, 'that poor guy didn't know the law.'" Since the operator was "only carrying out orders from the insurance company" and had already spent a night in jail, the judge said, "I'm going to give him a lecture on tolerance and civil rights, and let him off with a suspended sentence."[47] Poston narrated the incident in an amused tone; nevertheless, he pushed relentlessly the rest of his life for the abolition of discriminatory laws. When fair law got on the books, he insisted that the law be observed. He did not gloat when he came out ahead, but, in his offhand casual manner, he did enjoy victories.

Robert Weaver would one day eulogize Ted as "a keen observer of the political process. He understood its operation, and used it effectively to achieve clearly defined objectives."[48] But Ted's political mentor had been his brother. In an early history of Harlem politics that he wrote for the *Amsterdam News*, "The Rise of Colored Democracy," Ted turned to Ulysses as his main source, for Ulysses, says Ersa Poston, "like Old Man Poston, cared more for politics than for survival."[49]

Ulysses had become Harlem's most vaunted political journalist. J. Raymond Jones explained how he gained the authority that led to his column "The Political Buzz-Saw" in the *Inter-State Tattler*.[50] In the 1932 presidential campaign, Ulysses persuaded Vincent Daley, New York State's Democratic chairman, that with a little effort, black voters could "be converted to the Democratic cause," even though from the time blacks got the vote in 1870, they had cast their lot with the Republican party in tribute to Abraham Lincoln for having proclaimed emancipation. Daley listened, then "gave U. S. Poston permission" to create the Vin Dale Club on behalf of the Democrats. The club's efforts paid off, and the Democratic ticket won "throughout the state." As chair of the Vin Dale Club, Ulysses became "judge and jury" for postal laborers whose interests the club oversaw. That experience helped U. S. Poston understand "how the State and Federal patronage system worked."[51] Ulysses conveyed that knowledge of his political modus operandi to Ted.

Ulysses recognized how fickle a candidate's loyalty could be. In the New York City mayoralty primary in 1932, he preferred the somber John Hylan to the flashy songwriter Jimmy Walker, but when Hylan was defeated by Walker, Ulysses quickly switched his allegiance to Walker as a "friend who has done so much for Harlem" with traffic lights, jobs for Negroes in Harlem Hospital, the retention of the five-cent subway fare, and a local rent law. Ulysses dismissed Walker's attributes that he had so recently considered failings and asked, what if he "does overstay his vacation periods occasionally and is tardy in keeping his appointments?" for Walker was "quite the most colorful figure in the public life of America today" and his behavior as an official reflected "the spirit of New York City."[52]

With political acumen, as Franklin D. Roosevelt ascended on the national scene, Ulysses exulted because "already the name Roosevelt is in high favor with Negroes." Ulysses saw little danger in radical groups such as the socialists and communists, but he did not think they would ever gain the power of the traditional Democratic and Republican parties. He even praised the black attorney William L. Patterson, who allied himself with the communists to save Sacco and Vanzetti, the anarchist Boston shoemakers who were unjustly executed in 1927.

Ulysses' lack of fear of the communists influenced his kid brother's next exhilarating move. For service to the Communist party, William L. Patterson was "singled out and sent to Russia on a four-year scholarship," Ulysses said.[53] Subsequently, Patterson converted to "the faith" and later married another young Harlem intellectual, Louise Thompson, and when she found proselytism among her acquaintances difficult, she forsook propaganda and initiated a discussion group. At one meeting of her group, James Ford, an eventual Communist party candidate for vice-president of the United States, announced that a film was being made in Russia on American racism. Twenty-two "actors" were needed and all expenses would be paid, with Louise Thompson acting as intermediary.

Louise Thompson was working in the race relations department of the Congregational church at the time. Unsuccessful efforts had been made to secure travel funds for the "actors" through benefits. Then gifts were sought from famous blacks, again with no luck. Ted was not involved until Thompson sought "any Negroes who could pay their own fare." They would be reimbursed on their arrival in Russia, in rubles. To Ted, the project sounded like "a glorified tour and vacation." All announcements stressed that "Communist affiliation was not desirable" because the group was expected to bring back "an unprejudiced report on the Soviet Union."[54] Ted became the last of the twenty-two to sign up. He regarded the trip as "an excellent opportunity" to see for himself "the much publicized Soviet Union and possibly to write stories about it." His colleagues at the *Amsterdam News* gave a "Send Poston to Russia" party to help raise his boat fare.

In his "Political Buzz-Saw" column meanwhile, Ulysses portrayed communists as seeking to recruit Negroes to the party and warned the public, "If there is a continued recurrence of Scottsboro cases in America and the same brand of American 'justice' is dispensed," the Negro would resort to communism as a way out.[55] Ulysses may have feared that Ted might be swayed by the Bolshevik revolution. The week before Ted departed for Russia, Ulysses reminded his readers that using the vote was their one means of affecting their own lives and that the "Republican party is the party of class and 'privilege,'" whereas the "Democratic party is the party of the people. . . . It opposes in principle the concentration of the wealth of the nation in the hands of a few."[56]

The cynical and fun-loving Ted, his critical skills honed as a reporter, would avoid embracing communist dogma. The years under Ulysses' tutelage had confirmed in him a respect for American institutions, however gruesome their practices, and hope for progressive evolution.

Ulysses avoided criticism of the Communist party while Ted moved to its main turf. In fact, much of the communists' program coincided with the basic Socialist and Democratic party platforms, which Ulysses already promoted—concern for the common man.

T. Thomas Fortune had died in the spring of 1928, the year Ted Poston arrived in New York City.[57] He had foreshadowed Ted's mainstream success by his own life and the remark, "Genius will take care of itself," but Fortune had pleaded that the "masses of the colored race should receive preparation for the fierce competition of every day life that the odds shall not be against them."[58]

Fortune's mantle would pass to Ted Poston within a generation. As his initiation period into New York journalism ended, Ted retained his ardor for life experience and his eagerness to absorb and report. Now opportunity and curiosity beckoned Ted overseas, to a new country and culture.

5

Russia

1932

One lanky New Yorker, Ted Poston . . . was long
afterwards remembered as Daddy Long Legs,
because of his dancing prowess.
—HOMER SMITH, *Black Man in Red Russia*

Once the ice thawed on the Moscow River in spring 1932, the barge-restaurant Poplavok anchored upstream from the Kremlin. Its thrilling orchestra had the African American word "JAZZ" stretched across the bass drum.[1] The prospect of the arrival of twenty-two black Americans excited Russians as much as did jazz music. And America's race problem "intrigued . . . propaganda chiefs."[2] A German producer had just filmed *Flamingo* in Central Africa for Soviet audiences and imagined a need for a motion picture that would depict the social humiliations heaped upon the American Negro.[3] Premier Joseph Stalin, whose favorite pastime reportedly was watching Tarzan movies, appreciated film's potential for political proselytizing.[4] The locale of the planned film, *Black and White,* would be Birmingham, Alabama, its protagonists Negro laborers—the men, stokers in the steel mills, the women, domestics in affluent white homes. A progressive labor organizer would try to recruit poor Negroes and whites into one powerful labor union. Villainous steel mill bosses and absentee landlords from the North would bar the workers from the union by setting the races against each other. The Meschrabpom Film Corporation issued the invitation, and actors—"not a live actor in the group," according to Dorothy West[5]—and writers "jumped at the chance to travel abroad at someone else's expense," said Homer Smith, one of the twenty-two, "and to work in a medium that was all but closed to them at home."[6]

Americans in flight from the Depression were already flocking to Russia in hope of finding prosperity, according to Anna Louise Strong, and *Soviet Russia Today* painted an unusually rosy picture.[7] A Marxist scenario was being brought to life there in which the working classes were united in a proletarian internationalism that, ideally, overlooked racial and ethnic differences. This was a chance for blacks to gauge the experiment's success. American diplomat George Kennan, sent to Russia in the winter of 1932, had drunk it all in and intensely loved the cobbled roads and the dark evergreen forests but claimed that the Russian press suffered "poor type, poor print and paper" and the "propaganda is appalling," with its "hypocrisy [and] savage intolerance."[8]

Most of the planning for the journey of the twenty-two Americans took place at 44 West 66th Street, three buildings owned by the African Association for Mutual Benefit, a "workshop for the Harlem Renaissance," Ed Morrow terms it. Morrow was a black Yale graduate also trying to make it in New York journalism and remembers this interesting interlude in black American life. Moon thought that he and his roommates should all try to find the required boat fare and sign up, even though he himself "couldn't dance, and couldn't sing." Poston plunged ahead out of curiosity and the "chance to get a free trip with all expenses," a colleague at the *Amsterdam News* said.

Dorothy West, a tiny, vivacious, light-skinned would-be writer from Boston, had come to New York because "we all wanted to go to the magic city."[9] She was unique among the West 66th Street residents in having an income. Every Saturday a check for $17.50 came from her father, the "banana king of Boston." She was persuaded to make the trip to Russia when she went to a meeting of the Fellowship of Youth, Peace, and Reconciliation and met "nice, sane, simple people." At Zora Neale Hurston's apartment, West met Mollie Lewis, a youthful divorcee from Cleveland. Henry Lee Moon had been a playground instructor at Mollie's school when she was a girl. As Moon became better acquainted with the innocent Dorothy West, he suggested that she make the Russia trip but admonished her not to encourage Mollie. Ironically, West says, "Henry wanted me to get away from Mollie"; he thought Mollie was "a kind of wild one."[10]

Ted Poston, Thurston Lewis, Dorothy West, Henry Lee Moon, and Mollie Lewis all signed up to go to Russia. Others were recruited by W. A. Domingo, a onetime Garveyite, "militant Jamaican Socialist," and now chairman of the Communist Party USA. An interracial committee consisting of political journalist Bessye Bearden, white writer Malcolm Cowley, black communist attorney William L. Patterson, and designated trip leader Louise Thompson also spread the word.[11] Thompson, whom Moon termed "an energetic and brightly alert woman," already knew Moon from his stints reporting in the courts.[12] Ted was eager for life and had no wife, children, or mother to worry about him. He felt free to take off on adventures. The most prominent recruit among the twenty-two blacks was Langston Hughes. He and Moon had attended high school in Cleveland at the same time—Moon at Glenville High, Hughes at Central.[13] Moon, in a summer course at Central, had seen Hughes, whom he described as "neat and hygienic, not a guy who strutted around in a new suit showing off." [14] A few of the twenty-two were motivated to "get away from American race prejudice forever, being filled up with Jim Crow." Only two were known or admitted communists, Ted estimated. "Subsequent developments indicated that at least three others were then Communists or became Communists during the course of the trip." [15] Most of the twenty-two simply "thought they had found an exciting way to spend the summer." [16]

In preparation for the jaunt, Ted took a crash course in Russian from Maysie Stone, a sculptor whom he met through his sister-in-law, Augusta Savage. Maysie Stone's belief in interracial friendship as well as her skill and fascination with language had been fostered by her educated Russian Jewish parents.[17] While Stone and Poston practiced Russian vocabulary and grammar, Stone asked to sculpt Ted.[18] During sculpting and language sessions, they exchanged memories of childhood. Pauli Murray sometimes tagged along with Ted. Murray watched Ted's bust develop under Stone's hands. It showed his "huge ears, [and] full, sensitive lips." Ted had been Murray's "idol among the young writers in Harlem . . . a deity in my eyes." Murray was a junior at Hunter College in 1932 and "flirted briefly" with the idea of joining the travelers to Russia, "especially since Communism was beginning to attract Negro intellectuals" and one might "see the social experiment in action." She decided against it, however, because it would interrupt her quest for a college degree. But Pauli Murray, Maysie Stone, and Ted Poston's conversations contributed to both Poston's and Murray's determination to put the childhood experiences they had related to each other at Stone's studio onto paper some day.[19]

In June, the twenty-two African American travelers were ready and jubilantly "set sail for the Soviet Union," Ted wrote.[20] The interpersonal intrigues of the personalities in the group would provide juicy tidbits for gossip. The *Inter-State Tattler* headlined, "They're Off! Group Sails to Moscow to Make Black and White Film," and sketched the plans. A bon voyage telegram addressed to Theodore Roosevelt Augustus Major Poston, Nord

Deutscher Lloyd Line, from "a mischievous girl friend," did not reach Ted until mid-Atlantic. "With such an august address, Ted divined, the telegram had originally been directed to first class and filtered down through second class" to steerage.[21]

The group found a sometime nurturer of Harlem Renaissance writers, Professor Alain Locke of Howard University, on board, traveling with Ralph Bunche, the UN diplomat who would win the Nobel Peace Prize in 1949.[22] Locke lived in comparative luxury on board ship through the largesse of Charlotte Osgood Mason, who—until a recent estrangement—had underwritten the work of Louise Thompson, Zora Neale Hurston, and Hughes. Locke's shipboard activity seemed to be the penning of cryptic notes to "Godmother" Mason, concerning the activities of Hughes and Thompson and of his former students, Moon and the handsome Leonard Hill, whom the *Tattler* article called a "social service worker."[23] Locke scribbled, "how motley they are—how young and inexperienced," and remarked on "the inroads bad living has made," that Hughes, for example, "has coarsened and aged."[24] Locke persuaded Moon to promise to write to him from Russia. Moon kept his promise, then Locke copied Moon's words in his next missive to Mason. Moon wrote to Locke and Locke repeated to Mason: "Almost everyone in the party has been sick since we have been in Moscow: mainly due to the difference in food. . . . As yet we have not started to work. Our director . . . is having difficulty with Meschrabpom officials who it seems want more propaganda injected into the film."[25] But when Locke worried that the twenty-two might be left stranded in Russia without resources, he gave Moon no more forwarding addresses for his mail, for he did not want to have "several homeless and penniless derelicts on my hands."[26] Locke thenceforth read of the travelers in the press.

Langston Hughes's version of the ship crossing sounded more agreeable. The weather was "wonderful." Hughes did "nothing but sleep. . . . The boat was full of young people. . . . I practiced German, studied Russian, played deck games, and danced."[27] Arnold Rampersad paints Louise Thompson as the dominant figure and casts a poor light on the "giddy" twenty-five-year-old Ted Poston, who tested Thompson's authority even though "all had solemnly agreed to represent the race creditably." But Poston and Thurston Lewis, to Louise Thompson's mind, "seemed unhinged by their unusual freedom and, in particular, the many white women on board."[28]

They docked in Germany, which had "never had a year so 'dominated and bedeviled' by politics as 1932," a year "so pregnant with fate"—"nightly battles in the streets, frequent elections and mounting unemployment."[29] Arriving in Berlin by boat train, they found that "no Russian visas awaited them." The Russian consul knew nothing about the group. Thus the "twenty-two Negro Americans found themselves in Berlin without visas, without contracts and with fast-dwindling pocket money."[30] They were struck immediately by the absence of racism against them but also by general poverty, loose social mores, and turmoil unknown in America. Hughes noted that even though Negroes could eat "in any restaurant we could afford," Berlin seemed "a wretched city. Its beautiful buildings and wide avenues . . . [were] ringed with grey slums." Their hotel was near a railway station. Hughes put a coin into "what I thought was a candy-bar machine, but a package of prophylactics came out." The streets "teemed with prostitutes, pimps, panderers and vendors of dirty pictures." Hughes recalls that "some of the young men in our group got acquainted for the first time with . . . 'perversions.' Unusual sex pleasures" were offered "at pathetically low prices."[31]

The Russian consulate finally got visas and the twenty-two, the only blacks, boarded the *Ariadne* to cross the Baltic Sea. Hughes wrote that "the trip . . . was like a fairy-tale journey on a boat filled with amiable people." Coming from the poverty of the Depression, they partook ravenously of the smorgasbord—"creamed potatoes, smoked ham, sardines, salads, sturgeon, hot dumplings, stuffed rolls . . . spread buffet style on a long white table." But after they had eaten their fill, "dinner was served!"[32] The *Ariadne* reached Finland during the time of the summer's "white nights." The weather was "crisply cool in spite of the bright sun," and the group toured Helsinki in "*droskis*. . . . [They were] low, open carriages."[33] By night, they traversed Finland by train and entered the Soviet Union.

In St. Petersburg, which had been renamed Leningrad in 1924, they were greeted by a brass band that "blared out the Internationale" and by delegations from Meschrabpom Film and the city itself. In Moscow, a "puzzled official shook his head after shaking hands with several" of them, "their hands, so soft, they don't feel like workers' hands."[34] Muscovites welcomed the newcomers as Negro comrades.[35] They were whisked to the Grand Hotel—one block from the parklike, church-filled grounds of the Kremlin—for "a gala breakfast," Hughes wrote. Meschrabpom soon sent them film contracts. According to Russian buying power, their four hundred rubles a month was "about a hundred times a week" as much as Hughes had ever made before.[36]

Treated royally as marvelous representatives of the "downtrodden American workers," the twenty-two took advantage of the opportunities for enjoyment free of color lines.[37] Moon's daughter—Ted's godchild Mollie Lee Moon Elliot—remembered "Uncle Ted's stories" that the Soviets had not seen blacks before. "To them, the blacks looked very dark and very tall. Russians would run out to touch the hair of some of them." Another black would say, "Touch me, too." In Russia Uncle Ted made his color work to his advantage, Elliot concluded. Except for Hughes, the group was having too much fun to apply their talents to correcting the quaint stereotypes the Russians had of them.

After their humble abode in Harlem, Moon and Poston relished the Grand Hotel with its "enormous rooms, huge [old] beds, heavy drapes at the windows and deep rugs on the floors." But with famine in Russia, dining consisted of "whatever was available. Day after day . . . weak Russian borscht, some Irish potatoes, cabbage and black bread. No pork chops, no chicken, no ham and eggs, no butter." Vodka-fueled grumbling ensued, so "wheezy old trucks" were "dispatched into the countryside to forage for food." They returned, "loaded with chickens, eggs, vegetables and meat . . . bought from farmers, who despite collectivization and the shortage of food in the state shops, were stashing away provisions for such lucrative private trading." The goods were turned over to the hotel's kitchen "with strict orders that they were to be prepared and served only to the Negro *tovarischi*."[38]

The comrades were lionized as "representatives of the great Negro people." Their ruble stipends from Meschrabpom arriving on the Fourth of July made Ted's twenty-sixth birthday extra happy.[39] Ted, Moon, and Thurston Lewis occupied one bedroom with beds that sagged in the middle. They spent some of their largesse on a woman tutor who helped them with their Russian, although they had interpreters when they went out as a group. Homer Smith recalled that for the Negro *tovarischi,* "things had never been so good."[40] Romances abounded. Men flocked around the beautiful artist Mildred Jones, but she turned them aside with avant-garde frankness, saying, "Sorry, but I'm looking for the same thing you are."[41] At the home of Emma Harris, "the black mammy of Moscow," the group found homelike comforts.[42] The twenty-two were especially interested to see the veneration with which the premiere nineteenth-century Russian man of letters, Aleksandr Pushkin, was regarded. Pushkin's statue was located in the heart of Moscow where the trolley lines met. A descendant of the "Negro of Peter the Great," Pushkin was adored in Russia and his mulatto heritage was constantly played up in the press that summer. His verse-novel *Eugene Onegin* and his historical tragedy *Boris Godonov* were standard texts in Soviet schools.

Filming for *Black and White* kept being postponed. The unfinished script, which Meschrobpom based on a Mayakovsky poem, had incongruous scenes that amused Hughes to tears. He read the script the night it arrived and laughed so loud he woke his "two roommates . . . asleep in their beds, dreaming about being movie actors." Hughes sequestered himself to rewrite it. Director Karl Yunghans "became a nervous wreck after the first rehearsal" when "almost none" of the "supposedly naturally musical Negroes could sing." Meanwhile, for all except Hughes, by day there was sightseeing "or nude bathing in the Park of Rest and Culture on the banks of the Moscow River."[43] Nude bathing had not been a practice of the twenty-two at home so, Henry Lee Moon says, "Our people went in with their shorts on. The Russians asked, 'Why are they covered up?'" Ted Poston, "always forthright," Moon says, adapted and "didn't cover anything. But it was an experience that was new to us."[44]

Quiet, conservative Moon often seemed aghast at Ted's frivolous antics. They were opposites "as far as women were concerned," Ellen Tarry says. "While everybody else was having liaisons all over the place, sedate Henry was seeing an elegant English woman," Ted told Tarry. One night, Henry propositioned the woman. She broke out in laughter. He had asked her, "When are you going to give me some?" The woman had never heard it called "some" before. "And that's one of the lies that Ted would tell periodically on poor Henry," Tarry concludes.

Moon had a tale of his own with which he got revenge for Poston's teasing. One evening Moon visited three friends and "talked politics—international and national." It got late, and the friends suggested that Moon stay the night. Moon says, "I didn't turn up that evening, or that morning." Ted and Thurston were worried, thinking, "What the hell's happened?" They called Lovett Forte-Whiteman, a Negro American communist who had relocated to Moscow, for advice. He said, "Sit tight. Henry will be all right. The OGPU [secret police] will find out where he is." When Moon finally rejoined his friends, he implied that he had enjoyed a sexual rendezvous. He told them, "Man, you should have been with me. We had a delightful evening of discussion and we had wonderful strawberry jam for breakfast." Ted and Thurston "were envious as hell."[45]

The group's romantic forays continued when the twenty-one—Hughes was busy on the script—"idled away the hours" in the bar of the Metropole Hotel, where a little band "played jazz wretchedly and mysterious women . . . invited attention."[46] Apparently the women were government informers. Thurston Lewis and Ted "pursued the women crudely," Louise Thompson thought. She wrote home that Ted Poston had been a "malicious trouble maker . . . thoroughly irresponsible." Concerning white women, Ted and Thurston were "like two puppies, chained for a while and then let loose." Thompson added that Henry Moon had "not acted in the disgraceful manner" of those two, but had repeatedly backed them. Homer Smith's recollection was less harsh. He said that the *Black and White* crew were "demonstrating nightly Harlem's terpsichorean art with charming Russian girls . . . with such finesse and gusto as the establishment had never seen before," with Ted as dance floor luminary.[47]

A later colleague of Poston's at the *New York Post,* Fern Marja Eckman, who heard his Russian stories, thought he used a traditional Old South technique of "puttin' on ole massa" with the Russians, that his antics were a deliberate manipulation of the Russians who were at the same time trying to manipulate them. At parties Eckman would hear "Ted's own laughing stories about the Russian episode in his life." He reminisced about the Russian women who "flung themselves at him and the other males in the group." He regarded the women as enticements provided by the Russians to convert the Americans to communist dogma, and he "seemed to have enjoyed every minute of it," Eckman says. "Remember, Ted was young. And he *was* a nonconformist by any standard."

Savoring the chickens and vegetables trucked in from the farms especially for them, the twenty-two seemed blissfully unaware of the famine that in 1932 afflicted other parts of the Soviet Union. Joseph Stalin, as Ian Grey has written, had forced the peasant to "give up his land and join collective farms." He "sent teams of armed zealots into the countryside to requisition all the food they could find," including their seed grain.[48] An estimated six million Ukrainians perished.[49] Yet, judging from official reports, workers in the cities seemed to be treated well. Labor unions, which were becoming a Poston passion, provided benefits for Russian workers even as their decision making was taken over by the state. For example, the composer Dmitri Shostakovich was just finishing his opera *Lady Macbeth of Mtsensk District,* about a provincial dreamer who was a victim of the social order. Shostakovich lived with his mother in a cramped apartment, but then the new Union of Soviet Composers rescued him with "comfortable accommodations on Kirovsky Prospekt, in one of the best sections of Leningrad."[50] Unionism in that case benefited even a cultural worker.

Before the summer was over, the twenty-two blacks were invited to a party in the abode of Sergei Eisenstein, Russia's greatest filmmaker of the 1920s and a partisan of the black race. Eisenstein's aura was fading in 1932, however, because he was more passionate for art than for Stalin's favor. No union would rescue him. Eisenstein's reputation had been established with *October,* the 1927 film that commemorated the tenth anniversary of the Bolshevik revolution. (It was renamed in English-speaking countries for John Reed's book, *Ten Days That Shook the World.*)[51] Eisenstein's special interest in blacks had led, in 1931, to an idea that he would make a film on Toussaint L'Ouverture, the liberator of Haiti, and entitle it *Black Majesty.* He thought that a slave—one generation removed from Africa—who was capable of organizing an army and defeating the troops of Napoleon was more than a unique individual; "he must reflect the developing genius of the Negro people."[52] Because by 1932 Eisenstein had come under a cloud in

Stalin's regard, his housing suffered in comparison even with Moon and Poston's Harlem flat. Moon observed that their Harlem apartment "was far superior to any of the Russian homes I went into, and I went into a number."[53] Moon recalled of the visit to Eisenstein's, "We had a lot of fun—still it was barren. People seemed to endure it because it was a shared poverty."[54]

All Americans in Moscow heard of Anna Louise Strong and the English-language paper she had initiated there in 1931, the *Moscow Daily News*. Strong was two decades older than Ted Poston. She had sought a political vision that would overcome the chaos of the world and embraced revolution, immersing herself in unionism, child welfare, and the labor movement. She had covered the Everett, Washington, massacre for the *New York Evening Post* a generation before Ted Poston joined that paper as its first black reporter.[55] In 1921 Strong found herself in Moscow, "wrecked by four years of civil war and intervention," no streetcars running. "Water pressure only came up to the second floor" of the hotel and "the upper floors carried their water in pails." But by 1932 Strong marveled that Moscow, "a sprawling picturesque, semi-Asiatic town . . . is a world capital. Tomorrow it will be an example of what the workers of the USSR can build as the central citadel of socialism."[56] To serve the many skilled laborers who had "come from the West to the USSR for work," Strong wanted an "American type newspaper," a forum for their problems and a "source of information about developments in Russia and back home." It would carry baseball scores and be written in a "lively American manner."[57]

When the two visiting journalists, Poston and Moon, appeared with their vivid American style, she summoned them to the *Moscow News* office and invited them to edit one issue of the *News*. They did that for "Anna Louise and the four dwarfs," the nickname for the male staff members because they were all short. Ted would later relate that the issue he and Moon edited was a sellout. With typical embellishment, Poston said that he and Moon had "worked our way through France and pre-Hitler Germany, and anywhere else any solvent publications were willing to buy the free lance opinions of two unexcelled experts on the Great American Depression." Even though they realized that Strong's invitation was a "propaganda stunt," the bait she offered was too tempting. Anything that "anybody did to that four-page English language tabloid was bound to be an improvement." For instance, it had never had a streamer headline, and previous illustrations had tended to show "a stirring picture of a tractor being delivered to a collective farm." He and Moon, Poston recalled, "waded into Tass copy and came up with a gem. We made it the *Moscow Daily News'* first streamer: 'JIMMY WALKER FORCED OUT AS N.Y. MAYOR.' (Of course [a Russian editor] changed that later to read: 'DANCING JIMMY, CAPITALIST DOG, KICKED OUT.' " But the issue was a "one-day sensation." Strong rushed to the Mininskaya Hotel the next morning to tell them that their issue had enjoyed the first complete sellout in the paper's history. "I'm sure it's because of the new English classes they had started in the Red Army and the secret police schools," she said, and the two men "modestly accepted her compliments." Poston went on, "So it came as a shock to me and Moon three days later when we discovered that the Soviet Fish Trust was located next door to the offices of the *Moscow Daily News*. And on the day of our great triumph, the store had received a record shipment of fresh fish for immediate sale. How were we to know that the Soviet experiment had not advanced so far at that point that neither wrapping paper nor shopping bags were available to fish-hungry customers?"[58]

Poston had made advance preparations to ply his trade while abroad through Claude Barnett, Ulysses' friend who had founded the Associated Negro Press (ANP). Barnett emphasized "constructive news that would offer readers models to emulate and would win respect from both blacks and whites for the responsible black press."[59] When Ted offered Barnett his services, Barnett accepted but warned, "Pure propaganda is no longer acceptable, neither does it sell to the public."[60] As it turned out, since the ANP had practically no resources, Ted would not make money serving it. But when Meschrabpom suddenly canceled the film project, a disillusioned Poston sent Barnett "the complete and 'inside' story of the recent Soviet film fiasco."[61]

The group members' recollections about the failure of the film project reveal tensions related to various members' attitudes toward their Soviet hosts and show a variety of ways each of these creative people reconstructed what had gone on. On hearing of the cancellation of the film, the usually soft-spoken Moon said to the others, "Comrades, we've been screwed!" Moon says that one of the Russians who was producing the film replied, "Would you have said that if you were in Georgia, back in the USA?" Moon forgets how he answered but thinks, "I *should* have said, 'Comrade, did it occur to you to speak the truth in the Soviet Union?'" But Ted was "all in stitches." He liked the revised version of Moon's response best and exclaimed, "From now on, that's what you *said*. I'm going to spread that story from now on."[62] One of the places Ted would "spread the story" was in a profile of Moon he wrote a generation later when Moon's book *Balance of Power*, an analysis of how the Negro vote turned the tide for President Harry S Truman, was published:

A non-Communist liberal who might well have developed into a fellow traveler. . . . has never forgotten a scathing question put to him by A. Piatnitksy, a Comintern official.

"That's a very courageous speech, Mr. Moon," Piatnitksy said, "but I wonder if you would be so courageous in Atlanta, Ga."

"Oh, does it take courage to speak the truth in the Soviet Union?" Moon shot back.[63]

The different responses of the twenty-two "actors" to their treatment in Russia led to ideological arguments. Hughes recalled one instance when Ted "arose to call [Hughes] a Communist Uncle Tom" because he accepted the Soviet representative's explanation of the reasons for the cancellation of the film. Hughes wrote, in *I Wonder as I Wander,* that Ted "solemnly stated that my books in the United States had never amounted to much, so for that reason I had come to the Soviet Union to build a new literary career. And he closed his speech by terming me an opportunistic son-of-a-bitch. I arose to call him a similar name—so the meeting broke up in general vituperations. But later we laughed about it, made up, and from then on everybody jokingly called all of our meetings 'son-of-a-bitch meetings.'"[64] In the arguments, Hughes was joined by Mollie Lewis, Louise Thompson, Dorothy West, Mildred Jones, and most of the other thespians.[65] The minority of four—Poston, Moon, Thurston Lewis, and West Indian Laurence Alberga— resented their hosts for spying and for persecuting truth-tellers.[66] Despite the arguments, Moon concluded that the Russia trip was helpful "in developing my world view. . . . I could certainly write more knowingly about Russia after that."[67]

Robert C. Weaver thought that his friends "flirted with the Left; it was inevitable, because the Left was the only part of the white community that was not racist to the core." An FBI agent heard that Poston "came back from Russia thoroughly disillusioned . . . [and] has been opposed to Communists and Communism ever since." Ted himself said that upon their return to America, "we were vilified in the Communist press and handbills were distributed on the streets of Harlem denouncing us for expressing our opinions of the Communist Party and the Soviet Union."[68] Although Ted could see that communism's solutions would fail to alleviate American social ills, henceforth he would join one of their battles and fight for unions.

On October 13, 1932, Ted and Henry Lee Moon stepped back on American soil, "penniless, too late to register to vote and a dime between us." Ted called his brother, and Ulysses "picked us up and took us to the Dunbar apartments where we stayed in his spare room until we got settled."[69]

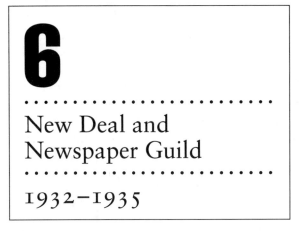

6

. . . .
New Deal and
Newspaper Guild
. . . .
1932–1935

This is my kind of union!
—TED POSTON to Heywood Broun

The election campaigns of 1932 were in their closing days, candidates frenziedly shouting their messages. America was in bad shape. The Republicans renominated Herbert Hoover, who believed in the basic soundness of the economy and that it would regenerate spontaneously. The widely read *World* columnist Heywood Broun championed Socialist Norman Thomas, who advocated laws against lynching and child labor; the admission of Negroes to juries; reduction of southern representation in Congress until all citizens could vote; unemployment insurance for all workers who were victims of involuntary idleness; and enforcement of constitutional guarantees of economic, political, and legal equality for the Negro.[1] The Democrats chose as their candidate the popular governor of New York, Franklin D. Roosevelt, who had surrounded himself with a small group of intellectuals, his Brain Trust, who advised him in many fields.

Ulysses Poston, publishing his regular Democratic campaign issue of the *Contender,* was "out rounding up votes in Harlem and elsewhere in New York City," Moon says. "Ted and I worked on his paper at Ulysses' home." The October 22 issue contained an array of material: a new addition to the Poston-Moon version of *Black and White*'s cancellation; some puff pieces correlated with ads; some racial uplift; some strictures of advice on saving face for the race; propaganda in the news columns; and an all-out editorial endorsement of the Democrats and New York City's Democratic administration of Tammany Hall. In a special feature, Ulysses exhorted that "Republican-bossed public utilities were the first to announce to the Negro, 'We are sorry but we can't use you after Saturday,'" whereas Tammany "walked steadily up and reached out its hand and beckoned the Negro to come this way." Roosevelt had "shown his great sympathy for the fight of the Negro citizen for full equality" by becoming a member of the board of directors of the National Association for the Advancement of Colored People. Ulysses advised, "The Negro citizen . . . can vote the Democratic ticket from top to bottom without reservations."[2] Roosevelt rolled into the White House when the country's economic structure was tottering. Because despair hung heavy, the crippled president declared, "The only thing we have to fear is fear itself."

The earnest political endeavors of both Ulysses and Sybil Poston left them frustrated with patronage, the main conduit to black career advancement until then.[3] Their experience contributed to Ted's distrust of the patronage system as an avenue for entrusting one's career.

Many Negroes' prayers were answered when Eleanor Roosevelt became first lady. Not long after the Roosevelts arrived in Washington, word went around that she was "one person who considered [Negroes] as human beings and whose sense of compassion and fairness embraced them." She invited a group to the White House, and they "talked until midnight when the President was wheeled in and said a few friendly words. The whole occasion was unprecedented in Negro history." When Republicans in the New York State legislature cut $21 million out of the appropriation for the Department of Public Works, then were "obliged to appropriate not only what they had cut out of the budget, but more for public relief," Mrs. Roosevelt wondered which would have been better—"to pay that money out in salaries for labor on public works, or to pay it in unemployment relief."[4]

The Roosevelts had aroused America. Though the Depression grew deeper, J. Raymond Jones remembers, blacks in New York politics "felt a subtle lift in our spirits."[5] That spring and summer of 1933, an exciting, "bustling sort of chaos, born of renewed confidence and new undertakings, filled the city [Washington, D.C.] and many a government corridor."[6] The lights burned late, and in the "vast new office buildings along the Mall there was sublime confusion as new jobholders arrived," Frederick Lewis Allen wrote. "Government departments were overflowing . . . the streets were full of apartment-hunters . . . [and] real-estate men of Washington rubbed their hands at the sudden boom in the housing market."[7]

No wonder, then, that Moon and Poston would seek respite from unemployment in government service. After the 1932 election, Moon says, "the

Contender folded, and we had to look around and scramble. Ted got a job back on the *Amsterdam News.*"[8] J. Raymond Jones's Penn Station Intellectual Gang met with U. S. Poston to reconnoiter. The *Contender* of 1932 was Ulysses' last effort as a publisher.[9] Perhaps Judge Samuel Seabury's investigation of Tammany, which brought down the debonair Mayor Jimmy Walker, caused Ulysses' final disillusionment with active politics.[10] He opened a real estate office.[11] Moon landed a job in the federal Public Works Administration under Secretary of the Interior Harold Ickes on a project called technocracy that attempted "to re-introduce bartering into society. You did some kind of work for which you would get something in exchange—food, a suit of clothes," Moon says. "Money has always been a lot of trouble—getting and holding and spending. But the program was terminated." Ted Poston then got Moon rehired at the *Amsterdam.*

After leaving Ulysses and Sybil's spare room, Ted and Moon moved in with Thurston Lewis again in the basement at 363 Edgecombe Avenue, with its bathroom, a hot plate, and one big living room where they held bull sessions. Ted assumed his normal role of resident raconteur. When somebody visited and Ted started up, Lewis and Moon would walk ostentatiously out of the room saying, "We've heard this." In a moment they would be back "laughing like hell." Ted would be recounting some adventure as if it were the first time. Moon nicknamed Ted "the great embellisher." Taylor Gordon, a popular Negro entertainer, stopped by one day and Ted launched into his Russian stories. After Gordon left, Moon asked Ted why he had not told about being a waiter on the railroad and how "that chef was cheating the railroad company by throwing out a ham every time he passed his home." Poston answered, "Hell, that nigger's worked on the railroad, but he's never been to Russia!"[12]

Exemplifying a serious conflict over Negro civil rights, and Poston's most memorable assignment for the *Amsterdam News,* the Scottsboro trial in Alabama was the first incident to awaken many white Americans of the 1930s to the extent of injustice to blacks. Hoboes had roamed the land throughout the Depression. In 1932, at Paint Rock, Alabama, nine blacks, ages thirteen to twenty, were charged with raping two white women who had hopped the same freight. The trial date was set for March 1933 in Decatur, Alabama. After a "hasty trial, held in an atmosphere of pervasive hostility," the blacks were convicted. All but the youngest boys were sentenced to the electric chair on the shaky testimony of the two female witnesses, one of whom later repudiated her statements. The *New York Post* castigated the "shameful course of the Alabama trials" for leading many Americans "to lose faith in the veracity of the state's officials."[13] The NAACP and the communist-led International Labor Defense (ILD) entered the case and spread news of the Scottsboro boys around the world, also revealing the rising tense relationship between black liberalism and communism.[14]

William H. "Kid" Davis, publisher of the *Amsterdam News,* posted news of the boys' sentence on the bulletin board outside the *Amsterdam* office and urged Harlem residents to march on Washington in protest. Thousands responded. The ILD embraced Kid Davis's proposal fervently, then tried to dominate, calling the now black-white protest a true "united front." Heywood Broun, in the Socialist party, was named a vice-chairman of the protest, but when he realized who controlled the group, he "quietly ceased active participation."[15] But Kid Davis sent Ted—with no expense account (he promised to send funds "later")—to Decatur to cover the boys' retrial in 1933. There were no television cameras to afford Ted a measure of protection. A black reporter in the Deep South had to watch his back and try to avoid attracting attention to himself. Ted was turned away at the first boardinghouse at which he sought a room when the landlady discovered the purpose of his visit. He was then advised by a railroad porter to "walk along up these tracks and . . . you'll find a woman by the name of Williams down by the river. Tell her the truth and she'll conceal you."[16]

In a talk to reporters thirty-five years later, Poston expressed his indebtedness to black Alabama townsfolk, to white reporters, and even to the defense attorney, Samuel S. Leibowitz, in helping him disseminate his Scottsboro stories. Poston said, "There were so many decent white guys working on papers who were willing to do the right thing but knew that their papers would never print what they knew *I* could print, and they wanted the truth to get out. I just happened to be lucky enough to be the conduit." No Negro reporters then were accredited. Every day, instead of taking a seat at the press table, Poston would "sit up there in the Negro gallery in ragged overalls pretending to be a country boy, looking, and I would make notes under the overcoat on my lap." Then he would go to the colored restroom next to the "white gentlemen's" room and put his copy on top of the partition separating the two men's rooms and Tom Cassidy of the *New York Daily News* would pick it up and wire it with his. When that was not convenient, after typing his copy on his portable typewriter at the boardinghouse, Poston would "sneak to the railroad tracks at night" and put his stories "in the mail car of the midnight special." When word got out that a Negro reporter was at the trial, a group of young whites caught him by the train, he said, and put a pistol to his back. He denied he was a newsperson and reached in his pocket for his phony credentials—"The Rev. A. Parke Williams of the African

Methodist Episcopal Church." [17] The ruse merited him a kick in the pants but may have saved his life.

During the time of the trial two white men in California were lynched for kidnapping the nephew of writer Bret Harte. The *Decatur News* made no editorial suggestion that lynch law should be practiced on the nine Scottsboro youths. It just printed an eight-column picture of the two bodies in California, stripped and hanging, and implied that a similar solution to the Scottsboro trial would be expedient and economical. Poston said that the caption to the page-wide picture was "30 cents worth of rope. This county is $130,000 in debt for the Scottsboro trial." At the end of the retrial, a reporter for the *Decatur News* warned Poston to "get the hell out of town, that . . . there were plans" to get him. Penniless, Poston, still awaiting the expense money that Kid Davis had promised but never sent, went to defense attorney Leibowitz, who gave him $100. Poston wrote, "God knows I lived on it." He went straight to the railroad station and reserved a seat on the day coach, "made sure the ticket seller remembered me," then sneaked out of town on a bus. Leibowitz, just as unpopular in town, also made a train reservation, "then slipped out in an automobile." [18] A master of trickster techniques would naturally outsmart wielders of power from the dominant culture. Leibowitz learned and told Poston later, "There were between five hundred and a thousand [people] . . . waiting at the depot to get both of us." [19] In a black community, his color provided Poston protection, but getting a story among whites in the South required an ingenuity unknown to white reporters.

Before leaving the South, Poston stopped in Hopkinsville to call on his Braxton cousins. They remembered that every time Ted came, whether by plane, train, or bus, he carried newspapers under his arm. "He had *read* all the way here." That seemingly ordinary gesture suggests the closeness of newspapers to his heart and the belief inherited from the generation before him that journalism righted wrongs. The Braxton cousins were still children then, but they knew Ted was a writer and they loved to listen to him tell them poems and stories. "We would be starry-eyed. Ted always used to say, 'Never forget the closeness of the family.' He kept that in front of us all the time." [20] Ted cherished what he himself no longer had.

Back in Harlem, Poston and his onetime *Courier* editor Floyd Calvin had spoken of forming a newspeople's organization. Their hope materialized when "a group of popular news hounds" met at Calvin's home and initiated the Harlem Newspaper Club. Officers included Poston as president and Corienne K. Robinson of the *Inter-State Tattler* as secretary. Calvin, Bessye

J. Bearden (*Chicago Defender*), Geraldyn Dismond (*Afro-American*), Thelma Berlack-Boozer (*Amsterdam News*), Henry L. Moon (*Amsterdam News*), and Obie McCollum (*Amsterdam News*) formed the executive committee.[21] This group was a black forerunner to a newspaper union, which was needed if reporters were ever to obtain reasonable working arrangements and wages.

The saga of Sidney Hillman, who during World War II would summon Poston to government service in Washington, may clarify the necessity for unions. Sidney Hillman came to the United States from Lithuania as a garment worker the year Ted was born. In 1910, Chicago garment workers struck Hart, Schaffner and Marx because of its intolerable working environment. Forty thousand people joined them and refused to accept "another cut in their meager pay," walking out in a general strike of the whole industry.[22] In 1914, Hillman was elected president of the Amalgamated Clothing Workers and introduced such union practices as cooperative housing and banking.

The wealthy and philanthropic capitalist Joseph Schaffner had not looked into his factories for years. He was satisfied with the quality of the firm's merchandise, but the strike troubled his conscience. He had thought his labor standards were in "a satisfactory state." But in 1915, the garment workers struck. Hillman led a delegation of prominent citizens to the mayor's office "to plead with the city government to mediate the strike, [and Mayor] Thompson refused to see them." One picketer was shot and killed. Three days later, ten thousand ragged workers marched silently through the streets carrying their dead colleague to his grave. They bore banners announcing their grievances and demands but "preserved a strange and frightening silence. No dirge sounded and not an outcry was heard." When the union's money was gone two months later, Hillman declared an end to the strike. But eighty-seven shops with five thousand workers had signed agreements with the union by then. And Joseph Schaffner, seeing the need for unions, became one of organized labor's "rare industrial champions."[23]

Two decades after the garment workers' strike, Ted Poston noticed that unions had made their lives bearable. Ted was gaining confidence in himself as a newspaperman at the *Amsterdam,* and he believed that the black press was giving its readers a feeling of strength and solidarity.[24] He thought the black press's public exposure of racism produced a cathartic effect much as had slaves' "oaths said against the master out of hearing of the plantation gate" in an earlier day. James Scott calls the "declared form of resistance" practiced by the black press a radical departure from the slaves' "disguised, low-profile, undeclared resistance" to racism.[25]

By 1935, Poston was city editor at the *Amsterdam.* His colleagues who most desired to promote a newspeople's union were Moon and Thelma Berlack-Boozer. The latter, college-educated on a $100 Madame Walker Scholarship after she graduated from high school with highest honors, was "a small, attractive, dark-skinned woman, most punctilious and precise," according to St. Clair Bourne.[26] The *Amsterdam* journalists bided their time on the question of unions while carrying on business.

Their own predicament, however, raised the issue of exploitation of black workers by black capitalists and the relationship of class to race solidarity. Black publishers, who had been editorializing that they supported workers, lost their passion when their own staffs sought to organize. Should reporters stick with their penurious class or, at any price, with their discriminated-against race?[27] The *Amsterdam News* staff struggled over the problem of wages and working conditions. Twenty-five dollars a week, no ceiling on hours, and no vacation pay kept the reporters insecure, overworked, and broke. Thus the idea of unionism that was being promulgated by Norman Thomas, Frank Crosswaith, and Heywood Broun held an irresistible attraction.[28] If unionism could help oppressed garment workers and white newspeople, black reporters thought it could work for them. Once Senator Robert F. Wagner's Wagner Act went into effect in 1935, establishing the National Labor Relations Board, some of the fear concerning bargaining collectively with management was lifted.[29]

In newspapering's unwritten tradition, the journalist would "sacrifice money, comfort, sleep, love, food, and hope of eternal salvation to the spirit of his craft." His compensation was to be "on the inside of things, to see how society functioned, and to promote justice."[30] But newspeople had no job security. Federal intervention was certainly needed. Through their efforts during the rest of 1935, Poston and Moon laid the foundation for benefits that would accrue to all later *Amsterdam* journalists.

Poston, Moon, and the *Amsterdam News* got involved in the Newspaper Guild in 1933, when Heywood Broun first called for a newspaper writers' union. Broun wrote, "Beginning at nine o'clock on the morning of October 1, I am going to do the best I can to help in getting one up."[31] Poston learned of the plan when he chanced to read of Broun's announcement in an issue of the communist *Daily Worker* that he picked up from a subway seat on his way home. He and Moon went to the meetings held in Broun's cluttered, book-lined study. The original group, whose membership spread by word-of-mouth, made four demands: a five-day, forty-hour week with consecutive days off; paid vacations; a minimum wage of at least $35 a week to newsmen who had one year or more of newspaper experience; and dismissal notice on a graduated basis (ranging from one month's notice for newsmen with three years' service on the same newspaper to six months for those with eight or more years' service).[32] Some reporters avoided the idea of a union; collective bargaining and rowdy strikes were beneath their dignity. Others, fearful of management reprisal, stayed away. But Broun said that unionization would bestow on journalists enhanced professional standing, "free of the chronic threat of arbitrary dismissal," and when adequately rewarded, reporters could "spurn proffered bribes" that tempted them to run or kill stories. The Newspaper Guild would gain independence for individual journalists.[33]

As an elder statesman of the Newspaper Guild, Poston in 1968 could tell young reporters his version of the Guild's origins. He says he asked himself, " 'What *is* this business? They talking about newspapermen demanding fifty dollars a week?' "

"We gathered at a hotel for some meeting and a [white] cat from Louisiana [saw us *Amsterdam News* staff], jumped up and said, 'Jesus Christ, you let niggers into this organization?'

"And Carl Randeau [of the *World-Telegram*] busted him right in the mouth. I said, 'This is *my* kind of union.' "[34]

Moon remarked that if there was any tendency toward discrimination within the Guild, they realized that Broun "stood like a bulwark against it."[35]

Poston and Moon persuaded the entire editorial staff of the *Amsterdam News* to join the new Guild. They assisted their white compatriots in picketing the *Brooklyn Eagle,* the newspaper that was "an institution like Borough Hall or Ebbets Field," according to William O'Dwyer. O'Dwyer was then serving on the Magistrate's Court and considered the *Eagle* strike "as much an expression of resentment against past wrongs as it was a determined effort to improve the miserable working conditions of its reporters." He could feel the "subtle pressure" being exerted on him to "make me see the consequences of Brooklyn without the *Eagle,* if I ever contemplated running for higher office."[36]

When the *Newark Ledger* struck, the *Amsterdam News* unit again "participated excellently."[37] By supporting fellow newspeople, the *Amsterdam* was gaining allies for its own coming fight. *Amsterdam* publisher William "Kid" Davis, champion of the Scottsboro boys, had by this time left the paper. He vanished from the scene when his marriage to Sadie Warren Davis, the widow of the former publisher, soured.

Sadie Warren Davis and her daughter Odessa Warren Morse now ran the paper alone and were not succeeding. They certainly worked hard. Percival L. Prattis was hired to save the paper, and he confided to Claude Barnett that

Davis "works all day on the switchboard and every morning when I come in, her daughter is cleaning up the office, with broom and dust rag." [38] Heedless of race solidarity, however, Davis "treated her employees in a feudal manner." She threatened to fire anyone who did not resign from the Guild; the unit voted secretly and unanimously agreed to strike "if necessary." Pleading financial necessity, Davis arbitrarily canceled all vacations. Poston and Moon asked the New York Newspaper Guild to undertake negotiations with her. Recognizing the economic difficulties faced by a Negro newspaper, the Guild representatives sought no wage increase but simply a contract that would assure the editorial staff of some job security. Davis refused to recognize the right of the Guild to negotiate for her staff and a crisis hit. [39]

Did she "lock out" the entire editorial department, or did the *Amsterdam* unit of the Newspaper Guild strike? The language used depends on whether one asks labor or management. Strike leader Poston felt that black publishers had no more business undervaluing their staff than did white publishers. [40] He declared that Negro publishers offered no incentive, that Negro newspapermen were among the lowest paid in the industry, many receiving no salary beyond payments from the sources of puff stories. He added that reporters who helped organize a Guild shop were sometimes denounced as "traitors to the race" and "enemies of Negro business" by publishers who had lavish summer homes, real estate investments, and high incomes. [41] Poston had no argument with Negro publishers' financial success except when they achieved it by exploiting their own people whom, editorially and simultaneously, they claimed to represent. The NAACP's *Crisis* editorialized that many Negro employers still clung to the race pride argument in the running of business: "It is true that many Negro businesses cannot stand absolute comparison with similar white businesses or be subjected to identical demands, but they should realize that employees, whether they be working for white or colored bosses, are entitled to fair wages, decent hours and some security." They should approach the ideal as closely as possible, and "the *Amsterdam News* strike has pointed the way." [42]

The Guild set up strike headquarters around the corner from the *Amsterdam,* at 205 West 135th Street, prepared picket signs, and made arrangements for financing the strike, including the payment of partial salaries to the locked-out employees. [43] In 1925 Frank Crosswaith, who sported a fresh boutonniere daily and sounded distinguished with his West Indian accent, had organized elevator operators, motion picture operators, mechanics, laundry workers, drugstore clerks, and grocery clerks into the Trade Union Committee. Crosswaith was aware of the power of united action and gave the newspeople moral support. [44]

In October 1935, Poston, Crosswaith, and Elmer A. Carter, editor of the Urban League's *Opportunity* magazine, distributed an invitation to selected Friends of the Newspaper Guild of New York, including the black municipal justice James S. Watson and Arthur A. Schomburg, curator of the Negro Division of the 135th Street Public Library, to help them in their fight. To combat Sadie Warren Davis's threat to dismiss the whole *Amsterdam* editorial staff, the voluntary citizens' committee tried to persuade the publisher to bargain collectively with the Guild.[45] Harlem's most noted citizens joined the Friends of the Newspaper Guild and sided with the reporters. A dozen ministers—including Rev. Adam Clayton Powell, Abyssinian Baptist Church; Rev. Shelton Hale Bishop, St. Philip's Protestant Episcopal; and Rev. William Lloyd Imes, St. James Presbyterian—preached sermons in support of the strike. Sympathetic picketers included Broun; writer Zora Neale Hurston; and Angelo Herndon, a victim of a Georgia chain gang.

The *Amsterdam* strike became the rage of Harlem. Newspeople from all over joined the picket line. Heywood Broun would arrive by taxi, bedraggled but earlier than the others, putting them to shame. Moon recalled that Broun "lumbered up and down in front of the *News* office . . . good-naturedly shouting our slogans." Broun attended committee meetings, joined the strikers in formulating plans, spoke for the group from the public platform, and contributed to their strike fund. Unlike some white liberals who drew the line at a race-based struggle, Broun had "nothing of the patronizing in his attitude."[46] Sadie Warren Davis, however, criticized Broun, saying that his associations with the Negro were so limited that he could not begin to understand all the angles of a situation involving the Negro people.

The Russia trip had crystallized for Ted the two passions he held throughout his life—union activity and civil rights. Proletarian solidarity was necessary in each endeavor. That meant taking advantage of white folks, such as Broun, who espoused their idea. He believed that the communists were willing to support the *Amsterdam News* workers because they hoped to win recruits for the party from among those workers as well as from others who might become involved, but Poston also thought that, whatever their politics, the response to the strike of fellow Guildsmen was splendid. Guild pressure caused the *Amsterdam*'s circulation to drop 50 percent even though its price was slashed from ten cents to five cents. A postcard campaign resulted in readers signing pledges not to read the *Amsterdam News* until it reinstated the Guildsmen.[47]

Mayor Fiorello LaGuardia had named blacks to important posts in his administration, treating Tax Commissioner Hubert T. Delaney as an unofficial ombudsman.[48] LaGuardia, who was admired in the black community, attempted to bring the publisher and the workers together. Sadie Warren Davis and her daughter were supposed to meet LaGuardia's representative and a Guild representative on October 14, 1935, but Davis's lawyer headed her off at the subway and advised her not to appear.[49] Thus LaGuardia's representative could hear only the Guild's side of the story. It seemed clear to the representative that these *Amsterdam* reporters were fired solely because of their organizational activities and their membership in the Guild. The real issue was a "determination on the part of the employers to defeat unionization."[50]

Davis declared that she would "cease publication rather than negotiate," and her daughter told the employees' representatives "We'll all go down together."[51] Indeed, within a month, Davis fired Poston and the other instigators of the strike, then she was forced to declare bankruptcy. On Christmas eve 1935, Dr. Clilan Bethany Powell and Dr. M. H. Savory bought the *Amsterdam News* from Davis, for a "pittance," Bourne says, largely as "a vehicle to advertise their new Victory Life Insurance Company." The publisher-physicians tried and failed to break the men and were forced to hire Poston and Moon back—but kept them only as long as the law required.

The doctors also turned out to be poor bosses, according to Bourne. Newspaper people made a living wage for 1935 only after they got a Guild contract. On buying the paper, the medical owners wanted to get rid of all the people who had headed the strike.[52] They told the FBI in 1941 that they were "forced to release" Ted Poston because of "his radical outbursts editorially." Poston had tried to dominate "in the same way he had when Mrs. Davis owned the paper" and had followed a policy of "fomenting Negro unrest by headlining and editorializing discriminations against Negroes in Civilian Conservation Corps camps and in the Works Progress Administration as well as in other state and governmental emergency set-ups." Sadie Warren Davis had been more irritated by Poston than by any other staff member. When an FBI investigator looked her up five years later, she was still "visibly disturbed and excited, with respect to any reference to Poston." She considered him dishonest, "sneaky and tricky, a fifth columnist" type, a "provocative influence," and "a considerable factor" in her ultimate loss of the paper. Another reporter from the *Amsterdam* strike period, probably Edgar Rouzeau, "made no effort to hide his dislike" for Poston when the FBI contacted him, yet he considered Poston "one of the most able colored writers in America." Poston's eventual firing was "occasioned by the impossible situation he created, and the unpleasant atmosphere attached to the paper as a result." A more moderate informant told the FBI agent that Poston was a gifted writer, "extremely well liked by the staff . . . editorially honest, and [that he] never angled his stories with personal sentiment." [53] Poston had started out in his *Courier* "Harlem Shadows" as flippant and carefree, but his personality had blossomed in the Soviet Union. The times, his own life experience, and traveling abroad had made him more aggressive. The question is whether Ted Poston had become more inflammatory or whether more people were taking sides in the class-race struggle and becoming more conscious of bias in the labor movement.

At the time of the strike, Poston, as leader of the *Amsterdam* Guild unit, was a glamorous character in Harlem and had attracted a female following. Miriam Rivers was one of "a group of young debs who got caught up in the glitter of the strike" and joined the picket line "so they could be seen and identified and hope to be photographed," recalls Bourne. "The strike was like a party, a social occasion. Everybody wanted to be there." Rivers, nicknamed Ming for her delicate, china-doll beauty, was "petite, cute," a "total contrast in looks and style to tall, rough, humorous" Ted, who was so "brassy, quick, loud, and sharp," says Archer Winsten, a white resident of the Harlem Young Men's Christian Association (YMCA) at the time. Ellen Tarry describes Ming as "a light brownskin girl who wore her hair straight back with a knot at the nape of her neck. She looked slightly Oriental. She came from a nice family. Her mother was a mulatto and her father brown." [54] Ming was charmed by Ted, and he became "just enamored of her," says Moon, but "she was not a member of our clique"; "not literary," adds Tarry. "Miriam Rivers was dating me," Ted's roommate Thurston Lewis mentions, "when she met Ted. I brought her along on a picnic. Then Ted began taking her to the home of a friend of his in New Jersey for week-end visits, and their friendship blossomed."

On November 13, 1935, Poston, age twenty-nine, shanghaied Henry Lee Moon over to the church—St. Philip's Protestant Episcopal—of one of the staunch *Amsterdam* strike supporters, Rev. Shelton Hale Bishop, for Moon to act as best man, and Ted married Miriam Rivers. On the marriage license, Ming gave her age as twenty. Moon celebrated Poston's first wedding day by reading his own name in the *New York Times* for the first time. The *Times* had found "fit to print" the news that strikebreaker Edgar T. Rouzeau had taken striking fellow reporter Moon to court for calling him a "Rat." [55]

7

Federal Writers' Project

1936–1940

Ted was a guy to whom a story was an art creation.
—HENRY LEE MOON

As Poston strove for unity among reporters through the Newspaper Guild, he and Ming did not succeed in nurturing unity at home. Journalism with its erratic stresses did not bode well for the health of marriages. St. Clair Bourne remarked, "Miriam married Ted in a burst of enthusiasm. Their romance earned the strike added attention. Then she found the pace too frenetic. Miriam was not ready to be the wife of a person like Ted Poston. Ted's pace and hers were too different. The most attention she ever got was when they married. From then on, she kind of faded away."

Ed Morrow looked back on Ming as "mousy, just a little girl. She never grew up. Ted was growing all the time." Ted took Ming to Hopkinsville to meet his hometown friends, and she failed to adhere to Kentuckians' expectations of mates. Allison Williams said that on a fishing trip, "She wouldn't set her own bait, then she raised the devil about cleaning the fish." [1]

In addition, Ted's private persona diverged from the public one. Ming told Ellen Tarry that Ted had two sides, the jocular one that the public saw and another that emerged "in the privacy of the bedroom," after drink, when "he was not always so convivial. He had a cruel streak." [2] Tarry remembered double-dating with Ted and Ming. Tarry's escort was Andrew Brunner, and she and Ming commiserated about their companions' jealous natures. "As we watched the two men come under the influence of whatever was being served, we said to each other, 'Oh, we're going to catch hell later.' Yet, when we were out, Ted was the life of the party."

Black marriages carried special burdens. In an atmosphere of poverty and white oppression, black men especially felt the need to seem "somebody" at home. In *Lonely Crusade,* Chester Himes depicted a wife who could not understand her fearful husband's "necessity for dominance" or his ego that "made a man beat his wife just to prove that he was stronger." The fear came from the husband's "being unable to support and protect" a woman. It caused him to do such things as "look inside of strange restaurants to see if Negroes were being served" before taking his wife inside.[3] Indeed, Poston told of an incident when he and Ming tried to enter "Aunt Dinah's Restaurant" and a buxom German proprietress physically blocked their way to the tables and told them, "I won't serve you in my dining room. . . . If you want to go back there in the kitchen, maybe the chef will give you something."[4] Ted's accumulated anger at society, at being fired from the *Amsterdam,* and at the Depression period in general may have erupted at home, causing a schism in what should have been a honeymoon period.

The Postons changed their address several times. In 1936, they lived at the classy 409 Edgecombe, where they shared an apartment with others.[5] Apartment sharing and rent parties on Friday nights were fixtures of life in Harlem. At a rent party, a tenant sponsored a dance evening and charged a small amount for down-home cooking and alcohol. The proceeds supplied that person's rent for the week.[6] But "409" was stylish beyond Ted's means.

Frank Crosswaith had helped Ted get a part-time job as an investigator for the New York State Temporary Commission on the Condition of the Urban Colored Population. For that commission, Ted wrote one exposé on how some house rent parties led to vice rings and another on how a landlord in his neighborhood boosted rents when white tenants were replaced by blacks.[7] At the same time, the dissatisfied Ted and Ming kept moving. Their address in September 1937 was 15 St. Nicholas Avenue, where rent was $40 a month for three rooms. On May 21, 1938, it was 50 West 124th. Later in 1938, they owed $27 in back rent at 479 West 152d Street on the $75 per month at that place. In fact, they were robbed there.[8]

It appears that the couple separated within three years, and Ming stayed at the West 152d Street apartment, where she would be closer to her mother and sister on West 153d, whereas Ted returned to his old compatriots, Moon and Thurston Lewis, at 15 St. Nicholas Avenue.[9] Bachelorhood was easier when earning one's daily bread was so difficult. St. Nicholas Avenue remained Poston's official address until April 1940, but by then he was seldom in town. The date of Ted and Ming's divorce is unknown, but by September 1940, Ted was finished with Harlem and his first marriage and on his way to Washington for the duration of World War II.[10]

Ted as bridegroom had failed to live up to only the first of three commitments he seemed to have made in 1936: to provide for his wife; through the labor movement to help the race find openings in the economy; and to use his unique abilities. An FBI informant described him at this time as "a liberal idealist, progressive, and a staunch New Dealer" and as a firm believer in legislation pertaining to "health, housing, and relief for the colored people." [11] Frank R. Crosswaith, Heywood Broun, and the New Deal helped Poston keep his latter two commitments.

Through the Newspaper Guild, Poston had developed a coterie of partisans among writers. In January 1936, he had joined the Executive Committee of the New York Guild.[12] Thenceforward, he went into the union movement in a big way. The New Deal's National Recovery Act of 1933 was intended to energize industry following the stock market crash of 1929. It led to increased power of the American Federation of Labor (AFL) and then the formation of the Congress of Industrial Organizations (CIO).

Frank Crosswaith, with Poston's assistance, set up the Harlem Labor Committee in July 1935.[13] A compelling orator, Crosswaith promoted the slogan "Union Hours, Union Conditions and Union Wages for the Negro Worker." It was effective, for Crosswaith was "respected in Harlem, a smart man but not demagogic," according to St. Clair Bourne.[14] "He would speak out sharply, yet not immoderately." Designed to bring together "existing organizations already having the support of the recognized organized labor movement," the Harlem Labor Committee strove to put unorganized black and white workers in their logical place in the AFL. Poston (for the Newspaper Guild) and A. Philip Randolph were among the twenty-seven people representing the key unions of the city on the Harlem Labor Committee. Its headquarters, called the Harlem Labor Center, had a large, beautifully arranged and equipped auditorium and classrooms.[15] Crosswaith said that the organization wanted its members to be "decorous and tolerant," "disciplined men and women," so that "we can feel that we are leaving a monument in procedure and intelligent deliberation." [16] Not all black workers saw their interests as represented by organized labor and unions.[17] Therefore, such a distinguished leader as the articulate Crosswaith was needed, with his oratory, immaculate dress, flower in buttonhole, and writing skills, and with the inviting Harlem Labor Center behind him.

In uniting with socialist Crosswaith, Ted Poston was not boarding a demagogue's bandwagon as his brothers had done when Garvey inspired them with his message of hope and action. Ted worked toward the same ends as his brothers but with a more low-keyed visionary. "Everybody believed in Crosswaith," Ed Morrow says, because "Crosswaith and the Socialists had the poor people's interests at heart." When Crosswaith ran against the communists for city councilman on the American Labor party ticket, Ted campaigned for him. The FBI would learn that the communists tried to get control of the Harlem Labor Committee and Poston opposed them. As a result, the communists "gave up their efforts" regarding Poston and made "every effort to eliminate him from the labor field." [18]

Perseverance was required for integrating blacks into the Jim Crow unions. In 1934, for example, the AFL had allowed "any local or national union to exclude Negroes on any pretext." [19] The Brotherhood of Sleeping Car Porters and the NAACP tried to persuade the AFL to "drop its color barriers, but their pleas were disregarded." [20] It was Crosswaith and Randolph who "broke the ice." [21] To pressure utility companies to hire blacks, a "black-out boycott" was instigated by the Greater New York Coordinating Committee for the Employment of Negroes. Every Tuesday night "electric lights gave way to two-cent candles." Then a Bill-Payers' Parade converged on the Harlem office of Consolidated Edison and Gas and residents "paid their bills in coins of nickels and pennies." [22] These civil rights actions proved the size and value of the black population and the importance of their dollars in the marketplace. In this movement of the 1930s Ted Poston found a role even as he struggled for self-fulfillment.

The federal Works Progress Administration (WPA) was cranked up just in time to buttress Harlemites' self-esteem with economic dignity. Eleanor Roosevelt, the WPA's "godmother," had recruited the administrator for the New York State WPA program—a hard-driving, militant social worker named Harry L. Hopkins—when her husband was New York's governor. [23] WPA workers constructed 116,000 buildings, 78,000 bridges, and 651,000 miles of public roads. The Federal Arts Project would support Poston's sister-in-law, Augusta Savage, and her art students. [24] The Federal Theatre Project opened avenues for Langston Hughes and others, and the National Youth Administration (NYA) under Mary McLeod Bethune was "Washington's prescription for enabling youth to weather the Great Depression." [25] All were offshoots of the WPA.

But it was the Federal Writers' Project (FWP) section of the WPA that saved Ted Poston, Ellen Tarry, Henry Lee Moon, Ralph Ellison, Richard Wright, and scores of other talented black authors. Based on the idea that unemployed writers, like unemployed carpenters, "had a right to jobs," the Writers' Project had more than six thousand citizens on its payroll nationwide at its peak. [26] To get on the project, Ted had to go through the humiliating process of applying for relief. [27] He listed his father, stepmother and long-lost oldest brother, Frederick Douglass Poston, as "dependents" on his application. A person had to be on relief to be eligible for a writing job. Ted was free-lancing for the *New York Post* by that time, but he needed a dependable income.

The FWP's administrative offices were in the Port Authority, a "Gulliver among buildings. . . . Its elevators alone were houses." Orrick Johns, who was in charge of six hundred writers, had to interview streams of folks who "filed past and related their sorry tales."[28] When Poston's group was hired, the FWP recruits needed assignments, so the unit supervisor, James McGraw, directed them to "scrounge the neighborhood for boxes and orange crates" to be used as desks and chairs and "whatever writing equipment they could muster," mostly paper and pencils. Although some of the writers had owned typewriters, "the machines were now in hock." Because anonymity of authors was the general policy for the finished products from the New York Federal Writers' Project, a researcher gets no hint, except through style, which sentences or essays Poston composed.[29] Roi Ottley edited the Harlem writers' work; then, unethically, Ottley later used their material under his own name for his prizewinning 1943 book, *New World A-Coming.*

A dozen unions represented various political affiliations and ethnic interests of the many FWP writers. National director Hopkins assured them of their right to "join organizations of their own choosing," yet political fights ensued, "sometimes with fists."[30] Communists were rampant on the New York project and allegedly controlled job assignments, Ellen Tarry recalled. She had difficulty getting on the project in the first place because she had not saved her rent receipts proving she had been in New York long enough to qualify. Novelist Claude McKay spoke up on her behalf, however, declaring, "If Miss Tarry were a Communist, she would be working!"[31]

Ted Poston and Henry Lee Moon remonstrated with the communists for their "disruptive tactics" and, with Philip Rahv and Harry Roskolenkier, published a broadside that addressed the fragmentation threatening the unity of the class-race struggle. They claimed that the mutually destructive warfare fomented by the communists "weakens the workers' unity and endangers the very existence of this project." They wanted "real unity for jobs and higher pay," not unity through joining the Communist party. "Rally to the defense of workers' rights!" they urged.[32] Even though Richard Wright participated in communist-led picket lines and protests, the FWP was more important to him as "an ideal brotherhood of intellectuals than as an arena for political and union combats"; it gave Wright a "spiritual family." Fistfights and disunity notwithstanding, one writer, Vincent McHugh, looked back on the project as "exhilarating" and thought that the New York City office was "more fun than anywhere else."[33]

After hours, Poston and his friends repaired to watering holes for story-telling soirees. Ted sometimes brought along white John Woodburn, a senior editor at Doubleday publishers, whom he had met through the Guild.[34] Ellen Tarry had written a children's book while she was on the Writers' Project, *Janie Belle,* about a black foundling who was adopted by a white nurse. Poston introduced Tarry to John Woodburn, then Woodburn coaxed *Janie Belle* through to publication. When one Doubleday editor objected to it because it would "offend southern readers," Woodburn persisted and said, "Ellen, we're pioneers!" From that time on, Woodburn regularly joined the black FWP writers for refreshments on payday. Poston, Tarry, Claude McKay, and Arnold de Mille—"some of the boys"—would go to the grill on the corner of Eighth Avenue and 42d Street for the free lunch that went with a round of beers. (Tarry was "one of the boys" until John Woodburn became smitten by her Alabama "cornbread and collard greens accent" and began seeing her as something more.) Sometimes they would gather at Frank's restaurant in Harlem to drink and talk. And, Tarry says, "Ted would talk, endlessly."[35]

Why was Ted Poston the raconteur around whom others gathered? "Because he was funny," said Tarry. "It was hard *not* to be attracted to Ted. You just want to hear what a person who is humorous is saying." She also remembered late day sessions at the Old Colony Club on Lenox Avenue that included white Archer Winsten, the *New York Post*'s movie critic who had attended school with John Woodburn. At the table, Ted acted out his *Dark Side of Hopkinsville* stories, especially the ones about "Knee Baby" and the "Evil Fairies."[36] Tarry said, "Knee Baby I never will forget. 'I don't *wanna* go to 'cool this mawnin'!' Always when Ted did that, we went into stitches. And Evil Fairy! I've seen Ted slay that little boy a thousand times, so that Ted could get the fair princess. He did it with gestures." And always, while Ted told his tales, somebody would call out to the waiter, "Bring another round of drinks!"

Claude McKay, who had preceded Poston to Russia, "did not enjoy" what Ted related about McKay's life there, according to Tarry. Poston said that McKay had accepted all the gifts and adulation the Russians could heap on him, but when they started telling him what he should write, he realized that he was under a dictatorship and left. Poston swore that in his getaway "McKay ran across Red Square so fast that his coattail was standing out behind him like a board." McKay, in turn, sniffed that Poston was vulgar. Tarry, however, saw Poston's storytelling as a "natural outflow from his personality. Ted saw the comical side of everything." She suspects that his stories might have been a defense mechanism, a method of dealing with harsh realities, but she "treasured for years the memories of when I used to sit at the Old Colony and hear Ted tell those lies about Knee Baby, with that 'I don't *wan*na go to 'cool this mawnin'!'"

In 1939, Federal Writers' Project workers received pink dismissal slips. White southerners had initially supported Roosevelt's programs out of Democratic "party loyalty and a dire need for aid," but when so much relief flowed to blacks, they objected.[37] Further, taxpayers resented the government funding writers; thus the Federal Writers' Project became history.[38]

Ted Poston and Henry Lee Moon dreamed ultimately of proving themselves on a level playing field, that is, on mainstream papers. A later reporter, Tom Johnson, recalled, "For many black journalists of my generation, the big city, white daily newspaper had been the goal. . . . The white dailies, from our have-not perspectives, loomed bright, shining and out of reach across a chasm of either outright, hostile denial or the polite and unspoken understanding that it was simply not for us."[39] But Poston and Moon assumed that merit should carry them across. When they were fired from the *Amsterdam News,* Poston, at thirty, felt it was time to break the color bar and move to a "white" daily. He encouraged Moon to try to do so too.[40]

All his life Moon had "expected to be involved in the struggle for parity, to level the barriers that excluded [us] from any area of life in America." Since Moon had a bachelor's degree from the best-financed and most noted black school in the country, Howard University, and a master's degree from white Ohio State University, he and Poston thought that Moon's skills were especially suited to the staid *New York Times,* which had long been editorializing for racial integration. Enraged by one *Times* editorial that praised the director of the National Urban League for promoting job integration, Moon questioned why the *Times* itself did not hire blacks except as elevator operators. He decided to "challenge [the *Times*] and try to break through."[41]

Moon addressed Julius Ochs Adler, the *Times*'s general manager, on May 6, 1936, to that effect, adding that "the *Times* has thousands of readers in Harlem from whose pennies it derives revenue, and whose varied activities are all but ignored by your publication." Moon concluded his job request with a question: "Is it that, according to the standards of the *Times,* we in Harlem are the source of scant 'news that's fit to print'?" Moon's application was turned down with a prompt, brief letter signed by the publisher, Arthur Hays Sulzberger. It said, "The point that you make merits consideration. On the other hand, it entails difficulties which cannot be overlooked." Moon theorized that the *Times* men "blanched" and said, "We can't have a nigger *Times* writer!"[42]

While Moon was bothering the *Times,* Poston sought a job on the *New*

York Post, which had been the most respected liberal American news organ when he was growing up. As a child, he had memorized "Thanatopsis," a poem by William Cullen Bryant, editor of the *New York Evening Post* for half of the nineteenth century. The *Post* had been founded by Alexander Hamilton in 1801 and under Bryant had developed its liberal attitudes. Bryant had promoted the presidential campaign of Abraham Lincoln and "supported organized labor [and]. . . . the extension of suffrage, free speech and abolition of slavery."[43] As Poston walked past Bryant Park after each day's work on the Federal Writers' Project, he would see William Cullen Bryant's statue in the park and be reminded of the *Post*'s venerable traditions.[44]

He knew *Post* history and that a descendant of abolitionists, Oswald Garrison Villard, had co-founded the NAACP, loaning it start-up office space, when Villard owned and edited the *Post.* After Villard, the *Post* had taken a turn for the worse under Thomas W. Lamont. Lamont entrusted it to an inexperienced Harvard professor, Edwin F. Gay, then, discovering a $2 million deficit, turned the ownership over to "a group of 31 public-spirited citizens . . . giving rise to the witticism that it was 'no longer a *Post* but a picket fence.'" When the *Post* came back to Lamont, he sold it to Cyrus H. K. Curtis of the *Saturday Evening Post,* and the deficits increased.[45]

On the horizon had loomed a potential buyer, a friend of labor, J. David Stern. Since World War I and the stock market crash, profits of industry had increased 100 percent while wages increased only 25 percent. Stern's financial adviser pointed out to him, "If factory workers do not have buying power, they cannot consume what they make. . . . We need strong trade unions to maintain the balance between wages and profits." Thus Stern, a former reporter himself, became a staunch union man.[46]

The *New York Post* finally devolved on Stern by a roundabout route. He had bought the *New Brunswick* (New Jersey) *Times* in 1911 for $2,500.[47] That investment and others profited. When Cyrus H. K. Curtis died in 1933, his son-in-law Curtis Bok asked Stern to save the ailing *Post.* Stern answered, "Thanks for calling, Curtis, but no thanks for offering to put the dying baby on my doorstep." Curtis pressed on, saying, "William Cullen Bryant . . . was the first champion of trade unionism in this country. If it had not been for his editorials in 1836, the movement might never have gotten under way."[48]

In December 1933, Stern took on the *New York Post* mostly because "newspapers fought for causes, molded public opinion, determined government policies, constituted the fourth estate," and such a newspaper, "with editorial purpose and force, is fast becoming extinct in these United States."[49] His enlightened attitude regarding workers' rights notwithstanding, Stern told an early meeting of his editorial employees that he would "sell the paper unless they immediately accepted a pay cut, to be repaid out of revenues—when there were revenues."[50]

By 1936, the *Post*'s losses "had been cut from $25,000 a week to $25,000 a month."[51] Perhaps it was Poston, as a researcher on the New York press for the Federal Writers' Project, who wrote in the WPA's *New York Panorama*, "The *Post* has made more impressive gains than any other newspaper in New York in the last few years."[52] However Poston's thinking evolved to make him decide to apply for work at the *Post*, he told Doris Willens at mid-century a fanciful story of how he gained entry there. One day in 1936, he said, he picked up a telephone book, closed his eyes, and thrust a pin at the listings in the yellow pages under "Newspapers" to decide where to ply his trade. "The pin hit the *New York Post*." He went there then and was hired on a space-rate basis.

Poston gave others a less fictitious account of his hiring: "I got my job through a perfect fluke." The softhearted city editor Walter Lister, a slight man with clear blue eyes behind horn-rimmed glasses, certain he would never hire a Negro, agreed to pay Ted thirty cents an inch if he could discover for the front page "*one* story that's an exclusive that any other reporter doesn't have." On his subway ride home to Harlem, Ted saw a white man jump over a turnstile and take cover in a phone booth from a group of shoving blacks. He and a transit policeman rescued the man, and Poston said, "It was only then that I discovered [that the white man] was a process server serving a summons on Father Divine, so, tired as I was, I trucked back down to the *New York Post* and wrote my first story."[53]

Poston struck it rich when Governor Thomas E. Dewey raided the numbers game in Harlem. "Nobody at the *Post* knew anything about the numbers game and I knew so *much* about it, that even at 30 cents an inch I was making more than Lister. Finally Lister said, 'What the hell! I'm going to give you a job.'"[54] Copy boy Paul Sann witnessed Poston's arrival at the *Post* and arrogates to himself the credit for his hiring. One of Sann's duties was to paste up Ted's stories, and "I tortured Mr. Lister over the notion that Ted was producing so much, he was earning *more* than a salary. After some time, Mr. Lister hired him, and that made us the first major American daily to hire a black."[55]

The *Post* matched Ted's talents and interests because it had championed abolition, racial justice, and labor and because Stern had been the first publisher to sign with the infant Newspaper Guild.[56] Poston would later tell Paul Sann how valuable the *Post* had been to him at the *Amsterdam News*. When the Harlem riot of 1935 occurred, Ted said, "although our own reporters were in the thick of it, we held up our press run until we could read the *Post* for our weekly edition." The *Post* was the first, and almost only, daily paper that stressed the economic and social factors that had precipitated the Harlem explosion, and "we unashamedly stole whole gobs of its stuff as thinly-veiled rewrite. . . . Most of the major Negro weeklies in the country began to subscribe to the *Post* by mail for the same reason." Robert L. Vann of the *Pittsburgh Courier* told Poston, "You can say what you want about the dailies, but we swear by the *New York Post*. It's the only way we can be sure of what is happening to our people." [57]

The *Post* was not yet a tabloid when Poston started there; its restrained front page resembled that of the *Times*. It sold three hundred thousand copies daily for three cents a copy, while the *Times* still went for two cents. News coverage of the *Post* and *Times* was similar otherwise except that the *Post* also contained some black news.

A perusal of Poston's career indicates that one of his major goals was simply to write what would sell. His material had to be agreeable to publishers. At the same time, however, he aimed to expose racial conditions and race relations accurately. His mission would be to interpret each race to the other. To get in print, Ted crafted his first stories to fit the stereotype of the amusing, cunning, Hambone-like Negro. He related the antics of the famous Harlem character Father Divine, the preacher who renamed his followers (e.g., "Faithful Mary"), required celibacy of everyone but himself, and took the paychecks of his flock in exchange for providing food and living accommodations—"heavens"—for all. Father Divine accumulated sufficient paychecks from his "angels" that during the Depression he was able to buy an estate on the Hudson River near President Roosevelt's home, Hyde Park.[58] Poston disdained Divine's shady financial dealings and sexual practices. When, years later, a book by one former "angel" came out, the *Post* assigned the review of it to Poston. He said that the book's author, "a comely young researcher who spent many months in Divine's Heaven . . . explains logically why thousands of whites as well as Negroes feel that an untutored ex-handyman from Baltimore is truly God on earth. Equally as fascinating as the picture of the followers is her portrait of Divine himself, a shrewd and conscienceless charlatan who well may have fallen victim to the hallucinations of his adoring angels." [59]

In another early story in the *Post*, "Harlem Limps on Bunions After Battle of Ballrooms," Poston told of the Savoy and the new Golden Gate Ballroom competing for the same "happy feet." He flavorfully described the difficulty of interviewing, on his newsman's pass, the Savoy manager about the truth of the rumor that his bouncer had defected to the competition: "'Look,' Mr. Buchanan said, grabbing the reporter by the arm and bucking inch by inch towards the jumping dance floor, 'haven't I got troubles enough? There's 2,300 people here tonight, the majority of whom paid their way in here. My job is to see that they have a good time. Who can worry about unimportant things on a night like this?'"

Using such colorful material, Poston provided the Depression-era *Post* with comic relief. His stories depicted blacks not as victims but as inventive blackguards of droll chicanery. Poston's carefree-sounding narratives reminded readers of life's amusing aspects. And Harlemites were delighted to read about their own community in the mainstream daily press, written by a trusted reporter from an authentic black background. In the field of journalism, Poston was proving that a black could be streetwise as well as literate and informed.

Of course, Ted encountered discrimination at the *Post*. Late in life he remembered having been sent, as a new hire, down to "the shack" at police headquarters and nobody spoke to him for two weeks. On a beat like that, he explained, "reporters pool everything." But not even the reporter who had been at the *Post* for forty years would talk to him in the presence of others "because I was breaking into a sacrosanct field." [60]

Poston gained access to the NAACP's struggles because he knew the adversaries. Thurgood Marshall had been his neighbor at 409 Edgecombe Avenue. In fact, one night during the late 1930s, Marshall called Poston to go out to Long Island with him "to check into reports that police were terrorizing blacks" in the Freeport and Kew Gardens areas, centers of Ku Klux Klan activity. Some of the police were members of the Klan. On that occasion Poston became impressed with Marshall's dedication. "The idea of a lawyer being that interested and involving himself in a case to that degree fascinated me, so I went with him and saw what a really courageous guy he was." Poston and Marshall interviewed victims that night in hopes of gathering enough material to win a "restraining order to close down KKK activities" in the area. They barely eluded the Ku Klux Klan policemen, and Ted reached home "damned scared and tired." Poston ventured that Thurgood Marshall was "fundamentally an actor, though a man with a deep understanding of people, a guy with a delicious sense of humor, and a helluva good teller of tall tales. His mannerisms and his southernness were part of his approach and strategy." [61] In mannerisms and in his dedication to making the American legal system work, Marshall resembled Poston himself.

Ted stayed close to the Newspaper Guild and was a delegate to its national convention in St. Louis in 1938. Moon credits Heywood Broun with challenging the Jim Crow barriers of the St. Louis hotels. Under Broun's auspices, Poston broke precedent, Moon says, and was housed in the Statler Hotel.

"All its facilities were opened to him—the until-that-moment segregated dining room, roof garden, ballroom and barber shop." Poston "used them all and no calamity befell St. Louis."[62]

Poston's now more prominent public position encouraged other blacks to take a chance on getting mainstream jobs, and it encouraged whites to risk hiring blacks. In the process of Poston's evolution from a young and carefree Harlem columnist to a reporter of consequence, the range of his writing deepened. At the *Post*, Poston knew he had a rostrum from which he could change racial perceptions. Rather than readers being afraid of blacks because they did not know any, through Poston's articles, such as his "Beloved Prophet Martin Makes Last Plea to Harlem," they realized that blacks and whites share a common humanity.

Even at the *Post*, Ted's future was not secure. The paper was still suffering losses, and shortly J. David Stern, like the previous owners, tried to shed it.[63] Again, a buyer stood ready. Dorothy Schiff Backer, a New York housewife and granddaughter of Jewish NAACP signator Jacob Schiff, was bored with normal upper-class female activities.[64] She had been one of Franklin D. Roosevelt's favorite volunteers in his 1936 campaign. When FDR said, "This generation of Americans has a rendezvous with destiny," the crowd "nearly went crazy," Dorothy Schiff Backer among them.[65] The day after that speech, she, "a recruit from the Republicans," reported at Val-Kill, Eleanor Roosevelt's hideaway, to "rehash the convention and get their marching orders."[66]

Schiff attributed her interest in politics to her second husband, George Backer. And "Grandpa Schiff, although a banker, was on a lot of liberal committees." Jacob Schiff had set up Hebrew schools in all five boroughs of New York City, sent many of the teachers to college to get their doctorates, and supported them while they were learning.[67] Dorothy Schiff would soon become a personal friend of President Roosevelt and would ride, snuggled next to him, in his V-8 Ford touring car over his Hyde Park estate while she worried what Eleanor, also her friend, was thinking.[68]

One of Ted Poston's concerns at the *Post* may have been that he worked for Jews, a subject of controversy in Harlem, for "in the Negro's view, the people with whom he has direct dealings are his chief exploiters; and his rental collectors, employers, merchants and money lenders are Jewish."[69] In the previous decade, Marcus Garvey had extolled Jews as a race that "rose from a position of serfdom, exclusion, and oppression" and were therefore worthy of imitation.[70] In 1931, however, Ted Poston's poem "Seventh Avenue Finance" denigrated Jews.

Ah! A Negro Bank?
Well . . . not exactly—
But a Negro works there . . .
See his broom?

"I'd like to borrow some money, sir,"
"I'm sorry—but not today—
. . . go to Mr. Cohenburg
Who lives across the way.

"He'll lend you all the cash you want;
Twenty cents on the dollar you give—
Of course, we only charge him six . . .
But even Jews must live." [71]

Poston heeded Elmer Carter's articles in *Opportunity* magazine about Hitler and the Jews in 1938 and perceived that blacks and Jews were kin.[72]

As Ted's brother Robert had preached in the *Negro World,* both Jews and blacks were noncombative, which put them at a disadvantage: the Jew "does not fight back more often in the defense of himself because both Church and State are united against him and if he made an effort at defense" the army and navy would "massacre him." The Negro, Robert had said, is similarly conscious that "at present there is no great government to protect him when he strikes back."[73] The treatment of the Jews in Germany brought "a full discussion of Negro-Jewish relations into the Negro press" in 1938.[74]

Jews were persecuted in New York in a way familiar to African Americans. On their way to synagogue on Friday nights, particularly in Brooklyn, they would "go around the block rather than pass the places where the anti-Semites held their meetings," William O'Dwyer says.[75] Knowing Jewish history, Schiff understood what blacks as an oppressed group suffered, but early in life she was conscious that blacks had it worse.[76] Schiff's sympathy toward blacks made Ted Poston feel more confident, yet the *Post*'s financial underpinnings remained shaky while Schiff was considering purchasing it.

J. David Stern and his wife had urged Dorothy Schiff to buy, saying, "Owning a newspaper is more than a financial investment. . . . It's an opportunity for self-expression, a chance to become a personality, a force in community, state, and national affairs." Schiff's attorney was Morris L. Ernst, "a fighting liberal," as well as Heywood Broun's best friend. Ernst told Schiff she had the "right to do what she liked with her money [but] that the risk was not too great for a woman of her wealth."[77] Asked whether she was influenced by the paper's history, Schiff affirmed, "You don't want to kill the oldest newspaper" in the country.[78] Thus Schiff, "an old-fashioned girl with a huge pile of old-fashioned money," bought the *Post* as a hobby for her second husband, George Backer.[79] The fates of the persistent Harlem journalist Ted Poston and his rich Jewish peer Dorothy Schiff converged toward what would for many years be a successful amalgam on the *Post*.

For the Thanksgiving issue of the *Post* in 1939, Poston foreshadowed his war work in Washington and touched on black-Jewish relations. He surveyed a cross section of the Negro press for its reactions to Hitler's Holocaust and found that it castigated the American government for ignoring racial proscriptions at home while denouncing Nazi atrocities abroad.[80] In his article, Poston cited the *Chicago Defender*, which saw in Germany "ominous signs of the dangers ahead for black America," and the *Norfolk Journal and Guide*, which noted that the five thousand lynchings of black citizens in the United States in the previous forty years were not too different from Hitler's designs on the Jews. Striking at the heart of America's social problem, Ted Poston had made a leap from his naive work at the *Courier* a decade earlier and even from his first pieces at the *Post*. He was developing into a journalistic heavyweight.

Aging, quixotic Heywood Broun became Poston's colleague on the *Post* for one issue. Broun took his liberalism too far at the Scripps-Howard chain and was fired. The *Post* immediately grabbed him in December 1939, "at a humiliating cut in salary," his son remembered, and "he seemed tired."[81] Broun wrote one column at the *Post* before he died. Twelve thousand persons jammed Manhattan Center for a memorial service for this champion of the vulnerable and mentor of most newswriters.[82]

Ted Poston was only starting his thirty-five-year-long *Post* career at that time. The state of the world was unsettled; so was the state of the *Post*. Ted's marriage had been disastrous, and he was still uncertain just what direction fortune would take him. He moonlighted as a feature writer for the *Pittsburgh Courier* while getting his bearings in the white press. Sometimes he used the same stories for both the *Post* and the *Courier*. In addition, the more he investigated the urban black population for Frank Crosswaith, the more informative his stories became for both papers. Before Christmas in 1939, Ted put together a careful study of the new law on Social Security—whom it would cover, whom it would not, how to apply for it, and what needed to be done so that the largest group of black workers, domestics, could receive its benefits.[83]

The weekly *New Republic* expressed interest in the childhood trickster tales Poston had been narrating orally for his friends, and it published one piece of his Harlem fiction, "A Matter of Record," about a broken boxer and his sister trying to get funds to return to their southern hometown. A few stories for the *New Republic* grew out of his straight pieces in the *Courier* on union organizing among southern blacks. With his *New Republic* work, Poston was inserting an articulate black consciousness into another white intellectual publication. In 1940 Ted Poston had all the work he could handle.

Billy Rowe was a plucky twenty-five-year-old columnist for the *Pittsburgh Courier* in 1940.[84] He, *Courier* publisher Robert L. Vann, and Poston agreed that the *Courier* needed a lively, up-to-date, on-the-scene look at black participation in social and educational programs along the eastern seaboard and that Poston was the man to write the series, Rowe to photograph it. Therefore, early in 1940, Poston and Rowe left their wives behind in Harlem.

In his weekly column for April 6, Rowe composed lightheartedly: "Ted Poston, our sleepin' companion, especially when we're driving, is definitely in a mood about Miriam Rivers, who holds a piece of Justice of the Peace paper over his head. Don't tell her we told you this, else she might have to change her hats and that would be too much for Ted after the mad rush down dollar-and-cents row." What did Rowe mean? Was Ted seeking affluence so that he could support his wife? Was she threatening divorce? Two weeks later, Rowe referred to both their wives in "Out of Billy Rowe's Harlem Notebook": "Despite the fact that Izzy and Miriam are separated from us by miles and time, our work is made most enjoyable by scores of interesting people."[85] If Ted and Ming were not actually divorced, it appears that they had agreed to be. By the time Ted finished his southern stint, his severance from Ming was permanent.

The Poston-Rowe journalistic enterprise, however, was an inspiring success, a series of realistic yet uplifting pictures of America's prewar black population. A comprehensive overview of their journey appeared in the *New Republic* as "You Go South"; the compelling details filled one hundred stories in the *Pittsburgh Courier,* making 1940 Poston's most prolific year.

As election season approached in 1940, government, according to John Kenneth Galbraith, was "the center of the world."[86] But this gets ahead of the story. After the Federal Writers' Project folded, Henry Lee Moon had found work in Washington through Robert C. Weaver, head of the Black Cabinet, Roosevelt's black "brain trust." Secretary of the Interior Harold Ickes had invited Weaver, a Harvard-educated economist, to assist him with labor matters. Moon had sent his friend and Weaver's secretary Corienne

Robinson his curriculum vitae and clips with the words, "Help! Help! Help!" Robinson showed the materials to Weaver, and "shortly thereafter," Moon says, "I got a telegram [from Weaver] that altered my life. . . . 'You have been named to be racial relations and press associate for the race relations unit. Report at your expense, if you accept.'" The job, at a salary of $2,600 per annum, so excited Moon that he telephoned Mollie Lewis, one of his and Ted's former Russian fellow travelers, for he and Mollie had agreed that when he could afford it, they would wed. "We hadn't told anybody about our plans, including Ted. . . . Mollie was elated. This $2600 was a hell of a lot of money." Henry Lee Moon married Mollie Lewis on August 13, 1938.[87]

After his call to Mollie, Moon phoned Poston; then as soon as he got settled in Washington, he says, "I began lobbying for Ted." When Robert C. Weaver left the Department of Labor to go to the War Manpower Commission, Moon pressured Poston, "See about getting a position." Weaver left the U.S. Housing Authority in 1940 for Sidney Hillman's National Defense Advisory Commission and again needed someone to do public relations and investigatory work. Weaver recalled, "Of course Henry could think of *no* one who would be better suited than Theodore Roosevelt Augustus Major Poston." Since Poston was traveling to Washington with Billy Rowe anyway, he would be able to see what Moon and the Black Cabinet were up to, and Moon wanted the Black Cabinet to have a chance to look Ted over and decide that they needed him.

On a cold March day in 1940, Billy Rowe and Ted Poston left Penn Station by train, courtesy of the *Pittsburgh Courier*. As a knowledgeable former railroad man, Poston cautioned northern-born Rowe that they would encounter discrimination in the South but they could not let it depress them or they would not get their articles done. With that, the two black journalists began their pre–World War II journey in a nonsegregated coach. Poston described it later in a typical light, intimate tone. Second-person voice gives an immediacy to how intrusive discrimination is to normal life. Poston wrote:

> You are amiably debating the race question with a Duke University student, also en route to Norfolk. You are so engrossed in the conversation that you look up blankly when the conductor taps your shoulder just after the train crosses the Virginia line. The Duke student prides himself on his liberalism and has settled the question to his own satisfaction. "It's only a matter of education," he is saying. "If all Nigras were as intelligent as you two, there would be no problem. . . ."
> Young Duke is still defending his view when the interruption comes.

The conductor is polite. His voice is pitched so low you can hardly hear him. "Won't you please move forward?" he asks.

Young Duke . . . starts to speak. He checks himself, however, and buries his face in his magazine after nodding an uncertain farewell. You gather your luggage and stumble forward to the Jim Crow car which has been switched on at the station. The car you are leaving is air-conditioned. Its dual seats are comfortable. It is clean and well-lighted and all its equipment is modern. The Jim Crow car is filthy.[88]

Poston and Rowe became so disgusted at train travel below the Mason-Dixon line that they turned back, Rowe to get his automobile, Poston to dally at Moon's digs in Washington. This was the time Robert Weaver and Poston became thoroughly acquainted. Poston found the self-disciplined Weaver a contrast to himself in personality and skin color. Weaver wore his clothes "with a stylish flair" and was of light complexion—"high yaller," according to Roi Ottley. He possessed a "refined intelligence" and was "not one of the boys in the hail-fellow-well-met sense. . . . He is the student, discerning, deliberate and removed." [89]

Moon had rented a third-floor apartment in Bob and Ella Weaver's home and arranged some social get-togethers while Ted was his guest. An assertive and striking six-foot-tall secretary from Weaver's office, Marie Byrd, overwhelmed Ted. Byrd matched her in-law Jessie Fauset's description of a cultured mulatto: "Her work . . . her dignity, her remarkable beauty, her distinguished clothes were bringing her a half-begrudged, half-admiring recognition. . . . She was someone choice, unique, different. She knew her beauty stirred him." [90] Marie's aunt, Crystal Bird Fauset, the first black in the Pennsylvania legislature, had sued the famous tenor Roland Hayes for breach of promise.[91] The family was clearly a power to be reckoned with.

Ted and Marie danced and drank, Marie Byrd dominated, and Ted enjoyed himself in the company of this glamorous woman of color with an ambitious and independent streak. She told him she had attended St. Francis de Sales—"Rock Castle"—the Catholic boarding school in Virginia founded by Mother Katharine Drexel. Ted told Marie he knew all about Rock Castle because his friend Ellen Tarry had graduated from there. Marie did not mention that she had been forced to withdraw from the school in February 1928 because she did not fit the requirement of obedience in convent life, and Ted had no reason to question her about such details. He had a fine time in Washington.

When Billy Rowe reached Washington to pick Ted up in his new Pontiac,

Poston and Rowe took to the road again and found that an appearance of affluence softened some white hostility. Poston described their next southern encounter:

> One day you take the wrong detour in Virginia. Your gas only carries you to the first filling station—a country store with a gas tank—so you pull under the shed and wait. You don't sound your horn for attention; you've learned that much. Five minutes later a white woman's face appears in the grocery window. She regards you silently and then disappears.
>
> You sit quietly for a full twenty minutes before a slate-faced white man steps from the store and approaches your car. He spurts a splash of tobacco juice near your front wheel and wipes his mouth on his sleeve. Then he asks abruptly: "Well, what do you want?"
>
> "I guess thirteen gallons will be enough."

The grocer cannot believe there are Negroes with enough money to buy thirteen gallons of gasoline at one throw. His tone changes, and he "almost chokes on his tobacco cud. 'You say *thirteen?* Yes, suh! Coming right up. Fine car you got there.'"[92] The green of money was more powerful than the brown of skin.

Pauli Murray and a friend were traveling by Greyhound in Virginia at the same time Rowe and Poston were wandering. Murray became incensed at discrimination on the bus. She and her friend protested and were thrown in jail. The combative Murray immediately contacted Eleanor Roosevelt, and Ted wrote the situation up for the *Courier* as another example of ordinary daily racial slights.[93] Otherwise Poston and Rowe filled the *Courier* with positive stories and pictures of black southern schools and businesses that had forged ahead despite the odds.

They made a stop along the York River in Virginia, at Capahosic, the summer home of Tuskegee Institute's president emeritus Robert Russa Moton. Poston interviewed the tall, powerful, very black Moton and his wife while Rowe took pictures of their home, Holly Knoll, to depict the Motons' lifestyle there.[94] Poston was enchanted with Capahosic. It had been an Indian village in 1600. Moton invited him to return and often; Poston gladly tucked the invitation away in his memory. Henceforth, members of the Black Cabinet would make Capahosic their vacation hideaway, and Ted would take his third bride there for a honeymoon in 1957. But Moton did not live to entertain Poston again; he died within a month of the 1940 visit.

The series of articles emanating from Rowe and Poston's travel carried datelines from Richmond, Alexandria, Norfolk, and Hampton, Virginia; Charlotte, Durham, Greensboro, Lexington, Raleigh, Sedalia, and Winston-Salem, North Carolina; Columbia and Orangeburg, South Carolina; Jacksonville, Florida; and Savannah, Georgia.[95] The men concluded their series in Chicago with a spread on the American Negro Exposition at the Coliseum in June. Robert L. Vann joined Poston in covering the exposition. Vann, a lawyer as well as *Courier* publisher, was at the time ill with abdominal cancer. The disease had been surgically arrested, but he was convinced that it was time for him to write his memoirs. Vann's political concerns overshadowed memoir writing, though, as evidenced by his attendance at both the Democratic and the Republican conventions that summer. Poston accompanied him.

At the Democratic convention, the party's nominee, "tired and weary" President Roosevelt, foresaw a crisis looming for America because of the war in Europe.[96] On the convention floor, Poston got a story unique for a black journalist. A southern delegate was so annoyed at hearing one plank in the platform that he turned to the man nearest him, a Negro, and "ordered him to remove his hat." Although the southerner himself and half of the men on the convention floor were wearing their hats at the time, Poston wrote, "The disgruntled white man snarled: 'Pull off that G—— D—— hat, N——r. Don't you know that white women are in the hall?'" The culprit—Poston, of course—"turned around in surprise," but before he could answer, "the man roughly knocked the hat to the floor." Poston promptly "floored the Southern delegate with a right to the chin and standers-by rushed the white man away from the rostrum." Chicago police looked on amusedly "but made no effort to arrest either party."[97]

The *Post* paid Ted $65 a week for his convention coverage. Walter Lister would tell the FBI later that Poston had done "an excellent job" covering the convention, "being clever enough to cultivate several of the colored chauffeurs of some of the delegates and to obtain from them inside information."[98]

When the Republican National Convention opened in Philadelphia, Poston was impressed with its platform plank that "discrimination in the Civil Service, Army, Navy, and all other branches of the government must cease." The Democrats had included mention of Negroes in their platform for the first time but "neglected to make any resolution about blacks in the armed services."[99] The Republicans' more progressive-sounding plank caused Robert Vann to switch his backing to the liberal Republican candidate, Wall Street lawyer Wendell Willkie.

Poston executed a coup for the *Courier* by gaining an exclusive interview with Willkie. Even in the North, it was not easy for a Negro reporter to gain access to major sources of news, Moon later wrote. "But true professionals like Poston . . . surmounted these difficulties." [100] Poston's sometime employer, Vann, did not live to see whether his candidate was elected; Vann died October 24, 1940.

With Miriam Rivers out of Ted's life, his thoughts turned to Marie Byrd, whose aggressive nature titillated him. Whereas Ming had looked to Ted to provide for her, Marie was self-reliant. Ted had jotted Marie a note from her hometown, Philadelphia, when he was at one of the political conventions. He enclosed a cartoon that showed a man going into a diner and saying to the waitress behind the counter, "Marie, I don't just come in here for the apple pie." [101] Marie, recently divorced from her steady, affable, fair-skinned, mother-approved husband, Albert Tancil, was interested in Ted. [102] But her career had become her passion. And Washington seemed full of possibilities, especially with the civil service laws that guaranteed job security even for blacks.

Ellen Tarry, on her way home to Birmingham, Alabama, had stopped in Washington, curious about the Rock Castle alumna of whom Bob Weaver had told her, "Ted Poston has a woman who's really got his water on. She tells him what to do and when to do it." Tarry discovered that Byrd was "Ted's match in anything. He couldn't flim-flam her. When I walked in the living room, this long, tall lady stood up and I knew, 'This is the lady.'"

Henry Lee Moon had made a point of making sure Ted impressed Bob Weaver and Will Alexander, FDR's white race relations expert, so that Ted would have an inside track for applying his wit and brain to the same racial reforms in government that Moon had been working on. [103] The avenues through which blacks made their entry into government were paved by "Dr. Will" and Secretary of the Interior Harold Ickes. Roosevelt had known Ickes, "a futile worker for civic betterment," since 1933 when FDR was building his regular cabinet, and he had "liked the cut of his jib." Ickes was the "original triple termite" in that he "wrote the platform, uttered the keynote speech, mapped the whole strategy and prepared an outline" for most of FDR's campaign speeches. Besides that, Ickes's "gift for lethal invective" came in handy. During election season 1940, he called Wendell Willkie "a rich man's Roosevelt" and "a simple, barefoot Wall Street lawyer." [104]

The Rosenwald Fund provided the bridge connecting Ted Poston to Ickes. Edwin R. Embree, a Yale-educated Kentuckian who headed the Rosenwald Fund, had lobbied for a government agency to be set up in FDR's first administration to see that blacks received fair treatment, much as the fund had done privately for "some of the most gifted men and women in the nation," including Augusta Savage and Ralph Bunche. Roosevelt was receptive to

Embree's idea and gave Ickes the responsibility for implementing it because he had "worked hard to end segregation in the Department of the Interior" by employing black architects and engineers.[105]

Ickes had always befriended the underprivileged but particularly "the blacks, whom he saw as the most oppressed of minority groups." Ickes ordered the Interior Department to provide him with "information and a certain measure of control over all New Deal agencies' relations with blacks."[106] He should be the intermediary because he was the only fellow he himself could trust. Ickes was "building for the long run." But in 1935, Roosevelt undermined his work by shifting funds from Ickes's Public Works Administration to Harry Hopkins's WPA because Hopkins had "promised to hire workers fast," and "people don't eat in the long run—they eat every day."[107] For six years Ickes had administered the Public Works Administration. He owed one of his nicknames of "Honest Harold" to the fact that "billions of dollars were spent under his supervision without a breath of scandal."[108] One critic said, "It is impossible not to feel drawn toward Mr. Ickes if you have ever met him. . . . He wants everyone in this country to be prosperous and happy."[109]

Ickes, Will Alexander, and Robert Weaver colluded in placing in government the men who would form Roosevelt's Black Cabinet. Ickes brought William Hastie to the Department of Interior as assistant solicitor in 1933.[110] Clark Foreman, a "young firebrand," became adviser on the economic affairs of Negroes, but because Foreman was a white southerner from Atlanta, many blacks saw his selection as "a continuation of the same old white-over-black condescending paternalism."[111] Ickes stood firm, and "the sounds of disapproval died down" after Foreman appointed Weaver as his assistant.[112] Will Alexander was the catalyst who convinced Robert Weaver that Ted Poston's place was in Washington. "Dr. Will" agreed with Ickes that the federal government must learn to work with African Americans, for the "shadow of war and the impetus of a burgeoning defense effort clarified the need to . . . incorporate Negroes and other minorities into the full fighting and laboring force of the Republic."[113] America's "most persistent and pernicious social problem" thus entered a new phase.[114]

During the 1930s Will Alexander and Harold Ickes had raised the subsistence level of all southern sharecroppers, black and white.[115] A specific concern, for example, had been whether southern farm families could ever have plumbing. The president thought plumbing fixtures unnecessary, whereas Mrs. Roosevelt "wanted the houses built with all modern improvements" such as water and electricity, Ickes wrote in his diary. With World War II looming, conservatives, who complained that too many of the New Deal

Farm Security Administration's benefits, which Ickes controlled, were flowing to Negroes, had a chance to "kill off some of its most innovative programs" under the pretext of "cutting non-defense expenditures"—those Ickes and Alexander promoted.[116] Therefore, defense work would be the new venue for an Ickes attack.

Into this Washington milieu came brash Ted Poston. "In September, 1940," he has said, "I got a three-months leave to go down to Washington as an 'information specialist' (press agent) for Sidney Hillman in the old National Defense Advisory Commission."[117] In 1940, Hillman had put Weaver in charge of the minority training programs of defense and war manpower agencies. Hillman shared Roosevelt's conviction that America was likely to become involved in the European war and had better prepare for it. He felt that the major problem was "how—in view of the chances of war—to conserve labor's gains and the new rights and instruments of social justice established under the New Deal."[118]

Poston filled out his application for "Field and Public Relations Assistant" assigned to Weaver's office and had his application notarized.[119] He listed his address as 2090 Seventh Avenue, which was Harlem's Theresa Hotel.[120] To the question, "Do you have any practical knowledge of a mechanical trade, name the trade or trades, and state the time you have worked at each, and when, where, and under whom, giving places and dates," Poston wrote that for five years, from June 1931 to April 1936, "I worked in the make-up department of a weekly newspaper. Have a knowledge of type, layouts, and composition." But Ted was "too ill to take exam on date scheduled," he wrote on the line asking the results of some exam. It is not known what the illness was or what the exam was.[121]

The FBI had to check out Poston's background. On October 12, 1940, the *New York Post* printed the official word from Washington: "Ted Poston Named to Important Post by Sidney Hillman." Billy Rowe bade Ted a Harlem adieu in his *Courier* column, saying that in times like these, Poston's talent is "badly needed" and bemoaning that "the government is breaking up that old gang of mine." But Rowe predicted that Ted would one day return to a newsroom, for "Ted Poston will never be happy without the smear of ink on his person and the eagerness which comes with the changing scene of each approaching news day." He exhorted Ted to "carry on the good work that surged up whenever you tried to prove that the pen was mightier than the sword" and commended him that "you kept yours swinging for the good of the race." Ted Poston was off on his next adventure.

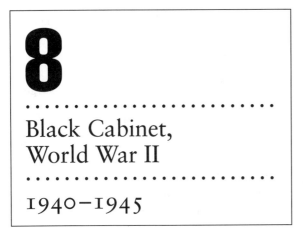

8

. . . .

Black Cabinet,
World War II

. . . .

1940–1945

Double V for Victory—Victory at Home and Abroad.
—*Pittsburgh Courier* slogan during World War II

Washington on the eve of World War II was a small town. With no air-conditioning, in the Senate "flies droned in the heavy air," David Brinkley recalled. Visitors' hand-held fans made the congressional balconies look "like fields of white poppies blowing in a wind."[1] Yet the city "buzzed with energy, excitement, and purpose." Washington "worked harder then—and drank harder," Jonathan Daniels noticed.[2] Ted Poston fit right into the "dark side" of the convivial fray as the Black Cabinet moved to integrate the government and society.

Negro intellectuals referred to discussions of the race problem as "beating the boy!"[3] In Washington, Negroes had been permitted to eat in no "white" public restaurant except the one in Union Station. There were no beds for blacks at any leading hotel, yet visitors from India "with the darkest skins," went, wearing turbans on their heads, to any place they desired.[4] Such continuing discrimination fueled blacks' cynicism about the war effort.

"I hear dem Japanese done declare war on you white folks," Horace Cayton heard a Negro draftee say, "Just put on my tombstone, 'Here lies a black man, killed fighting a yellow man, for the protection of a white man.'"[5] Tokyo Radio echoed such thinking, skeptical whether "18 million colored citizens of the United States would be so simple-minded" as to fight "just

because a few of them were appointed white-collar officials at Washington."
A Japanese broadcaster was told in the United States that "Niggers are
useless because their vote could be bought for 50 cents and a shot of gin."[6]
Attorney General Francis Biddle was alarmed enough by this enemy propaganda that he gave a Lincoln's Day address in Philadelphia, the City of
Brotherly Love, warning blacks that Negroes were the Nazis' next targets,
that in fact the Nazi Gestapo had issued an order for the "special registra-
tion with the Office of the Chief of Reich Security of all Negroes or persons
with Negro blood in German territory."[7] Malcolm X, "dressed in a zoot
suit, brushed his hair into a conk"—a hairstyle in which kinky hair is
straightened, usually by a scalp-burning chemical process—declared that his
argument was not with enemies abroad, and told the military's inducting
officers that "his ambition for the moment was to go down South and hunt
'crackers.'"[8]

The *Pittsburgh Courier,* trying to encourage black patriotism, came up
with the logo of the Double V for Victory, symbolizing "Victory at Home
and Abroad." Once "ignited, the idea spread like wildfire" among blacks,
says William Hastie's biographer.[9] The Negro press had thus found a way to
join the battle but at the same time to intensify its continuing efforts against
Jim Crow.

Idealistic Negroes, such as the Black Cabinet members, reckoned that the
eve of World War II was a chance for blacks to prove their patriotism. The
hero of Japan's December 7, 1941, surprise attack on Pearl Harbor, in fact,
which launched America's war in the Pacific, was a black mess steward,
Dorie Miller, "routinely going about his duties collecting laundry." Hearing
the strafing, Miller rushed topdeck, hauled his wounded captain to safety,
then "sprang into action" behind an antiaircraft gun he had never been
trained to operate, and "brought down four Zero [Japanese] fighter planes
before the cry to abandon ship."[10] Despite that example, military adminis-
trators in Washington feared white troops would protest if Negroes were
promoted beyond mess jobs.[11]

When Ted Poston joined the Black Cabinet, it was in transition from the
leadership of Mary McLeod Bethune to the aloof, private Robert C. Weaver,
thirty-two years her junior. Bethune, daughter of a southern sharecropper,
one of seventeen children, had been the only one of her family to secure any
education.[12] In the 1930s Black Cabinet, the gregarious, domineering woman
was a matriarchal figure.[13] The men spoke of her as "Ma Bethune" and of
themselves as her "boys." She asked her youthful associates to "develop positions" she would articulate. Sometimes they had done this "even before she
made the request." She listened to their ideas, "digested them, and then ex-

ploited them in her own dramatic fashion." [14] As a friend of Mrs. Roosevelt's, Bethune's main asset was her access to the White House. Whenever she went there she carried "a long budget of requests." [15] William J. Trent, Jr., recalls that when the Black Cabinet members wanted to press a point with the president, "Ma Bethune" urged them to exploit her relationship with Mrs. Roosevelt, insisting, "Use *me! Use* me!"

New times called for new techniques. When Bethune was a girl, the Negro who wanted to advance his people looked for benevolent white people. "Seek ye first some kind white folk," went the adage. But at the time Bethune was relinquishing Black Cabinet leadership to Weaver, she blessed the next generation, "which no longer had to beg for their future." [16] Jane Motz, in her analysis of the Black Cabinet, says that members made little mention of working relationships with whites. White help was sought "only after strategy had been worked out." The cabinet wanted to develop an image that would most advance its causes: "The ideal Negro leader is one who can appear to Negroes as absolutely uncompromising, and to whites as reasonable." Robert Weaver produced magazine articles, written in "a scholarly style, laden with statistics, rich with abstractions, and devoid of human interest." But together, simply by conferring, the Black Cabinet developed a united front. Their meetings would end with "that's the answer we'll give." Their white protector and chief, Harold Ickes, would then "go out on a limb" to support their decisions. Strategy called for stories in the Negro press. Then the cabinet cited the planted press stories to "prove the existence of a clamor for action." [17]

The members of Weaver's World War II Black Cabinet were among the best educated blacks in the world. Robert Weaver and quiet, industrious B. T. McGraw held doctorates in economics from Harvard; urbane and brilliant William Hastie, civilian aide to the secretary of war, had his law degree from Harvard. Alert, keen-minded Frank Horne, Lena Horne's uncle, was a doctor of ophthalmology and a poet. Hardworking William J. Trent, Jr., of the Department of the Interior, held a master's degree in business administration from the University of Pennsylvania. Campbell Johnson, executive assistant to General Lewis B. Hershey for Selective Service, held a law degree from Howard.[18] Truman Gibson, who would in 1943 replace Hastie in the Department of War, had a law degree from the University of Chicago, and Bob Ming would later teach law at Chicago.[19]

In a 1986 interview, Weaver identified the most active members of his Black Cabinet as Hastie, Horne, Trent, Moon, and Poston. "Other blacks in race relations in the government in the mid-thirties and early forties were occasional participants." Asked whether Ted Poston felt intimidated being surrounded by men with so many advanced degrees, Trent said, "I don't think Ted Poston ever felt inferior to anybody. The fact of a Ph.D. wasn't important. Ted had prestige in the community, a following, qualities that the others didn't have."

Poston described the cabinet's sometime modus operandi in a *Post* story that ran just before the 1940 presidential election. On one occasion, White House press secretary Steve Early, grandson of a Confederate general, had kicked a Negro cop in the groin in Pennsylvania Station. A White House aide called Weaver in a panic, and Poston later wrote up the resulting machinations: " 'This could cost us the Negro vote,' the [White House] caller bemoaned. 'So get the boys together and turn out a rousing pro-Negro speech which the President can give in Baltimore next Friday.' Weaver told him it might be difficult to get the boys together in the middle of the night (although most of them . . . at that moment were already assembled around the poker table in his basement)." [20]

"Anyway," Weaver told the White House, "I don't think a mere speech will do it. What we need is something so dramatic that it will make the Negro voters forget about Steve Early and the Negro cop, too." The "something dramatic" the Black Cabinet came up with was to convince FDR to name the first black general in the U.S. army, the former colonel Benjamin O. Davis, Sr.; the first Negro civilian aide to the Secretary of War, Bill Hastie; and the first Negro aide in Selective Service, Colonel Campbell Johnson. "And Roosevelt never had reason to regret the ballot box returns on the investment," Poston concluded. [21]

At age thirty-four, Poston began his three-month temporary appointment in Washington, taking the oath on September 17, 1940. [22] The whole country was going on the government payroll; war was the customer. Sidney Hillman argued that big business was "on the dole"; corporations "donated" their key men to government service for "a dollar a year," then continued to pay them their huge regular salaries. In turn, these donated men would make sure their own firms received the biggest government contracts.

Although Ted Poston recollected his Black Cabinet work with amusement in after years, at the time he was in earnest, and his three-month temporary appointment kept being extended. Poston and Weaver's umbrella agency name was changed to War Production Board. There Poston's job description contained a multitude of tasks, keeping

> the Negro and general public apprised of developments in Negro participation in war industries; to prepare special articles, news releases, radio scripts and speeches designed to encourage full and enthusiastic

action on the part of Negroes to prepare themselves for defense employment; to create in the minds of Negro citizens a true appreciation of current developments and thus to maintain their morale and their active support of the war effort; to inform the white public of the necessity of welcoming greater participation of Negroes in the war effort. To act as a trouble-shooter in specific cases of strained public relations and inaccurate interpretations of governmental policy and in cases of serious union disputes; to supplement, on special assignments, the work of field men; and to assist in planning.[23]

Ted Poston was a perfect candidate for such image-making.[24] As evidence of his strengths, Weaver pointed out that Poston had handled "social problems as a newspaper man" and "maintained contacts with the Negro press while successfully working for a New York daily paper." Therefore, Poston could "interpret the Negro to white persons and interpret programs to Negroes." As an investigator, Poston would be called on to go into "difficult situations and extract pertinent data with the minimum amount of local reaction to his presence."[25] That would be no problem. Former railroad porters and dining car waiters were masters of psychology.[26] Weaver had to convince the personnel office that Poston's job could be done by no one else, so he summed up, "In normal times it is difficult to secure" a person such as he described; "today it is almost impossible."[27]

Sidney Hillman, the man whom Weaver and Poston were enlisted to serve, had attained prominence after the 1929 crash as the "political leader *par excellence* of labor." His Amalgamated Clothing Workers of America were "imbued with his philosophy of . . . social idealism and practical common sense." Hillman had shown patience and resourcefulness in encouraging the democratic process to work "where others used their skill and power to win delay or frustration." He helped win passage of the minimum wage law of 1938 because of his "thorough understanding of the art of getting things done." Hillman was the driving force behind many of the measures attributed to the New Deal even though his efforts sometimes seemed minimal to blacks.[28]

Negro communities had resented having been barred from jobs in defense. Poston and Weaver would change the situation. They intended to ally Hillman's methods to their quest and incorporate social justice into industry. Weaver, Hastie, and Clark Foreman devised a formula for all government contracts, an early form of affirmative action. A stipulated percentage of the payroll should go to Negroes, a formula that had been used in all prewar public housing and slum clearance projects. "At least five percent of skilled, fifteen percent semi-skilled, and forty percent of unskilled workers" must be black. Weaver's staff checked weekly payrolls to ascertain that the goals were met. "It was my idea and Bill [Hastie]'s law," says Weaver.[29]

Ted Poston toured defense plants with Weaver to make sure that the equity formula was being applied. After they reasoned, cajoled, and threatened, trying to persuade employers to hire Negroes, they pushed government agencies to assure open racial policies.[30] "It is not enough," Weaver said, "for management to have an *inclination* to use Negro labor; it must have a *conviction,* and transmit this conviction to supervisors, foremen, and workers."[31] Going about the country, Poston and Weaver discovered Negroes with mechanical expertise or aptitudes underused, "driving delivery trucks, waiting on tables or operating elevators."[32]

The Civil Service Commission slowed Weaver and Poston's momentum, claiming Ted was a communist. The commission required a more intensive FBI check before it again approved Ted when War Production evolved into the War Manpower Commission. Then it reported that Poston should not be given security clearance, "pending outcome of appeal of character investigation," because of the appearance that he was a communist.[33] Poston, who considered himself a staunch anticommunist, was stunned.[34] Where had the FBI distortion come from? Agent J. R. Jones's March 1941 FBI report with its negative tone had stated that Poston had "misrepresented his financial status" in the past, that he had been evicted from his apartment for nonpayment of rent, that he was "living apart from his wife," was "regarded as immoral with women," and had been "arrested for illegal picketing." Yet Poston was "highly regarded from the standpoint of professional ability."[35] How did that information feed into the FBI machine and add up to his being a communist?

The affronted Poston set about to clear himself. First he called the *New York Post,* probably Walter Lister, who at once asserted that in no way was Poston a communist.[36] Poston articulated his politics in an apologia that reiterated his philosophy and the motivation of Negroes in journalism.[37]

> As a newspaper reporter, writer, and as an individual, I have never felt, nor do I feel now, that Negroes should be discriminated against, lynched, denied their civil rights or any other protection of our Constitution and laws. As a newspaper man, and especially as a reporter on a Negro newspaper, I have always attempted to expose any injustice which I thought was inflicted upon Negroes solely because of their race. Work of this sort has been and is one of the primary functions of the Negro Press. . . . Such activity, I contend, is not only legal but fol-

lows the highest precepts of our democratic form of government. . . . I do not believe that it is federal policy to regard as subversive any person who believes that the rights and protections of the Federal Government should be extended to all citizens of this country.[38]

Robert Weaver joined the battle, ruminating a half-century later, "The FBI had their minds made up. But we were able to put on enough pressure so that Ted was exonerated."[39]

White labor leaders of the 1930s had fought to get unions into industry, while black labor leaders had been fighting simply to get Negroes into unions. At Detroit's Ford Motor Company, a huge defense contractor, for example, the first step was more difficult than the second. Henry Ford was stridently antiunion, but he was certain he was the greatest employer of blacks in America. Black autoworkers and influential community leaders— the clergy—were pro–Henry Ford and therefore antiunion. Blacks' suspicions of unions were fueled by their memory that even such highly skilled technicians as bricklayers coming north after emancipation had been barred from them.[40] The problem for Weaver and Poston in their new assignment was to get headstrong industry, galloping government, and the bullheaded unions to work cooperatively rather than as adversaries. Poston had to explain the social persecution of black workers in such a way that employers would desire to alleviate discrimination and raise the morale of minority workers whose labor the war products factories badly needed.

Weaver had composed a "flying squad" of bright young men to deal with situations like that in Detroit. In Michigan, Poston made careful investigations, tactfully negotiated with management and unions, then politely prodded high officials in the manpower agencies and in the War and Navy Departments. The conflict over union membership was minor compared to the blatant white racism within the plants. Poet Jim Daniels articulated the factory ambience in a poem, "Time, Temperature":

> Our fathers worked with their fathers
> in factories in Detroit and Warren,
> brought their hate home in greasy lunch pails:
> *better watch out for that nigger.* . . .
>
> It spilled across the dinner tables,
> through the muddy alleys,
> across the concrete playgrounds,
> into the schools, and we learned our lessons well.[41]

Poston, as Weaver's "best-known staff member," called on white union leaders to counsel their workers to adopt more tolerant attitudes. He made a personal appeal before the United Auto Workers' International Executive Board, and that body vigorously reaffirmed its antidiscrimination policy.[42] Poston and *Michigan Chronicle* editor Louis Martin collaborated on a feature story, "Detroit Is Dynamite," for *Life* magazine, which pointed out the explosive potential of the sullen Detroit workers.[43] Ford's Willow Run plant "advertised the world over as a symbol of U.S. industrial might," they said, "has not completed one plane on its assembly lines and is working now at a fraction of capacity."[44]

Poston and Martin posited that Detroit had the "machines, the factories, the know-how as no other city in the world. . . . The weary months of conversion and retooling are over. If machines could win the war, Detroit would have nothing to worry about. But it takes people to run machines and too many of the people of Detroit are confused, embittered and distracted by factional groups that are fighting each other harder than they are willing to fight Hitler."[45]

In his own way, Ted was effective with all the adversaries, Weaver recalled later. He could, "when necessary, drive a hard bargain," for "each problem of training and each instance of recruitment or placement of labor was a challenge to him." And each success was "an occasion of deep satisfaction."[46]

Poston's efforts frequently had peripheral ramifications. The experience of his Hopkinsville pal Allison Williams proved that racism did not magically disappear as a result of government or employer intervention. Williams had been following a usual southern black employment track—bellhopping at hotels—when one day he got an occupational questionnaire from the Navy Department. On the skills line, Williams wrote "electrician" and "pipe fitter." He says he was sent to Wilmington, Delaware, for electrical school though previously "there had been a concerted effort *not* to hire any Negro electricians." The outhouse for Negroes was "way outside down on the corner. The white restroom was right inside." The instructor stopped him from using the white one several times, saying, "Can't you read?" Williams answered, "Sure, but I don't believe in no signs. You tell us about taking care of our health. But you don't care about our catching pneumonia going outside to the outhouse around the corner." Williams was resisting white dominance by defying it publicly. That his anger had to be aroused over an issue of toilet facilities illustrates the demeaning nature of discrimination. Poston was fighting over more comprehensive matters, but he was daily subjected to the same attitudes imposed by those in power.

During the summer of 1941, Poston, now well situated in Washington, was given as much respect as a black man could hope for. He was dating Marie Byrd in Washington, yet he kept thinking back to his childhood sweetheart, Mary Duncan. Mary's cousin Betty Ratcliffe, who lived near Mary in Indianapolis, told Ted that Mary was "not as happily married" as he thought; Ratcliffe neglected to mention that it was Mary's mother-in-law next door who gave Mary grief, not her husband, Clifford Wilson. Ted, however, felt spurred to travel to Indianapolis to check on Mary himself for the first time he had seen her since she left Hopkinsville to go to college in 1926. In Indianapolis, he proceeded to turn Mary's household upside down.

Ratcliffe entertained Mary's family and Ted at dinner. After dinner, Ted asked Mary to play the piano. She chose a Chopin Nocturne, Opus 9, No. 1. Ted seemed in ecstasy and kept begging her to "play it again." The two of them did not have a chance to talk that evening, but the next day Ted called Mary from her brother James's house and asked her to come over. She recalls, "I rounded up thirty-five cents, got on the bus and went." Ted took her child-care-worn hands in his and said, "I've been miserable without you. Does it make sense for both of us to be unhappy like this?"

During their conversation, Ted asked Mary why her father had opposed him so vehemently. Mary answered, "Because your mother, two of your brothers and one of your sisters died of physical sicknesses, and your other sister went into an insane asylum and died of tuberculosis. My father thought that if we had children, some of that would be hereditary."

Ted snapped, "Leave it to your father to think of genetics!"

As they talked, Mary's hands turned icy cold. Sensing her emotion, Ted murmured, "This is a time for me to use good judgment." He abruptly terminated their reunion by saying, "Well, if you are tired of this situation, let me know, because something can be done about it."

Mary concludes, "Then he kissed me good-bye and sent me home in a taxi."

Hell broke loose at Mary's house. She toyed with the idea of leaving her family to escape her domineering mother-in-law. Her husband said, "All right, I'll give you the money." But then Wilson came home every evening, drank, and refused to eat. Her three children later told Mary that their father would say, "Your mother's fixing to leave. You better start crying." Mary says, "Clifford acted so pitiful, and the kids put on such a show that I called the whole thing off. That is the closest that Ted and I ever came to being reunited. Down deep, my love for Ted was something that never got out of my system. But Ted was a man of the world. I knew he could make it. And we realized that for us it was just too late, too late."[47]

World War II started, and Poston married Marie Byrd. Four months later, his most famous story, "The Revolt of the Evil Fairies," appeared in the *New Republic*.[48] Its heroine was modeled on Mary Duncan but may show the influence of his relationship with Marie and her mother as well. In "Evil Fairies," a black youth never attained the light-skinned girl he wanted because of intraracial prejudice. Poston probably relieved some of his bitterness by portraying the hero as rebelling in swashbuckling manner and claiming his Sleeping Beauty.

Poston's second marriage endured longer than the first, but it, also, seemed programmed for failure. Marie's mother, Mae Byrd, disapproved of Ted because of his color. "Mae Byrd was color-conscious," Marie's friend Eloise Scott Reed says. Yet Ted was successful. That pacified Mae Byrd.[49] Marie usually got what she wanted anyway. She was brassy and well organized, a "take-charge girl." She would "not just be *in* a club; she would be in *charge* of the club." Although Mae Byrd, employed as a housekeeper, could never buy Marie beautiful clothes, Reed says, "Marie sewed her own.[50] When she would go to a dance, she would be written up in the newspaper because she had worn something so clever," says Reed. "She didn't have as much as most of the people she went around with, but you would never have known it from the way she looked, the way she acted, and the way she spoke." After their wedding, Marie and Ted honeymooned in New York. As a wedding gift, Ed Morrow gave them the use of his apartment for a week at the co-op at 43 West 66th Street.

St. Clair Bourne, who was in Washington working for the Fair Employment Practices Commission (FEPC) then, speculates that Marie, like Ted's first wife, married Ted to "advance herself. She was calculating," so "one could conjecture that she considered that advancing herself was a dividend of marrying Ted, not necessarily the only reason, but you don't throw that out the window." Some called Marie "stunning," others "conventional," but they agreed with Ted's secretary, Margaret Proctor, "When Marie walked in a room, you knew *some*body had entered." Proctor says, however, "Ted's and Marie's personalities clashed. They both liked the limelight." Philleo Nash's wife, Edith, who would soon come to know the Postons well, says, "Marie was not one who would subordinate her life's ambitions to support him."

Ted and Marie were married for fifteen years, but they were childless. A pleasure during the war years was the acquisition of three godchildren when two of Marie's friends, Eloise Scott Reed and Ruth Adams, had daughters and Margaret Proctor had a son. Both Postons enjoyed their responsibilities as godparents. Their friends claim that they loved children.

Ted Poston's next assignment in Washington following his work with Weaver was at the Office of War Information (OWI) as head of the Negro

News Desk. The story of how he came to be appointed is convoluted. Several noted men of letters, both black and white, had offered their services to the government when the war began—Archibald MacLeish, Malcolm Cowley, E. B. White, Richard Wright, and Langston Hughes, for example. As head of the Office of Facts and Figures, MacLeish had "the pick of a glut of applicants for writing posts."[51] E. B. White recommended anonymously that the information bureaus be unified under Elmer Davis, "the most trusted news broadcaster in America" and a person who could "get along with people."[52] On June 24, 1942, FDR announced that Elmer Davis would head the new Office of War Information, incorporating the Office of Facts and Figures.[53] Davis would have no boss but the president.

The "Negro problem" was interwoven through all war problems. For six months of 1942 the solution of how to deal with it was pondered.[54] L. M. C. Smith of the Department of Justice called a meeting of whites only to discuss it. The group considered censoring the black press. Milton Starr, a white who had represented black interests in the Office of Facts and Figures, had been a target of Walter White's NAACP epistolary attack for the previous six months. White said it was absurd to allow Starr to dominate policy on the Negro since his "sole claim to being an authority on the Negro . . . is his ownership of a chain of theaters in the South chiefly located in Negro slum and dive areas."[55]

On March 20, 1942, Poston attended, in Weaver's stead, an explosive meeting on the race question to which a few blacks were invited. Its purpose was "to provide counsel and advice for securing unity of thought and action in this war for democracy."[56] The meeting ended in pandemonium. But the "Negro problem" had been taken seriously enough in the earlier Office of Facts and Figures that Ulric Bell, an assistant, sought advice from Percival L. Prattis of the *Pittsburgh Courier* in naming an "informal advisory committee on the Negro question." The committee included Prattis; Claude Barnett of the Associated Negro Press; Carl Murphy of the *Baltimore Afro-American;* P. B. Young, Sr., of the *Norfolk Journal and Guide;* Mary McLeod Bethune; Walter White; A. Philip Randolph; Lester Granger of the Urban League; and, to represent intergovernmental groups, such men as Judge William Hastie, War Department, and Robert Weaver of the Office of Production Management. Theodore Berry, a Cincinnati lawyer, served as "chief liaison man." That group said there should be a Negro News Desk in the new OWI with a Negro in charge.

The search began for a Negro in charge. Richard Wright's name was eliminated because Prattis suggested that "Mr. Wright may have Communist affiliations."[57] Malcolm Cowley told MacLeish how impressed he was with

Ted Poston. Poston and Moon had visited MacLeish and mentioned "grievances now being played up in the Negro press." Cowley asked those two who would be a good man to work on questions of Negro morale. They put forth as their first choice "Roy Wilkins of the NAACP, who edits the *Crisis* under Walter White. . . . Alvin White, a Washington correspondent for the Associated Negro Press; Roy [*sic*] Ottley . . . [and] Obie McCollum, now of the Richmond *Afro-American*." Cowley added, parenthetically, to MacLeish, "Poston himself, by the way, is a talented writer." [58]

In the end, Elmer Davis secured for his OWI staff Philleo Nash, "an anthropologist of the liberal type," and Ted Poston, noting that "Will Alexander especially enjoyed Ted's keen sense of humor." Elmer Davis announced Poston's selection officially on October 29, 1942.

The assignment came none too soon. Ted was tired from his travels for the war production agencies. Weaver remembers, "Ted was energetic, but he didn't take care of himself. He drank too much. He smoked a good deal. He was never robust, but he would work hard and sometimes be exhausted."

The OWI was badly in need of Poston's help by the time he took the assignment. That week Elmer Davis had had to defend the agency against misstatements in stories accredited to the Associated Negro Press that the OWI employed only four Negroes. Poston drafted Davis's refutation: "The OWI does not make notations of racial identity on any of the personnel records of its employees," but "a quick check" showed that of thirteen hundred persons in OWI, "more than eight percent" were Negroes—"information specialists, organization analysts, field representatives. . . . These persons were employed on the basis of their training, experience, and background and not on the basis of their race." [59]

The makeup of the OWI staff was not the only concern. Intelligence services warned of imminent race riots in several cities. A deputation insisted to Davis that whites were unaware of "a Negro problem." If people "knew more, their generosity might gradually override their prejudices. (In factories where Negroes work alongside whites, prejudice is much less marked than among whites isolated from Negroes)." Therefore, "We should not . . . adopt the easy but dangerous line that in critical times it is better not to ventilate too much of the truth." [60]

Milton Eisenhower, associate director of the OWI, wanted the agency to "support the position of the more conciliatory elements" among white people by "promoting widespread understanding" of the "patriotism and participation of the Negroes in the war effort; [and by] assisting Negro media to obtain constructive material" showing the same thing. Eisenhower did not argue necessarily that the idea of censorship should be discarded. But the

Department of Justice should "keep an eye on the Negro press in publishing subversive or seditious material from time to time." [61]

Poston, back from troubleshooting for the War Manpower Commission, now had to take the heat from blacks and whites alike as head of the Negro News Desk. His new office was one of those that "spill[ed] out of the massive Social Security Building" into two adjoining buildings. [62] Margaret Proctor, the secretary found for him by Marie, was assigned to summarize items on Negro problems from twenty-five black newspapers around the country each week. Poston, Proctor, and the staff consisting of Bill Clark—formerly of the *New York Age*—and Bill Alexander would then prepare press releases for black and white papers and act as an informational resource for other agencies that wanted to know what Negroes were thinking. In a general city room at the OWI, every release was "dumped on the news desk where four or five editors" examined it "for policy conflicts and overall content." Then it went to a "six-man copy desk fortified by a research staff" before it was "mimeographed and given to newsmen." [63]

Proctor recalls Poston's working style, that he had "a cigarette forever dangling between his lips." Further, "You always knew Ted was around because he was so loud." [64] His office turned into a gathering place for all the black advisers in government. Sociologist Hylan Lewis, in Manpower then, "used to come down every day. Everybody would come by to talk to Ted" because he was "original, irrepressible, courageous, a person who feared no man," Lewis says. Ted was an "interesting combination in the way his quietness would suddenly erupt to a scatalogical explosiveness."

The black press was delighted with Poston's appointment at the OWI. Its members used his news handouts yet kept up their militant crusading against discrimination in and out of the armed services. Shortly, the FBI made calls on "the provocative *California Eagle* and the aggressive *Pittsburgh Courier*," challenging their militant tones. The *Courier* complained about the FBI's "obvious effort to cow the Negro press." It thought the FBI should "investigate those forces and institutions within America that are . . . treating Negroes as second-class citizens." To charges that Negro newspapers must be receiving subsidies from German or Japanese sources, the *Courier* declared, "For anybody to think that Negro editors need prodding from abroad to castigate and condemn the undemocratic practices to which their people are subjected, is to reveal an appalling ignorance of the intelligence and temperament of colored people." [65]

Poston telephoned his old friend Ellen Tarry, now a feature writer on the *Amsterdam News,* concerning her reports on seamen who had been discriminated against at the hands of their superiors. Tarry remembers, "OWI decided I was denigrating the war effort. Word got around that nobody could do a thing with me, so Ted called and said, 'Hey, Tarry, you're sabotaging the war effort! We're trying to get the brothers to understand that we're in this, too, and everything *you* write is turning them off.'"

Tarry retorted to Poston, "You can't muzzle me!"

He said, "You wanna bet?"

Ted contacted her managing editor, who finally persuaded Tarry to tone down her rhetoric. Tarry fears this may sound as though Ted was being an accommodationist when "actually he was just doing his job." [66]

In defense of the black press, Ted said that some government officials had accused it of "creating something to which it had only given expression: the American Negro's drive for the freedoms, rights, privileges and human happiness for which the war itself is being fought." [67] Poston and his fellow Black Cabinet members were treading a thin line as they advocated for blacks within the government yet also for the government among blacks. At least black citizens trusted the members of the Black Cabinet. Poston's close white associates did, as well. But Congress was another matter, as Ted soon found out.

With the assistance of his staff, Ted Poston acted as racial interface in correspondence not only with Congress but also with the public. Many letter writers requested copies of *Negroes and the War,* a pamphlet that described Negro contributions to defense. [68] It had been prepared by the Public Affairs Committee in New York, but the OWI distributed it and Poston absorbed praise for it at first, then blame. A constituent of Alabama senator John H. Bankhead berated him for "this Booklet printed in time of war" when "every dollar should take care of War expenses." [69] On Committee of Appropriations letterhead, Bankhead commanded Elmer Davis to inform him "how many of the booklets you have printed and the cost of same, and what method of distribution you have adopted or have in mind." [70] Davis's answer was that "2,500,000 copies cost $72,000 to print, 2.8 cents apiece," and "the principal distribution was through Negro organizations such as churches, high schools, colleges, etc. Except for sample copies to public libraries, the original distribution went only to Negroes." [71] Senator Harry F. Byrd of Virginia heard of the booklet through a white Richmond Boy Scout leader who said, "This mawkish, minority-glorifying handout . . . is a rank waste of public money." [72] Senator Byrd forwarded the letter to Elmer Davis, demanding an explanation. Davis soberly replied that the Negro is "the largest racial minority in the country and has a special interest in their part in the war. The pamphlet was written specifically to point out the stake that 13,000,000 American Negroes have in the war, and to help counteract

Japanese propaganda designed to foment racial discord in this country." [73]
Congress now placed the OWI on its unofficial hit list.

Attacks on Poston's work came from friendly partisans as well. John
Haynes Holmes of the Community Church of New York and a co-founder of
the NAACP, told Davis that "your *Negroes and the War* is an utterly disrep-
utable publication. . . . I can only believe that [it] is a propaganda attempt to
cover up the real facts pertaining to Negro life in this country." Davis referred
the complaint to Ted, and a reply came back, "Originated by T. Poston,"
phrased diplomatically. Davis signed his name over words Ted devised to
promote conciliation: "Dear Reverend Holmes. . . . I have read your criti-
cisms of this booklet carefully and while I disagree wholly with your inter-
pretation of its purpose, I recognize and respect the sincerity of your views. . . .
This pamphlet was distributed to most of the major war contractors and personnel in the country, and has been credited with playing an important part
in breaking down racial barriers against prospective Negro war workers." [74]

Rev. Holmes wrote again, in an ameliorative tone, that he was "deeply
grateful for the patient and kind spirit" of the Poston/Davis communication,
that it confirmed his "long-standing impression" that Davis was "a remarkable man." The letter had "reopened" Holmes's mind on "the whole question of the OWI in relation to the Negroes," and Holmes sympathized with
Davis in "perhaps the most trying office in Washington today." Elmer Davis
and Ted Poston, through such correspondence and press releases, aimed for
"national unity through true understanding." [75]

Blacks felt they had an ear in government with Poston responsible for
Negro communications at the OWI. A letter from a black minister, addressed
to President Roosevelt, was referred to Poston for an answer. Rev. O. W.
Connor of the African Methodist Episcopal Zion Church, Franklin, North
Carolina, wished Roosevelt

the best of health on your return from over sea [*sic*]. . . . I noticed that
you took time to visit our colored troops in Africa. . . . Your honor, to
me it is like Christ said to the young lawyer: "There is one thing yet
lacking if this nation will be perfect," that is the great need for more
respect shown to our Negro soldiers through the white press. [In white
papers] I never see one colored boy. . . . We are fighting for one great
cause . . . but neither freedom nor peace can be had as long as there is
war without and hatred within.

Poston replied with the gravity befitting an emissary of the president, yet
with sensitivity to Rev. Connor's concern: "The Office of War Information

is not empowered to dictate the policies of newspapers or to force the publication of any such material. . . . [But] the News Bureau, OWI, will continue its efforts in this direction and will do everything within its power to see that just recognition is accorded all persons who, in your words 'are fighting for one great cause—that of freedom.' " [76]

Even to some writers who used a peremptory tone in making requests of him, Poston's responses remained serious, thoughtful, and diplomatic. The *Ohio State News* public relations director demanded Poston to "send us all the available up-to-date pictures of the Negroes in the Armed Forces and Defense Industries" and "reply to the attached letter immediately." [77] Despite the tone, Poston responded graciously.[78] A youth for whom Poston had served as a reference in his job hunt, on May 11, 1943, asked Poston for eight new favors and added at the end of the list, "I should appreciate you giving us this information before Saturday, May 15." Margaret Proctor politely acceded: "In the absence of Mr. Poston from the office, I am taking the liberty of replying to your recent letter. . . . The enclosed carbon copy of a speech given by Mr. Poston will answer most of the suggestions listed in your letter." Proctor sent the youth the OWI's file copy of a Poston speech, asking merely that it be returned and hoping "that this information will be of service to you." [79] Poston had made sure that all the Negro News Desk staff provided the kind of "brownskin service" he had perfected during his years on the railroad. As a porter, he had done it for the tip. In Washington, he was doing it for the country and for the race.[80] Through correspondence during World War II, then, Poston tried to operate in a way to show that black hope for the realization of the American idea was not misplaced.[81]

Only a year after its inception, the OWI's work with Negroes was cut as a result of pressure from southern congressmen and hostile elements in the mainstream press. Photographer Gordon Parks, who worked briefly for the OWI, had planned to cover the black pilots' fighter group as a combat photographer, but Parks's credentials were canceled at the last minute. Poston later told Parks, "It's simple. . . . Several Southern congressmen are dead set against OWI giving international publicity to black airmen." [82] Congressmen had convinced their fellows that too much money was being spent on black concerns. Subsequently Poston had to explain the budget cut to new people requesting information and suggested they seek what they wanted from the Urban League or NAACP. In the end, Congress explicitly prohibited the OWI "from distributing any publications or printed material in this country." [83]

Following this congressional prohibition of Poston's work, he remained officially in the OWI but now worked out of the White House on minority affairs with Philleo Nash and Roosevelt's administrative assistants David K.

Niles and Jonathan Daniels.[84] The racially progressive Jonathan Daniels, son of Josephus Daniels—whom FDR had served as assistant secretary when Josephus was secretary of the navy during World War I—had been "borrowed by the White House" from the OWI in March 1943. Ted provided much the same kind of intercessory work in the president's office that he had at the OWI. He simply moved his public relations to the White House and joined FDR's men.

Philleo Nash, a loyal colleague and friend to both Ted and Marie Poston, had become the White House expert on Native Americans, having grown up in central Wisconsin, where Winnebagos were employed in the cranberry industry. Nash's doctoral dissertation in anthropology had concerned customs of the Klamath Indian tribe and its "shock at its first contact with whites."[85] David K. Niles had come on FDR's minorities scene as advocate for the Jews in the same way Nash did for Indians, Poston for blacks, and Daniels for minorities in general. Niles was FDR's factotum in monitoring congressional elections and promoting Roosevelt's fourth term. In 1944 Niles wrote campaign speeches and promoted a liberal coalition for the president.[86] Many in the American Civil Liberties Union considered that liberals shone during the Roosevelt administration because of Niles, whom they called the president's contact with do-gooders.[87]

In conjunction with his new team, Poston furnished information whenever anyone in the executive branch wanted to know anything about Negroes or what they were thinking. Nash's widow says that Nash, Poston, and Daniels bonded because "Roosevelt had changed from a social activist to 'Dr. Win-the-War,'" and they wanted to make sure minority interests were not overlooked in the quest for military victory.

In the summer of 1943 Attorney General Francis Biddle notified President Roosevelt that there might be racial explosions in Detroit, and he thought that the government should halt the migration of Negroes there.[88] Indeed, one Sunday in August, Detroit was "swept by racial strife more serious than anything since the first World War." Thirty-five people were killed, twenty-nine of them Negroes, and FDR sent in troops. The conflict had been triggered by a fistfight, but "racial bigots blamed Eleanor Roosevelt."[89] Philleo Nash recalled, "Fighting went on all night and in the morning, carloads of blacks, on their way to the war production plants, were attacked by gangs of angry whites."[90] Poston was not surprised at the incendiary confrontation when he thought of his own experience trying to integrate unions in Detroit in the 1930s and war industries more recently.

The Detroit riot convinced Poston, Nash, Niles, and Daniels that the Pentagon needed emergency information from all the mayors and governors who were "on the watch list of our race tension analysis." In a method Nash called "simplicity itself," he and Poston, to forestall further racial explosions, scanned their teletype tickers each day for news of "tension-revealing incidents in a city, a military camp, or a war production plant." Once they had pinpointed a problem, Nash and Poston together reported to Daniels, who would call the appropriate agency representative and ask for action. "The typical problem was a small one," Nash says: discrimination in assigned parking places; racially separate and unequal toilets; pay differentials; discrimination in hiring, promotions, and leave. The fact that the problems were being worked on was "often enough to reduce tension." The deprivation theory Nash had studied as an anthropologist led to good "preventive politics." And from his White House post, Ted could still keep the black press informed of what the government was doing and why.[91]

Black newsmen were not allowed membership in the National Press Club as late as World War II, thus Poston's Harlem cohort St. Clair Bourne at the FEPC and Alfred Edgar Smith of the *Chicago Defender* founded the Capital Press Club for black newsmen and Ted made a point of taking his White House comrades there as guests.

During National Negro Newspaper Week in 1944, Poston was asked to speak over radio station WINX. He quoted Frederick Douglass, "Who would be free themselves must strike the first blow." He praised black newsmen for their past accomplishments and exhorted them to keep up their efforts on behalf of "Victory at home and abroad."[92]

In all his endeavors, he never strayed from the ultimate goals of his family and himself. FBI agent R. E. Kehres noted, however, that Poston was "not particularly pleased with his job in Washington" because it was "of a conciliatory nature with the Negro race, which is not what he has been striving for in past years." He was "extremely race conscious and would take almost every measure or means to elevate the Negro race to what he thinks is its proper place."[93]

In November 1944, Jonathan Daniels spent election evening at the Postons' apartment, drinking "to the mounting returns for FDR."[94] The friends gathered again for FDR's last inauguration at noon on January 20, 1945. "An overnight storm had left a light fall of snow," and "the thermometer stood at one degree above freezing."[95] Daniels and his wife invited the Postons, the Nashes, and a few others for drinks before the inauguration, Edith Rosenfels Nash says, "Then we went out on the lawn and watched the ceremony."[96]

No one could witness the inauguration on television because that medium awaited postwar development. James Roosevelt propped his father into a standing position on the White House portico, then FDR stood bareheaded in a dark business suit while everyone else was "huddled in overcoats." Below, on the grounds and beyond to Constitution Avenue, several thousand of the public had gathered. The Postons brought with them pilot Hubert Fauntleroy Julian, "the black ace of Ethiopia," who passed around a "no pain cane" that, when you took it apart, had a long, thin bottle of whiskey inside.[97] "We all took a sip just to keep from freezing to death," Edith Nash remembers.

Three months later, Roosevelt was dead. Ted "felt as if I'd lost my own father. My wife cried . . . for two days."[98] Throughout the war, the *New York Post* had published a list of names of war casualties each week. The week of April 12, the president's name appeared in large type at the top of the list of soldiers dead in action—"Roosevelt, Franklin Delano, Commander-in-Chief."[99]

Harry S Truman was sworn in as president when the end of the war was imminent, and the coterie of Poston, Nash, Niles, and Daniels began reporting to this southerner whom they referred to as "the Chief." Truman was in charge for twelve days before being informed about the best-kept secret of the war, the atomic bomb.[100] Truman spent a whole month informing himself on the bomb, then he moved on to the next most important trouble, "the Negro problem."

On May 25, 1945, according to his schedule, Truman met with Senator William J. Fulbright; then, for fifteen minutes, at 11:45 A.M., with Walter White of the NAACP. But at 12:45 Truman had an appointment with the Negro Newspaper Publishers. Poston headed the list. Perhaps it was Poston who initiated the gathering of the publishers: John H. Sengstacke, *Chicago Defender*; H. H. Murphy, *Afro-American*; Alexander Barnes; C. A. Scott, *Atlanta Daily World*;[101] Frank Stanley; William O. Walker, *Cleveland Call and Post*; Mrs. Robert L. Vann, *Pittsburgh Courier*; Cecil Newman; J. E. Mitchell; L. E. Austin; Louis Martin, *Michigan Chronicle*; Charles Browning; Ira W. Lewis, *Pittsburgh Courier*; Dowdal Davis; Carl Murphy, *Afro-American*. All sixteen of these newspeople were allotted only fifteen minutes, whereas at 4 P.M., a half hour of Truman's time was turned over to just one white newsman, Arthur Hays Sulzberger of the *New York Times*.[102] Yet Truman heeded the blacks.

William Hastie said later that Truman may have been raised in Missouri and developed in machine politics, but "he was a person who had firm convictions, and when he reduced an issue in his own mind to a position that 'This is right; and that is wrong,' he would not allow political considerations to cause him to disavow the position."[103] And Truman did, indeed, quickly make up his mind on Negroes and take firm positions.

First, atomic bombs were dropped on Hiroshima and Nagasaki and the war ended. On August 31, 1945, Executive Order 9608 stated that "func-

tions of the Domestic Branch of the Office of War Information have ceased."
Ted Poston's job was terminated three weeks later.[104] The ideal that had
drawn Ted to Washington had been accomplished as far as Congress, the
South, and racism would permit it.

Poston has written that it was his disgust at racism in the nation's capital
that drew him back to New York.[105] But Henry Lee Moon says that it was
Marie who instigated the move. She got a job transfer to New York and
bade Ted, "I'll see you in New York." He had gotten in touch with the *New
York Post*'s managing editor at the time, Paul A. Tierney, who huddled with
executive editor Ted O. Thackrey, and they wanted him back.

They heard that the *New York Times* was also competing for this high-
profile White House alumnus, but Tierney was "sure Poston would be more
active and happier" at the *Post* than on the *Times*. Thackrey agreed that he
would be "an extremely valuable member of the Post staff and I should be
shocked and chagrined if we lost him to the Times for any reason, including
salary." The *Post* prepared to welcome Poston back at higher than union-
scale wages, $125 per week ($6,500 per year, slightly above his government
salary of $6,440).[106]

Ted's cohorts in Washington would not release him without a farewell
party. At it, one celebrant, Grant Lucas, M.D., teased Poston about the ma-
cho image he had projected. Lucas prepared a resolution that proffered September 27, 1945,

Ted Poston Day: Whereas, inasmuch as said Ted Poston has proved
himself to be (with reservations) a . . . thorough drunkard, adulterer,
poker player, crap-shooter, fornicator, teller of filthy stories, and Victory Gardener . . . that hereafter and henceforth September 27th be annually hailed and celebrated in the aforementioned Washington, D.C.,
as Ted Poston Day—this day to be observed by the populace with due
solemnity, inebriety, and hilariousness, and mourning for our departed
comrade. Be it further resolved that on each succeeding 27th day of
September, annually, said Ted Poston haul his black ass from wherever
it is, to join said mourners in his own damned obsequies.[107]

Such frolicsome souls as Dr. Lucas collected with Ted's more straitlaced associates to drink, dine, commiserate, and present Ted with a scrapbook of
parting letters.

W. J. Trent, Jr., as executive director of the United Negro College Fund,
wrote: "Dear Ted. . . . You've decided at last to cut loose from the public
teat! . . . I'm wondering how Mr. Truman is going to run his government
without your advice and counsel piped in through several exclusive inside

operators. I shudder for the 'brother'—you won't be on hand to charge in flamboyantly and save the day!"[108] Marshall L. Shepard, recorder of deeds, told him: "The place is dead enough as it is but a guy like you seems to hold things together and make life more bearable. It is so refreshing to have you around. . . . Wherever you are, I know you will be fighting for a better life for all people. You can't help but do that. It's what you live for. . . . I'll be seeing you, old pal." Tributes from these men and others lauded Poston's value to both official and unofficial Washington.[109] Indeed, the partnership Poston had developed with Philleo Nash and Dave Niles at the White House gave the *New York Post* for several more years an inside track in the office of the president that was the envy of other newspeople.

In his prime, Ted Poston was on his way to becoming a legend.

"Five years to the hour," he liked to say, from when he had left the *New York Post* for Washington, he returned. But the Postons would not reside in Harlem. In 1941, Ted's brother Ulysses, now fifty-six and without his old political fire,[110] had left Harlem with his wife, Sybil, for a quiet realty business in Brooklyn and bought a house at 101 Chauncey Street, in an area "preferred by the respectable and exclusive families. . . . There Aframericans were not herded together in a single quarter. The houses had spacious backyards and gardens." Ulysses found an apartment for Marie and Ted two blocks away, at 359 Stuyvesant Avenue. Under the East River by subway or over the Brooklyn Bridge Ted Poston would commute to work for the rest of his life. He never owned an automobile.[111]

Henry Lee Moon was already back in New York, with Sidney Hillman's Congress of Industrial Organizations Political Action Committee (CIO-PAC), and his cosmopolitan wife, Mollie Moon, was becoming New York's key African American hostess.[112] At the *Post*, Dorothy Schiff had divorced George Backer and married husband number three, Ted Thackrey, and named him executive editor.

Poston's new assignments would often draw directly on his wartime and White House experiences. In reviewing Jonathan Daniels's memoir, *Frontier on the Potomac*, about the "bright young men" who "flocked to Washington" during the war, for example, Poston would be telling his own story. He had "shared the frustrations, heartbreaks and the boundless exhilaration." He, too, had found American government "clumsily-great" with its "daily pressures from a hundred sources which create such democracy as we know."[113]

Poston was a seasoned insider after the war. No longer a black news upstart, he was now regarded by his journalistic peers as a venerable Washington veteran. Government service had given him a voice to be listened to.

9

. . . .

Postwar *New York Post*

. . . .

1945–1954

As a functioning liberal newspaperman . . . the
Post was one of the few places where I could
function.

—JAMES WECHSLER, *Age of Suspicion*

Poston recognized anew that New York was his city of choice when his father
visited him—his father who had "sued every agency" in Kentucky during
his "90-odd years" fighting discrimination. In New York in 1945, Ted took
Eph to a Broadway play and afterward tried to hail a taxi home. They settled
for the subway when "most cabs seem[ed] unavailable." Ted dashed into the
train to save a seat for Eph and was "startled a minute later" when Eph
leaped to his feet and took the strap beside Ted. Eph had "only realized then
that the seat . . . was next to a white woman." Ted wondered, "How can one
say to a father who has fought all his life for equality that: 'The crackers got
you anyway.'" New York blacks had rid themselves of such automatic adap-
tive responses to the racial facts of life. The incident, however, convinced
Ted that New York was his town.[1]

The postwar period brought more public concerns than civil rights. New
York City's population had increased by a million. Mayor William O'Dwyer
found that "smoke was choking [us], and the raw sewage had long ago discouraged fish." A smelly slaughterhouse stood at the site of the present
United Nations buildings. The rapid transit system, "once our pride and joy,"
was falling apart. Men and women dreamed of being "better housed; children . . . better fed and schooled; . . . Negroes and the populous Puerto Rican

community . . . lifted to opportunity. Crime [would] be prevented by more parks, more playgrounds, more schooling." O'Dwyer said the city must "deal courageously and progressively" with "housing, jobs, inflation and special problems affecting veterans."[2]

Poston's articles concentrated on city hall, sports, housing, and veterans. His relationship with Mayor O'Dwyer proved salutary. Analogies comparing blacks and Irish immigrants had been common since the nineteenth-century cartoons of Thomas Nast in *Harper's Weekly* and the *New York Times,* which depicted the Irish as "primitive, with features not unlike an ape."

When O'Dwyer became New York's mayor in 1946, there was no black in a leadership position in any city department. A black fireman or black policeman who "might, through dogged persistence, have qualified for such jobs, found ostracism awaiting him at the back room of the stationhouse or in the firehouse bedroom," O'Dwyer observed. Once elected, O'Dwyer hired Ulysses Poston's old compatriot J. Raymond Jones as his personal secretary. He regarded Jones as a smart, astute politician, and he liked Jones's accent, "the musical cadence of his native St. Thomas." Jones, nicknamed "the Harlem Fox," had performed skillfully as an O'Dwyer campaign manager and influenced O'Dwyer's winning of the mayoralty with the greatest plurality ever.[3] Afterward O'Dwyer proclaimed that Jones was his "eyes and ears in Harlem."[4]

Probably O'Dwyer knew of the Postons through Jones. But Ted would boisterously tell the tale that one of the first times he interviewed the mayor, O'Dwyer took him aside and gave him an exclusive. The next time Ted saw O'Dwyer, he asked, "Why did you do that, Bill? Why did you give me that exclusive?" O'Dwyer said, "Well, I figured if you were a Negro working first-string on a white paper that you must be a hell of a reporter and I wanted to get you in my corner right away."[5]

Staff bias and the country's readiness for movement on civil rights combined to make the *New York Post* America's most respected postwar liberal newspaper. The reputation that the *Washington Post* holds now was held then by the *New York Post.* In his niche there, Ted Poston, the moment, and the medium came together. Under Dorothy Schiff, James Wechsler, and a dynamic staff, the *New York Post* enjoyed its twentieth-century "golden age."[6]

The periods while Ted was at the *Post* can be divided into three parts—George Backer's paper (1939–43), Ted Thackrey's paper (1943–48), and Dorothy Schiff's paper (1949–72).[7] As Backer's paper, the *Post* had lost a million dollars a year and circulation by the thousands. Schiff later thought of Backer as a *Luftmensch,* insubstantial.[8] Paul Sann, the man who rose from copy boy to executive editor during Ted Poston's time, recalled the Backer period with "editorial meetings, no one in charge and nothing happening." Schiff wanted to make the *Post* a tabloid, with pages compact enough to be read on the subway; Backer thought tabloids vulgar. Schiff asked the top editors to present memos on what they would do to improve the paper, and the best ideas were Thackrey's.[9]

Ted Thackrey, then feature editor and a "cadaverous, harried man with gray hair, heavy glasses and a chain smoker's throaty voice," was "committed to the human cause." A peripatetic reporter, he had started at the *Cleveland Press* and made his way to China and the editorship of the *Shanghai Post*. James Wechsler described Thackrey as "a sort of dashing guy with . . . a hundred ideas a day, of which one was always good. But he got involved in politics of the left, a world he didn't understand." Thackrey sensed that Schiff's *Post* was "an expensive hobby." [10]

The night the Japanese bombed Pearl Harbor, Schiff went down to the office and immersed herself in producing the "extra," print journalism's form of "breaking news." She loved being in on such influential work, and once having tasted power she held onto it. From then on she involved herself closely with the newspaper and offered Thackrey the job of executive editor. Thackrey plumped for features, columns, the syndicating of some writers, and more international coverage. Wechsler was grateful that Schiff supported telling the story of southern civil rights.[11]

When Ted Poston came back on board in 1945, Schiff and Thackrey were married, bringing newspaper experience and economic underpinnings to the enterprise.[12] In this atmosphere of liberal camaraderie and the paper's prosperity, Ted Poston had license to work for the race on a periodical with a large circulation and at the same time to earn a reasonable living at union wages.

He maintained his close ties with the White House through Dave Niles and Philleo Nash as long as Truman stayed in office.[13] Marcy Elias Rothman says it was not unusual for the *Post* telephone operator's voice to ring out, "Ted, White House calling!" [14] That would be Nash. "Ted was a kind of *sotto voce* adviser to the White House," fellow rewrite man George Trow says. Nash used some of Ted's ideas as he "prepared research and program memoranda leading to both executive and legislative action" for President Truman.[15] Truman had determined that he would retain the few wartime advances that had been made in integration and that he would instigate more.[16] For example, in 1946 Truman appointed William Hastie governor of the Virgin Islands, and he created a national Committee on Civil Rights to investigate and make recommendations regarding racial injustices. That committee shook up the status quo with its pathbreaking report *To Secure These Rights*.

A mistake Truman acknowledged that he made in 1946 led to national paranoia—an executive order "subjecting the two million or more federal employees to loyalty investigations and discharging all found disloyal," even though Truman himself "believed the loyalty issue was 'a lot of baloney.'"[17] But that decree inspired Joseph McCarthy in 1946 to run for senator from Wisconsin; and so to Washington, like a bad apple, he came and in the next few years caused many people grief. But that gets ahead of the story.

Black concerns were a factor in the presidential election in 1948, and Poston was dispatched again to cover both parties' conventions. Truman approved such a strong civil rights plank in the Democratic platform that many southerners followed Senator Strom Thurmond in breaking away to form the Dixiecrat party. The Republican candidate, New York governor Thomas E. Dewey, "spoke so euphoniously that each word emerged polished and glowing like a jewel resting on its own little velvet pillow," David Brinkley remembers, but his "pomposity and condescension annoyed reporters."[18]

Press-watcher A. J. Liebling thought that the *Post* made Zionism the key issue of its campaign coverage. At the White House, David K. Niles had pestered Truman constantly on the Zionist cause, so emotional about it that "he would break into tears" over Palestine.[19] Truman felt touched by the arguments of David Ben-Gurion, the state of Israel's first prime minister, but he was irritated by the lobbying of Rabbi Abba Hillel Silver of Cleveland. Schiff and Thackrey liked Truman's positions against the Ku Klux Klan, but faulted him for his annoyance at the more aggressive Zionists.[20] Schiff shared that opinion until Fern Marja Eckman told Schiff that Menachem Begin's Irgunist group were terrorists. Then Schiff feared that Thackrey was walking right into the Zionists' hands. Schiff told Thackrey to ease off, then she eased out of her marriage to him. Thackrey was "fooling around with a young girl" anyway, reporter Joe Kahn remembers, so "Dolly just got rid of him."[21] That ended the short period of Thackrey's *Post*. It became Schiff's *Post* for the rest of Ted Poston's tenure there.

Dorothy Schiff and Ted Poston were on friendly terms. "Dolly respected him, certainly," Eckman says. As for Poston's regard for Schiff, "Ted took her in stride." With Schiff, he acted his normal, outgoing self, "affable, mischievous, serious when seriousness was called for." Occasionally Schiff would meet with reporters in her penthouse office that contained a well-stocked bar. If it were lunchtime, she sent out for sandwiches.[22] George Trow remembers, "We'd go up to her office, have a drink and Ted would give her a kiss." To Ersa Poston's hunch that Ted may have had an affair with Schiff, Ernie Johnston, Jr., says, "I've heard that rumor, too." Eckman protests, "The idea is preposterous. Ted's relationship with Dolly Schiff was like that of any other staffer."[23] Trow responds, "I have lived long enough now to know that almost nothing is preposterous, especially involving Dolly."[24]

Fern Marja Eckman became Ted's best friend at the *Post*. She had been hired fresh from college in 1943 as a copy girl (called "copy boy" then). By 1945 she was a cub reporter and Ted was a rewrite man, a "lofty figure," she says, "the *only* black reporter and/or rewrite man on any New York City daily for many years." Eckman and Poston "just clicked; we really loved each other," she says. The intelligence that stimulated Poston's was often Eckman's, whom he jestingly called his "office wife." [25] He would sometimes have to help her get organized and find her "copious notes" in the piles of paper on her desk in the reporters' section of the city room, she says. His desk was with the rewrite battery. Sometimes, on his way to the wire room, he would pause, kiss the top of her head as she sat typing, and remark lightly, "That's for nothing—now watch out," and they both smiled.[26]

In the *Post* milieu, Ted Poston lost any residual animosity he had felt toward "the Jews." [27] He was now soul brother to Fern Eckman, poker partner of Paul Sann, and employee of Dorothy Schiff and James Wechsler—all Jews.[28] Having visited in Nazi Germany during Hitler's rise and observing that German non-Jews and Jews alike seemed oblivious of the dangers of anti-Semitism, Poston developed an especial sensitivity toward that ethnic group. He became "obsessed by the Holocaust," Eckman says. He confided to her, "When I was a kid, some of my friends made anti-Semitic cracks. I told my mother about them and the next time my friends came over, she said to them, 'I want you to remember that Jesus was a Jew.'" [29]

In April 1949, Dorothy Schiff took "full charge of the paper." [30] It cost ten cents a copy and circulation reached 340,000 that year. Schiff brought the *Post*'s Washington bureau chief, James Wechsler, whom Randolph Churchill told her was "one of the best in the business," to New York, and he and Paul Sann commandeered the editorial helm.[31] More new blood came at that time when Trow from the ailing *World-Telegram* joined Poston on the rewrite desk.[32] Trow knew of Poston's work, that it was "damn good, so I looked at him with awe. I thought he was one of the glories of the *Post*. We didn't think of it as tokenism." Before affirmative action and the backlash it has generated, a black on the staff was not considered politically necessary. Other papers now reported occasional news of blacks but from a white perspective.

As rewrite people, Poston's and Trow's job was to "take the news from other reporters by telephone, and whip it rapidly into shape." [33] They had to "grasp the facts quickly and to write swiftly and accurately under enormous pressure," Eckman says. Rewrite people ranked highest in city room status though not necessarily higher in Newspaper Guild salary categories.[34]

Poston was sometimes sent out to cover "big stories" on his own.[35] The tone of his pieces changed from his prewar work. They were still generally upbeat, humorous when appropriate, hard-hitting when necessary, rarely bitter. Still committed to changing America's racial condition, he had an influential power base.

Of his career-long journalistic production, only those stories with bylines could be traced with certainty. They ranged in topics from personality profiles to book reviews and many multipart series. He had earned blacks' confidence in human interest "closeups."[36] Ralph Bunche, his fellow passenger on the boat to Berlin in 1932, won the Nobel Prize for Peace for his work on the UN Palestine Commission in 1949, and Ted profiled him.[37] When Bill "Bojangles" Robinson died, Ted wrote his first postwar obituary, reminiscing about what the tap-dancing "mayor" of Harlem had meant to the community when Poston had hit town as a newly minted college graduate in 1928.[38] Discrimination in housing was an ever-present topic. O'Dwyer designated J. Raymond Jones deputy housing commissioner, thus making him the highest-ranking, highest-paid black political appointee in the city, as well as the most powerful politician in Harlem.[39] With U. S. Poston in realty in Brooklyn and Jones now serving as deputy housing commissioner, Ted had inside sources whenever he needed to bring depth and perspective to a series on rent and housing.[40]

Poston enticed the mainstream white, ethnic readership to learn about black culture, and of course through his work, blacks could read of themselves in the context of the broad American spectrum. Explaining Negroes palatably to whites wearied him, but, Eckman says, "it was his race and he wanted to do that." He was not an Uncle Tom, Eckman emphasizes: "He fought politically for blacks." The *New York Post*'s editorial stand on race, which mirrored Poston's, was delineated by James Wechsler: "I do not know the words which can explain to a Negro that he is obliged to serve with equal hazard in the armed forces of the U.S. and accept the role of inferiority when he returns home. . . . [that he has] been put on the waiting list for full membership in American society, [and] that it may take another 10 or 20 years to win over some of the stuffy characters on the admissions committee." But in articulating the *Post*'s aim to "bring full emancipation to 18,000,000 American Negroes," Wechsler hoped he had not suggested "a simplistic view of life in which the wisdom of politics can resolve all the sadness and mystery of existence."[41]

Despite the risk to his own life, Poston insisted on traveling to the South for the Little Scottsboro trial of four Florida youths falsely accused of raping a teenage housewife. He and white reporters helped each other there, too, as they had in the Alabama Scottsboro story in 1933. Poston once said, "I never found being a Negro a disadvantage. Most white reporters have little or no contact with the Negro community and must depend on the

Negro reporter for insight. As a result, the Negro reporter finds twenty-five or thirty guys trading information with him in return for the single story he gives them." [42] White newsmen even physically protected him. Without their warnings and assistance, he said, "I could have been lynched," when he was chased out of town by mobs, one "led by three sheriff's deputies." [43] He owed his life "at least five times to guys that never saw me before." [44] Poston thus capitalized on his winning personality and rapport with sources and colleagues.

His work earned him nomination for a Columbia University–sponsored Pulitzer Prize in 1949. Wechsler's letter to the Pulitzer committee said, "The single all-round job of which we are proudest at the *Post* this year is Ted Poston's courageous coverage" of the Groveland, Florida, frame-up of a group of Negro kids. Florida prejudice against northern reporters notwithstanding, Poston "single-handed, obtained evidence which may save the defendants." [45] Wechsler's putting forward Poston's name for the Pulitzer angered the *Post*'s United Nations reporter, effulgent John Hohenberg, who lacked Poston's interpersonal skills. Hohenberg had desired the award for himself and when he was not nominated, he was heard to declare, "I will see that the *Post* never gets a Pulitzer." He resigned from the *Post* and went to teach full-time at Columbia University and from 1954 to 1976 served there as the secretary of the Pulitzer Board.

Paul Sann thinks that Hohenberg did block *Post* submissions. If the judges had "listed a *Post* story among its five recommendations," the trustees, especially "with Hohenberg's guidance," would have "tossed it out. . . . I do think that he would never let us come out into the sunlight." George Trow does not "believe in conspiratorial theories," but the committee was "not enthusiastic about giving us a Pulitzer. . . . It's too much of a coincidence." Ted Poston should have received a Pulitzer, Trow says, because he was documenting "in a very professional way, and from his own experience, one of the most agonizing aspects of American life."

Despite not getting a Pulitzer, Poston's "Horror in the Sunny South" series won other commendations. He accepted them modestly, explaining that he felt apologetic for the Heywood Broun and George Polk awards since the facts in his award-winning series "were not always a result of my reportorial brilliance" but given him by other frustrated reporters on the scene.[46] Poston's racial exposés did not end mockeries of justice but did help build a climate for the burgeoning civil rights movement.

Langston Hughes wanted Ted to do a book on "the American Negro looks at Africa" in 1952. But Ted felt that meeting daily deadlines at the *Post* precluded venturing on a sustained project such as a book would require. Further, "real understanding requires real and intimate knowledge of the people to whom the Dark Continent rightfully belongs. And no visiting specialist, white or black, can obtain such knowledge quickly." [47] Nevertheless, Ted Poston served as a historian for other blacks. Luther P. Jackson, Jr., vividly recalls Poston's help, while Jackson was a student at the Columbia Journalism School, on an early piece he was preparing about W. E. B. Du Bois, then running for the U.S. Senate on the American Labor party ticket: "Ted gave me a complete rundown on Du Bois's influence, involvement in the Niagara Movement, the man himself and his career. That was one of the best experiences I had in my year at Columbia."

Fern Eckman had many opportunities to observe how Poston handled prejudice. He awed and annoyed her when he seemed both to tolerate and to taunt being discriminated against at a nearby bar where they would sometimes go for a drink after work such as when they had a Newspaper Guild meeting to attend that evening. "It was still unusual for a mixed race couple to be seen together," she says. Frequently an inebriated white would stop at their table and glare. "Ted and I would ignore this until the idiot tired and moved on. How smoothly Ted managed this act of not noticing!"

At one restaurant, Ted felt service was deliberately slow for him, and he pointed it out to Eckman. Henceforth, Eckman avoided that restaurant but Ted persisted in going there. "When I bawled him out," she says, he laughed and said, "It annoys them more when I keep going." He had inculcated a facade that would hide his vulnerability. "If he was hurt, one could not detect it in his face," Eckman recalls. "He met situations and individuals with smiling smoothness—not *slickness,* but a polish, a luster." In manner, he was "unfailingly polite," and "except for those times when he told off-color stories, he did not have a complete Southern accent."

Most of his peers remember that Poston's ethnic bilingualism allowed him to switch from parlor to poolroom speech as the occasion demanded. Archer Winsten compared Poston and Moon, for example, as "intellectually in tune, though completely different in speech and aptitudes. Moon was a 'white nigger' as Ted would say, while Ted could be a 'fieldhand nigger' whenever he chose, whether as a joke or for protective coloration." Robert Weaver says Ted was not "crude, but with his capacity for dealing with all types of people, he could be a 'man-of-the-street.'" Once Ella and Bob Weaver went to a party at which Ted was a guest. Afterward Weaver asked his wife how she had liked the party. She said, "Fine until the poolrooms let out," referring to Ted's language.

Fern Eckman's visual memory of Poston at the *Post,* when he was not working on a story, was of him "striding toward the wire room on his long legs." As soon as any story broke involving black figures—whether in a legal or political context—Poston would read it on the Associated Press wire, then head directly for the telephone to call Henry Lee Moon, who was now public relations man at the NAACP. Poston used the telephone a lot, Eckman says, "an invention that was made for him." She recalls her pleasure in hearing him say over the phone, "This is Ted Poston of the *Post*."[48]

Joe Kahn says that Ted Poston inadvertently gave his career a boost. Kahn began at the *Post* as a copy boy, learned the craft "by going out with reporters—they are happy to help a kid who wants to learn." But because he once criticized the city editor, Kahn was shipped off to "the Bronx, like Siberia," to work on the *Post*'s subsidiary *Bronx Home News*.[49] Poston put Kahn on to a story concerning King's Park Mental Hospital. A mother had called Ted about her runaway son. Ted told her, "Oh, Joe Kahn handles everything in the Bronx." Kahn proceeded to write a series that exposed the hospital for keeping runaway children in with adult homosexual pedophiles. Because of the series, the director was dismissed, and Joe Kahn got his first award, from an association for better mental hospitals. He says, "I thanked Ted all the time for that." In hard-boiled reporter mode, Poston's laconic but humorous acknowledgment was, "If I had known you were going to get an award, I wouldn't have given you the story."

During its thriving years under Schiff and Wechsler, from 1949 to 1967, the *Post* was recognized for Schiff's special contribution to New York journalism by newspaper critic Peter Benjaminson in his book *Death in the Afternoon*.[50] There were nine New York dailies at the end of the war, three of them afternoon papers. Of these three, the *Sun* and *PM* quickly went under. As the only afternoon paper left, and despite its near-bankrupt condition and Schiff's inexperience, the *Post* had risen in circulation to seven hundred thousand by 1969–70.[51] One way the *Post* attracted readers was by filling an ideological niche. It "reflected Schiff at her best," as a fighting liberal, friend of FDR and of Adlai Stevenson. She spoke for ordinary people.[52] Readers were caught up in the *Post*'s concern for civil rights, unionism, and strong and assertive women and for standing up to Wisconsin senator Joseph McCarthy.

Post staff were inspired by a sense of shared mission. "We who worked on the paper in those days felt that being a *Post* reporter was something special, more than we had the nerve to admit," says Marcy Elias Rothman. "Fern, Ted, and I could use the *Post* as a battering ram." Rothman remembers an incident when Ted helped prove the innocence of a man accused of murder. Ted and one of the police reporters went over old ground and found the real killer. Afterward, "with awe in his eyes," Ted told Rothman, "I honest to God feel like I saved a life." [53] In his memoir, *Reflections of a Middle-Aged Editor,* Wechsler described the *Post* as a lost-causes gazette. [54] It took on a reputation as "a writer's paper" because writers were not confined to the "dry-as-dust style of, say, the *New York Times,*" says Eckman. Reporters trusted by the desk "could write with style and color in contrast to current dull and prosaic journalistic procedures. Most of us shared our paper's outlook and expressed empathy for the underdog." George Trow says, "What *we* had that the other papers didn't have was a spirit on the *Post,*" and "James Wechsler was its soul." [55]

The *Post*'s path was not always smooth. Truman's loyalty and security program got out of control in his second term and metamorphosed into the unfortunate McCarthy witch-hunt. [56] Senator Joseph McCarthy and FBI director J. Edgar Hoover scrutinized public figures and ruined lives by labeling some unfortunates "pink." [57] One target was James Wechsler for having joined the Young Communist League when he was a college student. [58]

Wechsler had been a risk-taking radical at Columbia University during the 1930s who idolized Heywood Broun for being a "bold journalistic spirit who despised stuffed shirts." [59] Wechsler's history included a teenage fling with communism. He had watched "admiringly" a freshman girl in the Young Communist League, Nancy Fraenkel, "handing out anti-Nazi handbills" and being "rudely interrupted," yet she appeared "imperturbably valiant." Daughter of a Civil Liberties Union lawyer, Fraenkel "stood her ground firmly but undemonstratively." [60]

In due course, James Wechsler married Nancy Fraenkel. They were both eighteen years old and, applying for their marriage license, they were "subjected to the indignity of having our parents accompany us to City Hall," but they figured that "if Communism were to be outlawed," they would "go underground" together. Their honeymoon was a one-day trip to New Haven for the Columbia-Yale game. It rained, "but we festively immunized ourselves with alcohol." [61] With his early reliance on alcohol and foolhardiness, Wechsler had the makings of a kindred spirit to Ted Poston. His adherence to communism passed, along with his adolescence, because he discovered that "no one could breathe or speak or think or write freely as a communist." [62] The Wechslers' marriage lasted a lifetime. [63]

Another *Post* victim of the McCarthy mania was a reporter on a bicycle, Murray Kempton—"mild in looks and manner, soft-spoken"—who, Eckman says, "writes like a dream." Kempton had come to the *Post* in 1947 as assistant to the small, explosive labor editor Victor Riesel. As a way "to escape the dreariness of Baltimore," Kempton had joined the "Communist faction of the sailors' union" one August, but within a year, "disillusioned by the Moscow trials, and other horrific news from the East," he abandoned the communists and joined the Socialist party of Norman Thomas.[64] Riesel and Kempton, the latter in his "customary three-piece suit and polished oxfords," used to "climb out onto the roof of the *Post* building . . . and mull over [each] day's story. 'Well, fellow-worker,' Riesel would say, 'whom do we hack today?'"[65] Riesel, a good friend of Ted Poston's, fell victim to his adversaries two years later when assailants threw acid in his eyes and blinded him. That act shocked the nation as well as the *Post* newsroom.

When Wechsler was subpoenaed to appear before McCarthy's Senate Permanent Investigations Subcommittee, the hearing room seemed "full of the dull, smirking faces" of McCarthy's staff "watching their bully-boy in action and trying to show him that they were on his side and getting a big kick out of his performance." Wechsler was reminded of Joseph Stalin's purges. New York senator Herbert Lehman was praised by the *Post* as "the lone and gallant Senate voice raised against McCarthy."[66] That Wechsler, Kempton, and the *Post* survived McCarthy's inquisition convinced Dorothy Schiff that she had, with steadiness, vanquished the enemy.[67]

Ted Poston repeatedly used the power of his typewriter to illustrate the inadequacies of communism. For example, when he read and reviewed Carl Rowan's book *South of Freedom,* he was struck by Rowan's analogy that prejudice is "near-gangrene" of the national body and that a wonder drug was needed, "not amputation of any apparently less-healthy part of the body."[68] Poston agreed that the cure for gangrene consisted of working within the system, not rejecting the system, as the communists proposed.

On another occasion, Philleo Nash contacted Ted from the White House when Frank Crosswaith organized a conference "to constructively meet the problems of the Negro workers." Nash wanted to know whether Crosswaith had been tainted by communism. Ted assured him that Crosswaith's credentials were just the opposite: "The Crosswaith conference is designed to counteract the recent Commie confab called in the midwest to set up a new Negro labor organization. . . . It will be a responsible occasion and one which may do good."[69] Nash trusted Poston's judgment and advised Truman to prepare a message for the group.[70] In such ways Poston lent his prestige to promoting a politics of moderation.

Poston never regretted supporting Truman, for the former haberdasher, now president, from another border state had proved his concern for blacks. Knowing the futility of trying to get civil rights legislation through Congress, for example, Truman had issued Executive Orders 9980 and 9981 creating the Fair Employment Practices Board, and Poston served as an informal White House adviser on the crafting of several such actions.

After Dwight D. Eisenhower was elected president in 1952 but before Truman left the White House, Philleo Nash reminded Truman that the Postons had been "helpful on many occasions and are enthusiastic supporters of the President." Marie Poston had asked for an autographed picture and Nash wanted for Ted "a letter." Within days a photo and letter were in the mail. Over Truman's signature went the words to Ted and Marie: "I want to express to you my gratitude for the many ways in which you have been helpful during the past seven years. The advance in *human rights* that has taken place in our country is a matter of satisfaction to me. . . . You can take justifiable pride in your personal contribution to it, for your unflagging efforts and wise counsel were always freely given." Up went the photo and latest letter on the wall by the Poston bar at 359 Stuyvesant Avenue. Ted touted "the chief" and his civil rights stand in a later book review.

"Many big men of vision knew" the problem of integration, Poston said later, but "none knew it better or did more about it than a stubborn little fellow from Missouri who had seen the 'why' demonstrated on battlefields of France in World War I."[71] Ted would compare the regard of African Americans for three presidents he had observed in his prime. Blacks "moved toward freedom under the adroit and suave FDR and the brusque but uncompromising Harry Truman of 1948—only to be slowed to a crawl under the euphoria of Eisenhower."[72]

The Postons' basement bar, where all their pictures of famous friends and Ted's journalistic awards were hung, was the locale for some white guests' encounters with blacks in a social setting. On occasion, indeed, the jovial host had to defuse awkward situations. Marcy Elias Rothman recalls an incident when Ted was telling a story about how he became, in the 1948 campaign, "the first Negro in history" to walk through the front door of the Muehlebach Hotel in Kansas City as a guest.

Rothman's husband, Ed, whose "wicked sense of humor matched Ted's irreverence," interjected, "Ted, you ain't got no call to go to a white man's hotel." At those words, Ted "rushed up, spread his long arms in front of Ed as protection and laughed out loud and exclaimed, 'He's only kidding!' The black listeners smiled uncomfortably, then laughed, too." Poston was merely encouraging fraternization between the races, perhaps lending it the weight of his and Marie's eminence. But in the changing times, people had to adjust their social rituals. Blacks and whites had particular senses of what was de rigueur and humor about the races was only borderline acceptable as a technique to draw people closer. Efforts at commingling were not a laughing matter.

Henry and Mollie Moon were the main confreres in the Postons' social set. A happy day for both the couples in 1948 was the day the Moons adopted their baby, Mollie Lee, and Ted became her godfather. "Ted took his Christianity seriously on the day of the baptism," says Moon. "Neither he nor his god-daughter took it very seriously the rest of the time." Mollie Lee became the darling of both families. As a child, she loved sitting on "Uncle Ted's" lap and listening to the stories he told "with all his gestures and mannerisms— his arms flailing and eyeballs rolling." She remembers that Uncle Ted called her father "Socks" because Moon would sit with his feet on a hassock and wiggle his toes while he was reading. Through the years, Mollie Lee remembered Uncle Ted coming over for Sunday dinner or to their many parties. He charmed his godchild as much as he did adults, although his swearing in front of her dismayed her father.

She also remembers Uncle Ted as "a ladykiller. He liked handsome, big women. They would get jealous of each other and Uncle Ted played that up." Poston called most of his female associates "Baby" or "Darlin'," and sometimes did indeed boldly flirt. Kenneth Clark believes that was because "Ted had to test." A sense of inferiority in himself or the racial prejudices he encountered required him to get some assurance that "in spite of his not being handsome, there would be women who would react to him as if he were."

Luther P. Jackson agrees: "Ted was dark-skinned, but he was not handsome. The happy-go-lucky manner he cultivated was a defense mechanism." Professor Hylan Lewis puts it, "Ted loved life. He had a sense of gusto." [73]

Ted and Marie both enjoyed the annual Beaux-Arts Balls, which Mollie Moon had launched in 1938 on behalf of the Urban League Guild. Held at the Savoy in Harlem for ten years, the Beaux-Arts Ball was the main event of the winter social season.[74] With the same compulsion to promote racial harmony that motivated Henry Lee Moon and the Postons, Mollie Moon's group raised money to assist the Urban League in opening jobs and housing to blacks. *Ebony* quoted Mollie as saying that the ball "brings together people of many colors, classes and occupations, mixes them up and everybody has fun." Ruth Banks says Mollie's theory was that "if you get the black and white people together, you can get them to understand each other." Through the balls, Mollie earned her reputation as "vivacious *grande dame* of Eastern Negro social life." [75]

Her coup was to involve in Guild projects one of the five sons of John D. Rockefeller, Jr.[76] Big Winthrop Rockefeller would sit cross-legged on her floor in Beaux-Arts planning sessions.[77] The 1948 invitations to the ball went out over their two names—Mollie Moon and Winthrop Rockefeller—and through Rockefeller's influence, the Beaux Arts moved downtown. Ed Morrow says that Rockefeller "took the Beaux-Arts Ball out of the Savoy Ballroom and put it in the Rainbow Room of the Waldorf Astoria."[78] Morrow adds that Rockefeller was "quite a bit in love with Mollie. That's the way to use a sweetheart." Mollie steered white folks in the same way Mary McLeod Bethune had done with Eleanor Roosevelt and the Black Cabinet. The Beaux-Arts Ball illustrated to Fern Eckman how "Ted and his crowd did things—in the grand manner." Ted housed his out-of-town guests "at the posh [now desegregated] Waldorf Astoria and provided the women with orchid corsages." Yet none of this was highlighted in any way—it was as though "doesn't everyone do this?"

At a ball during World War II, Ruth Adams and her soldier husband watched and were mesmerized by one "magnificent couple on the dance floor" who turned out to be Ted and Marie. The Postons, the Adamses noticed, were "both tall and striking in carriage, danced beautifully together and seemed completely engrossed in each other." It seemed to Ted's *Post* colleagues that he lived a more upper-middle-class life than any of the rest of them, Eckman thought.

Henry Lee Moon required a book party at Harlem's Schomburg Center for Research in Black Culture in 1948 when his book *Balance of Power* was published.[79] While on the road as field representative for the CIO-PAC, he had produced the manuscript detailing how the Negro vote would provide the plurality Harry Truman needed to win the election, and the book's publication gave Poston an occasion to write a profile of his friend.[80] From the CIO-PAC Moon then moved to his job as public relations director of the NAACP.[81]

The Moons' lives were in a state of transition in several ways in 1949. They departed Harlem's Sugar Hill that year for a housing community across the East River in neighborly Long Island City. Its level tree-lined streets were more suitable for strolling with their daughter. Mollie Moon's partner in elegant entertaining, Winthrop Rockefeller, became unavailable henceforth for the Beaux-Arts Ball because he moved to Arkansas, where he would in 1967 become governor, but he continued his work for amity between the races.

Mollie Moon's social successes were not mirrored in her husband's professional life. Henry Lee Moon's amenable temperament was valued more highly by the public than within the recesses of the NAACP staff offices.[82] Moon had been named to the NAACP executive staff at Walter White's suggestion. But at the time Mollie was planning the next extravaganza, "Shakespeare Goes to the Beaux-Arts Ball," Henry Lee was pleading for a raise in salary to $8,000, even though he feared that Roy Wilkins, the assistant executive secretary then, considered him "incompetent, inept and blundering." [83] Ted later explained the interpersonal dynamics and machinations of the NAACP to the curious James Wechsler in a confidential long memo. [84]

Moon envied Ted Poston his supportive superiors at the *Post*. Moon did not get similar encouragement at the NAACP, thus his alliance of friendship with the increasingly well-known Poston seemed essential for his own self-esteem. Moon had left the CIO for the NAACP job at a "ten per cent cut in salary," even though he insisted that "money was never the most important thing." He did not have "all I needed" but "enough to maintain a . . . decent apartment, with books and friends." [85] Moon was committed to the NAACP's goals. He just wished its pecuniary rewards were not so minuscule and that its hierarchy was more appreciative.

Marie Poston, whom Mollie Moon had taken under her social wing, continued to rise professionally in her career as an examiner-hearing officer for the National Labor Relations Board (NLRB). From the Postons' Brooklyn base, Marie traveled between the NLRB offices in New York, Washington, Detroit, and San Juan, Puerto Rico. Marie liked the New York milieu, her godchild Rosemary Reed claims, because she "had a husband who knew all kinds of people and she enjoyed that public life." Marie continued to boss her social clubs—the Girl Friends, the Continentals, and the Moles—and was involved in good works with the Northwest Settlement House Auxiliary, Council of Black Appointees, and the Hands Across the Sea scholarship committee. [86] But Ellen Tarry observed that after Mollie Moon introduced her in New York, "Marie became very very society. Her personality would change with the environment." [87] Marie Poston and Mollie Moon were two "smart and socially ambitious women," says Viola Trent, wife of Bill Trent of the United Negro College Fund (UNCF). Another of Marie's godchildren, Lea Adams, remembers "Aunt Marie" saying that her favorite store was Lord and Taylor because it was "one of the first upscale retail outlets to welcome blacks; because they carried the latest fashions without catering to trends; and because they never changed the rose logo on their packaging. In that order." A frenetic energy required that Marie stay in motion. Eloise Scott Reed found Ted "gregarious and interesting, a flexible person who went along with what Marie liked. But Marie could not settle down and have a quiet evening." The phone would always be ringing; someone would be dropping by; or she would be having a cocktail party.

In December 1952, Ted enlisted Marie's aid in preparing a series of articles on integration of nightclubs when New York passed a stronger civil rights law. Entertainer Josephine Baker had been barred from the Stork Club, so

Ted used Marie as a plant to test the revised law.[88] He sent her and a dark-skinned neighbor to the Stork Club, El Morocco, and Gogi's LaRue night-clubs, then wrote sarcastically of their experiences. For example, when the two were isolated in an empty room at the latter cabaret, they told the host they would prefer the main dining room—"This is a little too exclusive in here." The reply: "We assign guests by the number of people in the party," although Marie and her escort had noticed that few tables in the main dining room were occupied when they were whisked through. Poston quipped, "When going to Gogi's Larue, get up a party. They are not so well equipped to handle odd groups like couples."[89]

In summer and winter Ted and Marie vacationed in the Virgin Islands, where their Black Cabinet compatriot Bill Hastie was now governor. Each Labor Day, Ted always tried to head to Capahosic, Virginia, for fishing, reading, and storytelling vacations with other illustrious friends. He told the *Post* that he went for the annual board meeting of the Robert Russa Moton Memorial Foundation.[90] Moton's son-in-law and successor at Tuskegee, Frederick D. Patterson, had reiterated Moton's invitation to Poston to "come anytime."

The Moton home was staffed by Tuskegee Institute after Moton's death, and it served as a gathering place for many black thinkers. For example, Bill Trent's UNCF and the Phelps-Stokes Fund—concerned with black American and African education—held their conferences there. But during World Series time, Ted and "the boys" gathered there to listen to baseball on the radio. Marcy Elias Rothman understood from Ted that at Capahosic, "a handful of the most prominent blacks in law, medicine, government, media, etc., gathered to plan the course of 'Negro strategy' for the next year." When Ted returned from Capahosic each September, his impressive tales let Rothman know that "there were areas of his life that would make a lot of us at the *Post* stare in disbelief."

Whenever he passed through the South, Ted revisited his alma mater. In 1950 the Tennessee State College *Bulletin* reprinted an article from the *Post* about Ted's winning the American Newspaper Guild award for 1949. A picture of nonsmiling Ted wearing rimless glasses and looking down at the college photographer adorns the article. He is nattily attired in his customary well-tailored suit, white shirt, and tie.[91] In a later yearbook, he appears again dapper and smiling, a cigarette hanging from his mouth, long fingers holding pad and pencil and making notes while he jokes with a laughing student wearing a strapless formal.[92] The photograph also shows him clutching a newspaper under one arm in the manner of his father and brothers before him.

Ted and Marie took a long vacation in Hopkinsville during the summer of 1953. Seeking relief from fast-paced, crowded, and polluted New York and slowing to a gentle Kentucky pace, they stayed with Ted's cousin Mary Belle Braxton Fleming and talked about how Ted and Mary Belle used to fish and go blackberry picking on Uncle John Braxton's farm.[93] Evenings that summer, Ted would amble over to Allison Williams's house to swap stories, encouraged by the regional beverage of choice, Jack Daniels bourbon and branch water. Ted's cousin did not approve of alcohol in her home so Ted had to escape to Williams's house to drink. Williams says that he and Poston always got along well because "we both liked to drink; and we both liked to bullshit." The bullshitting was often about "pussy," their premarital sexual escapades, and the wives and side girls of everyone else. They prided themselves on their stereotype of being of the sexier race, and Ted still relished any opportunity to embellish a story.

Whenever Ted was in Hopkinsville, he wanted to hear about the old school rapscallion Rat Joiner. Ted and Rat's teacher Rozelle Leavell referred to Joiner as "just a little old thoroughbred Negro boy." But Joiner had matured to become a hardworking, playful father of ten. He spent years on the Louisville and Nashville Railroad until his eye was put out by a flying fragment. After that he supported his family often by cleaning a doctor's office or gardening for wealthy whites. At the bottom of the Joiners' Billy Goat Hill, Ted would walk by the stockyards on his visits home and laugh. There Rat Joiner would be entertaining his children or grandchildren by riding the cattle. Philip Joiner says, "Daddy would get on and they'd buck him off." By the time of his death, Rat Joiner's descendants numbered more than three hundred grandchildren and great-grandchildren. "Mama said if she had a buck for every grandkid she would have no bills to pay," his son Philip claims.

Allison Williams had sired two little boys by 1953, and "Marie and Ted were attentive to the children," he says. "They took them on picnics at Cherokee State Park. They bought them little bathing suits." Ted and Marie regarded with longing Rat Joiner's and Allison Williams's offspring. Marie was forty-two, and her biologically fruitful years were passing. Ted's Braxton cousins say that Ted "felt a void that he had no children, loving family as he did. He wanted to adopt a relative. He tried to get all of us to come to New York."

When Lydia Braxton Moten finished college in 1942 and started teaching, "he invited me." Another summer, Ted and Marie tried to persuade his cousin Alberta Braxton Bell to let her daughter Bernice (Bell Torian) come to New York. But Alberta was afraid to let her go, and Bernice "missed it by one inch. I nearly got a job there," Bernice says, "but my mother said, 'Stay here with us.' I listened to my mother. If she had not spoken, I think I would be in New York right now."[94]

Reorienting himself from fishing and family back to journalism at the end of the summer of 1953, Ted made a last call in Hopkinsville on Francis Eugene Whitney. After World War I the Whitney family had run a black newspaper when the Postons put out their *Contender.* The only extant Whitney now was on the city council. He says that Ted "put an article about me being a councilman in the paper in New York. He was so happy to go over to the municipal building and see the names of the black servicemen that had finally been put on the memorial plaque" there. Ted also took a story back that local Negro prisoners of war, returned from Korea, were being honored in town, though belatedly, with a parade.[95] Finally, from Kentucky, Ted could report that his home state university had at last opened its doors to Negroes.[96] The South had changed much in the quarter-century since Ted had left.

Throughout his life Poston kept his eye on his professional base, the black press. As a genre it had enjoyed a period of prosperity before the civil rights movement brought black activists into mainstream journalism. Afterward, Poston felt the black press was still essential, for still too few of his white counterparts were "qualified, by recent experience, to speak of the sufferings and aspirations of the Negro people." When John P. Davis launched a black picture magazine, *Our World,* Poston did some writing and editing for it. Davis's son Mike mentally pictured Poston in his "little round wire glasses," working with his father. "I can see him yet, smoking a cigarette, eyes popping out of his head."[97]

The black press, in its turn, treated Poston as a celebrity. John H. Johnson's elegant picture magazine *Ebony* featured Ted and Marie in one issue as racial pace-setters. In a story in August 1955, Marie is shown languorously stretched out on a chaise longue on their Brooklyn patio, and Ted smiles as they converse and "relax with a cool drink while awaiting guests for their famous barbecued squab dinner."[98] In another issue of *Ebony,* Poston is paired with Roi Ottley in a mock essay-debate on whether Chicago (Ottley) or New York (Poston) was the better environment for Negroes. In that dialogue, Poston's punch line was, "Chicago businessmen have organized some of the largest and most efficient funeral and burial societies in the world. But some people would see in this the final contrast between New York and Chicago. . . . New Yorkers are interested in a more abundant life rather than in a glorious pre-paid death."[99]

The *Reporter* magazine asked Ted for a critique of the black press in 1949. It was scathing. Poston said that "the average news story is badly written, poorly edited, and often based on rumors which could be easily checked."[100] A specific irritant to Poston about much of the black press was its diatribes against mixed marriages. When fair-skinned Walter White of the NAACP, for instance, married dusky Caucasian Poppy Cannon, black papers raged at his apparent sacrifice of race solidarity to "selfish ambition" and demanded that he be fired as NAACP head. Only the *Black Dispatch* of Oklahoma City reacted with what Poston considered "a well-reasoned editorial." It said, "When we can think in terms of women and men and not in terms of colors we will have reached the abstract ground we should stand upon in human relationships and marriage." [101]

Poston's association with the NAACP through Moon made him a natural for writing a profile of the organization's legal light, Thurgood Marshall, for *Survey* magazine when Marshall was gaining notoriety arguing for desegregation of education before the Supreme Court.[102] Poston's and Marshall's affinities in lifestyle gave them a natural rapport. Marshall, like Poston, was a storyteller. Although Marshall had a "profound respect for the law," he too could relax and "carry on" outside the courtroom and, like Ted, "indulge in black English" in bantering with the press.[103] Marshall and Poston also shared a devotion to poker and drinking whiskey.

Ted would be sucked in as more than an objective reporter on several civil rights cases which Marshall argued. In 1950, federal judge J. Waties Waring appealed to Ted rather than the law for safety. In Charleston, South Carolina, Waring and his wife were suffering political vandalism—dirt put in their car's gas tank, bricks thrown through their windows, obscene phone calls, bomb threats—in 1945 after Waring ruled that a black teacher must receive the same pay as a white teacher. In 1946 Judge Waring could not believe it when a jury declared that no brutality was involved when police yanked black veteran Isaac Woodard from a bus and put his eyes out with their nightsticks.[104] In 1948, South Carolinians had had enough of Judge Waring when he became "the guy who let the nigger vote" by ruling that Negroes must be included in the primaries. Ostracism greeted the Warings, even from Waring's nephew, segregationist Thomas Waring, who edited the *Charleston News and Courier*.[105] But J. Waties Waring stated that people must choose "to be comfortable and tuck [their] principles and conscience in the corner, or be uncomfortable outside and be happy." [106]

In 1950, Waring planned for the pathbreaking Clarendon County school desegregation case, on the docket for early 1951, which advocates predicted would launch the end of "doghouse education." The judge and his wife had been informed of a plot to kill them. Not knowing who to turn to locally, they entrusted to Ted a confidential statement of the plot, "only to be disclosed in the event of his violent death." Poston put one copy in a safe deposit box and gave another copy to James Wechsler, who passed it on to the FBI.[107] Poston and Wechsler assured the Warings that "the facilities of our paper are at your disposal at all times." During their darkest period, Mrs. Waring wrote Poston, "You are truly a good friend, a joy, comfort and Rock of Gibraltar to us in our loneliness."[108]

On May 28, 1951, Poston was in Clarendon County when the school desegregation case opened. He observed the mood and conduct of the local Negroes in Judge Waring's courtroom as persistent and dignified. Many had driven in from the country in "battered looking automobiles," and started lining up at 5 and 6 A.M., "quietly, two abreast, down the hall and out the steps. Everyone knew how important it was and that an incident of any kind could be disruptive and damaging. Whenever there was any seat vacated, the line inched forward."[109] Waring, too, marveled at the country people coming to the trial as if on a pilgrimage. Their attendance showed him that they felt "a little whiff of freedom."[110]

Poston marveled at the NAACP's legal staff as well. For example, Spottswood Robinson, when challenged on a local statute, "recited it verbatim from memory, didn't miss a comma or semicolon—and he put them in when he spoke it." Poston mentioned that performance later to Thurgood Marshall, who scoffed, "Ah, he does that all the time."[111] Marshall also scoffed at social psychologist Kenneth B. Clark's use of dolls for testing black children to show that in segregated schools they developed a poor self-image. Marshall "chewed Clark out for 'wasting our time with all that irrelevant stuff,'" Poston told Richard Kluger, a young *Post* reporter who eventually wrote *Simple Justice,* which chronicles the process leading up to the *Brown v. Board of Education* school desegregation decision.

Ironically, in the final Supreme Court opinion, Chief Justice Earl Warren singled out Clark's doll study as the number one argument disemboweling the "logic" of the 1896 *Plessy v. Ferguson* decision case that "separate but equal" was fine law.[112] Kluger considers that the "only soaring passage in the opinion" was Warren's allusion to Clark's testimony: "To separate [children] from others of similar age and qualifications solely because of their race generates a feeling of inferiority as to their status in the community that may affect their hearts and minds in a way unlikely ever to be undone."[113]

At the end of the hot, grueling days in the tense Charleston courtroom, Poston and the NAACP lawyers were feted by the Warings at the couple's "graceful old mansion" on Meeting Street. That the Warings invited black guests to their home caused Poston to laugh, "Oh, my, the KKK and that crowd were up in heaven."[114] When the court case was over, Waring moved to a New York bench. He and his wife survived the death threats against them, and Ted never had to reveal their confidential note.

Poston's book reviews showed that the racial climate was continually improving, though not by much. More black authors were being published as the civil rights movement heightened public awareness. In ten book reviews he wrote in 1953, Poston revealed his own racial philosophy. Of *Seekers,* he suggested that one must work for the cause where one finds oneself: "Will Thomas found the personal solution to his problems in Vermont. To other troubled Negro Americans who can't afford such a drastic step, there is an alternative. They can take Booker T. Washington's advice to 'Let down your buckets where you are.' And also join the NAACP." [115]

Poston commended Hubert Creekmore and his novel *The Chain in the Heart* for refusing to minimize the horrors of Negro existence in Mississippi.[116] Richard Wright's *The Outsider* suggested that Negroes' search for inclusion in America was Sisyphean. Cross Damon was "no uncomplicated, slum-shocked Bigger Thomas. He is a highly literate, well-read product of our civilization who becomes a cold-blooded killer because he rejects the very civilization which created him." [117] Poston had some praise for *Cast the First Stone,* by Henry Lee Moon's cousin Chester Himes. Based on prison life, it was, he said, "no quickie attempt to capitalize on a current situation" but a serious and sensitive effort to portray the "day-to-day life of men shut off from normal relations with society." Poston credited Himes for his forward-thinking — for 1953 — portrayal of homosexuality, "which is common to any prison, or prison tale" but was still a taboo in the establishment press.[118]

Poston did a feature on William Bradford Huie's shocking story of Ruby McCollum, the Florida woman who had finally killed the white physician who had taken advantage of her sexually every time she or her children needed medical care. Subsequently, the *Post* serialized Huie's book.[119] In his review of J. Saunders Redding's *On Being Negro in America,* Poston let white readers in on the secret that "one's heart is sickened at the realization of the primal energy that goes undeflected and unrefined into the sheer business of living as a Negro in the United States." Beneath his own seemingly happy-go-lucky demeanor, Poston exposed a heaviness that was always with him when he concluded that Redding, as a Negro, had not the courage "to tell the whole truth." Still, he gave pause to "those writers who proclaim the wonderful advances made in American race relations, and to those Negroes who know too well but would never admit what Redding has brought into the light." [120]

Hodding Carter had won a Pulitzer prize for his bold editorials in the Mississippi *Delta Democrat-Times,* but when his novel *Where Main Street Meets the River* came out, Poston cautioned that Carter was no "liberal" or spokesman for the new South but "a new spokesman for the Old

South," with traditional rationalizations for "separate but equal" treatment of blacks.[121] Poston educated his readers to the history that he had known since childhood in his review of Benjamin Quarles's *Negro in the Civil War.* Negroes had "supplied the bones and sinews" of combat. Until northern commanders recognized their importance—and stopped returning them to their masters—"the slaves maintained transport, built the forts, dug the entrenchments, and freed white Southerners for battle."[122]

West Indian George Lamming's autobiography, *In the Castle of My Skin,* compared British and American racism. Through Trumper, a Barbadian who developed race consciousness after he had migrated to Harlem, Lamming illustrated British colonial accommodationism, how England had enslaved the minds of its subjects as well as their bodies, and "how America—through its very harshness—has awakened the Negro people to their own power."[123] In November 1953, a book on Father Divine was published.[124] No longer did Poston treat Divine lightly as a passing cult; with his mature commitment to solid reporting, Ted turned his jaundiced eye on that man and, by extension, on other cults and rackets engaged in by magnetic blacks. Through his many book reviews as well as articles, Poston thus educated many readers of New York City on what it is like to be black.

The year 1954 was a landmark for African Americans and for the country. The NAACP realized the fruit of its 1909 aim, to "create an organization so effective and so powerful that when discrimination and injustice touched one Negro, it would touch twelve million."[125] Thurgood Marshall and the NAACP won a unanimous Supreme Court victory in *Brown v. Board of Education,* and the nation's schools were finally required to desegregate.[126] The joy that ruling brought to the black community was that of a frontier between their hidden and public transcripts being "decisively breached," James Scott puts it. "The result is a charged political impact."[127]

Ted Poston heard the news at the *Post* and later told Richard Kluger that the decision being unanimous was "a big surprise to me. It came over the wire one sentence at a time. Everybody was all excited and yelling and screaming, and there I was gettin' this stuff fed to me and being very happy and not being able to hear myself think. I remember climbing up on the desk and shouting: 'Will you goddamn niggers shut up so I can write this story?' Of course I was the only Negro in the room."[128]

10

. . . .

Integration by Law

. . . .

1954–1957

By refusing to give this Talented Tenth the
key . . . can any sane man imagine that they
will lightly lay aside their yearning.
 —W. E. B. DU BOIS, *Souls of Black Folk*

James Wechsler sent Poston into the South to check the effect of *Brown v.
Board of Education* on local governments and schools. For the "Dixie's Fight
for Freedom" series, he talked with black and white teachers and politicians. Governor Herman Talmadge of Georgia had declared, "Segregation
forever."[1] Ted made an appointment to interview Talmadge. After keeping
Ted waiting for four hours, Talmadge's secretary ushered him into the governor's office through the back door. They had never met, but Talmadge
immediately called Poston by his first name. Poston aimed for typical humor in describing the encounter: "'You say you were born and raised in
Hopkinsville, KY.,' [Talmadge] said. 'Well, I'm sure they don't have any
mixed schools in Hopkinsville. And it doesn't seem to have hurt you none.
You seem like a pretty smart boy.' 'But, Governor,' I remonstrated quietly,
'I'm inhibited.'"[2]

Four days later, the Hopkinsville school board announced that the elementary and high schools there would be integrated, "and an effort will be
made to start the program next September."[3] Poston, now back in New
York, concluded his last article of the southern series by applying familiarity to Georgia's governor: "I felt less inhibited already—and I wanted to tell
Herman about it."[4]

That southern trip may have been the one on which social psychologist Kenneth B. Clark accompanied him. Clark exulted in listening to Poston on the long drive. As they passed one new school for blacks, Ted said that a taxi driver had told him that "when the white folks put up a brand new school for black children, they would soon find some way that it wouldn't be for them." Indeed, whites, cognizant of the inevitability of integration, finally put up a decent school for blacks because, with integration imminent, they knew that their children would get to use the modern facility.

Clark associates many such satirical stories with Poston. Clark was a guest on a few television programs with Ted during the 1956 Montgomery bus boycott and remembers Poston telling him that Birmingham's sheriff Bull Connor had a black mistress, and the blacks made her feel guilty when Connor set dogs on them in Birmingham.[5] With such inside stories, Clark says, Ted "made many situations bearable."

In 1955 Poston was given a boat trip to Nassau in the Bahamas by tourism promoters. He learned that racism was dying hard in the British Commonwealth. Twelve African American journalists were invited for the two-day sojourn in the hope that the Bahamas would benefit from rising black American prosperity. Evelyn Cunningham, one of the twelve, recalled Poston's fury when he saw the filthy, cramped "guest" accommodations on the SS *Nassau*. She said: "Ted called my 'stateroom' the 'black hole of Calcutta.'" On the island, Ted found that the major hotels maintained strict bans against Negro patrons.

Perhaps it was the Nassau visit that was bothering him in an incident mentioned by Marcy Elias Rothman. On his first day back in the office, with "coltish enthusiasm" she headed over to greet him, but Fern Eckman warned her that Ted was not in a good mood: "He was jim-crowed in the Caribbean." Later, Poston explained to Rothman, "The trouble is that often I forget I'm black and when something like this happens, I'm too painfully reminded."[6]

A sad event in 1955 for Ted was the death of his brother Ulysses, at age sixty-four, after a long illness. Sybil had died in 1951. Ted arranged a service at their Concord Baptist Church in Brooklyn, then buried Ulysses at Long Island National Cemetery. The *Amsterdam News* and *New York Age* published obituaries saying Ulysses had written for *Current History,* the *Atlantic Monthly,* and the *American Mercury* magazines. A perusal of these publications has not turned up any such articles; they may have been unsigned. Ted was aware that Ulysses, through his work in education, journalism, and finally business, had upheld the family imperative of attaining a livelihood while working for the advancement of the race.

He inherited Ulysses' 101 Chauncey Street house in Brooklyn, so Ted and Marie moved, with Marie's mother, Mae Byrd, around the corner from 359 Stuyvesant Avenue.[7] The neighborhood at the time was "posh, upper-middle class," and "a kind of a black oasis," Fern and Irving Eckman claim.

Ted's family concerns were interrupted in spring 1955 by the lynching of Emmett Till in Mississippi.[8] The *Post* sent Ted to cover the trial. Murray Kempton was there, too, and found "a kind of majesty in the spectacle of the State of Mississippi honestly trying to convict two white men on the word of four Negroes." As was the custom, however, the all-white jury overlooked Mose Wright's testimony and acquitted Till's murderers.[9]

Each time Poston returned to the *Post* from the South, a "bevy of editors and reporters would surround him with questions," Eckman says. This time Poston told them of the deputy who checked him for weapons before he could enter the courtroom. The deputy spent "an undue amount of time fondling Ted's genitals." Ted slyly suggested to the deputy, "Want to go steady?"

In a tale from his coverage of the Bloody Sunday march across the Pettus Bridge in Alabama, Poston related affably how he handled one situation. He "went right in" to introduce himself to Selma's mayor. The mayor called in Sheriff Jim Clark, a "big potbellied guy with his holster, chewin' his tobacco." The mayor told the sheriff, "This is *Mister* Ted Poston from one of them big-city papers up north." Sheriff Clark shifted the wad of tobacco in his jaw and said, "Is it a white paper you work for or one of them nigger papers?" Poston answered, "I understand that here in the South if you got one drop of Negro blood then you're a Negro. Well, I'm the one drop of Negro blood on the *Post*, so I guess it's a Negro paper." [10]

As 1955 ended, the civil rights movement was gaining a hero through the oratory of twenty-six-year-old Martin Luther King, Jr. In the next twelve years, King rushed toward his death, and Poston documented it. But the energy of the aging Poston was slackening.

If 1940 was Ted's most prolific year, when he wrote for both the white *New York Post* and the black *Pittsburgh Courier,* and 1949 was his happiest, then 1956 must have been his most stressful year. He had reached his pinnacle in the profession and was swamped by pressure. His immoderate lifestyle and drink affected his relationship with his wife. Marie's ingrained sense of life's proprieties and black Philadelphia middle-class values did not accommodate themselves well to the capricious mode of a working reporter. And both Postons, with their forceful personalities, could be "irascible as well as charming," says St. Clair Bourne. Murray Kempton thought Marie was too haughty and high-society for Ted. In "Breathless Reporter Gets His Story as Dodgers Hit Town," Ted related how he spent one evening in the company of a redhead rather than at a dinner party Marie had planned because the city desk sent him to Penn Station to get human interest on the return to town of the Brooklyn Dodgers.[11] When the team's train was delayed, Ted called Marie from a phone booth, and Marie overheard the giddy girl from whom Ted was eliciting "local color" ask him, "You really a reporter? You can get me down on the platform?" Marie demanded, "Who's *that?*" Marie was not amused. The Postons' courtship had been carried on while Ted was in government service with regular hours. Marie could not accept that even reporters who have worked in the White House are subject to the authority of a city editor and fitful hours.

Normal journalistic interruptions to their marriage were exacerbated by the issue of the Postons' failure to reproduce. Ted thought more frequently now of his status as "the last Poston." Paul Sann says, "I know Ted brooded that he had no offspring and his brother had none. He felt deeply about the fact that there would be no more Postons." Marie told friends they had wanted children. She "went through various fertility things," says Rosemary Reed. Their barrenness added to conflicts over their strenuous careers. When they were together and Ted was off duty, alcohol sometimes clouded his good sense. An undated note to Ted accusing him of physical violence would come into the hands of Henry Lee Moon as executor of Ted's estate after Ted's death. Apparently it was from Marie.[12]

> Ted, you didn't appear to be in condition to discuss anything when you came home tonight. . . . I retained an attorney when I realized the extent of the injuries I had incurred as the result of your insane and absolutely unprovoked actions on Friday at the Laurels. In case you would like to "glow" in your cowardice. . . . due to extreme head pains I had to stop on the highway en route home and received aid from the State Police. I told them eventually what had happened and why I was traveling alone at 4:30 [A.M.]. . . . Due to the left ear damage, I had to go Saturday to an Ear Specialist because I had vertigo trouble. . . . This, of course, does not take care of the left side and back injury where you put your knee in my side and back to hold me down on the bed as you tried to pull my hair out and to disfigure me. . . . I just have gone as far as I can and cannot take your violent abuse any longer. . . . My attorney will contact you about a conference on the separation procedure. . . . I'm sorry it has to end this way but I continued to hope—.

The note is unsigned. Ed Morrow, who still saw the Postons socially, confirms that "there would be a swinging battle every now and then. They were both aggressive and combative and would bring that home to the dinner table. Anyone can take a cheap shot, especially at a mate."

In any case, by the end of 1955 Marie had left. Their divorce was granted on January 17, 1956.[13] Even Marie's exodus, however, added to Ted's repertoire of tales. She "stripped him blind," says Sann. Marie backed a moving van up to the house and took every stick of furniture so that he had not even a chair to sit on. Ted's laughter over Marie's sudden departure, however, covered a sense of sadness and personal failure. Sociologist Hylan Lewis surmises that "each of Ted's wives probably saw something in him that he could give. He had connections. Marie was an upwardly mobile gal. She had a sense of power and of how to use gender so that she was able to parlay and move into a good spot. There was a chemistry in how she used Ted before, during, and after their marriage."

Marie Poston was injured in a fall sometime in the decade after she decamped. Ted told Fern Eckman that Marie had been in an accident and needed medical care—for plastic surgery?—so "he sent her money." Nevertheless, Marie continued her impressive career.[14] Ten years later, she achieved marital happiness with a third husband, elderly and distinguished Alexander L. Jackson of Chicago, a onetime track star and class orator at Harvard, class of 1914.

For Ted, loss mounted upon loss. Within a month after his divorce, in February 1956, he was notified that his father had died at age eighty-eight in Paducah. Ephraim Poston had retired in 1941 from West Kentucky Industrial College, resigning at that time also as a director of the Kentucky Negro Education Association. Ted went home to bury Eph, then he brought his stepmother, Susie, back to New York, probably out of guilt for, as a teenager, having run away from home at the time Susie married Eph.

The *Post* soon assigned him to cover Autherine Lucy, the black student whose entrance to the University of Alabama Governor George C. Wallace barred at the doorway. The Lucy story provided grist for Ted's narrative mill during his friends' annual retreat at Capahosic that year. "Ted knew every detail," Viola Trent says. "We would sit spellbound while he told us inside stuff."

When Poston got home, Martin Luther King, Jr., came to Ted's Concord Baptist Church in Brooklyn. A female reporter was so impressed with the young minister that she whispered to Poston of King's charismatic oratory in support of the Montgomery bus boycott, "I'm sure glad he's not mad at the IRT [New York subway], for if he said so, I'd walk back home to Harlem tonight."[15]

In 1956 "Negroes" leaped to prominence in the mainstream press. Reporters from around the globe descended on Montgomery, Alabama, to learn about Rosa Parks, the Reverend King, and their bus boycott. The *Montgomery Advertiser* tried to sidestep scrutiny of the South with a series,

"Tell It Not in Gath," that chronicled the horrors of black-white relations elsewhere.[16] Editor Grover C. Hall, Jr., snarled to reporters, "Aren't there enough cases of discrimination and racial pressures up North to keep you busy?"[17] But Hall was open-minded and phrased his defensiveness as a challenge. He broached the idea to James Wechsler that the *Post*'s Murray Kempton, whom some southern journalists called a "wild-eyed bleeding heart with a pulpit under his arm," "handcuff himself to me for a week in New York illuminating race conditions there."[18] Wechsler agreed that some alliance of the *New York Post* and the *Montgomery Advertiser* would be intriguing but that Poston rather than Kempton should accept Grover Hall's challenge. Wechsler wanted the racial scene from his black reporter's point of view.

First, Wechsler made Ted the writer on a series, "The Negro in New York," with six other reporters doing legwork. That group's conclusion fingered housing, again, as the main sore spot of discrimination: "No matter what his economic status, cultural attainment or educational achievement, any Negro here is subject to . . . rude rejection if he seeks to escape from the ghettoes to which the majority of his fellow colored citizens are confined."[19] For the first time Ted penned autobiography in other than humorous anecdotes. He told of his youthful life on the railroad, his arrival in New York when he waited table and ran elevators, and discriminations he encountered then. That compelling series kept the *Post* sold out at New York City newsstands in April 1956.

Poston concluded the "Negro in New York" series with a "Letter to an Alabama Editor" in which he dared the *Montgomery Advertiser* to reprint the series, then to join him in a similar series on the Negro in Alabama. Grover C. Hall, Jr., still preferred to work with Kempton or with "my opposite number," editor Wechsler; but Wechsler insisted that Poston do it.[20] Wechsler did not want Poston to court martyrdom, however, so he sent him on his way, admonishing Poston to check in by phone every few hours. Wechsler's anxiety caused Hall to guffaw: "Now what kind of reporting has been done on Montgomery that after five billion words by reporters from all over the world, a foremost New York editor is so grotesquely ignorant of Montgomery conditions that he wanted daily assurance that his reporter was among the living?"[21]

Yet Hall cordially welcomed Poston to Montgomery and offered him the use of all the *Advertiser*'s facilities—office space, typewriters—and of his city editor, Joe Azbell, "the best friend the Negro ever had," as guide.[22] Because of Poston's affinity for "fun and laughter," he "hit it off fine with both editor and news staff." Other *Advertiser* reporters took to calling Azbell

"Ted Poston's chauffeur." [23] Ted himself called Joe Azbell the father of the bus boycott because it was Azbell who found one of the leaflets that the Montgomery Improvement Association distributed in the black community announcing the boycott starting "tomorrow" and reprinted it on the front page of the *Advertiser*. Without that notice, many Negroes might never have heard of the projected boycott and it might not have enjoyed such success.

Just as Hall would have preferred that Kempton come to do an Alabama series with him, so Poston would have preferred collaborating with Hall's more progressive father, "one of the great editors of his era." [24]

In his Alabama series, Poston documented moments of beauty; some surprisingly unprejudiced whites; human interest touches as he rode with Negro maids boycotting the Montgomery Bus Lines in their improvised station wagon brigade; and the atmosphere around the sensational Martin Luther King, Jr. During the three weeks of Poston's stay, Joe Azbell asserted that Negroes "hold the same jobs that white men hold," but Negroes countered privately to Ted that their jobs were "anything that's hard, hot or heavy." Poston's strongest impression was that since the bus boycott began, the local Negroes "walk a little straighter," heads "held a little higher. . . . They're no longer afraid." [25]

The love-hate relationship with Grover C. Hall, Jr., would continue as Ted extended his stay in Montgomery to do another series, this one on the rise of the Reverend King. Wechsler, back in New York, lamented that King had no equal in the white ministry, "graced with" such "wisdom and restraint." [26] For "Fighting Pastor," Poston compared King and Hall in a public epistle to Hall:

> I couldn't help but think . . . that two of the men who had impressed me most in Montgomery could not be real friends and associates because of . . . myopia. . . . You and Rev. Martin Luther King Jr. . . . are the two best-dressed men in Montgomery. . . . You are the two best tennis players in town—although King is probably rusty since he is not permitted to practice on any of the six city courts. . . . And, intellectually, you are on a level—although King holds a doctorate and you chose to pursue your newspaper career instead of obtaining a college degree.

On leaving Montgomery, Ted thanked Hall for his hospitality but added, "I was constantly shocked by the realization that while you and similarly situated whites were willing to accept me—an outsider—you were quite unable to even see the Negro fellow citizen in your midst as other than an indistinguishable black mass." [27]

Poston's series elicited letters from both North and South. A *New York Post* reader who apparently did not know Ted's color, wrote, "To the Editor, I get tired of Ted Poston's articles on the Negroes of Alabama. . . . If Ted Poston was the father of three or four little girls, would he be happy and contented to have his girls play with colored boys?"[28]

A *Montgomery Advertiser* reader cajoled Grover Hall: "Based upon much that I have read . . . Ted Poston would be the least desirable person to want to be associated with on anything. . . . There has never been anything constructive in anything I have read from the pen of this Poston."[29] Those letters contrasted with one from a *Post* reader who said: "Ted Poston was never better. A great story-teller, as well as a great reporter. Why not combine his talents in a weekly column on adventures in bringing discomfiture to the bigots—and joy to the rest of us?"[30]

Stories on racial changes tumbled thick and fast from Poston's typewriter that summer and fall. In September 1956, Ted wrote a vernacular feature about a decrepit Virginia-born woman buying chitterlings in the Little Gray Shop in Poston's Brooklyn neighborhood. She was ecstatic to see the headline on the *Post* under Ted's arm: "Bayonets Hold Off Ky. Mob." She told him she was thinking of "going back [South] just for spite. . . . And I'll be going first class. . . . Them crackers. . . . The Lawd sure lays it on them. . . . They got troops right down their craw both in Tennessee and Kentucky. And, mark my words, they gonna have 'em in Virginny, too. . . . Now if Mr. Roosevelt was in there, we wouldn't a-had all this mess. There was a man for you." After discussing Roosevelt's "guts," the decrepit woman proved how up-to-the-minute she was by reminding Poston of the integrating of Little Rock Central High School. "Guts?" she says. "What about them little colored kids who went to that white man's school every living school day in spite of that mob and all them crackers. You say something about guts?" Poston brought the NAACP into the conversation, and the old woman turned to him. "Son," she said, "you belong to the N double-A C P?" When Ted mumbled "Yes'm," she said: "I joined up years ago. Cost only $1. then. Now it's $2. I call that Eisenhower's poll tax up in Brooklyn. If he done his part, then the N double-A-CP wouldn't have to spend all that money to get what the good Lord already done give us but what the crackers don't want us to have."[31] That story obviously cheered Ted Poston, in contrast to a scenario that involved him in another eatery.

In October he arranged to meet a group of his scholarly friends for breakfast at the train station lunch counter in Richmond, Virginia, on their way to a United Negro College Fund conference at Capahosic.[32] Ted's light-skinned companions had been allowed in the restaurant because the hostess thought they were "Filipino." When Ted arrived, the waitress told him politely, "We are sorry, sir, but we can't serve you here. We will be happy to serve you in the colored dining room." Famished, Ted answered resignedly, "That's all right." Then he waited for his friends to finish eating. In his article, he made clear what classy people the whole group were, but because of their pale skin, his friends got served only because the waitress thought they were Filipinos.[33]

Able to slow his frantic pace by fall, Ted thought about his stepmother, Susie. Having brought her to New York, he tried to get another transplanted Paducah native, Ersa Hines Clinton, to take Susie to a World Series baseball game. That incident resulted in a couple of whimsical stories. One was "The Day Mama Put the Whammy on the Yankees," about Susie's "secret weapon"—prayer—which caused Jackie Robinson's team, the Brooklyn Dodgers, to win. The "Mama's whammy" stories, however, got tied up with the story of Ersa Hines Clinton, whom Ted seemed to be courting through the newspaper. Ersa, fifteen years Ted's junior, had seen Ted on his visits to Paducah, in church with Susie and Eph. She and other residents had admired Ted for his success in New York journalism.[34] Ersa had not realized that by taking Susie to the game, she would become fodder for Ted's typewriter. Ersa Hines Clinton Poston now says that when she was at the World Series, "I was supposed to be on sick leave. When I went back to work the next day, they said, 'Ha! You sure got caught on that one. Clinton was at the ball game!'" Ted's two articles on Mama at the World Series are the only written record of his romance with his third wife, Ersa.

In December, the Negroes of Montgomery marked the first anniversary of their bus boycott with fasting, services of thanksgiving, and workshops on nonviolence. Ted closed the year by returning to Montgomery and doing a feature on the sublime Mahalia Jackson, who served as sustenance for the boycott. He said that listeners "started packing St. John's at noon. And by nightfall, stragglers could hardly force their way into the basement." When Mahalia arrived, "cognizant of the fire regulations and the possibility of a riot if she started them swinging too soon, she opened up with a soft number called 'I've Heard of a City Called Heaven.'. . . The applause was thunderous."[35]

In the mid-1950s, Ted Poston had experienced personal unhappiness in the interstices of professional success. At work, he clarified complex issues with articles infused with reader-friendly dialogue. His prose was not ponderous even if the subject was. He knew how to excite attention, to surprise, and to please. On occasion he could move or shock; ordinarily, he told sad things straight. His talents were being fully used under James Wechsler to advance civil rights and improve the human condition in those great days of the *New York Post*.

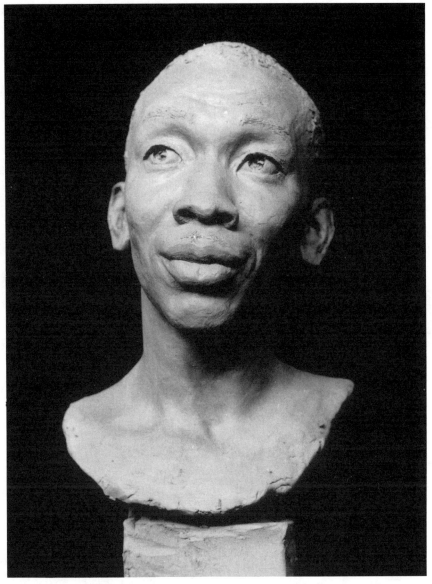

Bust of Ted Poston, 1932. Sculptor Maysie Stone. Bust at Schomburg Center for Research in Black Culture. Photo by A. B. Bogart. Photo used courtesy of Deborah Stone and Kate Kolchin.

[*above*] Bell's Station store and railroad station, 1895. Ted's mother, Mollie Cox Poston, came from Bell's Station. It is now part of Fort Campbell, one of the largest military installations in the United States. Photo courtesy of William T. Turner, Christian County historian.

[*opposite top*] Principal and teachers at Booker T. Washington School. Front row, seated man is unidentified. Seated woman is Fanny McReynolds Robinson who taught fifth grade. Row 2, Mrs. Fannie Bronston Postell; Emma Majors, who taught fifth and sixth grades; Lottie Dade, second grade; Mrs. Steele, first grade; Rosa Morgan, who married Claybron Merriweather; Olivet Poole, third grade. The last person in the row is not identified. Row 3: Jennie Poole; Cornelia Evans; Bessie Walker. The dark-skinned woman standing in front of the window is H. Belle LaPrade, who cast the Poston brothers as evil fairies because their skin was so dark. Willa Glass taught second grade; unidentified; Louise Glass; and Virginia Ritter McNeil. LaPrade became principal of Jackson Street School (precursor of Booker T. Washington School) when Postell went to teach at Attucks. Photo courtesy of Rebecca Quarles Clark.

[*opposite bottom*] Booker T. Washington School, 1954. Photo courtesy of William T. Turner.

Class of 1924

The Senior Class of

The Attucks High School

Commencement Exercises

Friday Evening, June Sixth

Nineteen Hundred Twenty-four

at eight o'clock

Auditorium

Invitation

Class Roll

Class Motto:

"We build the ladder by which we climb"

Class Colors:
Lavender and Gold

Class Flower:
White Carnation

Class Roll:

DOROTHY ANNALICE RUSSELL
MARGARET HOPE SLEET
FRANCES LOUISE WAGNER
WILLIE AUGUSTA BRONAUGH
EVERETT ROOSEVELT JOHNSON
DOROTHY LOUISE BRYANT
ARLETTA LORENZO MACKEY
ALBERTHA AUGUSTA BRAXTON
FANNIE BELLE SHELBY
ELIZABETH BEATRICE GARROTT
RHEDA BELLE SALLEE
JAMES MADISON WILSON
CORRIE AUGUSTA BROADY
ZELA LUCILE SLAUGHTER

MARY ELIZABETH LARKER
BETTIE ANNIE MAE ROBERSON
JOE HENRY GANT
LOUISE DOLORES SIMMS
NANNIE MAE QUARLES
PATRICK HENRY BAKER
BESSIE MAE WALKER
VIRGINIA ELAINE REDD
ANNIE ANITA McADOO
THEODORE ROOSEVELT POSTON
MASALIAR TALLIFERIA LYNCH
OWEN LEE JONES
ORA BELLE PAYNE
BESSIE LENA TANDY

Class Roll

P. Moore, Superintendent

[*opposite*] Graduation announcement for Ted Poston's class, 1924. Courtesy of Roberta Mabry Wooldridge.

[*above*] Attucks High School, built in 1917. Photo courtesy of William T. Turner.

[*right*] View from Belmont Hill of the house where Ted took care of the fireplace grates. Hauke photo.

Rex Theatre, 1912, where the children from the dark side of Hopkinsville sat in the balcony every Saturday from 10 A.M. to 5 P.M. Photo courtesy of William T. Turner.

James Duncan, Mary Duncan, Sina Duncan, Dr. James R. Duncan, and William
Duncan, about 1924. Photo courtesy of Mary Duncan Wilson.

Jennie Knight's 1925 graduation photo from Fisk University. Chicago Portrait Studio photo courtesy of Jennie Knight Baker.

[*above*] Twenty-two black American intellectuals traveled on the *Bremen* to Europe to make a film in the Soviet Union on American racism. Seated on the deck, Louise Thompson, Dorothy West. Seated on chairs and bench: Mildred Jones, Constance White, Katherine Jenkins, Sylvia Garner, Mollie Lewis. Standing, row 1: Wayland Rudd, Frank "Curly" Montero, Matt Crawford, George Sample, Laurence Alberga, Langston Hughes, Juanita Lewis, Alan McKenzie. Standing, row 2: Ted Poston, Henry Lee Moon, Thurston McNary Lewis, William L. Patterson, Loren Miller. Leonard Smith and Homer Smith were on the tour but did not appear in the photograph. Photo courtesy of Schlesinger Library, Radcliffe College. Dorothy West Collection.

[*left*] Ellen Tarry, late 1920s. Photo courtesy of Ms. Tarry.

Mollie Moon, founder and president of the National Urban League Guild. National Urban League photo, 1962. Schomburg Center for Research in Black Culture, New York Public Library.

Henry Lee Moon. *Our World* photo by Ricci Byrd. Schomburg Center for Research in Black Culture, New York Public Library.

Ted Poston, 1952. Photo courtesy of *New York Post*.

[*above*] Kenneth B. Clark, psychologist, 1970. *New York Post* photo.

[*right*] Irving and Fern Marja Eckman. *New York Post* photo.

James A. Wechsler, editor of the *New York Post,* 1953. *New York Post* and Associated Press photo.

Dorothy Schiff, publisher of the *New York Post* during Ted Poston's tenure there. *New York Post* photo.

Black Cabinet reassembled for stag "Dinner and Tall Tales" at the Waldorf Astoria when President John F. Kennedy appointed Robert C. Weaver administrator of the Housing and Home Finance Agency in 1961. Seated left to right: Frank Horne, Campbell Johnson, Robert C. Weaver, William Hastie, Robert Ming, Ralph Bunche. Standing, left to right: A. Maceo Smith, B. T. McGraw, Frederick D. Patterson, Farrow Allen, Donald Wyatt, Ted Jones, Roy Wilkins, Ted Poston, William J. Trent, Ralph Lanier, Truman Gibson, Henry Lee Moon, Al Smith, Lawrence Oxley. Weaver says that the active members of the Black Cabinet were Hastie, Horne, Smith, Trent, Poston, and Moon. Other blacks in race relations in the government in the mid-1930s and early 1940s were occasional participants. Bill Anderson, photographer. Photo courtesy Schomburg Center for Research in Black Culture, New York Public Library. Robert C. Weaver Collection.

Ersa Hines Poston, Albany, New York, 1967. Ruth Andrus photo, used courtesy of *New York Post.*

Nancy Hicks Maynard. *Oakland Tribune* photo courtesy Mrs. Maynard.

[*above*] Diana Bonnor Lewis, Ted Poston's last love. Hauke photo, 1983.

[*left*] Ruth Banks, who took care of Ted Poston in his final illness. Hauke photo.

Dean of
Black Journalists

1957–1964

Hunch up and take it. You'll get 'em in the end.
—LYNDON B. JOHNSON

At age fifty, Ted Poston, at the top of his form, was held in esteem by most journalists in New York and by knowledgeable blacks across the nation. He was reporting history in the making as the civil rights revolution rolled along. His wife, Marie, was gone, but Ted still enjoyed a comfortable lifestyle. He tried to be a good son to his stepmother as he had had no chance to be to his own mother, dead since 1917.

Because Poston shared with his publisher a quest for "honest unionism, social reform and humane government programs," the *Post,* aimed at a middle-class readership, was still the right place for him. Dorothy Schiff had been trying to lure Eleanor Roosevelt and her column, "My Day," to the *Post* since 1939 and succeeded in 1957, when the *World-Telegram* dropped it. In 1949 Roosevelt and Poston had been winners of the Geist Award for fighting bias. Roosevelt won first prize and Poston and the *Post*'s Oliver Pilat shared second prize.[1]

Eleanor Roosevelt and Ted Poston were old friends. He told an ABC producer about the time during the war that he was walking through Washington's "Negro section . . . near Seventh and New Jersey," at three in the morning and saw Mrs. Roosevelt walking ahead of him. He said, "It was a pretty rough section of the city. I caught up with her and . . . said, 'What are you doing out here this time of night?'" She had been visiting her friend Mary McLeod Bethune and they talked late. She was certain she was quite safe and figured, "I'll get a cab at the next corner." He admonished her, "What if someone came up behind you and didn't recognize you! . . . If the wife of the President of the United States were mugged in a Negro section at 3 in the morning . . . you'd set the cause of race relations back a thousand years!" [2]

At a banquet given by the American Jewish Congress in honor of the *Post*, Thurgood Marshall extolled the paper for its "accurate and courageous reporting." Marshall said, "If one wants to know the status of civil rights in our nation today, it is essential that he read the files of the *New York Post*." [3]

Ted updated the Virginia integration scene by hailing Vivian Carter Mason as "the Harriet Tubman of Norfolk," a woman who had known the real Harriet Tubman and had "heard from her own lips the stories of the fantastic exploits of the Union Army spy who led hundreds of Negroes to freedom during the Civil War." Mason, sister of Elmer A. Carter, head of the New York State Commission Against Discrimination, was then a "greying matron who prepared 17 Negro children for their successful assault on Virginia's 'massive resistance'" to school desegregation. [4]

Ted did three compelling series on black figures in the news in 1957, each illustrating the proverb that "it takes a village to raise a child." "Fighting Pastor" was a continuation of the drama of Martin Luther King, Jr., his leadership of the bus boycott, and his prospective future. In the final article on him, Poston asked, "Where Does He Go from Here?" King told Ted, "One of the frustrations of any young man is to approach the heights at such an early age. . . . No crowds will be waiting outside churches to greet me two years from now." Poston caught King in June at the former Kentucky Normal and Industrial Institute, now Kentucky State University, when King admonished graduates, "We stand between two worlds, the dying old, and the emerging new." [5] Ted felt he was on a similar threshold. On September 21, the black movement suffered a blow when King was stabbed in New York while signing copies of his book *Stride Toward Freedom* and was rushed to Harlem Hospital. His daily medical report was the city's biggest story until his life was out of danger. [6] Neither King nor Poston could know that the 1960s held in store for them and the country much more tragedy.

While an articulate tomboy, Althea Gibson, prepared for the U.S. Open tennis matches in 1957, Poston broke through this first black Wimbledon champion's diffidence toward the press and did a six-part series on Gibson's evolution from Harlem street urchin to college-educated "lady," who was proud that she could "beat the hell out of anybody in the block." [7]

After he finished the Gibson series, Ted made a last stab at achieving personal happiness by more actively pursuing Ersa Hines Clinton, the thirty-six-year-old professional woman from Kentucky who was smart, fun, good-looking, and stable and whose career was moving fast. Ersa had been appointed area director of the New York State Division for Youth in 1957. She was also taking care of her grandfather at her home in St. Albans, Long Island, and "Granddaddy couldn't stand Ted." He didn't want Ersa seeing someone fifteen years older and who had already been married several times. Further, "Granddaddy very much liked my first husband, John Clinton. He said hard things about Ted but I let it pass."

The Reverend Gardner Taylor married Ersa and Ted privately in the living room at Ted's Chauncey Street home on August 21, 1957, with Henry Lee Moon as Ted's witness for the third time. Ersa says, "We had a big reception later, after Labor Day. One hundred people came, wall-to-wall people, and we ran out of ice."

What was Ersa like? "A card," says Elizabeth Tarry Patton, "a Murphy Brown type. She can get with the guys in a bar or the stock market and talk about what's going on in Congress and the Senate, yet there's an elegance about her where they would defer to her." When Patton's uncle Dunbar McLaurin died, Ersa was working for Governor Nelson Rockefeller. She had a state car and driver, but she went in the back way, rolled up her sleeves, and "washed dishes. One man there started ordering her around, to get him a cup of coffee," Patton says, but "Ersa gently put him in his place."

Ersa had been a roommate of Urban League director Whitney Young's wife, Margaret Buckner, at Kentucky State, class of 1942, and had matchmade the Youngs. At State, one friend recalled, Ersa was "president of everything but the school."[8] Ersa's Cherokee mother had died of tuberculosis when she was four so she was raised by her paternal grandparents.[9] Her grandmother taught Ersa what she had learned as a child when her mother had worked for a wealthy white Paducah family. Passed on from that family through the generations to Ersa were "what young ladies do" and "this is what young ladies don't do." No one in Ersa's family had completed high school except her mother. A better future for Ersa was something that "was driven into me every moment of the day. . . . They even got me private typing lessons because they figured I'd find it useful later on."

Ted was "startled" when he first encountered the adult Ersa and her circle of professional friends, for their "absolute professional confidence." He said, "They were unlike any Negroes I'd met before in Kentucky. . . . They came out of school during World War II when jobs were opening up for Negroes in government and industry. They all took it for granted that, since they were bright and well-trained, they would get the jobs they wanted without a struggle. And, the odd thing is, they always do." [10] Ted, whose career had reached its zenith and in 1960 would begin its descent, was pleased that the dynamic Ersa had responded to his attentions. Ersa, in her turn, was not surprised that this noted journalist—an intellectual equal, who had been operating at high levels of government and communications yet who came from a similar Kentucky background—was attracted to her.

St. Clair Bourne, who knew Ted and all his wives, says, "Ersa was even smarter than Marie. Marie was capable, but Ersa's capabilities were at a higher level." [11] Ted's godson Bill Proctor, who as a little boy was "in love with my godfather's wife," Marie, thought Ersa "seemed like a rough lady." Ed Morrow says, "Both Marie and Ersa had to fight like hell to get where they got. They were battling the women's fight and also the civil service fight. A weaker man would have been caught in between, but a weaker man Ted was not." Ersa had a coterie from college with whom she remained lifelong friends. "That indicates character," Robert Weaver says. Marie "had friends who were useful. Marie was ambitious, a ruthless person in getting what she wanted. She may have married Ted for upward mobility. Ersa didn't, although she capitalized on Ted's contacts." Ted's godchild Mollie Lee Moon Elliot compared the two wives: "When I, as a grown woman, saw Marie, I was tickled at her pushiness. Ersa was never so aggressive. There is a soft side in Ersa. She's big but her carriage is such that she looks handsome."

For their honeymoon, Ted took Ersa to the nicest spot he could think of, Capahosic. She says she "fell in love with it. I walked down to the York River. It was almost sunset—a beautiful place. I like to have died, though, when I went inside the house. It was so male—rustic, a pool table in the living room. The beds in some of the bedrooms were like army cots. The Moton family bedrooms were comfortable. As honeymooners, we got one of the bedrooms. Later I slept on those cots. You didn't tarry long in your room!"

Capahosic then became a favorite vacation spot for Ersa and Ted, Bill and Viola Trent and their daughters, and other old members of the Black Cabinet. The main event there was "to go crabbing," although what Ted wanted to do most was relax. He would withdraw to a screened-in gazebo at the end of the pier to read, smoke, and "watch us and make sure nobody got hurt. [12] If the little ones [Trent girls] had too heavy a net, Ted would get the crab into the bucket for them." Frequently Ted would procure his fishing gear from the boathouse, where he had it stored, and "sit with us, but on the other side of the pier where the water was deeper. He would cast out from there, a book in his left hand, his fishing gear in his right. If he got a bite, he would put the book down, bring the fish in, then go back to reading," Ersa says. In the evening Ted cooked the crabs in beer. Viola Trent recalls, "Over crabs we developed long-lasting relationships."

As a career woman, Ersa knew how she wanted to run her new household, but Ted's stepmother did not relish relinquishing control to her. Ersa discovered that, despite Susie Poston's Christian proclamations, she was "a horrible woman. She consumed Ted. She put all this guilt on him, that she had looked after his father. I told Ted, 'Your mother or me.'" So in 1958, Ted took Susie back to Kentucky, where she lived until her death. Fern Eckman's assessment of Ted's stepmother confirmed Ersa's: "She was a pain. She plagued him. She would call him and ask for money, things that were outrageous, far more than he could afford. But Ted would smile and shrug his shoulders. He was very giving."

In her new home, Ersa told Ted that "as long as I go out to work, as you do, there are a few things I will not do," including "clean a house. And I do not in*tend* to do laundry." To please her, Ted had the kitchen remodeled so she could have a dishwasher. Ted borrowed the money for the renovation from the *Post* credit union.

Ted's friends Fern Eckman and Marcy Elias delighted Ersa as much as they did Ted. "Marcy was Ted's cub. And Fern was one of those top career women," Ersa says. "Both were byliners in the competitive world of that *Post* with mainly white males. Oh, Lord, I remember when I got 'em married." Marcy, too, remembers when she got married.

Marcy was subjected to merciless teasing from Ted, who had seen her through several romances. Even after she got engaged to Ed Rothman, she tried to give back the ring. Ted told her, "I'm a helluva fisherman but I have never seen any fish fight the line like you." When Marcy gave birth to Jimmy, the third person Ed Rothman called, after their mothers, was Ted Poston. Ed remembers telling him, "Ted, Marcy had a boy. The hair's black but the face is white." Ted said, "Never mind that shit. Is the hair kinky?" Poston insisted on calling the baby Bobby. Every time Marcy corrected him, Ted would shrug, "To me, he's Bobby." In exasperation, Marcy declared, "I'm going to have another son and call him Robert so that once in a while you'll be right." Two years later, she had another son and named him Robert Ted Rothman. She says, "We were told that when Ted received the birth announcement, tears came to his eyes. We did it because Ted never had any children and, in our own way, we wanted to honor him."

On October 4, 1957, the world creaked into a new era when the Soviet Union put its satellite Sputnik into orbit, crucially damaging America's self-image. How could the American educational system be so derelict that the Russians shot ahead in math and science? The *Post* saw a connection. The United States had been worrying about who sat next to whom in classrooms and whose sister one might marry, rather than about what children learned. Ralph McGill, editor of the *Atlanta Constitution*, scolded the South for its resistance to the Supreme Court's school desegregation decision, " 'We will abolish our schools, if necessary, to save segregation.' Yeah. You can. But within a few years you won't have many people who can spell the word." [13]

Poston went to Arkansas when Little Rock made a stab at integrating Central High in the fall of 1957. Of the hundreds of reporters there, he had unique access because his headquarters was the spare room in the home of L. C. and Daisy Bates, who ran the *Arkansas State Press* and the Little Rock NAACP. Situated in the nerve center of the integration battle, where the students gathered daily for moral support and strategy sessions, Ted observed, interviewed, took notes, then retreated to his room to type out his stories on his portable typewriter. He called the room "Ted's Post." [14]

The saga of Little Rock would continue for three years, and Ted stayed involved both on the scene and from New York. [15] Initially, Ted did personality sketches of the integrating teenagers. They had been selected as leaders of the struggle for their aptitude for school, their mental toughness, and their likely support from home. "Little Gloria Ray," whose goal was to be an atomic scientist, amused Ted with her disgust at all the reporters. "How do you expect me to get an education if I have to spend all my time telling you how things are in Central?" When Ted left after their interview, Gloria Ray called after him, "And you smoke too much." Poston figured that she "probably will be an atomic scientist." [16]

In his Little Rock articles, Poston caught for readers the daily lives of ambitious and brave young people thrown suddenly into an international spotlight. [17] The Bateses had to turn their house into a fortress with revolvers and private guards who "politely chided" Ted once or twice "with a soft gunbutt rap on his front bedroom window for failing to close his side window drapes while reading in bed late at night." [18]

One installment of Ted's Little Rock series was a profile of group leader Daisy Bates, whose drive came from a lifetime of anger. Bates's mother had been raped and murdered by three white men when Bates was three years old. In the Bates home, Ted felt the hostility that local organizers faced. [19] Around-the-clock phone calls were disruptive. Ted answered one when Bates was busy with a group of white teenagers who wanted to ease the black young people's transition. A girl on the phone yelled hysterically in Ted's ear, "Don't you try to convince me of nothing, you black nigger bastard, you." Then the phone went dead. The next caller sounded like a teenage boy. Ted "silently listened to 45 seconds of uninterrupted epithets and vilely unprintable denunciations until the exasperated caller concluded with: 'Nigger, you say something. You answer me when I'm talking to you.'" Ted hung up the phone, and Bates called to her maid, "Johnny, it's after 10. Take the phone off the hook." [20]

Poston and the *Post* became more personally enmeshed in the Little Rock scenario in January 1958. Effervescent Minnijean Brown was singled out as a special target of white harassment. Poston conferred behind the scenes with Moon and Roy Wilkins at the NAACP and psychologist Kenneth B. Clark about whether any other educational options were open to Minnijean. "She had one of the best voices at Central and had practiced 20 hours with the Glee Club" but was then called in and told she couldn't sing in the Christmas program because the White Citizens Council had protested; nor could she sing in chapel, either.[21] In French class, one boy tripped her every time Minnijean came up the aisle. In the cafeteria a boy poured a bowl of hot soup down her back. A white girl followed Minnijean from class to class one week yelling, "Nigger, I just hate you; I just hate your guts." At that week's end, Minnijean turned and told the white girl, "Say nothing else to me, white trash." The white girl then hit Minnijean in the head with her pocketbook, yelling, "Don't you ever call me white trash, you nigger bitch."[22] Superintendent of Schools Virgil Blossom "took no action" against the white girl but suspended Minnijean for two weeks and "recommended to the board that she be expelled for the rest of the term," and the school board expelled her.[23]

Roy Wilkins sent the Little Rock Board of Education a telegram saying that "as responsible citizens you cannot approve of this tactic." Within a week, Poston announced that Minnijean would attend New York's experimental New Lincoln School, which had offered her a scholarship. And Kenneth and Mamie Clark invited Minnijean to live with them and their children—Kate, seventeen, and Hilton, fourteen—and their Finnish exchange student. Ted and the *Post* thus intervened on behalf of one of the victims in the battle for integration.

A Little Rock story Poston and Wechsler tried to keep out of the *Post* concerned Minnijean Brown's father, who, during those stressful times, killed a man after a bar brawl. The *Post* wanted to help Brown in his defense although Ted had to explain to Arkansas civil rights lawyers that the NAACP, which they perceived as rich, would not spend "thousands" or even one cent to defend Brown in this case, which was unrelated to civil rights. Poston quietly flew to Arkansas over the Labor Day weekend of 1958 and hid out in the Bates's basement. There, people concerned with Brown's case came to talk with him. Brown had been intending to escape prison and flee town. Thurgood Marshall counseled Poston that the FBI would get him the minute he crossed the state line. Back in New York, Ted filled Wechsler in with a detailed memo. The *Post* cared so much that the outcome of Little Rock school integration be successful that in this instance the paper abandoned objectivity and killed any thought of publishing a story on Brown's trouble.[24]

Little Rock Central High stayed in session through May 1958, when its first black, Ernest Green, graduated. During the subsequent summer, however, Governor Orval Faubus ordered all the city's high schools closed for the entire year because the courts had insisted that integration proceed. After one year, Faubus's actions were declared unconstitutional and the high schools were required to admit both races on August 12, 1959. Ted returned to Little Rock, along with a horde of other reporters. Bates remembered that "many reporters were afraid. Ted told them, 'I'm missing that dread' because 'whites have been doing these things to me all my life.'" Bates related one occasion when Poston was typing in the front bedroom late into the night and a rock crashed through the window. Subsequently he used "Ted's Post" only to work in during the day and slept at night on a couch in the recreation room downstairs.[25]

Lynching by tar and rope in the South had been replaced by car chase and torture, and guns were coming into play. The evening before Central High's reopening in 1959, the police chief's "fears were realized," Bates has written. Four shots were "fired from a passing car at . . . a group of reporters. They included Ted Poston . . . and Carl Rowan, then with the *Minneapolis Tribune.*"[26] Poston's version of the incident was that a car filled with white men "roared down the street" past the Bates home "spraying bullets." The shots missed them but entered a house on the corner where three white children were watching television. None was injured.[27] When Bates's book *The Long Shadow of Little Rock* was published in 1962, Poston extolled "this disarmingly dramatic story" with its "suspense of a thriller." He commended Bates for her restraint in this "best account—and the most human—of all the chronicles of the struggle" at Central High.[28]

During 1958 it became more difficult for Ted to manufacture an upbeat tone in his work. Many activists similarly struggled hard against the current. New York's white City Housing Authority police chief committed suicide because he had been taunted as a "nigger lover" simply for carrying out his charge to integrate public housing.[29] Ted reviewed *An Epitaph for Dixie* by Harry Ashmore, editor of the *Arkansas Gazette*, "a breath of fresh air from a badly ventilated section of our country," but he said that Ashmore's liberalism was behind the times. Ashmore claimed that southern whites alone understood the Negro. Poston disagreed and warned that "the Negro they understood . . . was old Cuffey, singing in the cotton fields" but that Cuffey's son "is a sullen . . . dark-skinned man in a lawyer's blue suit . . . demanding his people's rights. . . . And he is an ominously quiet man with a switchblade knife standing squarely in the middle of an empty sidewalk."[30]

In 1959 Poston traveled less and worked more by telephone. He did a closeup on twenty-eight-year-old Lorraine Hansberry when her *Raisin in the Sun* made her "Broadway's latest Cinderella girl." The title of the play came from Langston Hughes's line, "What happens to a dream deferred?"[31]

Poston had urged the *Post* to add Hughes to its stable of columnists with Jess B. Semple, or "Simple," the Harlem character who had become popular in the *Chicago Defender*. To help the *Post* promote "Simple," Ted went uptown to visit Hughes for a profile. His pleasure in their friendship and in being in his old Harlem stamping grounds were reflected in his article. Proud of Hughes, with whom he and Moon had long since reconciled after their son-of-a-bitch meetings in Moscow back in 1932, Poston stated, "There is a certain school . . . who insist that no such character as Langston Hughes exists." But the "plump pixy of a man . . . . has lived so many lives that it has already taken him two autobiographies." Shortly afterward, Ted reviewed *The Langston Hughes Reader,* in which he acknowledged that Hughes was "the unchallenged spokesman of little people everywhere . . . who love life and live it with love."[32]

Poston produced for the *Post* a thorough history of the NAACP on its fiftieth anniversary, February 1959. It contained sketches of the people who had kept the organization going since 1909. Of Arthur Spingarn, Ted could write from personal knowledge, "No living person has enjoyed a longer, livelier, more effective association with the organization than this energetic, chubby little lawyer whose twinkling eyes and erect carriage belie the 81st birthday which he will share next March 28 with another fighter for the liberal cause—Herbert Lehman."[33] Poston knew the NAACP people and story because he had absorbed their history through his family, associates, and work. Langston Hughes was putting together a young people's book of NAACP history at this time and congratulated Ted on his articles in the *Post.* He said that Ted, with his "vivid style," should have been the one writing the NAACP book: "I'm sure you'd have the whole story at your finger tips. Me, I had to research. . . . WHEN are you GOING to WRITE a BOOK, anyhow?"[34]

Ted was working on writing short stories of his childhood in Kentucky which he hoped would be published in a collection to be called *The Dark Side of Hopkinsville.* But the constant demands of daily journalism precluded its completion.

Nigeria had just thrown off colonialism. At the inauguration of Hughes's former Lincoln University classmate Nnamdi Azikiwe as Nigeria's governor-general, Azikiwe quoted from a Hughes poem: "We have tomorrow / Bright before us / Like a flame."[35] The poem foreshadowed a new day for a generation of blacks throughout the African diaspora, but Ted Poston's and Langston Hughes's careers, at that stage, did not have a lot of "tomorrows."

To add to the melancholia of simple decline, the harmony that Poston had earlier enjoyed with his superiors was gone—the wordless understanding that he and the *Post* were one. Wechsler was into "causes"—race above all. Paul Sann, now executive editor, was into news as entertainment. Acrimony between Sann and Poston never surfaced, but Ted brought his displeasures to the attention of those in charge.

In a May 1958 memo to Wechsler, Ted protested the race tag on crime stories. He had been "pestered and damned at home as well as in the office" by callers who complained of the use of "Negro" identification in crime news, "even when the accused person is in custody and when, the callers contend, no useful purpose can be served by identifying the race of the suspect." The practice of race labeling had been halted after NAACP pressure, then re-instituted, apparently under a direct order from Dorothy Schiff.

Poston and Moon attended a reception at Averell Harriman's house; Schiff was also there. Moon confronted Schiff. "Why do you stick these 'Negro' tags on crime stories?" Schiff answered, "People want to know. If I'm an Irish reader, I want to know if it's a Negro or not." Moon said she should be consistent then, and he illustrated with a tagline on that day's copy of the *Post*. Moon had written in "James Levine, Jewish, stole such and such." Schiff "got so furious." But when Ted told an "Interracial Reporting" audience about it years later, the audience recognized the discrepancy and chuckled knowingly.[36]

Early in June 1959, at age fifty-three, Ted was not in a mood to cajole racist officialdom down South. He was no longer so patient when he was kept in trivial public ways from "getting the story." The *Post* sent him to Tallahassee, Florida, for a trial in which white men, for the first time, faced the consequences for raping a black coed at Florida Agricultural and Mechanical College. He was forced to view the proceedings from the gallery three flights up, which was hard on his aging legs.[37] He had to "dash downstairs to call my City Desk from the outdoor corner telephone booth" during five-minute recesses. Just before the testimony of the black coed, however, when Poston was heading for the phone booth, "a white courthouse lounger saw me coming and beat me to it." The lounger made no call but "just held the phone in his hand and grinned evilly at me."[38]

By the time Poston climbed back up to the third floor, the sheriff's deputies would not let him in because the girl had begun speaking.[39] That treatment of Poston impelled Wechsler to assure readers in an editorial that that "inconvenience will not hamper his coverage; Poston has overcome far more formidable obstacles." But Wechsler chided Tallahassee's law enforcement officials for "so cruelly disgrac[ing] themselves."[40]

All through 1959, Ted followed the fortunes of escaped Florida chain gang convict Willie Reid. Reid fretted to Poston and the NAACP that he would be shot if he were extradited to Florida. Poston and the NAACP pleaded with New York governor Nelson Rockefeller not to send him back. Rockefeller conferred by phone with Florida's governor, who assured him that Reid would be treated justly. Rockefeller allowed Reid to be extradited. And Reid was executed.[41] Despite Ted's failed intervention, one reader wanted to thank "men like Mr. Poston who will stand up against great opposition and speak the truth."[42]

The journalism department at Lincoln University, a historically black school in Jefferson City near St. Louis, Missouri, awarded Poston citations in 1956 and 1963. His Braxton cousins, the remnants of the Poston family who lived in the area, regretted in later years that they had not offered Ted the support of their attendance at either ceremony. But some of the faculty gave Ted directions and "Ted came and took us out to dinner," they recalled with chagrin. They loved the dinner and being with Ted once more, but they were sorry that they had not acknowledged his professional stature with their presence when he received those public honors.

The whole African diaspora was starting to claim American attention. During the communist scare, Poston had profiled a noted African National Congress leader, South African educator Z. K. Matthews, when he was on a one-year visiting professorship at Union Theological Seminary. In "The Strength of Non-Violence," Poston showed a South African who was involved in rearing a generation that would wipe out apartheid and not through Marxism. Professor Matthews told Ted, "Ever since the Bantu encountered the Europeans on the banks of the Great Fish River, long before the Communist Manifesto was even thought of, they have struggled for equal rights in the land of their birth. They will . . . not allow themselves to be browbeaten by smear tactics in their determined fight for their liberation."

When Ghana became a nation, Poston had the opportunity to write a "closeup" in July 1958 of Kwame Nkrumah, prime minister of the recently decolonized Gold Coast. Nkrumah, as a student at Lincoln University in Pennsylvania, had only recently "wandered the streets" of Harlem, "homeless, and slept in the only bed he could afford—a five-cent seat on a subway train"; "peddled fish (to which he was allergic) from a pushcart"; and attended nightly street-corner meetings where "step-laddered Negro nationalists preached the 'Africa for Africans' doctrine of a Marcus Garvey they had never met."[43] Poston was thrilled that Nkrumah had risen from the African soil and acquired an American education and then become head of government of the first African country to free itself from European domination.

Garvey was remembered again in a Marcus Garvey Day celebration in Harlem during Adam Clayton Powell's congressional campaign against Earl Brown. Powell appeared at a rally with J. Raymond Jones, his campaign manager, who, Poston wrote, "is . . . the wiliest political figure who ever held a Tammany leadership there." Ted recognized that nearly "every present Harlem district leader . . . was trained in [the former Garveyite] Jones' club."[44] Powell had been cited recently for not paying his income tax. Yet such luminaries as A. Philip Randolph and Jones supported Powell's reelection because of his seniority in Congress and therefore power, which no new black congressperson would be able to attain for at least a decade.[45]

An office highlight during the 1960s was when Fern Marja, after a couple years of marriage to Irving Eckman, added "Eckman" to her byline. Ted congratulated her when she won the Lasker Award for a series, "Children in Trouble: The Problems of the Mentally Ill." Another series Eckman wrote was on James Baldwin, after which several publishers called her and asked her to do a book on Baldwin. She thought she needed to be assured of Baldwin's cooperation or there was no point in agreeing. Ted Poston helped. She says, "Ted called me one night at about 12:30 and told me, 'Jimmy Baldwin's standing right next to me and he said to go ahead and sign the contract.' So I did. Then, Jimmy Baldwin told his friends not to talk to me. I still remember, though, that Ted was so delighted, then annoyed at Baldwin," for telling his friends not to talk. Eckman's appointments for interviews with Baldwin over twenty-nine months were frequently aborted, but she got the information she needed, and in 1966 her *Furious Passage of James Baldwin* appeared.

Also in 1960, Pete Hamill, a kid from Brooklyn, came on staff, starry-eyed at entering the old *Post* building on West Street, its city room "more exciting . . . than any movie," for "this was the *Post,* the smartest, bravest tabloid in New York."[46]

Publisher Schiff had married her fourth and final husband, Rudolf Sonneborn, in 1953, and written giddily in her *Post* column that he was "gray-haired and handsome, with a beautiful speaking voice," and "a liberal Democrat!" In 1959, however, Sonneborn suffered a stroke, needed constant care, and Schiff decided to end the marital aspect of her life.[47]

Poston seemed happy in his own marriage. Ersa, who found her job with the New York State Division for Youth challenging, made sure that she and Ted usually dined together and that when they had company, the food and conversation sparkled. They attended the seventy-fifth birthday celebration for Harry Truman at the Waldorf's Grand Ballroom in May. Weekends, Ted went fishing. He and friends would charter a boat and go out on Long Island Sound or off the Jersey shore.

The importance of fishing in Poston's life must not be minimized. He liked the quiet time for thinking, he enjoyed the quest, and he was pleased to be able to present his friends with some of his prize catches. He and Ersa never returned from Capahosic without a batch of fish for others. She says they transported the fish to New York in dry ice. "We'd put some in our deep freeze and the rest we would give away around the neighborhood. Folks used to wait for us to come back." George Trow agrees. One time Ted gave Trow a "lovely, beautiful fish," and Trow, who commuted by train to Connecticut, fell asleep on the train, awakening only after "my station had run off and left me. I jumped off the train at the next station, without the fish." He did not know how to face Ted, so he prevaricated and told Ted "a fish story of my own" about how delicious the fish had been. Ted kept giving him more, and Trow never lost another.

Fern Eckman had a less agreeable fish story. She says, "I'm not that mad about them. Ted came back from one trip and presented me with a bluefish—which I dutifully brought home. On a Sunday morning, before I had had breakfast, my husband, who was madly enthusiastic, scaled the bluefish in the kitchen. For months afterwards I was cleaning bluefish scales off the wall." She continues, "After we prepared the bluefish, Irv and I found that we detested it. I thought maybe it was the way I prepared it." Trow interjected: "Maybe it was, Fern." Eckman ignored Trow. "Anyway, I told Ted I would never forgive him and never to give me a present like that again. I'm not polite."

Sometimes Ted accompanied Ersa when she was called to Albany to lobby state legislators as part of her job. The two of them would stop in Saugerties, upstate in the Hudson valley, to call on Ted's sister-in-law, Augusta Savage, who now lived there at a farm studio. After Savage's brief marriage to Robert Lincoln Poston in 1923, she had spent the rest of her life as his widow, devoting herself to art. Dying of cancer now, she still "loved Ted to death," Ersa says, because he was the baby of the family. One of Savage's sculptures, *Laughing Boy* or *Gamin,* is modeled on Ted.[48] Ted lost his last link with his nuclear family when Savage died in 1962.

Poston's major assignment at the beginning of 1960 seemed minor—to follow the action, by phone, of white Tennessee denying to Negroes who voted such essentials as heating oil, food, and even employment.[49] The major national news was the presidential campaign and John F. Kennedy's challenge to Vice-President Richard Nixon. Poston documented a few incidents that heralded Kennedy's appeal to blacks. Tom Mboya, a Kenyan labor leader and politician, had obtained scholarships for eighty-one Africans to study in America, and prominent black Americans had arranged for their living costs. The Eisenhower-Nixon administration was asked to defray their $100,000 travel expense; it declined. The Kennedy Foundation then offered to pay. When the press spread that information, immediately candidate Nixon interceded and said that the State Department would underwrite the travel costs after all.

Locally, Poston compared the campaigning of Kennedy and his wife with that of the vice-presidential nominee Henry Cabot Lodge and his wife in Spanish Harlem on the same day, three weeks before the election. The Lodges shook hands with hundreds of people and Lodge addressed them in English; but the Spanish-speaking crowd was won over by Jackie Kennedy, who greeted them, "like a child reciting for her elders in the parlor," in Italian and Spanish. A third incident turned to candidate Kennedy's favor among blacks when Martin Luther King, Jr., joined a student sit-in at the Magnolia Room, the elegant dining room in Rich's department store in Atlanta, and he and fifty-two other Negroes were arrested.[50] When Kennedy heard that King was in jail, he telephoned King's pregnant wife to express his concern. Subsequently, Poston reported, King praised Kennedy's courage "and his willingness to take a stand in my unjust arrest." King said that Kennedy risked losing white votes; therefore, "if a man would do this while the campaign is going on . . . you can expect something forthright and positive from him."[51] At that juncture the *Post* decided to endorse Kennedy and Johnson.

Following Kennedy's election, happy news emanating from his transition team made the holiday season especially pleasant for the Postons and their friends. Kennedy had expected to end discrimination in housing with "a stroke of the pen" by initiating a housing department in his cabinet and naming Robert C. Weaver as secretary. But the southern-dominated House Rules Committee abhorred the idea of a black cabinet member.[52] Therefore, Kennedy would "try first for a department of urban affairs." Ted could report that his former colleague "will accept the highest federal post ever held by a Negro. . . . Administrator of the U.S. Housing and Home Finance Agency."[53] Ersa delighted in the event's social aspects. She says,

> The night when Kennedy offered Bob Weaver the spot, Bob was at our house. We were having a dinner party—Ken Clark and his wife, Whitney Young and his wife, and Bob Weaver and his wife.
>
> Oh, you couldn't have a more interesting gathering; you wouldn't want to leave the table.
>
> But we knew the call was coming, everybody except Bob and Ella Weaver. When it came, we all laughed. The agreement was that if we could keep Bob Weaver at the table until the president called, then Pierre Salinger would let Ted have the exclusive.
>
> Ted, naturally, went into his room then and started writing.[54]

Following the announcement, Bill Trent arranged a "Dinner for Bob Weaver" for January 14, 1961, at the Waldorf Astoria, inviting members of the old World War II Black Cabinet. The invitation that went out on Trent's UNCF letterhead said, "Advice: stag, informal, and no publicity; just the gang getting together to honor one of its own!"

The Postons were invited to Kennedy's inauguration in January and got snowbound outside Baltimore. "The state police made *all* the cars get off the highway," Ersa says. Margaret Proctor's family "had chains and they came and took us to their house and kept us overnight until the roads could get cleared the next day." The Postons suggested that Ted's godson Bill Proctor go with them to the festivities, but Bill remembers, "It snowed that day. Let's be real! A fourteen-year-old is not interested in going over to D.C. and hobnobbing and seeing the president and getting cold," so he declined the invitation.

Poston's name was bandied about as a possible assistant press secretary in the Kennedy administration. Ersa was thrilled at the thought of "going to elegant dinners." But Ted said he was too old for the stress. He asked her, "Do you know what it's like to never have a moment when you can sleep soundly, without that phone ringing?"[55] So the man who had interpreted blacks and whites for each other under Franklin D. Roosevelt swore off similar work for Kennedy two decades later.

The legend of Ted Poston was still evolving in 1960, but his career was on a plateau, reaching a stasis because of the ascension to the *Post* managing editorship of Alvin Davis, a Paul Sann protégé and until then one of Ted's closest friends at the paper. Al Davis had come to the *Post* during the war and was night managing editor from 1957 to 1960. Davis, Eckman, and Poston had been called "the three musketeers," George Trow remembers, because "they were inseparable." Eckman says, "Al was bright, able, ambitious."[56] But when he was promoted, he severed their relationship.

Managing editor James Graham died suddenly in 1960, precipitating the editorial shakeup. George Trow was transferred from rewrite to night editor; James Wechsler was moved from executive editor to editorial and column writer; Paul Sann was made executive editor; and Al Davis became managing editor. Schiff said she changed editors because circulation was declining, and she attributed that to too much opinion in news articles.[57] Some people had been caricaturing the *Post* that anytime anybody got arrested, "Jimmy Wechsler would come out and want to start a police brutality story before the guy had a chance to be beaten up at the station house," Trow says.

Wechsler was "more of an intellectual than Sann, liberal, more articulate. But they both had wit and flair; and both appreciated good writing." Sann, now in charge of the whole show, "wore cowboy ties, affected a drawl and hung out with a Broadway crowd," says Eckman, whereas "Jimmy Wechsler's associates were political buddies. When these two were working together, they were beautifully balanced. We were getting the best of both worlds."

Tony Mancini came on staff after the shakeup and found that Jimmy Wechsler "was not a constant presence in the city room anymore. He had lost his power struggle for the day-to-day operations of the paper to Paul Sann." The staff felt they were being divided, Wechsler people against Sann people. But Sann liked the new arrangement. He says, "I was comfortable with Wechsler taking all the flack from Dolly Schiff and me out in the city room putting out a newspaper. Dolly would have eighty or ninety thousand questions every five minutes. And Wechsler dealt with that. He and I were not rivals by any means." Poston had been close with Sann and his wife, Birdye, Sann says. Ted was "always in our immediate circle, in our weekly poker games." [58] Nevertheless, the staff noticed, Trow remembers, that with Wechsler moved upstairs at the paper, "part of the 'soul' was lost."

With the positions of Sann and Wechsler rearranged in the hierarchy and Alvin Davis, then thirty-five years old, as managing editor, Poston sank into near oblivion from 1960 to 1964. He was no longer getting important assignments. His clipping files in the archives are lean, in contrast to the previous dozen fat years. Eckman says that she and Ted both felt that his stories were deliberately assigned to be "minor, back-in-the-paper stories." The setting aside of Poston continued "just long enough for both Ted and me to feel depressed and blame the switch on Al Davis." [59] Years later, Poston, in a tired voice, described Davis and one of his abrupt changes; Davis arbitrarily proclaimed, "No more police brutality stories." Therefore, Poston gave one gruesome story of the police beating of a black electronics engineer to "a guy at the *Times,* because, even though we were supposed to be a liberal paper, the editor had just decided there was no such thing as police brutality. Later in the week we picked up and rewrote the same story from the *Times.*" [60]

Other reporters were also disgruntled with Al Davis as editor. Jerry Tallmer alluded to the period in remembering Ted. "Even before I got to the *Post* or ever met him," Tallmer had written about Ted's courage in covering stories in the South. He describes the Poston he met now as "a proud, genial, ever helpful (to me), sometimes cranky man who in his last years was treated shabbily and used mostly only to write short filler stories." The shabby treatment was Al Davis's doing.

Ersa Poston saw a psychological link between what was happening at work and her husband's deteriorating health. "Ted had been on senior rewrite status, but now he would no longer lock up one of our rooms and do his research. He used to not even let me come in that room when he was working on big stories. His stacks of books and papers were all over then. He would put up a big sign for the housekeeper, 'Don't open this door.' But he wasn't being put on those assignments any more."

Marcy Elias Rothman had moved to the *Los Angeles Times* but tried to see Ted on her visits back east. She found him withdrawn. Ed Rothman, a lawyer with Universal Pictures, twice called Ted to tell him that a television executive was looking for "a crack black journalist for a commentator's spot—it would have been a television first." Marcy says, "The word was out that one of the networks (CBS I think) wanted to hire as a major personality a black man in the news field. Ed and I talked it over and knowing that Ted was unhappy at the paper, we agreed that Ed would call Ted and tell him about the offer. It's my distinct memory that Ted turned the idea down out of hand or agreed to talk to Ed's contact in such a desultory way that he was given the impression that Ted wasn't interested. Actually, we thought he was scared shitless to take it."

Rothman and Eckman both thought Ted would have soared on television—"articulate, colorful, knowledgeable, witty, and so bright," but they also think he was afraid to venture into the new profession. Poston did do some TV. Ersa would go with him to Washington, for example, when he appeared on Martin Agronsky's news and comment program, *Agronsky and Company.*

The Postons capitalized in another way on their renown during this leveled-off period of Ted's career. *Jet* magazine in March 1961 carried an advertisement for Smirnoff Vodka featuring Ted and Ersa.[61] The same ad appeared in the May issue of *Ebony.* The photo showed Ersa placing a tray of highball glasses on the coffee table, with Ted looking fondly on. The caption read, "Noted Reporter, Ted Poston, Gives a Vodka Party. Mr. and Mrs. Ted Poston prepare to welcome guests to their New York apartment with a batch of Smirnoff Screwdrivers."[62]

A shadow fell over the Moons' and Postons' social life during the early 1960s when Chester Himes published his roman a clef, *Pinktoes.* The novel mocked Mollie Moon, the Beaux-Arts Ball, and Mollie's interracial activities.[63] Himes's fictional creation, Mamie Mason, was "a 39-year-old, big-boned, hard-drinking, ambitious, energetic woman with the instincts of a lecherous glutton."[64] Ersa asserts, "We boycotted *Pinktoes!*" One critic claimed that the people of *Pinktoes* "purport to be crusaders, leaders in the sacred fight against the demon racism, but in reality they are . . . preoccupied with the sex act."

The Moe Miller character in the book seemed to be based on Poston since Ted was noted for telling his Rat Joiner stories in *Dark Side of Hopkinsville.*

In *Pinktoes,* Moe Miller is a "distinguished black journalist, who drags himself reluctantly away from Mamie's parties . . . to take up once again the fight
against the giant rat that infests his home in Brooklyn." [65] Himes derided
Moe Miller's departure from one party: "One might assume that Moe Miller,
blessed with such a formidable talent and charged as he was with strong
whiskey and fried chicken, would certainly have passed the night in some
creative activity, such as increasing the population. But no, Moe was a home
man, and even though his wife. . . . was in Baltimore, he went straight
home. . . . Moe was writing a series of newspaper articles on the Negro Problem, mornings after parties being the best time for such creativity, and on the
side he was trying to catch a rat." [66] Perhaps "catching a rat" also referred
to the investigative reporting which Ted often did, smoking out the culprits
in the fields of race relations, journalism—Walter Winchell, for instance—
and government.

For six months of 1961, Poston observed southern sit-ins and the freedom-
riding phase of the civil rights movement. He seemed older than his fifty-
seven years because he had been abusing his spindly body with smoking and
drinking for so many decades. His story assignments on civil rights were
passing to a new generation. [67] Ted had lost the drive to chase around the
South. In addition, he regarded some of the new black militants as frightening upstarts.

He had weighed in on the strident blacks in his review of C. Eric Lincoln's
scholarly *Black Muslims in America.* In one of his strongest professional
statements, Poston warned, "Few Americans . . . face up to the fact that un-
counted thousands of our colored citizens—some 100,000 of whom call
themselves Black Muslims—have given up on the American dream. Many
whites . . . find it difficult to believe that a sizable segment of the population
hates them—individually and collectively—because they are white." [68]

In 1962, Ted's clippings were even fewer, but he composed two fat memos
to editor Sann, perhaps feeling that this was the only way to reach the eche-
lons of power. Sann had suggested to Ted that a series on Negro society would
be "interesting." Unwilling to exploit his friends, Poston spelled out racial
subtleties that had not arisen in conversation in spite of the years of Sann's
and Poston's close after-hours poker association. Poston pecked out to Sann
that "the very term 'Negro Society' is anathema . . . when it is used to designate some ultra-ultra exclusive group." Ted's father used to tell him a story
of the "pathetic efforts" of some "to establish a Negro Society which would
set them aside from the mules under them." The most exclusive group was
the Coachman's Club, founded by Negroes who drove the coaches of New
York's Four Hundred and who were, therefore, "arbitrars of manners in the

Negro community." Poston said, "We passed that stage a long time ago." For emphasis he added, "Negroes are goddam tired of being 'interesting' to white people."

Poston scored the *Post* for the current direction it seemed to be taking toward blacks, saying that it was not keeping step with the new dignity they commanded on the American stage and that was causing the newspaper to lose black readers, most of whom "had at one time . . . a deep regard for the *Post*." [69] Poston reminded Sann that his own most valuable asset to the *Post* was his acceptance by every stratum of the Negro community and a series by him on Negro society would "affect the *Post* adversely and thereby my own bread and butter." He ended his memo with an apology for its length: "This is the first time that I have written a series *against* a series."

Sann felt affronted at Poston's intimating that the *Post*'s Negro readership was falling off for, two weeks later, Poston had to elaborate in another expansive memo to Sann how important the *Post* had once been to African Americans. "No daily paper outside the old *New York World* ever enjoyed the esteem in the Negro community here that the *Post* held for years." This memo alluded to the negative direction Al Davis was taking. When Poston was city editor at the *Amsterdam News* in 1935, the *Post* was "the only daily paper which stressed the economic and social factors which had precipitated the Harlem explosion and we unashamedly stole whole gobs of [the *Post*'s] stuff as thinly-veiled rewrite." John H. Johnson of *Ebony* and *Jet* had subscribed to the *Post* religiously over the years but lately had wondered to Ted whether it was "worth it. Have you all lost interest in The Brother?" [70]

Before the 1960s, blacks had felt that if anyone understood what African Americans were up against, "it was the *New York Post*." Ted wrote Paul Sann a memo saying that Negroes had come to believe that "no matter where other Negroes were in trouble . . . they had only to buy the *Post*" to get the straight story, but now there was growing resentment against the *Post* "for what many regard as a patronizing attitude towards the Negro and an effort to segregate him from the rest of the larger community as something different and bizarre." Again, Ted apologized for the length of his memo, signing off, "It seems that I find it hard to stop when I discuss something about which I have some deep feelings also. Ted." [71]

All of New York City's newspaper presses stopped for three months beginning on December 8, 1962. The Publishers' Association had refused the unions' latest demands and declared a lockout. Christmas advertising revenue was lost; fans of the glamorous Kennedy family in the White House lost their daily fix. A long-term result was that New Yorkers broke their addiction to the daily newspaper.[72] For many citizens thereafter television provided their news. Although Dorothy Schiff was pro-labor and pro-union, the cost to her of reducing hours, raising wages, and promising job security while the city room was undergoing automation threatened the existence of the *Post,* America's oldest newspaper. Efforts to salvage it consumed her. Because of its pro-labor policy, Richard Kluger says, the *Post* "came to contract sessions with one arm tied behind its back." Until then, it had "survived on grit and the personal bankroll of its publisher."[73]

During the layoff, reporters received small stipends from the Newspaper Guild, funded by the union dues they had been paying for years.[74] Eckman says of the antiunion backlash that occurred in the 1980s and 1990s, "I am annoyed with the stupidity of the current crop of youngsters who contend they can do without unions. Wait until they get their wish!"[75]

After eighty-six days, on March 4, 1963, Schiff broke with the Publishers' Association for good and reopened the newspaper. Pete Hamill was thrilled to be back at work, but Paul Sann told him, "Don't get used to being too happy. . . . No matter what happens . . . newspapers will always break your fucking heart."[76] Just as unions' achievements were scorned by later generations, so too Poston's generation found its struggles denigrated for political reasons. Adam Clayton Powell began pandering to the new black generation with exaggerated, militant rhetoric.

The NAACP spent much of 1963 planning the March on Washington scheduled for August 28. Although Martin Luther King, Jr., would gain the fame from the march, the titular chairman was Moon, with Bayard Rustin as organizer.[77] Adam Clayton Powell, Jr., who was not invited to the march, felt "humiliated and angered" at his role as "eminent spectator. . . . [He] grabbed the nearest headline by declaring war" on his recent campaign manager, J. Raymond Jones. In relaxed moments, Powell referred to other Negroes as "my slaves."[78] Ted Poston's stories on Congressman Powell over the years had portrayed him as likable but deceitful and unworthy of the trust the Harlem electorate had put in him. But Poston withheld personal rancor toward Powell, whom he needed on his side as a valuable news source. He seemed to regard Powell as just one more of God's infinite varieties.[79]

James Wechsler, no longer executive editor but now the *Post*'s chief editorial writer and columnist, took an editorial stand on the side of the behind-the-scenes power-wielder Jones over the charismatic—"He could charm a band of Ku Klux Klanners"—but ethically shaky Powell.[80] Poston's Hopkinsville pal Allison Williams explains that Adam Clayton Powell "wasn't educated as no Negro nohow. He just became a Negro because he wanted to be. It was to his advantage." Through the years, Powell had actually done much good for Harlem. During the Depression he procured jobs for his constituents. From his pulpit at Abyssinian Baptist Church, "Sunday after Sunday, he stood in the pulpit . . . shouting: 'If you want to change Harlem, then you've got to vote.'" But in March 1963, when black militants were cropping up all over, Powell sought to align himself with the apparent new Negro leadership. He attacked the old-line NAACP, the Urban League, and the memory of Eleanor Roosevelt, and thus, Wechsler said, "invited his own doom." In a "blunt rebuke to Powell's racist harangues," his now opponents in J. Raymond Jones's Carver Democratic Club approvingly cited NAACP chief Roy Wilkins's declaration chiding Powell that "we cannot call for integration while advocating segregation."

Wechsler mourned that Powell "finds himself locked in combat, not with the legions of oppression, but with men who have fought long and hard for Negro emancipation."[81] Racial advocates were losing solidarity. The young attacked what they saw as their elders' inaction and called them Uncle Toms. The elders witnessed the alienated young undermining the progress that had been made at such a high cost. And even northern whites were becoming scared of the brash blacks with the big bushy hair.

Martin Luther King, Jr., was busying himself getting arrested in Birmingham. On April 16, 1963, he wrote "Letter from a Birmingham Jail" to white ministers who had accused him of inciting violence by his activity, and the *Post* was the first newspaper to publish the letter. King told the ministers, "You asserted that our actions, even though peaceful, must be condemned because they precipitate violence. . . . Isn't this like condemning the robbed man because his possession of money precipitated the evil act of robbery?"[82] Neither the *New York Times* nor the *New York Post* discovered King's letter until a month after it was written, then both scrambled to print it.[83] The *Post*'s edition came out first, so the *Times* scrapped it.

The shooting of Medgar Evers, NAACP leader in Mississippi, outside his home in June 1963 marked a turning point in the civil rights struggle. Ted wrote of the Evers family, and on NBC's *Meet the Press* program, as a panelist, he praised the day's guest, Attorney General Robert F. Kennedy, for arresting Byron de la Beckwith but asked him whether the Justice Department had taken any steps to protect Evers after earlier threats and assassination attempts. Robert Kennedy answered Ted curtly: "We are not a national police force. We do not have the authority to go around and provide protection for everybody who happens to be involved in these kinds of operations." Kennedy could not imagine that shortly the situation would be reversed and the FBI and the press would attempt to placate him, assuring him, too, that they had done "all they could" to protect President Kennedy.

Ted and the *Post* were especially concerned about the children Medgar

Evers had left. Thus when Mississippi's governor Ross Barnett became focus of a chain letter scheme, Poston made a big thing of it. He reported on the widely disseminated anonymous letter that proposed "to flood Gov. Barnett's desk with envelopes containing checks for $1. which will automatically make him trustee of money that he can only deliver to the Evers family." Letters poured in and were being sent back because, his secretary said, "Gov. Barnett is not a trustee of any such fund." Poston concluded his article, "But the NAACP has assured the college education" of Evers's three children because the fund had reached fifty thousand dollars.[84]

Ted was there when the trial of Byron de la Beckwith for killing Evers began in the Hinds County Circuit Court House in Jackson, Mississippi. A humane series under his byline went back to New York. Poston described Evers's killer as slender, smooth-haired, and smiling; he "shook hands with deputies and court officials throughout the preliminaries." The assailant had lived in a run-down mansion before his arrest, but he "indicated his expectations when he demanded his gun collection as well as his TV set while being held. . . . 'I'll need them when I get out of here,' he told his jailer."[85] Evers's wife thought that Beckwith might well have been "one of the three white men who walked slowly by our house day after day, staring and smirking, shortly before it happened."[86]

Through his NAACP connections, Ted found a "worn, dog-eared copy" of a "letter to the editor" from Evers's killer that had been published in the *Jackson Daily News* in April 1957. In it, Beckwith had clearly stated his intention to combat the evils of integration. Beckwith had written, "I shall bend every effort to rid the U.S. of the integrationists, whoever and wherever they may be. Segregation is a right and a privilege. I live by it, respect it and appreciate it." The clipping had been filed away by Medgar Evers in 1957. Poston surmised that that letter "may have been the first curious link between the two men."[87]

The judge at the Beckwith trial, "towering, scraggily handsome" Leon F. Hendrick, held out hope for a just verdict. Even though the district attorney addressed Mrs. Evers as "Myrlie," following the local custom of never addressing a Negro woman as "Mrs.," Judge Hendrick called her "Mrs. Evers."[88] Poston thought, "Other subtleties seemed discernible" as well in Judge Hendrick's decorum. He "never once rebuked District Attorney Bill Waller for his insistent use of the word 'nigger.' But he often took over the questioning from the prosecutor at just that point and pronounced the word 'Negro' rather pointedly."[89]

Poston got to know the judge personally and included his reader in the experience by using second person, the intimate "you," a beckoning approach, a frequent technique of Poston's so that whites could sense how blacks feel.[90]

> You run into some strange things on stories. . . . I was walking down the corridor on the third floor of the courthouse, and the judge was in front of me. He said, "I'd like to talk to you."
>
> I explained to him that I had to walk 52 blocks a day to get to meals. . . . Way down on Lynch St.—nicely named—and he said, "Come in to my chambers."
>
> He sent out and got lunch for us, sandwiches. It turned out that this judge was a member of the number one committee in the Presbyterian church which was working for integration all throughout the South, but, he explained to me, "Of course, you mention that, and I'll get run off the case."[91]

It came as a great disappointment to both Poston and Judge Hendrick when the Evers jury declared a mistrial.[92]

Commenting on the deaths of four Sunday school children when a bomb exploded at a black church in Birmingham, Alabama, Poston wrote, "The murders were in Birmingham. But Harlem had a victim too. . . . the philosophy of nonviolence."[93] Events were overwhelming Ted. His and his family's quest to create a just society, what Martin Luther King, Jr., called "the beloved community," seemed stymied.[94]

In three months, the man in the White House who had defended their struggle became another victim of violence. The news of Kennedy's assassination made the late afternoon edition of the *Post* on November 22, and most of the *Post*'s reporters were sent out on JFK-related assignments. Ted quoted one black citizen: "Our jobless rate is still twice as high as theirs despite everything [President Kennedy] tried. But one thing you've got to say: he might not have got us the jobs yet, but he's sure helped create the atmosphere which might get more of us the jobs someday." Poston pointed out that before his election, Kennedy had had no discernible record in support of civil rights. But as a candidate Kennedy had spoken out for the jailed Reverend King when Nixon had "decided to play it cagey—and silent." After Kennedy was elected, "big and little things" all "wove the picture of the man." On Inauguration Day, Kennedy had observed audibly that there were no Negro officers in the Coast Guard contingent that marched by.

JFK's life ended as hope arose for the first meaningful civil rights legislation since Reconstruction and, to blacks, "the best and last bulwark against a Republican hopeful who would leave their fate to the tender mercies of those who had oppressed them." In addition, at his death, Kennedy "knew personally more Negroes . . . than any other man who had ever occupied the White House." Kennedy had "integrated social affairs and invited more Negroes in a month than his predecessors had done in years." Man-to-man, Kennedy made a black "feel you are discussing your problems on a basis of equality" because "it's obvious that he regards you as an equal." [95] In December 1963 it seemed there was no Christmas; the nation could not shake its feeling of being under a cloud following the death of its leader.

Ted Poston was on the minds of Dorothy Schiff and James Wechsler as they pondered how best to use the staff in December 1963. They had both noticed that Poston was not getting the plum civil rights assignments since Al Davis became managing editor. Wechsler wrote Schiff a memo saying he had urged Poston to try a column. Ted, of course, had been a columnist for the *Pittsburgh Courier* thirty years earlier, but in 1963 he was displeased with his new efforts, "would not show the dry runs" to Wechsler, and "his wife concurred." Wechsler thought that if Ted approached the typewriter "with lack of confidence in himself. . . . I would be hesitant to press the matter," but that he needed to be regarded as more than a routine rewrite person. Another paper was running stories on how Negroes in New York felt about the progress of the civil rights battle, and Wechsler was "sure that [Poston] could have done a similar series with far greater skill and depth." His evaluation was that Poston was "under-employed and that a column is not the only medium through which his knowledge and abilities could be more effectively utilized" because Poston's early energy had been replaced by knowledge and perspective.

Perhaps Schiff and Wechsler's concern was resolved in 1964 when Al Davis, questioned by Schiff, prevaricated. Nora Ephron, a staff member then, recalls "a famous story" at the office to the effect that Ted went to "the loathsome managing editor" to tell him of a major meeting that Robert F. Kennedy had held with black leaders in New York. "Al didn't think it was a story. Two days later the *New York Times* ran the story on page one. And Al Davis was fired." According to Joe Kahn, Schiff had asked Davis why he had not assigned Poston to that story and Davis had said, "He refused to cover it." Schiff called Poston in to ask him whether that was true. Ted was surprised and protested, "I never turn anything down." Schiff removed Davis as managing editor.[96] Ted Poston, who had been figuratively put in the corner in 1960, was thus revivified in 1964.[97]

During the four years of Ted's near oblivion at the *Post,* Ersa Poston had been catapulted into the eminence she had earlier anticipated achieving through Ted's career. As confidential assistant to New York's governor Nelson Rockefeller, she proved her mettle. Helen Dudar wrote a "Closeup" for the *Post* on Ersa and described her as "a striking figure of a woman" who, like her husband, "in repose, appears to be contemplating the world with serene detachment and faint amusement." But, Dudar said, Ersa was "neither detached from nor amused by the dire problems she sees." That attitude accounted for Rockefeller's appointing her director of the Office of Economic Opportunity and sending her to Washington to get funds for the state so that it could begin meeting more of its citizens' needs.[98]

Simultaneously, Ted was embarking on his final most important professional function, that of journalistic mentor. In 1979 Bob Maynard would become the first black editor and publisher of a so-called white American newspaper, the *Oakland Tribune,* and a nationally syndicated columnist, but in 1956 he was age nineteen and first visited the newsroom at the *Post.* He reminisced, "One of Ted Poston's principal preoccupations was assisting young blacks who wished to have careers in daily journalism. He held impromptu seminars on how the *Post* worked. He read examples of our work and made constructive suggestions." Ted would expand that teaching function in his final years.

The sense of a new recognition of blacks in the media was conveyed with Ted's profile of Carl Rowan when President Johnson appointed Rowan to head the United States Information Service (USIS).[99] Poston used a humorous racial euphemism, saying that Rowan had been the only "club member" in a training unit of three hundred sailors when he joined the navy. It was inevitable that the question would be raised as soon as his USIS appointment was announced: "A Negro as the Voice of America?" But for Carl Rowan, Poston said, "it was nothing new," for he "met this question in every step of his . . . rise from dingy Congo St. in McMinnville, Tenn. . . . He long ago learned to shrug it off and get on with the work at hand." After the Cosmos Club in Washington blackballed Rowan, "one of the first calls of support came from [President] Johnson, who advised him: 'When they start shooting at you, act like a Texas jackass. Hunch up and take it. You'll get 'em in the end.' "[100]

Poston had always tried to shrug off daily reminders that being Negro in America carried a stigma. He liked Johnson's idea, but he was beginning to doubt whether he and the race would, in his lifetime, "get 'em in the end."

12

· ·
The Torch Passes to a
New Generation
· ·
1964–1972

The reality of race relations in this country is so
terrible that none of us dares . . . admit the truth.
—TED POSTON, review of
Crisis in Black and White

The assassinations of Medgar Evers and John F. Kennedy in 1963 seemed to rob Ted Poston of strength. In 1964, he was back covering major stories, but arteriosclerosis and apathy interfered. Moving more slowly, he concentrated on personality profiles of public figures close to home, for example, of Kenneth B. Clark, Mary Parkman Peabody, Earl Warren, and Martin Luther King, Jr., again, when King won the Nobel Peace Prize. By 1964, Poston felt that integrated education lacked "the dedicated Negro guidance counselors in the South" who had given "their all" to their students, in contrast to many northern counselors "who make little effort to raise the sights of the Negro pupils." [1]

On the tenth anniversary of *Brown v. Board of Education,* Poston reviewed Charles E. Silberman's *Crisis in Black and White* with a new directness. Reiterating Silberman's thesis, he forthrightly stated his now disillusioned viewpoint: "Let's face it. We never have. . . . This is the crux of our tragedy. . . . White America has no intention of granting the Negro his full and equal rights, and all the Negro can hope to get is what he is willing and powerful enough to take. . . . All of us have fearfully rejected reality and created illusions which mask our dread of what we will not admit. We've spoken in partial truths, shrouded the inadmissible facts."[2]

The day after that review was published, Ted was pounding out a memo to Paul Sann on "the current furor over the so-called Blood Brotherhood and anti-white violence in Harlem." He argued that the media instigated racial fear by publicizing rumors. The *New York Times* had created a myth of supposed Blood Brothers who conspired to "maim or murder every white person in Harlem." The *Times*'s evidence was four instances of whites attacked for various reasons, and it featured a college student who slashed himself with razors, then implicated the Blood Brothers. Then the *Times* "buried the Blood Brothers as abruptly as it had created them."[3] The contradiction was that "the *Times* denounced the Blood Brothers. . . . [It] didn't seem to recall where the Blood Brothers was born," when in fact, "Nothing like the Blood Brothers ever existed." The guy who slashed himself with razor blades? "We looked into it. . . . The guy just didn't want to go back to school."[4] The media, Ted insisted, were partially responsible for implanting in the nation a mood of racial fear.[5]

This alarming climate guaranteed more riots. One sparked by the issue of police brutality was touched off in July when a building superintendent sprayed three Negro boys with a hose, saying, "I'm going to wash the black off you." The boys protested. An off-duty policeman saw the dispute and tried to intervene, but James Powell, a remedial reading summer school pupil at Robert Wagner Junior High School across the street, went at him, the police report said, "with a knife in his hand." The policeman fired and killed Powell. Four students testified that "Powell only had a can in his hand and that he was holding it at his side when shot." The principal of the school, Max Francke, was looking out the window when the incident occurred, and he "blamed the [building] superintendent for precipitating it, that Powell was a quiet youth 'who had had no trouble in school.'"[6]

Yet that fracas touched off a reign of violence that went on for three nights in Harlem, then rolled into Poston's own neighborhood, Brooklyn's Bedford-Stuyvesant.[7] Clearly the ridding of segregation from public life through the legal system had not rid society of racism. Martin Luther King, Jr., had preached nonviolence; when its results were paltry, the alternative looked more appealing, and militance vied for dominance.

Nationally, the summer of 1964 was called "Freedom Summer." Multitudes, black and white, joined the Students' Non-Violent Coordinating Committee and the Congress of Racial Equality volunteers and went south to register "as many voters as possible among Mississippi's 900,000 blacks." Three volunteers were killed—Michael Schwerner, Andrew Goodman (both white Jews), and black James Chaney. Schwerner was "marked for death by the Klan nine days before he was killed for having eaten and slept in the homes of Negroes." [8] Poston called on Schwerner's family and listened to his father say what blacks knew all along, that "the majority of us white Americans do not regard our Negro brothers . . . worthy of human rights." Had Jim Chaney died alone "few would have cared," Ted wrote. "Remember the dismembered Negro bodies uncovered elsewhere during the long search?" [9]

The unsavory national temperament paralleled Poston's sorrowful writing tasks in 1964. He found himself composing as many obituaries as profiles. The reality of the danger of cigarette smoking struck when the gentle singer and pianist Nat King Cole died of lung cancer in February.[10] Less than a week later, Malcolm X was gunned down in Harlem's Audubon Ballroom. The public had not known how to regard Malcolm, his strident rhetoric, and his rough and tragic past. Malcolm talked tough, but he was obviously intelligent, race-proud, and passionate to achieve constructive change. Poston wrote that Malcolm X had "predicted his own murder nearly a year ago. 'They've got to kill me,'" he told Poston when Malcolm publicly broke with Black Muslim leader Elijah Muhammad—"they can't afford to let me live." [11]

In a retrospective piece, Poston reiterated that Malcolm had said in a *Saturday Evening Post* article that he had been a "big time dope peddlar and hustler in Harlem," but Poston checked with his own sources among Harlem hustlers and no one corroborated Malcolm's claim. The word on Malcolm was that he had emerged from the Black Muslims and become "their most effective organizer, orator and spokesman." Poston thus found that Malcolm's "bark was worse than his bite," that he once urged Negroes to organize rifle clubs to protect themselves against hostile whites, but the only such rifle club Malcolm himself founded was "his armed bodyguard—to protect him against what he thought were black former colleagues." [12]

With Al Davis out at the *Post,* race again became an emphasis of the paper. White reporters—Jerry Tallmer and Roberta Brandes Gratz—did a series, "Mixed Marriages," but they used their resident expert, Ted, who knew of many such unions and their subsequent fortunes.[13]

Gratz gained more from Ted, she says, than help on reporting assignments. In 1965, she was struck by Ted's warmth for her as a new reporter. Many *Post* people were famous in New York journalism, but "Ted seemed to be the most accessible." Gratz noticed that he had "a way of laughing at life." He had "suffered all the hard knocks, yet he came through with humor," an "important message for a reporter like me who felt overwhelmed at times. He put it in perspective and said, 'It will get behind you.' He looked at the good side and the bad side and laughed at the bad."

Robert Weaver verified that Poston's humor "attracted people to listen to Ted who otherwise might have turned him off. Once you get a person in a good mood, you can do a hell of a lot more with him," Weaver explains. "Charles Rangel has done it in the House of Representatives. It's a technique indigenous to Negroes in this country." Sometimes it has been "a matter of sublimating manhood, but that wasn't true in Ted's case. His humor could be biting—first laugh at himself, then laugh at a situation, then laugh at the damn fool who created the situation."

With Poston's *Dark Side of Hopkinsville* stories, readers first laugh then recognize that they have learned lessons—of friction between the races, within the race, and between classes and of children understanding the importance of getting along anyway. Langston Hughes included several of Ted's stories in his anthology *The Book of Negro Humor*. When that volume's reviews were published, Hughes jotted Poston a note saying that his contributions "stole the show" and admonishing Ted to get busy on his autobiography.

Ted soon had an excuse to write positive profiles. President Lyndon B. Johnson made an initial move in July to get Thurgood Marshall onto the Supreme Court by naming him solicitor general, and Ted sauntered over to Foley Square and asked Marshall why he was willing to take a job that meant a cut in salary. Marshall replied: "Because the President asked me." [14]

Ted next enthusiastically greeted the news of the appointment of Robert Weaver as secretary of housing under Johnson. He allowed himself an optimistic note in this article, rare in the often dismal 1960s, by quoting Weaver: "This is the most exciting period in which to live. There is at long last a realization of the importance of urban life, articulated by a President who not only talks about it but gets legislation to facilitate it. Human dignity, equal opportunity and civil rights are on the agenda of America." [15] Lady Bird Johnson felt the same because of Weaver's arrival in the cabinet. In her diary she wrote, "It was one of those moments when a sense of history hung in the air." [16]

Dorothy Schiff shed her last husband in 1965, and the *Post* too was undergoing change. Press watcher Peter Benjaminson found it "descend[ing] into blandness, enlivened only by froth, gossip, and columnists" during the 1960s, after "Schiff had defeated all the men who had once threatened her" and the last competing afternoon newspaper, the hybrid *World-Journal-Tribune*, perished, "squeezed by union demands and pessimistic advertisers." [17] Ted Poston was using his remaining energy to encourage a new generation of activists.

Aging Ted and Henry Lee Moon pondered who of those in the wings might play roles in the future. Moon says, "Julian Bond would have been my own personal choice . . . if there is a future for the NAACP, and I hope there is." [18] So Ted's first byline of 1966 went above a profile of the boyish Horace Julian Bond, who shrugged off the fact that, although he had been elected, "the Georgia House voted 184–12 . . . not to seat him because of his opposition to U.S. policy in Vietnam." Bond told Poston, however, "I'll be back in that seat sooner or later." [19]

In April 1967, Ted was mugged in the park across from his house as he walked from the Fulton Street subway. The newspapers, particularly the *Daily News*, had been featuring, in lurid detail, stories of muggings by "big burly Negroes," says Marcy Elias Rothman. The *Post* tried to refute them by checking out the reality. It found that muggers were frequently white, "anything but black and burly." But that night, after winning at poker, Ted got about one hundred yards from the subway and was "punched out and robbed of every cent," says Rothman. "He struggled to a bar and borrowed ten cents from the bartender" to call the police. The white detectives who met him later, at his home, "collapsed with laughter. As he told it, they said to him, 'No big, black burly muggers, eh, Mr. Poston?'" [20]

Ted was happier at work with Al Davis gone, yet his health fluctuated. What initially seemed to be an alcohol-related disorientation turned out to be "arteriosclerosis with an organic brain syndrome," Ersa says. It caused memory loss, blackouts, and weakness in his legs. Ersa, headquartered in Albany now, came home weekends and tried to fix Ted's favorite foods. "It was difficult emotionally to cut his food up and feed him," she says. "At that point there was no alcohol." Robert Weaver thought Ted "showed signs of senility early. Now it's called Alzheimer's."

An initiative by Kenneth and Mamie Clark in 1967 contributed to Ted's last pleasant spring. Clark had spearheaded the formation of a group called Metropolitan Applied Research Center (MARC) and put Ted on its board. MARC sought to "serve as a catalyst for change and as an advocate for the poor and powerless in American cities" through research, analysis, strategy development, and intervention. [21]

Spring 1967 was also a time of awakening in the lives of a crop of young black journalists. A few had been hired on white papers, and they gathered together for mutual support. One, Nancy Hicks, was hired by the *Post* for Saturdays while she was still at Long Island University. She did not meet Poston during her first year because there was no regular staff on weekends. After she graduated, she says, "I arrived on my first day of [regular] reporting and suddenly, here he was, this wonderful man. He was lanky, a cigarette hanging out of his mouth, and as bright a human being as you would ever want to meet, *so skilled* at what he did, but *so protective*. What Ted meant to my success was something I didn't know for ten years afterwards."

There were six other black journalists on white newspapers nationally in the 1960s—Nancy Hicks, Tom Johnson, Paul Delaney, Gerald Fraser, Earl Caldwell, and Mike Davis, says Davis.[22] A biographer of Thurgood Marshall and son of the publisher of the mid-century black picture magazine *Our World*, John P. Davis, Mike Davis met Poston in 1963 when Ralph McGill and Eugene Patterson hired Davis as first black reporter on the *Atlanta Constitution*. Ted was considered the "dean" by Davis and the five others.

They concocted a standing joke, that they were being assigned collectively to all the black national stories such as on the NAACP and Urban League conventions and the civil rights movement. In Ted's hotel room one night— with drinks supplied by Nixon aides Robert Brown, Arthur Fletcher, and General Chappie James—Ted observed, "Look! All the colored reporters on white papers are here in my room!" Thereupon he coined the acronym that they were on the RUINS beat—"a tongue-in-cheek remark to mean that black reporters covered Riots, Urban affairs, Indians and Niggers," said Davis.

What struck Nancy Hicks, the only woman on the RUINS beat, was some *Post* editors' attitudes toward black rookies. They perceived black males especially "almost as alien." They interpreted anything racial in a "dire, negative way. It became reinforcing, an encampment mentality." The first substantial wave of black journalists rode in after the riots, according to Murray Kempton, when "city editors were chary of sending white reporters to the scene. They have ever since been treated as special people." Hicks covered the Newark riots and school integration, and "You're *out* there," she says. "My father asked me, 'Who *goes* with you into these areas?' Of course it was a danger."

The initial impression that Nancy Hicks had of the *Post* was not of race but of office conditions at the 75 West Street office, "godawful, a mess—filthy and noisy; not enough desks for the reporters—six places and five chairs." Schiff replaced the squalid *Post* building and its foul-smelling toilets in 1968 when she bought the *Journal-American* building at 210 South Street overlooking the East River and the Brooklyn Bridge.[23] The new quarters were cleaner and more spacious, but 210 South never gained the same affection in the hearts of the old-timers. Joe Kahn, reminiscing, says of the paper's move, "I can't believe it's all over. When we were down at 75 West Street, it was like home."

Home it was for Ted, whose wife was no longer on Chauncey Street. He was having mixed feelings about Ersa's rise to political prominence. Governor Nelson Rockefeller celebrated his trusted assistant, but her loyalty and dependability made her unavailable to Ted. Sometimes Ersa arose early to fly from New York to Buffalo, then down to Rochester, and would arrive home just before she "heard Ted come to the gate. I knew that the family meal was important to him." When she could not manage all that in one day, Ted "was not pleased. He was very much a homebody." She says Henry Lee Moon thought she should have left her job and "assumed the role of nurse-maid." But she was fifteen years younger, "and I had *my* life ahead of me."

A white woman entered Ted's life at this time to assuage his feelings of attention deprivation. Mollie Moon asked a wealthy friend, Diana Bonnor Lewis, to host a book party for Ann Fairbairn upon publication of her novel *Five Smooth Stones,* then Mollie pressed Ted to attend. He said he did not want to go to "no party with no rich bitch," but Mollie prevailed. Ted went, drank, told stories, flirted with the hostess, and left. But a springlike interlude in his life had opened.

Diana Bonnor Lewis and her husband, Salim, lived at 778 Park Avenue. Salim was a Jewish philanthropist who headed the Wall Street firm of Bear, Stearns and Company and had helped pioneer the concept of block trading.[24] Diana Lewis recalls the party and that Ted's yarns sounded interesting so she sat down next to Moon to listen. As Ted was elaborating on something, Henry whispered to Diana, "He's the biggest goddamned liar that ever lived." Ted heard that, Diana remembers, "never batted an eye and said, 'Isn't that so, Henry?'" Henry agreed, "Yes, sir." That is the way they always did, Diana explains. "Henry or Mollie would be a stooge for Ted."

After a while, Mollie asked Diana, "Sugar, could we have a fire in the fireplace in the library?" Diana said, "Sure," and stood back to let her guests exit first. She recalled, "Ted waited gallantly for *me,* and as I started, he looked down and said, 'You better keep away from *me* or you're going to get in trouble.'" Diana thought, "Wonderful!" In the library she gave everybody another drink, "many of whom did not need another drink." When everyone was seated, there was no place for her so she sat on the floor. Ted, with a twinkle in his eye, murmured to her, "You oughtn't to be sitting at my feet."

After that party Diana Lewis did not see or hear of Ted until she was on a television program discussing disturbed children and telling about one of her sons who had been successfully treated in a residential treatment center and "the six marvelous grandchildren I had from him." Just as the program went off the air, the telephone rang. "I picked up the phone and Ted said, 'Braggin' about your grandchildren is not going to save you, either!'" The next day she received a bouquet of violets with a red rose in the middle. The card contained one word, "Insidious." This friendship brightened the later years of both these people. They looked forward to the comfort of talking, and occasionally on Friday nights they drove to a place up the Hudson for dancing. "Course he'd be the only black person in the place," Diana says. "I *know* he was self-conscious, but he brazened it out."

At the office, Fern Eckman heard about Diana from Ted. "His romance with the wealthy socialite was high drama," Eckman says. "He would tell me about it with a kind of breathless joy. I had never seen Ted in such a state in all the years I had known him. Tingling from top to toe, he would tell me, swooning, 'We read poetry to one another.'" And Diana Bonnor Lewis listened to Ted's Hopkinsville stories. Since she knew some publishers, she tried to get the stories collected into a book. In addition, the tales made her eager to see Hopkinsville. She asked Ted to take her there. He answered, "What you tryin' to do, get me lynched?"

In May 1967, Diana Bonnor Lewis went to London for two months. Ted sent flowers to her plane. While she was gone, Langston Hughes died. Immediately the *Post* called on Ted to write an obituary and tributes. That assignment essentially marked the end of Ted's quest for telling the African American story in writing. Hughes and Poston had long helped and promoted each other. Hughes had landed in Harlem at about the same time as Ted's brothers. Ted journeyed with Hughes to Russia in 1932. Now, he went to Hughes's funeral and quoted a "middle-aged woman who had traveled from Yonkers." The woman tried to explain what Hughes's work meant to her. She said, "I didn't know him. . . . But he knew us." [25]

The passing of Langston Hughes hit Poston like an earthquake. How much time was left for him? Diana Lewis remembers Ted calling her every evening at 2 A.M. London time. "Langston's death was an excuse for Ted to go on a bender," she says. He would put a record on, Ray Charles singing "Baby, It's Cold Outside," then "go off and get himself another drink." Transatlantic, Ted was reaching for closeness while his world shrank.

Ersa found a letter to Ted from Diana on one weekend home and felt hurt. At what point they became estranged is unclear. In Moon's collection of Poston's papers is an undated, unsigned handwritten note to "Dear Ted" from Ersa. She wrote him at some point during this period, "*Remember always—You* ordered me out of *your* house and even extended me the courtesy of a deadline, of which you reminded me daily. Why do you refuse to recognize that we do truly love each other but need the counseling of a professional who could assist us in not destroying our future? . . . How can you be bitter? You *drove* me away with your brutality, and unwillingness to ever believe anything except those things which could handle your ego needs." [26]

When were Ersa's hopes for the marriage dashed? In retrospect she says, "I did not anticipate a future when I first met Ted because I had not realized the complex nature of this man. If Ted and I had courted longer, some of this might have been revealed. But that's behind us now."

The turn that Poston's third marriage took by the late 1960s did not surprise Fern Eckman, for "Ted could be difficult. When in the last year or two I would tell him about something that upset me, he would brush it aside. He was changing." Roberta Brandes Gratz corroborates Eckman: "I remember at the end Ted being not pleasant, becoming distant, not the same fun-loving person, certainly not someone whom you could joke with or socialize with in the same way, and you'd have to back off." Ted was "not cut out to be a good husband," Robert Weaver thinks. "No one could domesticate him. He and Ersa had the best of his marriages." Apparently, Poston's dark side, revealed after drink, contributed to the breakups.

Ted went to Montgomery, Alabama, in 1967 to cover the Democratic gubernatorial primary, "the first big test of the Voting Rights Act of 1965." This was the last trip from which Ted came back with usable material.

At the office, he unofficially trained new reporters and shared bylines. With the talented black Earl Caldwell he wrote of Adam Clayton Powell, Roy Innis, and militancy.[27] His faithful friend Fern Eckman was given an assignment to sit in on a Black Studies class at Fordham University, where the professor sneered at the quaint, becoming old-fashioned designation "Negro," which had been a dignified term for African Americans throughout Ted's heyday. Poston's name was raised during the provocative class discussion. The professor said, "Head Poston; he's a Negro," and the students laughed. They were "Black!" Eckman says, "I had apoplexy and dropped my observer role." She stood up and said that if any two or three of those students together could ever do one-half of what Ted Poston had done for his race, they would do themselves proud. Looking back, she reflects, "This may have been something that Ted was suffering from—being put down by his own people."[28]

Ted called the rising race-conscious blacks "the fuzzy-wuzzies." When younger folk said nothing was different, that segregation, discrimination, and racism still existed, he and Henry Lee Moon dismissed their ignorance. The young had not had to live through the period of monolithic segregation, total exclusion, and lynch terror. When Poston and Moon dined one evening at their favorite restaurant, some fuzzy-wuzzies came in and, passing their table, cracked to the old-timers, "It's Uncle Toms like you who have been holding the race back all these years." The now "old" Moon and Poston had thought they had been "doing everything that was right and cogent," says their friend Ruth Banks, "that they had served the race well."

Profiling H. Rap Brown in July 1967 was an unpleasant task for Poston because Brown seemed to be a harbinger of the future. His lead read: "When Black Power advocate Stokely Carmichael surrendered the reins of the Student Nonviolent Coordinating Committee in Atlanta last May, he said—

only half-jokingly—of his successor, H. Rap Brown: 'People will be happy to have *me* back when they hear him.'"[29] Rap Brown barred whites from covering the Newark Black Power conference, which turned out to be a blessing for the future of minorities in journalism, for suddenly papers all over the country avidly sought black reporters.[30] Cub reporter Emile Milne (pronounced MIL-ney) remembers, "It was a time, like today, when they claim they can't find black people. There were few experienced reporters around then unless they robbed the *Amsterdam News*." Paul Sann agreed: "Hiring the competent black was not that easy. They didn't have the opportunity to get basic training. It's like the business about blacks not being good swimmers. They can't get near the water."

But the press itself had "set up bugaboos," Poston asserted, which created such radicals as Rap Brown. In 1968 Ted told a group of practicing journalists how the *Times* took teenage boys to a gym, stripped them to their waists—"they were practicing jujitsu—paid them fifty cents a piece, took pictures and captioned the photos as Blood Brothers getting ready to kill the next white person." Poston said, "You're playing with people's lives when you do this." He and Abe Rosenthal of the *Times* "almost had a fist fight once" when Poston accused the *Times* of "covering Harlem like a police beat."[31] The press "created Rap Brown and the Blood Brothers," he sighed. "Now they're frightened of these creatures they created."

Poston summed up his experience in the journalism profession in an essay, "The American Negro and Newspaper Myths." The substance of the change in race news, he theorized, was that southern editors and publishers had been "cynically defending" the myth of "white superiority, Negro indolence, and a baseless contention that the region's magnolia-scented values would triumph over the moral and legal might of the federal government." Poston singled out only one white southerner for resisting the prevailing view, Grover C. Hall, Sr., and the *Montgomery Advertiser* of the 1920s. They had "stood as a beacon light" when they courageously "castigated and ridiculed the hooded riders" of the Ku Klux Klan, even though it meant that Hall had to meet their "daily threats by wearing his holstered pistol" to the office. Hall had mobilized the "responsible citizens of the community by citing the real threat to lawful government." After thirty-five years of trying to improve race relations in his northern milieu, Poston felt discouraged that so many editors would designate as a race leader "any nonwhite citizen who makes preposterous statements about race relations," for that gave "respectability to irresponsibility." The "sporadic hiring" of "a handful of Negroes" did not help either, Poston complained, to pierce "the silken curtain between the major Northern newspapers and their Negro readers."[32]

Poston worked with Nancy Hicks on a story at the end of February 1968, when Manhattan borough president Percy Sutton admonished that unless Negro soldiers in Vietnam were taught "useful civilian skills—both in and outside the Army—returning veterans might be forced to utilize the one skill they had developed—killing." [33]

On the side, Hicks and Poston discussed the broad spectrum of the situation of minorities in journalism. She would point out to Ted some absurdity in the paper and say, "Look what they did!" Then Ted would pressure an editor. As she surveyed the journalistic scene, Hicks thought "the pattern didn't look human. If a white screwed up, 'They've had a bad day.' The minority journalist screws up, 'You're incompetent.' That's the way it played."

Poston saw "tremendous potential" in the ambitious and angry Hicks, according to Kenneth B. Clark, and he tried to enlist Clark's assistance in helping her fulfill it. Poston took Hicks to meet Clark, and, Clark says, "one could see that here was someone. Ted was happy that I took Nancy on as a kind of protégé. He would be her mentor at the *Post,* and I was sort of an unpaid therapist. When Ted felt it was time for Nancy to move on to the *Times,* he gave her every encouragement. This balances the cliché about Ted as a womanizer. Nancy adored Ted because he demonstrated a genuine concern."

Hicks insists that her relationship with Ted was professional, not social. She never heard that Ted was a womanizer, and "I didn't give it a thought. He was not a physically handsome man, but that was of least concern. Some people you look at and say either 'Yuck!' or 'Yum!' but for me, Ted was a total character and his appearance fit his persona." Ted's introducing her to Clark had a long-term effect. "Ken is almost my second father," she says. "He has taught me things over the years that I couldn't have learned otherwise, and Ted was the entry point. When we formed an association of black journalists, Ken let us use MARC's facilities. There were all of these concentric circles."

Before newspaper editors realized they needed blacks on their regular staffs, most newsrooms had no black perspective. The American Newspaper Guild published a pamphlet containing an article, "A Newspaper Pro, Ted Poston," about Ted and the few other blacks who by then had made it into the mainstream press in some cities. Poston declared in the article that there was no monolithic viewpoint emanating from "the Negro." Negroes were as various as the community at large. When Ted heard whites say of the NAACP head, "Why doesn't Roy Wilkins control his people?" he pointed out that the president of the City Council was an Italian named Screvane, yet whenever Italian-Americans got into a melee no one asked, "Why doesn't Screvane control his people?" [34]

President Johnson created the Kerner Commission to investigate the reasons for urban riots and to make proposals for preventing further unrest. "The only genuine, long-range solution," Johnson had exhorted, "lies in an attack—mounted at every level—upon the conditions that breed despair and violence. . . . We should attack these conditions—not because we are frightened by conflict, but because we are fired by conscience." [35] Upon publication of the commission's findings, newspapers were importuned to be more active in seeking black reporters. Jack Rosenthal, who helped put the 650-page Kerner Commission report together, said, "Our Nation is moving toward two societies, one black, one white—separate and unequal." [36] Black reporters were essential throughout the profession, for the white media had failed to communicate to whites "a feeling for the difficulties and frustrations of being a Negro in the United States." Whites showed "no understanding or appreciation for Negro culture, thought, or history," with the result that the white press was "at best mistrusted and at worst held in contempt" by black Americans. [37] The *Report* recommended the infusion in journalism of just what Ted Poston had been providing in his long career and what he continued to nurture in young colleagues.

Ernie Johnston, Jr., was Poston's next beneficiary after Nancy Hicks. As a boy, Johnston had lain in bed at night and "put stories together in my mind, picture stories." He studied journalism at North Carolina Agricultural and Technical State University in Greensboro. On being hired at the *Post,* he was grateful to Ted "just for the opportunity to work on the same staff." When Johnston did the legwork and Ted the rewrite, "Ted would bust you back to get details." Johnston remembers observing Ted "take a story on the phone, cigarette dangling from his mouth, always with a cigarette holder. Between stories, he had a book to read, and he'd be sittin' there reading, tapping his cigarette, waiting for the next story. He didn't get rattled or shaken. He took pride in being a chief rewrite man, because he *loved* journalism." Johnston noticed especially how Poston dealt with racial slights, and he told of one time that Ted took a story over the telephone from a guy in the South who was ranting about "the niggers." Ted listened to the fellow go on, and finally Ted said to him, 'You're talking to a Negro, now.'" The way Ted related it, Johnston remembers, "when the guy heard that, he was fit to be tied."

The *Post* tried to give blacks more opportunities to try out for the paper. One "half-black" tryout for whom Ted's mentoring did not seem to take "leaned way over to be all-black," Eckman says. "He would come in with such distorted stories that made blacks look good no matter whether it was true or not." Ted never did that.

As a beginning reporter Tony Mancini shared some bylines with Ted and says, "He and I were of different generations. Our careers overlapped—the dawn of mine, the twilight of his." Ted was over the hill by then, "with a pot belly, an old man's paunch," despite his thin frame. But Mancini also noticed that Ted would "take new African American reporters under his wing and show them the ropes."

Poston did not confine his mentoring to blacks. George Arzt would become City Hall bureau chief for the *Post* in 1972 and was press secretary to Mayor Ed Koch when he was tracked down for this book. Arzt says, "Ted was *so* nice, helping me when I was a cub reporter." He was "patient, knew exactly what I was supposed to get, and how to coax the story out." In covering a hearing on drugs in 1970, for example, Arzt interviewed politicians but "ignored this 12-year-old drug addict who got up on the stand." An experienced photographer was there and snapped the youth. Seeing the photo, Poston pressed Artz for details, saying, "George, the boy *is* the story." Ted asked enough questions of Arzt that they came up with the lead: "A 12-year-old sat twitching nervously before a legislative investigating committee today and confessed he was a dope pusher." [38] Arzt says that the next day the *Post*'s rivals—the *Times* and the *News*—had the same story on the front pages. "Their experienced reporters, like Ted, knew what the story was."

Poston coached Arzt through another reporting stint trying to devise a catchy lead for a piece on Mickey Mantle. With ten minutes to spare, over the phone Poston nudged Arzt, "Give me a baseball lead." Arzt struggled and the words came out: "Mickey Mantle tried to field the high hopes of business, but somehow the ball got past him." Poston pressed, "Try a little bit more," then sharpened the lead himself and guided Arzt through the structure of the story. "To this day, those lessons have stuck with me," Arzt says.

Because Martin Luther King, Jr., was the biggest race story of the latter half of the 1960s, Nancy Hicks was annoyed at the *Post* for not putting a full-time reporter on the King beat. On April 4, 1968, she left the office early for a meeting for organizing black journalists, and when she arrived at the meeting she learned that King had been shot. She wanted to go to Memphis herself, but when she heard that Ted had been dispatched, "I just remember being less angry, because Ted got to go. But, also, that day I began looking for a new job." [39] Did Ted come back with a good story on King or the funeral? There was none in the *Post*. "He just got drunk," Diana Bonnor Lewis says. "That's when he began to slip badly."

Ted Poston had become the elder statesman of black journalists. Columbia University's Journalism School professor Luther P. Jackson invited him to speak on interracial reporting on October 16, 1968. Aware that they were about to hear a "legend," Jackson taped the talk. On the tape, Poston's voice sounds gravelly and deep. One can hear in it a lifetime of cigarettes and bourbon. In its boisterous exuberance, the voice verges on laughter. Professor Jackson—whose grandfather was president of M. and F. College in Hopkinsville, where Poston's father and brothers once taught—introduced Ted: "Today we are privileged to have the fabled Ted Poston. So few journalists reach the fabled status. Ted came today out of a sense of obligation. He's suffering a virus and says he's only half a man, but half of Ted Poston is good enough for all of us."

Commencing his swan song presentation, Poston began, "When Luther called me, he said I should tell some of my experiences." There was sobriety in his cautions. He did not want to speak so much "about the plight of Negroes as what I feel for the plight of this country. We are in a dangerous period. Anything that any of us can do to make us stop and think twice might be helpful." The meeting was filled with questions, answers, and laughter. The journalists told Ted of their attempts to promote better race relations in their own communities and asked his advice—what would help, what hindered. Poston found himself mentoring again, passing on the philosophy his career had embodied for forty years.[40]

The following month, Richard Nixon was elected president, and in his lavatory Henry Lee Moon hung a picture of himself taken with Nixon. Ersa Poston was asked but declined to join Nixon's administration.[41]

Was there life for Ted Poston after 1968? His final years became an anticlimax. Emile Milne, a journalistic heir, appeared at the *Post* for tryouts and became "much closer to Ted than any of the other youngsters," Eckman remembers, "truly like a son to Ted—present at all his parties, helping with drinks, helping Ted when he needed it on other occasions." He was a "quiet young man, very intelligent."

Milne's memory is that he was "a total neophyte." He says, "I would call raggedy, disjointed telephone notes into Ted and he turned them into wonderful little stories that sounded so good." Milne inadvertently ran roughshod over one of Ted's endeavors. Schiff sent Milne a note about a black comic strip and asked his opinion of it. Milne says, "In my arrogance, I wrote, 'This thing is not relevant.'" Later, Ted chastened him, "What did you *do?* I've been working for years to get that strip in the paper." Milne reflects, "Despite his renown as a civil rights reporter, Ted took on little personal campaigns like that, and worked quietly. This asshole, me, screws up."

After work, often one of the rookies would give Ted a lift home, stopping at a store to pick up cat food. Ted now lived alone, except for his cats, whom he referred to almost as characters in his life. Milne was usually invited in for a drink and supper, Ted doing the cooking, but the drinking lasted longer than the eating. "Ted told me hilarious stories about going to Russia and getting run out," Milne says, "but because we consumed so much Jack Daniels, I have lost the stories. Most of them evaporated with the alcohol." Milne does remember being impressed with Ted's jokes about having had a lot of wives. Ted's was "a larger than life story. In my mind, he had had maybe a dozen wives." He spoke of his marriages "not with sadness or tragedy, but as an episode that happened."

This detachment was a lesson Poston conveyed to those who followed him. "He dealt on a higher professional, social, and political level than most all the other reporters at the *Post*," Milne says. "What I got from him was a sense of style in living. I was impressed with his savoir faire and brashness, his charm. During those long evenings we spent drinking Jack Daniels, he talked about his amorous adventures with rich white people. For someone of Ted's generation, that sort of thing was unheard-of. Whether or not these stories were true, he told them in such a way, like jokes, that I believed everything he said."

Alcohol may have interfered with Poston's functioning by this time, Ernie Johnston, Jr., says, because "Ted came from the old school where you put together the story then go to the bar for a drink. Talk to any old-time journalist; the bottle was a part of life." At social affairs, such as the Beaux-Arts Ball, "You got free liquor, and Ted was a happy-go-lucky person. If he had problems, you couldn't tell it." Even so, alcohol had stopped giving him a lift.

Just twelve stories carried Poston's byline in 1969. None was distinctive. Helen Dudar heard that now Ted's fingers were hitting the wrong keys, "producing garbled words and sentences which he did not seem to recognize." George Arzt called stories in to Poston, then would see quotes that "didn't come out quite right." Arzt spoke to the city editor about it, and the city editor said, "Did you have Ted before or after lunch?"

At lunch, Poston was often accompanied by Fern Eckman. His habit was to have a cocktail, Eckman says. "He would order a drink and an entree, take a few bites, then gracefully drape his napkin over the food, effectively concealing the large amount he had not eaten," then he might order another drink. As he got older, "one drink made him tipsy. His speech would slur. But that was just before he quit."

Editor Paul Sann remembers that in his last years, "Ted was in bad shape." The rewrite desk was "a place to stay in out of the cold and do a day's work to collect his salary." Roberta Gratz had the feeling that Ted was "both used and abused" by the *Post* then. Watching him slowly cross the city room to his desk, Eckman says, "was almost more than I could bear. He had always been so lithe and quick, and merry." Kenneth Clark and Hylan Lewis were witnesses to Ted's failing health. "We never talked about it except here [at our office]. But it still sticks with us."

One of Ted's final bylines is mistakenly labeled "Ed Poston," suggesting that a newcomer was writing the headlines and that Ted was already a has-been.[42] That mistake, "Ed Poston," had also been made when he started out at the *Post* in the 1930s as an unknown. Had he ended up unknown? According to the quantity of his co-bylines and their dates, he was at work all of 1969 except from mid-August through September. Perhaps he went to the Virgin Islands that summer or to Capahosic. He used to come back from vacations with a sheaf of book reviews. This time there were none. Maybe he was not being asked to review books anymore. Certainly, he needed vacations. America seemed to have stopped making sense for him. It was hard to foresee a positive future for himself or for the race.

From May 1970 until mid-1974, the *Post* lay under the burden of a suit against it brought by Bill Artis and the two other beginning black reporters. And Poston took the side of the reporters because "I was the *Post*'s alibi Negro for 25 years."[43] As James Scott says, "The initial act that publicly breaks the surface of consent owes a part of its dramatic force to the fact that it is usually an irrevocable step."[44] Ted thought that twenty-five years of him as sole black reporter had been too long even for a liberal newspaper.

The complainant, Bill Artis, had trekked to the *Post* from a cotton plantation in the South via Columbus, Ohio, where an uncle provided him lodging so he could attend Ohio State University. When Artis got to the *Post* for the normal three-month tryout, Poston informed him that once the paper had three blacks as permanent reporters, the trend was not to expand beyond that, and the paper now had its full complement—Ted, Emile Milne, and Ernie Johnston.[45]

Artis sued the *Post* claiming that he was discriminated against because the paper had a quota system, thus it was impossible for him to get beyond the tryout stage. "My outlook was that this case involved far more than me," he says. "It was the issue of black reporters in the media. I was a stalking-horse." The *Post* had not kept most of the blacks it briefly brought on staff, "including some who went on to do prominent work elsewhere." Artis had "an illustrious list" of reporters Ted helped him round up and trace to get comments to support his side.

Oddly, Paul Sann was completely unaware that Ted had been acting as a counselor/mentor for the young. When Sann was asked about Bill Artis's suit, he said his impression was that Ted had "done either nothing or little to help the guy. I didn't recall Ted *ever* going out of his way with the other black reporters, either."

George Trow, assistant managing editor in those years, relates that the *Post* was always "trying out" reporters, many black ones after the Kerner Commission *Report*. With Bill Artis, "We wanted to find out if this kid could write, how much he knew." The editors were under constant pressure about budgets. "You could only have so many reporters and could only hire the best," Trow says. "I saw some of the copy of this fellow. It wasn't bad." When the ninety-day tryout period was up, Trow was asked about Artis and said, "No, he's going to have to go."

So Artis went, to the Human Rights Commission. "He said I fired him because he was black," Trow remembers clearly. "The case lasted four years and went to the high court." Dorothy Schiff hired civil rights attorney Morris Abram to defend the paper, an inspired choice considering that Abram grew up in backcountry Georgia yet had become "the patriarch of American Jewry."[46] Abram's humble beginnings resembled those of both Poston and Artis—although his white skin allowed Abram to be admitted into his local library. Still, Abram, too, knew the stigma of ethnic discrimination.[47]

Artis won the first round of his suit, and the *Post*'s blacks took joy in the open declaration of their hidden transcript of resistance to domination in the teeth of power—a moment when truth was finally spoken.[48] The *Post* was required to reinstate Artis, but Schiff appealed the decision and, according to Artis, paid Abram's law firm a quarter of a million dollars defending itself.[49] The state of New York represented Artis.[50]

By the last round of the fight, in 1974, Artis lost, the *Post* won, and Ted was dead. Trow reflects, "I think what Ted was thinking was, 'Hell, we should have had more black reporters over the years. And, hell, I should have gotten further here than I did.'"[51] Roberta Gratz comments, "If you *want* a black reporter, you find one who is bright and trainable. If you are just going through the motions, you say, 'We interviewed and haven't found any.' Yet the *Post* was doing more than all the other papers put together."[52]

Fern Eckman remembers how Ted was treated once the suit was under way. The warmth and friendliness were gone; Ted was overlooked. Sann felt annoyed with him. Sann says, "I was the guy that got Ted hired and I was the guy that hired all the other blacks—more than any other major newspaper in those early years."

By the 1970s, the *Post*'s financially good years had passed. Dorothy Schiff told Newspaper Guild leaders that if she were required to pay the 11 percent increase due under all union contracts on March 31, 1972, "the *Post* would be in serious financial trouble by the end of the year."[53] Ted and the *Post* seemed to be going down together. Tony Mancini says that now "Ted felt cynical about the *Post*. He was aware that he was a token." Joe Kahn said,

"Ted wasn't walking well." Rita Delfiner saw him "getting frailer and frailer," but he would still "come to work and do *work!*" Larry Kleinman, on rewrite with Ted in his final year, recalls, "Ted was getting the most rudimentary kinds of assignments, and took a while to do them, no more pressured deadline situations."[54] In self-defense, Sann claims, "As long as I was there, I would have kept Ted on until he fell down dead at his desk. Whatever meager salary he was earning up to that point, the *Post* owed him enough of a debt to carry him forever."

In March 1972, Ted retired.

It would have been hard for those standing on his shoulders to measure up to Ted Poston's legacy. Who could claim prior experience, as a child, helping his family publish the *Contender;* writing a column for the *Pittsburgh Courier* while a dining car waiter; editing the *Amsterdam News;* starting up the American Newspaper Guild; frolicking in Stalin's Russia; working on the New Deal WPA, then in the White House? A modern black could not come out of journalism school and duplicate the breadth of training Ted Poston had brought to the *Post* in 1936. But for the new generation, he had laid the groundwork. "Ted didn't get out and wave the flag," Ernie Johnston says, "but he worked consistently toward improving race relations."

Each generation has its own battles to fight. "Ted fought hard in his own way," George Trow sums up, "as Booker T. Washington did in his. Now we tend to think of Booker T. Washington as an accommodationist. But we forget the times in which he lived and what he had to put up with. When Ted came along, some of the younger guys said, 'Why didn't you do more?' But Ted Poston paved the way for these kids and they don't even know it."

13

. . . .

Retirement, Death

. . . .

1972–1974

My sword I give to him that shall succeed me in
my pilgrimage, and my courage and skill to him
that can get it.

    —MR. VALIANT-FOR-TRUTH,
      Pilgrim's Progress

On his retirement in the spring of 1972, the *Post* gave Ted Poston his union-required severance pay—two weeks for every year on the paper up to twenty-five years—and "with undaunted spirit," he set out to "catch all the catfish" in Hopkinsville, then to sojourn in the Virgin Islands. He told Fern Eckman, Roberta Gratz, and his other friends who were, according to Eckman and Gratz, "longing to see his outrageous, humor-filled reminiscences put into print," that he would work on his autobiography.[1]

Kentucky's *Louisville Courier-Journal* got the news of his retirement from its *New York Times* syndicate and allotted the state's son one paragraph: "Ted Poston, dean of Negro journalists, has retired from the *New York Post* after a journalism career of more than 40 years."[2] Moon described the Poston style for *Black Perspective*: "At the end of a two-and-a-half hour session of tall tales (all with a kernel of authenticity undergirding massive embellishment)," Ted always explained, "plaintively, to his enthralled and envious listeners: 'I can't help it if I've lived an interesting life and remembered it—in detail.'"[3]

Post people circulated invitations for a "party honoring TED POSTON . . . April 15 at 8 P.M." Ten dollars per person would cover "plenty of food and drink" and a "gift." Roberta Gratz opened her brownstone on 87th Street for the party. Paul Sann did not attend, although, he says, "Ted went out of his way to personally invite *me;* but the rift between us had become too deep." Eckman comments, "Paul Sann ignored Ted after Ted testified against the *Post.* Overcoming his anger was not a Sann trait!" Poston's single act of public insubordination had "pierced the smooth surface" of his apparent consent regarding *Post* policy. His strategy for keeping the racial dialogue going may have used the regular trickster techniques at times, of disguise, deception, and indirection, while he maintained an outward impression of willing adherence to the paper's direction.[4] But the farewell party, even without the executive editor, was "spirited and loving," Gratz remembers. Bestowed on behalf of the Executive Committee of the Newspaper Guild of New York was a "declaration of merit" on "retiring after some four decades as an honest reporter. . . . 38 years a member of the Newspaper Guild."[5]

Eckman acclaimed Poston as "the first black man to crack the alabaster front of a major New York daily. . . . during the long period when black signified anything but beautiful." Delineating the way Poston tantalized listeners when he reminisced, Eckman reported: "Pretty copygirls were beguiled by his Soviet saga (did the ballerina chase Poston and Henry Lee Moon? or was it the other way around?). . . . Hostility was not Poston's weapon. He scored points—for his race, his country, his paper, his world—on the basis of reason and humor. . . . [He] managed to peel every major award except the Pulitzer."[6]

Post colleagues connived on a "gift." Trow suggested a tape recorder into which Ted could tell "his marvelous stories." Eckman agreed. She wanted the "endless stories about Russia" preserved.

Within a month, after Ted recovered from the *Post's* retirement party, Robert Weaver, Moon, and Ernie Johnston, Jr., plotted another "Party for Ted Poston by his Many Friends." This testimonial would be at the Playboy Club because, Ernie Johnston says, "*This* is Ted!" The invitation pictured a black Playboy bunny. People poured out of Ted's past: St. Clair Bourne, Morris Abram, Thelma Berlack-Boozer, Kenneth and Mamie Clark, Diana Bonnor Lewis, Joel Dreyfuss, Nancy Hicks, the Eckmans, Wechslers, Mal Goode, Bill Hastie, Frank Horne, Tom Johnson, Ted's physician Arthur Logan, Emile Milne, Frederick D. Patterson, Billy Rowe, Rev. Gardner Taylor, Bill Trent, Roy Wilkins, Franklin Williams, Whitney Young's widow; Vernon Jordan, Georgia state NAACP director then and a non-fuzzy-wuzzy; and many others.[7]

The Many Friends also presented a gift—another tape recorder. Emile Milne explains, "You know, 'Ted, talk into this?'" Diana Bonnor Lewis wanted him to record his tales of waiting tables in the dining cars, the ones he had fancied collecting as "The Little Red Cars." She says, "I don't think he ever wrote those down."

When *Black Perspective* asked Poston for a retrospective, he couldn't do it. Ted told the editor, "I have been handcuffed to a typewriter so long to earn my daily bread that I *hate* writing." He would try a few paragraphs on the autobiography but was unable to finish, Ruth Banks says. Luther Jackson thought it was probably "eating his heart out that he hadn't done a book." Kenneth Clark identified Ted as, like many blacks, a "truncated intellectual," whose true passion was in the arts. At least through journalism and *The Dark Side of Hopkinsville*, "Ted received a bit of recognition."

Poston's association with Kenneth and Mamie Clark's MARC group continued after his retirement. Under its auspices, a select group of distinguished black Americans gathered at the Clarks' beautiful offices at 60 East 86th Street, at the Clarks' home in Hastings-on-Hudson for a picnic, and at cocktails and dinner at the Hotel Carlyle. These statesmen of the race talked about how to negotiate with the tide of novice black scholars who were taking over the universities in their demands to be heard.

Clark was rebuffed by the upstart new generation as an "outdated 'colored' intellectual" when a City University of New York student admonished him that he failed to recognize the "many levels of psychological strain that are imposed upon the 'integrated' black intellectual today." The brazen CUNY scholar defied Clark's moderate stance, saying she was "not in the university environment 'to be some white person's "black experience."'"[8] Clark answered her that the angry young blacks would have to test their strength and the depth of their own humanity by doing what "our forefathers had to do; namely, to stand and affirm their being in spite of the limitations and the cruelty and the lies of the racist." Clark thought that "soul and random rage are not substitutes for courage."[9]

Although Poston was sick, he dutifully supported MARC by attending its meetings during his last two years, years that were for him, Clark says, "pretty sad." Hylan Lewis found Ted "psychologically impaired" by then, although "he would smile and laugh. His humor was a blessing."

During the summer of 1972, Ted made his way back to Hopkinsville to catch catfish. Bliss eluded him. He telephoned Allison Williams, "You be home. I'm coming over," then he shuffled the four blocks from Mary Belle Fleming's to Williams's home. Williams recalls, "We went fishing down at the Devil's Elbow, a crook on the Tennessee River, where it's hard for steamboats to get through. Ted fell and rolled down the embankment toward the water. That's when I realized how sick he was." Jennie Knight Baker, who had proudly procured Hughes's anthology with Ted's stories in it for the Crispus Attucks school library, remembers that last visit. "I saw Ted sitting on Mary Belle Fleming's porch and went over to talk to him. Ted didn't know me. He was out of it—like in a coma."

In New York, Poston and Moon attended a few Silurian Society luncheons. Silurians were senior New York newspaper people joined together for "no political or social causes" but "to encourage and support the press of New York in the cause of truth, fair play, liberty and human dignity." [10] Ted spent Sundays at the Moons', Diana Bonnor Lewis says, because "Mollie cooked chicken gizzards." Then Moon and Poston would watch a ball game.

One Sunday Mollie also invited their friend Ruth Banks. Banks, an Ohio State University graduate and former city editor of the Cleveland edition of the *Pittsburgh Courier,* was teaching psychology then at the New York University Graduate School of Business. Banks felt sorry for Poston. She had seen him around lately, "always alone," and looking forlorn as he drank coffee and smoked. Because of Mollie Moon's affinity for bringing people together—in this case, Banks—Mollie would enable Ted to spend his last two years as a kind of protagonist of Hughes's poem, "Sylvester's Dying Bed," with Diana Bonnor Lewis, Ruth Banks, and Ersa as "the womens." Even his second wife, Marie, would play a role. Hughes had written,

> Sweet gals was a-moanin',
> "Sylvester's gonna die!"
> And a hundred pretty mamas
> Bowed their heads to cry. . . .
>
> So I hollers, "Com'ere, babies,
> Fo' to love yo' daddy right!'
> And I reached up to hug 'em—
> When the Lawd puts out the light. [11]

Ted could not bask in the pleasure of desirable women concerned about his welfare because arteriosclerosis was making him feel sick and mentally confused. He was in and out of New York Hospital and Gracie Square Hospital. Several *Post* colleagues visited him there. Bill Artis remembers that "off and on he'd know who you were and what you were talking about. He would chuckle about how he had been able finally to stand tall and let the *Post* know how he had really felt in all of those years of their holding him forth as the only black in the metropolitan area on a major paper." Emile Milne thought Ted was "losing it; I didn't know what the hell was wrong with him. Even after he left the hospital, I went to see him at his house and he didn't recognize me."

But when Ruth Banks visited him in the hospital, Poston seemed lucid. Ted had visited and read to her when she had fallen and suffered a brain concussion. Now Ted was in need, so she offered her help. With Henry Lee Moon's blessing, she became his caretaker and drove him about on errands. Banks, fluent in French and Spanish, well-traveled and literate, stimulated his fondness for repartee. She chortled at his acronym, TRAMP—Theodore Roosevelt Augustus Major Poston—and would call him Ted "except when I had something of importance to tell him at which time I used all the names."

Poston and Banks developed a way of life that agreed with them both. A regular stop on their rounds in Manhattan was the Washington Beef Company on Ninth Avenue between 41st and 42d Streets. Even Fern Eckman remembers that Ted "swore by the meat" there. One day the two of them drove there, Banks dropped Poston off, then she went to park the car. In the store, Poston's legs failed him, he fell down, and, Banks says, "the people there who all knew him were helping him up when I came in the door."

In a letter dated January 15, probably in 1973, Ersa wrote Ted from Albany expressing her concern and love. She told him she was glad he was getting therapy for his legs, what she had been "trying to get you to accept when I visited Burke Rehabilitation Center" with the facilities that could assure progress "if a prescribed course of therapy is followed." She signed her leter, "With love—always, Ersa."

On the days of doctor appointments, Poston and Banks ate afterward at "The Library" on Broadway. They both drank—he Jack Daniels, she Beefeaters gin and vodka. "TRAMP was determined to keep me at his side as long as he lived," Banks relates, "so he kept me on that habit and joined me. I joined him by going fishing with him in Sheepshead Bay—quid pro quo."

Diana Bonnor Lewis came through when Banks needed a reprieve. In Banks's absence, on one occasion, Lewis offered to take Ted to the doctor. Ted was charmed at the thought of black him being chauffeured from Bedford Stuyvesant to Harlem by the woman whom he had referred to as a "rich bitch" before he met her. Diana says that she drove Ted through one seedy street at 9 o'clock in the morning, and they encountered a drunk standing on the corner who stared at them, then "began singing at the top of his voice." After the light changed, the drunk "watched us drive on and laughed." Ted told her, "That was for you. He was singing for you."

A younger Ted would have enjoyed having women friends hovering over him, but at this stage he felt addled. He could not make it to Mollie Moon's New Year's soul food party that year. Banks went alone, found Diana there, plus Marie Poston Jackson. The three of them chatted about Ted. Marie asked Ruth what emotional ties she had to Ted, such as, "Do you love him? Why are you taking care of him?" Ruth said she admired Ted, that he had never made any sexual moves on her, and that she saw him as a lonely man who had had three wives and perhaps needed a family. "So we—my daughter and the 'grands' became his family," Banks says.

The U.S. Virgin Islands beckoned. With quiet beaches, tropical beauty, and a year-round pleasant climate, the islands seemed to Poston and Banks like a place where life might be serene. Banks's daughter had just finished law school and was moving from California to New York with her three children. "As grandmother," Banks says, "I opted to take Holly B., age three, so that day care would not be a problem." When Poston was well enough, Ted, Ruth, and Holly B. packed up and moved to the Virgin Islands, although Ted first made out a will, naming Henry Lee Moon as executor of his estate.

When Ted, Ruth, and Holly B. got to Coral Bay, Ruth kept Moon informed of their settling in. She wrote, "Ted and Holly B. are a pair! She mothers him." Three-year-old Holly B. remembered, years later, "skinny-dipping and snorkeling," playing poker with Ted, and eating pigs' feet. Some days, when Ted didn't feel well, "he'd put his chair on the beach and just sit there." Holly B. elaborates, "I didn't know how to swim then so I would play by the shore and collect seashells, all that good stuff, then go back and eat more pigs' feet. Sometimes we'd sit up all night playing cards, and Ted told stories. Sometimes we went into town to shop. From where *we* lived you could see the candy store across the water. A daily event for me and Ted was to go and see the guy at the store. I must have had a tab because I could get anything I wanted and didn't have to pay for it."

Ted had brought his cat Ramses with them. "That cat," Holly B. says, "would leave fur all over and just wait for us to clean it so he could do it again." Ruth Banks recalls how much Ted loved Holly B. "This was the only time he had had a young child around every day, and he tried to be a grandfather to her. He spoiled her." She would lean on him and roll her eyes. In Holly B., Ted, in turn, "had someone who loved him unconditionally," Banks thinks.

The peace and pleasure that Ted and Holly B. enjoyed together was the last before daily events snowballed past him enveloping him in their inexorability. In October 1973, Marie Poston Jackson lost her third husband and, by coincidence, came to the Virgin islands in mourning.[12] At Thanksgiving, Ted heard she was there and telephoned her to offer sympathy. Later, Ted wanted to do something nice for Banks so he brought her whole family to the islands to visit. People surmised that Banks's daughter and her grand-children were also his. "When folk stopped and said to him, 'What a won-derful family you have,' Ted would just switch on his great smile and say 'Thank you.'"

Perhaps the surfeit of "family" overwhelmed Ted, for he became disori-ented again. He told an acquaintance of Ersa's who lived in the islands that he loved Banks. The acquaintance phoned Ersa to relay that news. The next day, Banks says, Ersa served papers on Ted for separation and was threat-ening to sue him for divorce. That upset Ted and put him in the hospital. He would "not let anybody near him and swore at the doctor, 'Ya little sonofabitch. You're not gonna hit me with that needle.'" Banks, her daugh-ter, and grandchildren, for eleven consecutive days, "went to the hospital to see that man, and to wash his clothes because the hospital was most unsani-tary." Marie Poston Jackson called on him as well.[13] When all the women were in Poston's room, the doctor begged Ted, "Can't you give me just *one?*"

The news of Poston's hospitalization made the *Post* and the *Amster-dam News* back in New York with stories that he had wandered around St. Thomas for three days "as victim of a mild case of amnesia," in and out of stores. When friends found him and spoke to him, he "looked at them with a blank stare, unaware that they were addressing him." The papers said that "his estranged wife, New York State Civil Service Commissioner Ersa Poston, had instituted separation proceedings against him." Hospital authorities had contacted Ersa and she had spoken with him by phone, af-ter which "nurses reported an improvement in his health."[14] Ersa says that Ted's amnesia was "a continuation of his memory loss and arteriosclerosis."

Banks and Diana Lewis say that it was Ersa's suit that precipitated Ted's crisis and that Ersa had named the two of them as "co-respondents" in sepa-ration proceedings. Ersa protests that she never took legal action. The two women became incensed, however. Lewis thought, "All I need now is to have my picture on the front page of the *Amsterdam News.*"[15] When Ted got out of the hospital, Banks took him home to Brooklyn, "to answer Ersa's peti-tion." Lewis got a lawyer, and "Ted and Ruth came up to the house. By this time, Ted could barely lift his feet. He was shuffling and mumbling. He could hardly speak." Diana adds, "My lawyer said that Ersa would be laughed out of court." Ted changed his will at this point to leave his property to Banks. Banks comments, "Had Ersa not filed for separation, I am sure he would never have changed it." His only remark to Banks regarding Ersa was, "I'll see to it that she doesn't get anything!"

In shaky handwriting, on December 13, 1973, Ted signed the papers leaving his estate to Ruth Banks and stipulated, "I make no mention of my wife, Ersa Hines Poston, and direct that she not share in any portion of my Estate, since she has long since abandoned me and abandoned our marital relationship." Subsequently his condition stabilized, says Banks, "and we resumed our usual pattern of doing errands around New York."

A bleak midwinter storm—snow, sleet, freezing rain, and a cold, gray drizzle buffeted New York City on January 10, 1974, "delaying rail and mass-transit commuters" and "snarling traffic on icily hazardous highways." [16] The snow from that storm made streets crunchy the next morning, slushy by evening. Poston and Banks were not thrilled about going out in it, but Banks had made an appointment for Ted with her psychiatrist. "I hoped he and I could get Ted interested in writing again. People who retire do not always have a viable plan to deal with the aging process."

The morning of January 11, they read the *Times*. Perhaps Poston felt some solace that blacks were finally being accepted in the profession when he noted that the young journalist who had integrated the University of Georgia, Charlayne Hunter, had a front-page story.

Later in the morning, Poston and Banks left for their appointment. Despite the weather, they had "a fun day." They had shopped, eaten downtown, then parked Banks's Volvo station wagon a couple of houses down on Chauncey Street. Carrying their purchases through the slush, they dropped two fifths of Beefeaters Vodka in front of a neighbor's house, "so we quickly hied ourselves into 101," says Banks. Ted went to the bathroom while Banks tidied his bedroom. He came back, approached the bed, and appeared to Banks to be faltering but managed to turn around to sit on the bed, "when he started to fall," she says. "I caught him. He died in my arms—like zap!"

Banks called the police and the Moons; they called Ersa. Then Moon phoned the *Post,* and Fern Eckman and Roberta Gratz pounded out an obituary for the *Post*'s late night edition: "The first black man to write for a major New York daily died today at his Brooklyn home after a long illness. He was 67." They said that Poston had returned to New York at Christmastime and "visited the *Post,* still kind of a home for him even after retirement." [17]

Responsibility for Ted's body devolved on Ersa. Banks's role in Ted's life was over. Upset, she called Diana Bonnor Lewis and said, "I really need you now." Ruth left for the Virgin Islands, Diana flew to meet her there, and they grieved together.

Ersa knew that Ted would have wanted to be buried in Hopkinsville, the town for which Robert Weaver called Poston the "one-man Chamber of Commerce." Ted's surviving cousins there made the arrangements. Paul Sann in New York thought Ted "deserved a burial with honors," and Ersa saw that he got it. Weaver delivered the eulogy at Benta's Funeral Home in

Harlem: "I was flattered and surprised when Ersa asked me to speak of Ted tonight. . . . My surprise was occasioned by my recognition of the uniquely close friendship and affection which existed between Ted and Henry Lee Moon." But Moon simply could not utter "what would have been an expression of love and devotion," Weaver thought. Luther P. Jackson, Jr., "kind of wished a newspaperman had talked. Weaver is formal and stiff." But Moon found Weaver's eulogy perfect and made copies for all Ted's friends who could not be there. Emile Milne felt honored that Ersa asked him to be a pallbearer. James Wechsler, also a pallbearer, said regretfully to Eckman, "Why didn't I make Ted an editor?"

Ersa accompanied Ted's body by air back to Hopkinsville, where Rev. A. R. Lasley conducted the service at his old Virginia Street Baptist Church. Bill Powell, a columnist from the *Louisville Courier-Journal,* drove down, then wrote:

> The skinny kid who didn't know he was licked from the beginning and went on to win, came home. . . . The funeral was in the . . . Church which Ted joined as a boy. . . . Ted had told [Rev. Lasley] that no matter where he went . . . he would never "move his letter" and he never did.
>
> It had turned warm, and some of the stained glass windows of the spacious church were open. From the street came the sound of car horns, of trucks roaring and gasping and voices of people working across the street at a tobacco warehouse. . . . Occasionally, the sun broke through haze and lighted up the stained glass windows. . . . symbolic of Ted Poston's personality—coming through just at the right time. . . . Mrs. Mattie Sue Ford sang in a voice as clear as Ted Poston's writings of "coming to the end of the road." [18]

After the service, the hearse and a few cars drove down First Street, past Billy Goat Hill, past Allison Williams's house and Attucks high school, then wound out to the colored cemetery, Cave Spring, where Ted's body was placed next to that of his brother Robert, who had symbolically waited fifty years for Ted to fulfill the family promise.

Ted's modest estate now had to be settled. Details took two years of careful attention from executor Moon. Ruth Banks was grateful that Ted had changed his will. Ersa, annoyed that Ruth had intercepted her marital prerogatives, fought back in court. The court decreed that Ersa should get half of Ted's estate.[19] His property included the house on Chauncey Street, carried on the tax rolls for $30,000, and Eph and Susie Poston's house at 1003 North Tenth Street in Paducah.[20]

Moon, seventy-two now, had not been well. Handling of the estate was complicated as well as aggravating. At the office, the NAACP wanted to move him from number four man to number eight man in salary so he retired.[21] He felt empty at not being able to talk everything over with Ted. He wished he could show him communications that arrived after the funeral, such as Maurice A. Dawkins's "Ode to Ted Poston," written for the melody of James Weldon Johnson's "Lift Every Voice and Sing." It included,

> . . . his dreams inspire us! . . .
> Catalyst, irritant and bon-vivant
> Humor and satire too—parody all came through
> Communi-ca-ting thoughts to make men change.
> Sing a song—of faith that young men will follow
> Taking up—the torch Ted Poston laid down-n-n. . . .

Dawkins testified to Moon that "I met Ted Poston in the pages of the *New York Post* and empathetically escaped with him from death at the hands of the Ku Klux Klan terrorists who chased him out of Florida. . . . The hair-raising 95 mile per hour careening automobile ride. . . . caught me up in the spirit of courage and adventure. . . . It turned me on and dialed me up and made me feel that 'fighting for freedom was my fight,' that in brief, 'I wanted to be like him when I grew up.'"

After that, Moon tried to write his own life story, which was also Ted's. Luther P. Jackson's interviews with Moon, subsequently placed in the Columbia Oral History Project archives, helped Moon articulate some of it. The story neither Moon nor Poston completely succeeded in relating was each one's role in the American Negro saga, "which teaches one to deflect racial provocation and to master and contain pain."[22]

Despite Poston's jovial mask, Pauli Murray—who would eventually become an Episcopal priest—had felt, when Poston first came to Harlem, that his "eyes smiled but hinted sadness."[23] Kenneth Clark agreed: "Behind his tremendous humor, Ted balanced inner sadness with a broad perspective of the sadness of his fellow human beings. When Ted was ill, I used to visit him and he indicated that human beings had a helluva time being human."

Ersa Poston thought her husband was "a complex person who harbored many feelings of inferiority" and that his story "The Revolt of the Evil Fairies" depicts the problems that, "even in childhood, haunted and confused him. Ted was a beloved person who never felt he had achieved his potential."[24]

Had Ted Poston achieved his potential? Joe Kahn says no. "The only thing I didn't know was whether it bothered him." Kahn "never had the feeling that Ted wanted to be an editor." Nancy Hicks is convinced that the *New*

York Post missed out because of Poston's conceptualization. She says, "I won't say unkind things about former bosses, but it burns me up that they might have had Ted's intelligence at the wheel. There are few good conceptual editors who are sensitive, bright, quick, and who synthesize well. Ted had more intelligence, more sense of style in New York than a lot of those people pushing pencils."

Hicks credits Poston for having nurtured her to the point that eventually she got involved in journalism training. In 1977, she and her husband, Bob Maynard, founded the Institute for Journalism Education in Berkeley, California, "a program sponsored by Gannett and others aimed at training minorities for jobs in journalism." [25] They would train Poston's heirs. Nancy Hicks Maynard says she has "a small, wonderful mental picture of Ted passing a mantle." It's like, "OK, *you* take it. Go and see what you can do."

Notes

ACKNOWLEDGMENTS

1. Charles H. Nichols, ed., *Arna Bontemps–Langston Hughes Letters, 1925–1967* (New York: Dodd, 1980), 122–23.

CHAPTER I. CHILDHOOD: 1906–1917

1. W. E. B. Du Bois, *Black Reconstruction in America, 1860–1880* (1935; rpt. New York: Atheneum, 1992), 125.

2. Ibid., 14.

3. Ephraim was born in 1863, according to the Christian County census for 1900, but in 1865, according to Frank Lincoln Mather, ed., *Who's Who of the Colored Race, 1915* (1915; rpt. Detroit: Gale, 1976), 221.

4. The Red River met the Cumberland at Clarksville and became the locus of a silkworm culture business intended to replace tobacco. See *Picturesque Clarksville, Past and Present: A History of the City of Hills* (Clarksville, Tenn.: Titus, 1887), 227.

5. Ibid., 164.

6. Ibid., 151. John H. Poston was a man "of clear head and fine intellect," president of the board of trustees for "the old Male Academy," and president of Branch Bank of Tennessee. He represented Montgomery County in the legislature, "kept a hospitable home," which was "ever an asylum for the worthy in distress . . . more than one orphan has been indebted to his generosity for a home and education" (ibid., 274–75). Another white, Charles Debrill Poston, was a journalist who lived briefly in Nashville during the period that Ephraim was growing up; he emigrated west and became foreign correspondent for the *New York Tribune* (*Dictionary of American Biography,* S.V. "Poston, Charles Debrill").

7. Charles Edwin Robert, quoted in Alrutheus Ambush Taylor, *The Negro in Tennessee, 1865–1880* (Washington, D.C.: Associated, 1941), 32.

8. *Jeanes Supervision in Georgia Schools: A History of the Program from 1908–1975* (Atlanta: Southern Education Foundation, 1975), 2.

9. Du Bois, *Black Reconstruction,* 665. Those white teachers were assaulted verbally, excluded from white society, and denied service in local businesses. See George C. Wright, *Life Behind a Veil: Blacks in Louisville, Kentucky, 1865–1930* (Baton Rouge: Louisiana State University Press, 1985), 29–30.

10. Du Bois, *Black Reconstruction,* 667.

11. Although Mollie was born October 1, 1872, her parents were not married until she was a year old, probably because of the difficulty of raising the "marriage bond" of one hundred dollars which guaranteed that both parties were free to marry. Joseph Cox and Hettie Pea [*sic*], Marriage Bonds: Negroes and Mulattoes, Book No. 6, Aug. 1873 to Dec. 1874, Commonwealth of Kentucky. The surname of Mollie Cox's mother, Hettie Pea, came from the owners of the Peay plantation. One Peay descendant was governor of Tennessee from 1923 to 1927, years which overlapped Ted Poston's years at college in that state.

12. In *The Dark Side of Hopkinsville* (Athens: University of Georgia Press, 1991), hereafter cited as *DSOH,* Ted says that his father was "the first Negro college graduate in Hopkinsville, Ky.—he'd finished Walden College down in Nashville long before the turn of the century." But *DSOH* is fiction. Frank Lincoln Mather, who edited *Who's Who of the Colored Race, 1915,* surely obtained his information from Ephraim Poston directly. Mather says Eph graduated from Roger Williams University, Nashville, in 1886. Ted's older brother, Robert, attended Walden. Perhaps Ted used "Walden" for Papa, since Roger Williams had ceased existence and Walden had replaced it, absorbed eventually into Meharry Medical College.

13. Wright, *Life Behind a Veil;* 28, 34–35.

14. Ephraim Poston and Mollie Cox, Christian Co. Marriage Bonds and Licenses, Book 10, p. 364, December 22, 1887, Christian County Court, Kentucky.

15. Thomas Sugrue, *There Is a River: The Story of Edgar Cayce* (Virginia Beach, Va.: Association for Research and Enlightenment, 1973), 9–10, 71; also see Emma Parke Wilson, *Under One Roof* (New York: Funk and Wagnalls, 1955), 78–79.

16. Sugrue, *There Is a River,* 51. In 1900 Stevenson ran for vice-president with William Jennings Bryan heading the ticket.

17. Mary D. Ferguson and William T. Turner, *A History of Newspapers of Christian County* (Hopkinsville: Southern Printing, 1980), 19. Ulysses Poston noted the spotty record of the nineteenth-century Democratic presidents on the "Negro problem." James Madison (1809–17) attacked slavery; Martin Van Buren (1837–41) resisted abolition; James Polk (1845–49) said that minorities had rights; Franklin Pierce (1853–57) believed that the federal government should not interfere with the rights of slaveholders; and James Buchanan (1857–61) thought the states should solve their own problems over slavery. Abraham Lincoln was not an abolitionist in Ulysses Poston's opinion but "an excellent statesman and crafty politician"; the abolitionists believed in "immediate freedom with all of the rights and privileges enjoyed by other American citizens," whereas Lincoln thought that the freed slave would "never be granted his constitutional rights" and that his presence was "a source of mutual embarrassment." See Ulysses S. Poston, "How Some Presidents Expressed Their Attitude Toward the Colored Man," *Inter-State Tattler,* March 13, 1925, 4.

18. Wilson, *Under One Roof,* 3.

19. Ferguson and Turner, *History of Newspapers,* 20.

20. Sugrue, *There Is a River,* 69, 38.

21. Charles Mayfield Meacham, *A History of Christian County, Kentucky, from Oxcart to Airplane* (Nashville: Marshall, 1930), 241.

22. Sugrue, *There Is a River,* 70.

23. Alice Allison Dunnigan, *The Fascinating Story of Black Kentuckians* (Washington, D.C.: Associated, 1982), 269.

24. Ulysses S. Poston, "The Political Buzz-Saw: Georgia Goes Lily-White," *Inter-State Tattler,* March 31, 1932, 4.

25. Meacham, *History of Christian County,* 343.

26. Ferguson and Turner, *History of Newspapers,* 20.

27. Wilson, *Under One Roof,* 150–51.

28. *DSOH,* 10.

29. Interview with Johnella Braxton Palmer and Lydia Braxton Moten, July 3, 1983. See bell hooks, *Talking Back: Thinking Feminist, Thinking Black* (Boston: South End, 1989), 10, for how poetry came into a girl's life at Virginia Street Baptist Church.

30. The Church Covenant which Virginia Street Baptist children signed challenges the believer to "walk together in Christian love, to maintain family and secret devotion," to "religiously educate children," to "seek salvation," to "walk circumspectly," be "just in our dealings," to "abstain from intoxicating drink," and to "watch over one another in brotherly love." Ted Poston heeded the covenant except about intoxicating beverages.

31. For example, see *DSOH,* 93.

32. Poston referred to his elementary school as the Booker T. Washington Colored Grammar School, but it was Jackson Street School when he was there and later the Second Street School. Ted was gone before it was renamed for Booker T. Washington (Allison Williams, personal interview).

33. In her big stone house on South Virginia Street, Postell laid "pure white and blue carpets on the floor," according to Williams's aunt Rebecca Clark. Postell and her husband, Peter, were the most prominent citizens in Hopkinsville's black community because of their money and light skin. The promiscuous Peter had inherited the Postell building, which housed a grocery, a feed store, and a saloon, but he eventually lost his inheritance because of gambling and wild living. Postell adored her profligate husband although she was preoccupied with educating the next generation of Hopkinsville's colored society. See Roi Ottley, *New World A-Coming* (Boston: Houghton Mifflin, 1943), 168–69; and Wright, *Life Behind a Veil,* 135.

34. "E. W. Glass," advertisement, *New Age,* April 25, 1924, 2. Allison Williams said: "Ed Glass was a leader among the Negroes. He did a lot of free work. A guy died in The Cedars, a residential section, when I was working for him. Ed said to go get the man and wash him up. 'There's a new suit of long underwear. That's good enough for a county burial—$50.' Then Ed said, 'Hell, no sense putting this clean underwear on him. Mine's full of holes. Where he's going he's not going to need to keep warm anyway. I'll give him mine and take this.' I chuckled, 'Ed Glass, you're a bastard'" (Williams, personal interview).

35. Black businesses were economically marginal; during the Depression, Hopkinsville lost most of them (J. T. Lynch, personal interview).

36. Allison Williams remembers Will Knight's kindness in letting him come in out

of the cold after Williams had become a teenage hobo and was riding on the outside of the train one cold winter day.

37. The house was Number 643 then but has since been renumbered 809. Later, the second story was damaged in a fire; the house was reconstructed as one story.

38. The murder took place on Attucks school corner in April 1919. In "The Werewolf of Woolworth's," Poston claims that the Mays's house was haunted (*DSOH,* 9).

39. See *DSOH,* xxii, and "Mr. Jack Johnson and Me," 1.

40. See *DSOH,* xxviii, 97. To prepare for fishing, Ted's friend Marcus Quarles says, "We got fishing rods off the creek bed and put string and safety pins on them, a cork from a bottle, a marble or BB for a weight, and worms for bait."

41. Sugrue, *There Is a River,* 38.

42. See *DSOH,* xxii, 2, 15, 52, 53.

43. Ferguson and Turner, *History of Newspapers,* 46.

44. Henry Lee Moon, "Ted Poston: A Creative Journalist," *Black Perspective,* Spring 1972, 11–12, 40. Also see "Rat Joiner Whips the Kaiser," *DSOH,* 83–91.

45. Jane Maguire, *On Shares: Ed Brown's Story* (New York: Norton, 1975), 28.

46. Ted Poston (hereafter cited as TP), "Harlem Shadows," review of *Battle of the Bloods,* by John Louis Hill, *Pittsburgh Courier,* March 21, 1931, sec. 1, p. 1.

47. See TP, "Horror in the Sunny South," *New York Post,* September 12, 1949.

48. Board, tuition, and room cost forty dollars a year. Walden students had to adhere to strict social rules. For example, a male student was allowed to talk with a coed "only at the weekly social on Saturday night" (George C. Wilson, "Footprints in the Sand," MS. 7, 1982, Blazer Library, Kentucky State University, Frankfort).

49. Robert L. Poston, "Is There a Race Question in America?" *Negro World,* March 31, 1923, 4.

50. See W. T. Brooks, "Editorial: The End of Education," *Kentucky Normal and Industrial Institute Students' Bulletin* 3 (Frankfort, Ky.: Institute Press, 1916), n.p.; Barksdale Hamlett, *Biennial Report of the Superintendent of Public Instruction of Kentucky for the Two Years ending June 30, 1915* (Frankfort: State Journal, 1915), 85.

51. Mather, ed., *Who's Who of the Colored Race, 1915.* No copies of *Pastoral Poems* have been found. Issues of the *Kentucky New Era,* during premicrofilm days, were stored in the newspaper's basement and destroyed in a periodic flooding of the Little River.

52. On June 3, 1915, John and Fannie Braxton had sold their lot on Hayes Street to E. Poston. But on January 15, 1917, an "indenture," or contract, was recorded in the office of the county clerk, "by and between Mollie Poston and Eph Poston . . . and L. E. Foster and V. E. Barnes" for the "consideration of the sum of One Dollar cash in hand paid." The property was that which Eph Poston had "conveyed" to Mollie on March 1, 1916 (Foster to Barnes, Deed Book 157, p. 376, Christian County Court, Ky.). E. Poston, conveyed to L. E. Foster and Vego E. Barnes property on south edge of Hayes Street, northeast corner of lot 318 (Register of Deeds, Deed Book 122, p. 301, ibid.). Frank and Sara McD. Rives conveyed to Mollie Poston

property on the south edge of Hayes Street (ibid., pp. 302–3). John A. and Annie Gunn conveyed to E. and Mollie Poston property on south side of Hayes Street January 1, 1902 (ibid., Deed Book 108, pp. 1, 2). Also see Deed Book 140, pp. 50–51, ibid. Since Eph and white Vego E. Barnes were both Democrats, probably Eph borrowed money from Barnes, using the property as collateral (Jennie Knight Baker, personal interview). Foster was the superintendent of schools, "thus the employer of all teachers. . . . The dollar mentioned is a legal device only. All deeds tended to be written that way" (Brooks Major, personal interview, Feb. 22, 1984).

53. *DSOH*, 35. The only record of what Robert Poston did during this period is his *Negro World* obituary, which says he "engaged in teaching at the M. & F. College, Hopkinsville, Ky., for four years [until] the call came for men to serve in the world war, [when] he answered and served with credit" ("Distinguished Workers Whose Names Will Adorn Our Honor Roll, No. 6, Robert L. Poston," *Negro World*, October 23, 1923, 4). Robert Poston would have provided the information for this profile.

54. Cause of death was stated as "acute parenchymatous nephritis," which is characterized by albuminuria and high blood pressure. Antibiotics could treat it today (Mollie Poston, age 43, Death Certificate No. 13362, June 2, 1917, Bureau of Vital Statistics, Commonwealth of Kentucky).

CHAPTER 2. END OF INNOCENCE: 1917–1924

1. Billy Goat Hill got its name from the smelly billy goats and the stockyard at the foot of the hill (interviews, Jennie Knight Baker and Allison Williams).

2. Bishop Charles H. Phillips, introduction to Claybron W. Merriweather, *The Voice of the Soul* (N.p.; n.d.), xi.

3. The "Big Six" borrowed the nickname of leaders of the 1920s black Republicans. Mary's "Big Six" are pictured on the cover of the paperback edition of *DSOH*. They are Cudella Gaines; Jennie Knight; Mary; Dorothy Leavell, who married Joseph Stevens and was the sister of Rozelle Leavell, Ted's high school shop teacher; Virginia Bronaugh; Julia Bronaugh, who married M. L. Morrison, of Montgomery, Alabama; and Inez Stuart.

4. *DSOH*, xvi, xxiv, 5, and "The Birth of a Notion," ibid., 72.

5. In 1964 in a profile of Carl Rowan, director of the Voice of America, Ted said that Rowan, in Tennessee, had "mowed lawns, swept basements, unloaded boxcars of coal, dug basements, hoed bulbgrass out of lawns and did scores of other menial tasks that fell to Negroes by default. . . . The community expected it of us" ("Closeup: Carl Rowan, The Next 'Voice of America,'" *New York Post*, January 26, 1964). Ted had worked at similar jobs in Kentucky.

6. *DSOH*, 27, 38, and "High on the Hog," ibid., 62. Uncle John and his wife, Fanny Cox, sister of Mollie Cox Poston, had three daughters and four sons—Alberta Braxton Bell, Iona Quarles, Mary Belle Fleming, and Leslie, Alonzo, James, and John Braxton, Jr. Williams says, "The Braxtons were all short, heavyset and black. Ole

man Braxton was famous through this part of the country for makin' barbecue. There ain't nobody can cook it like he used to. You dug your own pit and put the meat in; the moisture in the ground tenderized it. Now they say you catch germs that way." Uncle John spent the night barbecuing and singing such Christian songs as "Life Is Like a Mountain Railroad." That song's lyrics are "Life is like a mountain railroad, With an engineer that's brave, We must make the run successful, From the cradle to the grave. Watch the curves, the fills, the tunnels, Never falter, never quail, Keep your hand upon the throttle And your eye upon the rail" (Allison Williams, personal interview). Also see Dunnigan, *Fascinating Story,* 25.

7. See *DSOH,* 44–46, 100.

8. In 1924–25, *Caron's Hopkinsville Directory* listed at the 927 Seventh Street residence Amos and Clara Tunks; J. William Tunks, student; Mary L. Tunks, student; and Sarah E. Tunks, no occupation. Christian County historian William T. Turner says, "All the Tunks are deceased now with no living descendants."

9. "Ted used to say, 'I didn't know what in the *hell* to think. I wasn't doing nothing that nobody else wasn't,' but 'I didn't have *time* for nothin' else when I had *her*'" (Allison Williams, personal interview).

10. The doctor's name on the death certificate is illegible, but it does not appear to be Moore, Duncan, Leverett, Mays, or Bassett, the doctors who had played roles previously in the Postons' lives.

11. "Frederick Poston, son, male, black, age 22, single, sailor, marine. Not out of work" (U.S. Census Bureau, Thirteenth Census of the United States, 1910, City of Hopkinsville, File P235, T1266–129, Drawer 518, Kentucky State Archives, Frankfort).

12. Harry A. Ploski and James Williams, eds., *The Negro Almanac: A Reference Work on the Afro-American* (New York: Wiley, 1982), 860, contains a concise list of important dates concerning Negroes and World War I. Du Bois was angered that blacks had to prove their "manhood" through warfare (*Black Reconstruction,* 110).

13. For his later uses of the word, see *DSOH,* 93; and his articles "'Robin Hood of Soviet Zone' Just Imposter from Minnesota," *New York Post,* March 30, 1949, 54; "Fake Robin Hood Also Posed as a Russian Count," *New York Post,* Apr. 1, 1949; "Ted Poston in Alabama: The Negroes of Montgomery," IV, *New York Post,* June 14, 1956; "Letter to an Alabama Editor," *New York Post,* June 24, 1956, 5, 16; "Fighting Pastor: Martin Luther King", III, *New York Post,* Apr. 10, 1957, 4, 65; and "Fighting Pastor: Martin Luther King," IV, *New York Post,* Apr. 11, 1957, 4, 46; "Beckwith's Day in Court: A Smile Suddenly Fades," *New York Post,* Jan. 28, 1964; "Leading Harlem's War on Poverty: Livingstone Wingate, Arthur C. Logan," *New York Post,* July 12, 1964, 24; "Closeup: Unseated Legislator" [Julian Bond], *New York Post,* Jan. 19, 1966, 24; and "Closeup: 'Equal'" [Clifford L. Alexander], *New York Post,* Aug. 2, 1967.

14. William G. Frederick, "Radcliffe to Be in Charge," *Louisville Courier-Journal,* July 25, 1918, 12.

15. TP, "Judge Lynch Presides," *Amsterdam News,* Mar. 23, 1935, 9.

16. Du Bois, *Black Reconstruction,* 645.

17. Arthur E. Barbeau and Florette Henri, *The Unknown Soldier: Black American Troops in World War I* (Philadelphia: Temple University Press, 1974), 61; also see 191.

18. Robert L. Poston, 3,104,018, and Ulysses S. Poston, 3,104,058, World War Historical Record, Kentucky Council of Defense, National Personnel Records Center, Military Records, National Archives and Records Administration, St. Louis, Missouri. The nonbylined feature on Robert Poston, "Distinguished Workers," in Garvey's *Negro World* gave information that could not be confirmed because, according to the Military Personnel Records archivist, "the records were destroyed by fire on July 12, 1973." The *Negro World* account was most likely accurate because both brothers were editors of that paper at the time. Yet when Ulysses died in 1955, Ted supplied the information on him: "In World War I Mr. Poston served overseas for nine months as a sergeant in the Eighth Illinois Infantry. . . . [It was] one of four American Negro regiments under French command. All four received a regimental Croix de Guerre from the French government" ("Ulysses S. Poston, Real Estate Man," *New York Times,* May 16, 1955, 23). Extant official records do not indicate that Ulysses was ever sent overseas.

19. "Distinguished Workers."

20. See Wright, *Life Behind a Veil,* 171, 200.

21. Ottley, *New World A-Coming,* 270–71.

22. That summer was called "Red Summer" across the country because of the bloodbath of race riots in seven major American cities. See Luther P. Jackson, Jr., "Popular Media: Part I, The Mission of the Black Newsman," in *Black American Reference Book,* ed. Mabel Smythe (New York: Prentice-Hall, 1976), 850.

23. "Tallaboo Tonight at Tabernacle," *Kentucky New Era,* May 17, 1920, 5. A search of many African American, state, and local libraries failed to turn up a copy of the script, and Sylvester Russell's review could not be found. Therefore, little is known of the plot. Rebecca Quarles Clark had a copy of the program, which listed Lillian as one actress. It said that the adult Poston brothers initiated and produced the play. Also see "Tallaboo Once More: In Answer to a Request from Prominent White People," *Kentucky New Era,* May 22, 1920, 7; and "What Colored Ministers Say about 'Tallaboo,'" *Kentucky New Era,* May 24, 1920, 5.

24. No copies of the *Hopkinsville Contender* are extant. The *Contender* is not mentioned in the Christian County histories by Perrin, Meacham, or Turner; probably no issue of a *Hopkinsville Contender* was placed in any archive. Issues of the *Detroit Contender* and *New York Contender* are in the Detroit Public Library and the Schomburg Center for Research in Black Culture, New York Public Library, respectively.

25. "Distinguished Workers." Running the *Detroit Contender* was not pain-free; see "And Yet We Smile," *Detroit Contender,* Nov. 13, 1920.

26. The Postons editorialized that people of color had a duty to practice the virtue of hope: "We must stop applauding that apostle of tough luck, who goes upon the

vaudeville stage and sings, 'I feel so blue I dunno what t' do.' Certainly we are not going to give up" ("Quit Singing the Blues," *Detroit Contender,* May 7, 1921, 2).

27. David Levering Lewis, *When Harlem Was in Vogue* (New York: Knopf, 1981), 37.

28. A Poston first appeared in the city directory under the listing, "Ulysses S. Poston, Mgr., Universal Grocery Store, Res. 54 W. 135th," in *R. L. Polk & Co.'s Trow General Directory of New York City, Boroughs of Manhattan and the Bronx, 1922–23* (New York: R. L. Polk, 1922), 1425.

29. John C. Walter, *The Harlem Fox: J. Raymond Jones and Tammany, 1920–1970* (Albany: State University of New York Press, 1989), 40.

30. Quoted in Claude McKay, *Harlem: Negro Metropolis* (New York: Dutton, 1940), 179.

31. McPherson [first name missing], "Tallaboo," *Negro World,* Jan. 21, 1922.

32. Robert A. Hill, et. al., eds., *The Marcus Garvey and Universal Negro Improvement Association Papers,* Vols. 1, 2, 4, 5 (Berkeley: University of California Press, 1986), 5:11. T. Thomas Fortune's biographer feels that his "most important journalistic work during the last years of his life" was as editor of the *Negro World.* From 1879 to 1900, Fortune was "the only national leader the Negro people had" (Emma Lou Thornbrough, *T. Thomas Fortune: Militant Journalist* [Chicago: University of Chicago Press, 1972], 359–60; also see Ottley, *New World A-Coming,* 279).

33. Richard Kluger says the *Sun* was prosperous "but stuck to a kind of backstairs disreputability that kept it beyond arm's length from the educated and the prosperous" (*The Paper: The Life and Death of the New York Herald Tribune* [New York: Vintage, 1986], 80). In the 1930s, the Federal Writers' Project reported that the *Times* was the best all-round newspaper, "a distinction previously held by the *Sun,* in the heyday of Richard Harding Davis," and by the *World* when it had Heywood Broun. "Portrait of Harlem," in *New York Panorama: A Comprehensive View of the Metropolis, Presented in a Series of Articles Prepared by the Federal Writers' Project of the Works Progress Administration in New York City* (St. Clair Shores, Mich.: Scholarly Press, 1976), 304.

34. Hill et al., eds., *Garvey Papers,* 4:878, 1008.

35. Ibid., 787, 789.

36. Ibid., 943.

37. James Scott, *Domination and the Art of Resistance: Hidden Transcripts* (New Haven: Yale University Press, 1990), 94.

38. Hill, et al., eds., *Garvey Papers,* 5:174. Agent Andrew Battle quoted D. T. Tobias as saying that Garvey was "very foolish to make the remarks . . . [that he] would not be responsible for anyone who started out against the UNIA, if they should lose an eye, an arm, a leg, or head. . . . For the UNIA are all over the world and they know you." From the time that the federal Bureau of Investigation began overseeing Garvey, its black agents mingled at the UNIA offices, feigning interest as UNIA members. Battle, for example, would listen, ask questions, then write reports on what he had learned for placement in the files of the precursor to the Federal Bureau of Investigation (ibid., 30).

39. Ibid., xxxiii–xxxiv.

40. Ibid., xxxiii.

41. Ottley, *New World A-Coming,* 75.

42. Robert L. Poston, "The Reason Why I Accepted the Garvey Program," *Negro World,* May 12, 1923, 4. Robert had first published the poem in the army's *Trench and Camp Magazine* during the war.

43. Quoted in Roi Ottley and William J. Weatherby, eds., *The Negro in New York: An Informal Social History* (New York: New York Public Library and Oceana, 1967), 171.

44. Hill et al., eds., *Garvey Papers,* 5:510.

45. Floyd Calvin, "As Able a Young Man as the Race Has Produced," *Negro World,* Apr. 5, 1924, 2. Many poems and eulogies were printed in the *Negro World.* For example, see G. Rupert Christian, "Has Written Name High on Scroll of Negro Endeavor," Apr. 5, 1924, 2; A. H. Bisphan, "His Loss a Bitter Affliction, Says Member of Cambridge," Apr. 5, 1924, 2; and "Eulogies and Resolutions: Bishop McGuire's Sermon," Mar. 29, 1924, 2.

46. Tony Martin, *Literary Garveyism* (Dover, Mass.: Majority, 1983), 73.

47. Ted Poston, "Muslims—Myth or Menace?" review of *The Black Muslims in America,* by C. Eric Lincoln, *New York Post,* Apr. 30, 1961. Chester Himes parodied Garvey in his novel *Cotton Comes to Harlem* (1965; rpt. New York: Vintage, 1988). Himes's protagonist, Deke O'Malley, tried to fleece Harlemites: "The con-man's real genius [was] to keep the suckers always believing. So he had started [a] Back-to-Africa movement, the only difference being when he had got his million [dollars], he was going to cut out—he might go back to Africa, himself" (27). Fern Eckman thinks that Ted disagreed with the whole Garvey movement: "He never mentioned it. Even though he loved his brothers, he was probably embarrassed that they were connected with it." George Trow says: "He wanted to change things and make them better, but not in Africa. Here!" (George Trow and Fern Eckman, personal interview, Oct. 13, 1984).

48. O. H. Bartlett, U.S. FBI Agent, Nashville and Hopkinsville, Report on Theodore R. Poston, Dec. 30, 1940, File No. 77-102.

CHAPTER 3. COLLEGE: 1924–1928

1. The Postons borrowed this motto from a black Hopkinsville newspaper operated by politician Phil H. Brown, using it as a streamer across the top of the *Detroit Contender.* Robert Poston said he had served his journalistic apprenticeship under Brown.

2. Dunnigan, *Fascinating Story,* 222.

3. The Braxton cousins remember "Uncle Ephraim" always getting off the train "with a little brown satchel with two handles. It was *well-worn.* And always, there was a newspaper under his arm."

4. Ted's only written references to Lillian are in "Mr. Jack Johnson and Me" and "The Werewolf of Woolworth's," *DSOH.*

5. Hooks, *Talking Back,* 28–30, 76, 99. Bell hooks would earn a Ph.D. at Stanford, teach at Yale and Oberlin, and is now Distinguished Professor of English at City College of New York. In her works she discusses psychologically detrimental attitudes within Hopkinsville's black community.

6. "Hopkinsville in Brief," *New Age,* Apr. 25, 1924, 1.

7. Jews were portrayed in stereotype; also see Chester Himes, *Lonely Crusade* (1947; rpt. New York: Thunder's Mouth, 1989), 159–60.

8. Regarding shoes, see Alice Allison Dunnigan, *A Black Woman's Experience— From Schoolhouse to White House* (Philadelphia: Dorrance, 1974), 18–19.

9. Du Bois addressed such "stealing" in his study of Philadelphia Negroes: they "take food . . . but they don't consider that stealing, and are perfectly honest about money" (*The Philadelphia Negro: A Sociological Study* [1899; rpt. Philadelphia: University of Pennsylvania Press, 1967]). Williams's aunt Rebecca Quarles Clark used to recite to him and Ted a Paul Laurence Dunbar poem, "Accountability," regarding stealing. See *The Complete Poems of Paul Laurence Dunbar* (1895; rpt. New York: Dodd, 1980), 5.

10. Scott, *Domination and the Art of Resistance,* 188.

11. Charles Ball, quoted in Peter Kolchin, *Unfree Labor: American Slavery and Russian Serfdom* (Cambridge, Mass.: Harvard University Press, 1987), 242.

12. A Holy Ghost priest "used some technical phrase which meant that [such stealing] was a compensatory thing where people had been deprived," Ellen Tarry says. "They saw nothing wrong in helping themselves to the other fellow's worldly goods so as to make up for what they had been deprived of."

13. "Unfortunately, I don't have the retiree's name" (Georgianna Cumberbatch-Lavender, telephone interview).

14. State of Tennessee, *Annual Report of the Department of Education for the Scholastic Year Ending June 30, 1929,* 225, 276.

15. DePauw was also the alma mater of Vernon Jordan, eventual Urban League head, who during his college years became a surrogate son to Mary Duncan Wilson. Gore served as dean from 1927 until 1950, then went to Florida Agricultural and Mechanical University as president, retiring in 1968.

16. John A. Hardin, *Onward and Upward: A Centennial History of Kentucky State University, 1886–1986* (Frankfort: Kentucky State University, 1987), 242.

17. TP, "Harlem Shadows," *Pittsburgh Courier,* Mar. 28, 1931.

18. Poston was "athlete, Beau Brummell and student" (Moon, "Ted Poston").

19. "Eight Links Club," *Radio,* 1926, 66.

20. See "The Revolt of the Evil Fairies," *DSOH,* 92.

21. TP, "Mother's Day Reflections," *Blue and Gold* (Nashville: Tennessee State Agricultural and Industrial Institute, June 1927), 7.

22. The correlation between genius and insanity was in vogue. The *Courier-Journal* reported that "genius and insanity are twin brothers. . . . The master mind has mental and physical degeneration 'in its blood'; certain of the greatest geniuses of the world have lived in madhouses. . . . Buddha, Byron, Schopenhauer . . . hovered on

the brink of insanity. . . . To be creative, as genius is, means to be abnormal. . . . Giants in mind, like giants in body, do not propagate themselves and are generally childless" ("Insanity and Genius Hailed," *Louisville Courier-Journal,* Nov. 3, 1918, 4).

23. Wilma Dykeman and James Stokely, *Seeds of Southern Change: The Life of Will Alexander* (New York: Norton, 1962), 18.

24. Marie Byrd came to the school from 108 Ruby Street, West Philadelphia, Pennsylvania, on September 5, 1926. Her parents were listed on her records as "John Smith" and Mae Byrd. Marie had attended the Sisters' Holy Providence School in Cornwells Heights (Bensalem) for one year previously; she left Rock Castle in February 1928 (Sister Margaret M. O'Rourke, Archivist, Sisters of the Blessed Sacrament, letter to author, Oct. 25, 1991). Eloise Scott Reed says, "Rock Castle had the prettiest girls, many with red hair. A lot of them were daughters of wealthy men from New Orleans." Tarry confirms that Rock Castle "used to be the repository for children of mixed-race relationships, white father, black mother—so most of the students were rather light." Marie's mother had attended Rock Castle before her. By working "in-service" as Mae Byrd did, women "were able to acquire the manners, polish and social graces attendant to upper class behavior" (St. Clair Drake and Horace R. Cayton, *Black Metropolis: A Study of Negro Life in a Northern City* [New York: Harcourt, 1945], 232–33).

25. O'Rourke, letter.

26. John A. Hardin, author of *Onward and Upward* and of *Fifty Years of Segregation: Black Higher Education in Kentucky, 1904–1954* (Lexington: University Press of Kentucky, 1997), was asked whether he found any records of the Postons' employment at West Kentucky Industrial College. He replied that "the best place to [look] . . . would be the Board of Trustees Minutes for West Kentucky Industrial College from 1924 to 1934 (typescript). These documents were listed in the Archives Report of the Kentucky Department of Education (for the years) 1810–1967, catalog number 378.769 We. They *may* be located now at the Kentucky Department of Libraries and Archives, Frankfort. According to a partial copy of these documents, a salary of $810 for nine months work was approved for Mrs. S. E. Poston and $200 for summer school instructor E. Poston on May 5, 1927 (page 75). S. E. Poston appears again on the salary schedule for the 1930–31 school year (page 118) with a payment of $937 for nine month salary. On November 5, 1931, S. E. Poston's name appears on a list of staff due salaries on November 14, 1931. S. E. Poston appears again on July 15, 1932 as one of the deficit salaries" (Hardin, letter to author, Sept. 4, 1992). A trip to the Kentucky state archives did not lead to the Minutes for West Kentucky Industrial College, nor did checks of the Department of Education archives. Ted's widow, Ersa Poston, was asked whether she remembered Eph Poston from Paducah and his employment at the college. She replied, "I'm sorry I do not remember much about Mr. Poston. He always appeared to be 'retired' with Mrs. Susie being the main bread winner" (letter to author, Nov. 7, 1997).

27. "Wanted," *New Age,* Apr. 25, 1924, 2. Ted was one of thousands of educated black men whose only method of earning a living was the railroad. He acknowledged

those limited job opportunities in a 1964 article, "CCNY's Hello and Goodby to Gov. Ross Barnett" (Gene Grove and Ted Poston, "CCNY's," *New York Post,* May 21, 1964). For college students' summer jobs waiting tables and bellhopping, also see Lawrence D. Hogan, "The Gift of Alvin White: Sharing a World That Jim Crow Kept Apart," *Commonweal,* Feb. 10, 1984, 84; Jessie Fauset, *The Chinaberry Tree: A Novel of American Life* (1931; rpt. College Park, Md.: McGrath, 1969), 156; and Drake and Cayton, *Black Metropolis,* 239.

28. Wright, *Life Behind a Veil,* 87. The New York Central claimed that its dining cars were not run for profit: "They exist solely for the convenience and comfort of travelers" ("In the Dining-Car," advertisement, *Detroit Free Press,* Nov. 24, 1920, 22).

29. Williams laughs, saying: "If you worked in a hotel and gave brownskin service, you did whatever the client wanted done. If they wanted you to go get some whiskey, all right. If the lady wanted some lovin', you done that, too." Another way of looking at brownskin service: "A [black] Pullman porter will make the most insipid, insignificant white man feel like the President of the United States" (Bennie Butler, "This Harlem Urge, I," *Inter-State Tattler,* Mar. 10, 1932, 12; also see Gail Lumet Buckley, *The Hornes: An American Family* [New York: NAL, 1986], 119–20. Whites generally accepted "brownskin service" as their due; e.g. see Taylor in Robert Towers, "A Master of the Miniature Novel," review of *The Old Forest and Other Stories,* by Peter Taylor, *New York Times Book Review,* Feb. 17, 1985, 26.

30. David D. Perata, *Those Pullman Blues: An Oral History of the African American Railroad Attendant* (New York: Twayne, 1996), xiv; also see xviii.

31. Claude McKay, *Home to Harlem* (1928; rpt. Chatham, N.J.: Chatham, 1973), 140. On Pittsburgh layovers, the porter or waiter would retire to the sleeping quarters and, "tormented by bed bugs," lie on his berth "on his Negro newspaper spread out to form a sheet" (ibid., 152).

32. TP in Paul L. Fisher and Ralph L. Lowenstein, *Race and the News Media* (New York: Praeger, 1967), 64.

33. A. Porter, "The Voice of the Porter," *Messenger,* Sept. 1927, 205.

34. Andrew Buni, *Robert L. Vann of the Pittsburgh Courier* (Pittsburgh: University of Pittsburgh Press, 1974), 162.

35. Ibid., 138, 178.

36. U. S. Poston delineated his duties with the Universal Negro Improvement Association, his plans, why the venture failed, but that it "in a way did not fail. The young men who were employed as tailors . . . have entered private businesses and have retained the uniform business developed through the organization. . . . Many of the little grocery stores inspired by the association are carrying on" ("Harlem Economist Tells Needs of Community," *Pittsburgh Courier,* Oct. 15, 1927, sec. 1, p. 4).

37. Frank R. Crosswaith, "The Trade Union Committee for Organizing Negroes," *Messenger,* Aug. 1925, 296–97; "Crusading for the Brotherhood," in Philip S. Foner and Ronald L. Lewis, eds., *The Black Workers,* Vol. 6: *The Era of Post-War Prosperity and the Great Depression, 1920–1936* (Philadelphia: Temple University Press,

1981), 206–7; "Toward the Home Stretch," ibid., and "The Porter Asserts His Manhood," ibid., 234.

38. The Dunbar's six separate buildings, six stories high, were grouped around a central garden with a playground for children. It encompassed a whole block between Seventh and Eighth Avenues from 149th to 150th Streets. The Dunbar was conducted on a cooperative basis until 1936, when, "as a result of many defaults in payment," Rockefeller foreclosed (*The WPA Guide to New York City: The Federal Writers' Project Guide to 1930s New York* [New York: Pantheon, 1982]).

39. Jervis Anderson, *This Was Harlem: A Cultural Portrait, 1900–1950* (New York: Farrar, 1982), 138, 189.

40. Theodore R. Poston, Civilian Personnel Record, National Personnel Records Center, St. Louis, Missouri (hereafter cited as CPR).

41. O. H. Bartlett, FBI agent, Nashville and Hopkinsville, Report on Theodore R. Poston, Dec. 30, 1940, File No. 77-102.

42. "Poston of the Post," *Newsweek*, Apr. 11, 1949, 62.

CHAPTER 4. JOURNALISM APPRENTICESHIP: 1928–1932

1. Arthur Krock, *Memoirs: Sixty Years on the Firing Line* (New York: Funk and Wagnalls, 1968), 71; E. B. White, "Here Is New York," *Holiday*, Apr. 1949, 35.

2. Ottley, *New World A-Coming*, 59.

3. Stanley Walker, *City Editor* (New York: Stokes, 1934), 64.

4. The *Contender*, "A Weekly with a Program," sold for five cents. It promoted the five-cent subway fare and better housing in Harlem.

5. TP, with Henry Beckett, Peter J. McElroy, Marcy Elias, Joseph Kahn, Irving Lieberman, and Edward Katcher, "Prejudice and Progress: The Negro in New York," I, *New York Post*, Apr. 16, 1956, 4.

6. George Britt and Peter Kihss, "The Silurians' Story, 1924–1984," *Silurian News*, Apr. 1984.

7. TP, "Harlem Shadows," *Pittsburgh Courier*, Apr. 4, 1931, sec. 2, p. 1.

8. Kluger, *The Paper*, 146.

9. John K. Hutchens and George Oppenheimer, eds., *The Best in the World* (New York: Viking, 1973).

10. E. J. Kahn, *The World of Swope* (New York: Simon and Schuster, 1965), 244; also see Ottley, *New World A-Coming*, 280.

11. Kahn, *World of Swope*, 244. Walton stayed at the *World* until its demise, then joined the *Herald Tribune* to "cover Harlem happenings" and "conduct a column in the Sunday paper on interracial topics of national interest. . . . [He was then] the only member of the Race writing on a New York daily" ("Lester Walton Joins Herald-Tribune Staff," *Chicago Defender*, Mar. 21, 1931, 3). But the *Pittsburgh Courier* noticed that Walton was not receiving bylines for his work ("Walton Gets No By-Line in N.Y. Herald Tribune," Apr. 18, 1931, 4). *Amsterdam News* columnist Romeo L. Dougherty thought Walton "upstage and snobbish" ("My Observations," Aug. 10,

1932, 8). Aubrey Bowser, son-in-law of T. Thomas Fortune and Henry Lee Moon's predecessor as book reviewer at the *Amsterdam News,* responded to Dougherty that Walton's "coming to New York in 1908 raised Negro theatrical criticism to a dignity that it had never had before" and that people who "see the capital N in the word Negro in the daily press do not know what a fight it took to put it there. That fight was begun and carried on by Lester Walton" (Dougherty, "Observations," *Amsterdam News,* Aug. 17, 1932, 8). After serving as "Ambassador Extraordinaire Plenipotentiary to the Republic of Liberia," in 1942, Walton returned and was "boasting that he is going to be the czar of all race relations offices in the Government." Other Negro leaders rebelled because Walton was "a lightweight" and "is no longer conversant with current problems" (R. G. Herrick, confidential memo to Ulric Bell, May 4, 1942, Record Group 208, Box 40, Entry 7, National Archives, Suitland, Maryland).

12. "Broun to Address Hospital Meeting," *Amsterdam News,* Feb. 22, 1933, 1.

13. "Broun Urges Negro to Become Radical," *Amsterdam News,* Aug. 17, 1932, 9.

14. Kahn, *World of Swope,* 241–42.

15. Hutchens and Oppenheimer, eds., *Best in the World,* xx, xxiii.

16. "The Passing of 'The World,'" editorial, *Pittsburgh Courier,* Mar. 7, 1931, 10.

17. Allan Nevins, "Past, Present, and Future," in *The Greater City: New York, 1898–1948,* ed. Allan Nevins and John A. Krout (1948; rpt. Westport, Conn.: Greenwood, 1981), 14. Lena Horne's grandfather Edwin Horne supported his children through his association with the black Tammany organization. He taught for three years in the New York public schools, but "Teaching and writing did not pay black men in the big city—and Tammany did" (Buckley, *The Hornes,* 58–59).

18. Before the union, once a reporter was assigned a story, he or she was expected to "stick with it" as long as was necessary "even if this meant a 15-hour day. Rarely did he receive overtime or compensatory time off." One reporter remembers that "from time to time I would get so tired I could not tumble down to the office and would spend the day in bed; I was always docked for the lost day" (Daniel J. Leab, *A Union of Individuals: The Formation of the American Newspaper Guild, 1933–1936* [New York: Columbia University Press, 1970], 7).

19. For example, see Anderson, *This Was Harlem,* 244.

20. TP, "Harlem Shadows," *Pittsburgh Courier,* Feb. 28, 1931.

21. Richard O'Connor, *Heywood Broun: A Biography* (New York: Putnam, 1975), 178.

22. McKay, *Harlem,* 118.

23. Cab Calloway and Bryant Rollins, *Of Minnie the Moocher and Me* (New York: Crowell, 1976), 71.

24. *WPA Guide to New York City,* 264; "Portrait of Harlem," 146.

25. TP, "Harlem," *New York Post,* July 26, 1964. During Prohibition, Harlem was "a vast gin mill"; in the Depression, "a city of evictions, relief bureaus and bread lines, where half the people lived on 'the Relief.'" Riots "permanently rubbed out" the community as a dwelling place of a "dancing, laughing, happy-go-lucky, child-

like people" (Ann Petry, "Harlem," *Holiday,* Apr. 1949, 110). Harlem was popular among whites who flouted segregation mores: "The most law-abiding get a thrill out of breaking some law. . . . Unlike the white man, the white woman invading Harlem was sympathetic and sought to alleviate" (Bennie Butler, "The Harlem Urge, II," *Inter-State Tattler,* Mar. 17, 1932, 9).

26. Alfred Connable and Edward Silverfarb, "J. Raymond Jones," in *Tigers of Tammany* (New York: Holt, 1967), 340. Also see Ralph Ellison, "The World and the Jug," in *Shadow and Act* (New York: Random House, 1964). When he was with the Work Projects Administration, Ellison was told by a Pullman porter, "Some folks drinks to cut the fool. Some folks drinks to think. I drinks to think" (Ann Banks, ed., *First-Person America* [New York: Knopf, 1980], 250–52). *New York Post* writer Archer Winsten, who is white, spent "two happy years at the Harlem YM" during the Depression, with "hours at the Savoy Ballroom" (letter to author).

27. Quoted in Anderson, *This Was Harlem,* 323.

28. Pauli Murray, *Song in a Weary Throat: An American Pilgrimage* (New York: Harper & Row, 1987), 89; and TP, "Age Meets Youth," in "Harlem Shadows," *Pittsburgh Courier,* Jan. 24, 1931.

29. TP, "Interracial Reporting," speech, Oct. 16, 1968, cassette audiotape by Luther P. Jackson, Jr. Puff pieces were an early form of public relations. The *Inter-State Tattler* scolded the National Negro Business League for wanting publicity in the paper yet not being willing to buy advertising ("The Business League's Inconsistency," editorial, *Inter-State Tattler,* June 23, 1932, 4). Bessye J. Bearden, mother of artist Romare Bearden, was a shrewd Democratic political operative as well as head of the New York bureau of the *Chicago Defender.* She hired Ed Morrow to do legwork and to ghost her column occasionally. In that capacity, he was the recipient of some of the puff pieces' rewards, free passes to entertainments and nightclubs.

30. Bartlett, Report on Poston, and TP, "American," in Fisher and Lowenstein, *Race and the News Media,*

31. Jackson, "Popular Media," 859.

32. TP, "Harlem Shadows," *Pittsburgh Courier,* Jan. 24, 1931. The "stupid" appellation, which Poston used more than once, was probably derived from the *New Yorker*'s popular circulation campaign. A series of ten advertisements, which E. B. White wrote, showed photographs of Sterling Finny and his wife, Flora, window-display mannequins that White "borrowed from Wanamaker's department store and dressed and posed in a variety of situations." The ads parodied "culture-made-easy" advertising prevalent then. In war-between-the-sexes ads, the husband greets his wife, "Good Morning, Stupid!" Readers needed only to subscribe to the *New Yorker* to learn to converse brightly, "exchanging badinage on topics of sport, current events, and the arts" (Scott Elledge, *E. B. White* [New York: Norton, 1984], 134).

33. This was not Ted's problem alone; see Broun's August 11, 1934, column in Heywood Hale Broun, ed., *Collected Edition of Heywood Broun* (Freeport, N.Y.: Books for Libraries Press, 1941), 318.

34. "Harlem Agog over Newspaper 'War,'" *Pittsburgh Courier,* Apr. 25, 1931, 3.

35. On the *Amsterdam News* see TP, "Inside Story: Newspaper Is Mirror of People It Served 25 Years," *Amsterdam News,* Dec. 22, 1934, 3; and Ottley, *New World A-Coming,* 275.

36. St. Clair Bourne said: "I met Henry in 1931 and was just starting on my first newspaper job, with the *New York Age.* In addition to being several years older than I, Mr. Moon also had my great respect when he subsequently contributed stories to the august *New York Times.* This was like winning a Pulitzer Prize. The stature of the *Times* as a model of excellence in literate prose and factual accuracy was such that the acceptance and publishing of Henry Moon's occasional stories automatically established his reputation as an accomplished journalist. In those days, the *Times,* like all the other dailies in New York City, had a lily-white staff" (telephone interview, Dec. 5, 1990). A search of the *Personal Names Index to the New York Times* did not turn up byline pieces by Moon.

37. Henry Lee Moon, interview by Luther P. Jackson, Jr., Columbia University Oral History Project.

38. Petry, "Harlem," 116.

39. Moon, "Ted Poston," 12.

40. Moon, interview by Jackson, 139.

41. Moon, "Ted Poston," 12.

42. Moon, interview by Jackson, 140.

43. Walter White went to see the Roosevelts about the antilynching bill. FDR said he could do nothing because he needed southern votes (Joseph P. Lash, *Eleanor and Franklin* [New York: Signet, 1971], 672).

44. TP, "Judge Lynch Presides," *Amsterdam News,* Mar. 9, 1935.

45. Thurston Lewis, born in 1901, was the son of teachers. When he came to New York City, "I worked with professors of social work at New York University and at the Millbank Memorial Fund where I did a study of Puerto Rican mores of the early 1940s for Mrs. Eleanor Roosevelt, then had a brief foray in the theater before my Russian trip" (Lewis, telephone interview).

46. Moon, interview with Jackson.

47. TP et al., "Prejudice and Progress: The Negro in New York."

48. Robert C. Weaver, "Eulogy for Theodore R. Poston," Benta's Funeral Home, New York, New York, Jan. 14, 1974, in Henry Lee and Mollie Moon Papers, Schomburg Center for Research in Black Culture, New York Public Library.

49. TP, "The Rise of Colored Democracy: Black GOP Begins New Tammany Hall Organization," *Amsterdam News,* Apr. 6, 13, 1932.

50. The *Tattler* wanted abolition of the Eighteenth Amendment (prohibition); a Negro congressman for the Twenty-first Congressional District and a Negro magistrate for the Washington Heights Court of Manhattan; the employment of Negroes as clerks and workers in all establishments in the Negro communities; improved living conditions and normal rents in all Negro communities; nondiscrimination by public utility corporations in the advancement of their employees; and more public schools for children ("*Tattler* Platform," *Inter-State Tattler,* Jan. 14, 1932, 4). Iron-

ically, the *Tattler* advertised its hiring of Ulysses, "U. S. Poston, Writer, Editor, and Political Analyst, Joins the *ITS* Staff Beginning Next Week" (Aug. 6, 1931), yet in March 1932, while Ulysses was writing for the *Tattler,* the paper editorialized against the very type of campaign sheet for which Ulysses made his reputation: " 'Campaign Flashes' that blossom forth like so many Easter lilies five or six months before the election . . . enjoy a brief and precarious existence" ("The Phantom Press Again," *Inter-State Tattler,* Mar. 17, 1932, 4).

51. The Vin Dale Club was not part of Tammany but "a hybrid employment agency and local court of appeals for the Post Office Department employees" (Walter, *Harlem Fox,* 56–57).

52. U. S. Poston, "The Political Buzz-Saw: Mayor James J. Walker, Whole Life and Works Symbolize the Spirit of New York," *Inter-State Tattler,* Feb. 11, 1932, 4.

53. U. S. Poston, "Political Buzz-Saw," *Inter-State Tattler,* Apr. 28, 1932.

54. TP, letter to War Production Board, Apr. 13, 1942, FBI, Record Group 208, National Archives, Suitland, Maryland.

55. U. S. Poston, "The Political Buzz-Saw: Communism and the Negro," *Inter-State Tattler,* May 19, 1932, 4.

56. U. S. Poston, "The Political Buzz-Saw: An Open Letter to Negro Voters," *Inter-State Tattler,* June 9, 1932, 4.

57. Maurine H. Beasley, "T. Thomas Fortune," in *American Newspaper Journalists, 1873–1900,* ed. Perry J. Ashley (Detroit: Gale, 1983), 124. Fortune wrote editorials for the *Negro World* until his death. He decried the necessity of a journalist having to listen to so many people, "often cranks with axes to grind." Addressing the 1926 convention of the National Newspaper Publishers' Association, Fortune criticized the "recent trends in journalism, especially the amount of space devoted to sports and entertainment." He advocated the "supreme importance of the editorial page." Kelly Miller, dean of Howard University, said that Fortune represented "the best developed journalist that the Negro race has produced in the Western World. . . . His editorials were accepted . . . as the voice of the Negro" (Thornbrough, *T. Thomas Fortune,* 363, 364, 367–68).

58. Ibid., 75.

CHAPTER 5. RUSSIA: 1932

1. S. Frederick Starr, *Red and Hot: The Fate of Jazz in the Soviet Union, 1917–1980* (New York: Oxford University Press, 1983), 107.

2. Homer Smith, *Black Man in Red Russia* (Chicago: Johnson, 1964), 22.

3. Faith Berry, *Langston Hughes: Before and Beyond Harlem* (Westport, Conn.: Lawrence Hill, 1983), 168.

4. The cinema was Stalin's "only innocent form of relaxation" (Adam B. Ulam, *Stalin: The Man and His Era* [New York: Viking, 1973], 648). He had his own projection room at the Kremlin, and he made the Politburo members join him in watching films at night. He sat behind them in his own row, making them all nervous. See

Dmitri Shostakovich, *Testimony: Memoirs of Dmitri Shostakovich,* ed. Solomon Volkov (London: Hamilton, 1979), 194; also see Peter Kenez, *Cinema and Soviet Society* (New York: Cambridge University Press, 1992).

5. Dorothy West, interview by Genii Guinier, May 6, 1978, 63, Black Women Oral History Project, Schlesinger Library, Radcliffe College.

6. Smith, *Black Man in Red Russia,* 23.

7. Anna Louise Strong, "A New World in the Caucasus," *Soviet Russia Today,* Nov. 1934, 7.

8. Kennan accompanied, as interpreter, America's first ambassador, William Bullitt, "a young, handsome, sophisticated graduate of Yale who lived on the European continent in the manner of F. Scott Fitzgerald's characters" and who "married John Reed's widow for a while" (George Kennan, speech, Brown University, Providence, Rhode Island, Nov. 18, 1983).

9. West was in a writing group with Harlem Renaissance figures Wallace Thurman and Bruce Nugent, all "totally obnoxious. We . . . stuck together and everybody hated us" (Jane Knowles, "Dorothy West Describes the Harlem Renaissance," *Radcliffe News,* Apr. 1982, 8). Zora Neale Hurston wrote to West when West started *Challenge* that she was "too delighted at your nerve in running a magazine. . . . You have learned at last the glorious lesson of living dangerously." Boston-bred and born (1907), West was raised in the middle class, attended the Boston Latin School, and won a prize for a short story in the *Boston Post* at age seven. Reaching "sweet Harlem," she "realized that for her black people were the interesting people. . . . 'You sat around and talked about the great books and poetry you were going to write,' or rather, 'the women sat and listened and the men talked: the women knew their place.'" (West, interview by Guinier, 73).

10. West, interview by Guinier, 73. Henry Lee Moon proposed to West in Russia, she says, but "I was [already] going with a handsome man."

11. Someone thought Mollie Lewis had been Thurston Lewis's sweetheart on the Russia trip. He says, "Mollie told people that we were brother and sister since we had the same last name. That gave Mollie the protection of a relative to fall back on when it was needed, instead of her standing out as a lone woman" (Thurston Lewis, telephone interview).

12. West described Thompson as a social worker, "a little bitty woman," a chain smoker, who was "out of tune. I was the only one who had any sympathy for her" (Knowles, "Dorothy West").

13. The Moons were the first blacks beyond 105th Street, Cleveland's Superior Avenue ghetto, scene of riots in 1968 (Chester Himes, *The Quality of Hurt: The Autobiography of Chester Himes,* Vol. 1 [New York: Doubleday, 1972], 38).

14. Moon, interview by Jackson, 56.

15. TP, letter to War Production Board, FBI.

16. Langston Hughes, *I Wonder as I Wander* (New York: Hill and Wang, 1956), 70.

17. Her family's friend Olga Smyth remembered Maysie telling her about taking

air baths—no clothes—when she was in Russia, although when her niece knew her, "she was exceedingly modest." Probably Ted also heard of Russian air baths from Maysie. Deborah Stone thinks it was a great frustration for her Aunt Maysie "that her work wasn't recognized." Maysie lived at her father's place—414 West 118th Street—all her life. "She stayed up at night and slept in the day," Deborah says, "her way of making her own space. Maysie's studio had high ceilings, a sooty New York City look. It was a great privilege to go there. When she was at her studio, she was *at work*. It was private" (Deborah Stone, personal interview, May 11, 1992).

18. When Maysie Stone died, her cousin Ellis Kolchin gave her bust of Poston to the Schomburg Center for Research in Black Culture, New York Public Library. In 1992 it was sitting in the chief's office not far from Augusta Savage's bust of W. E. B. Du Bois. Ted Poston was probably introduced to Maysie Stone at Savage's studio. Savage's assistant, Angela Straeter, was another artist and friend of Maysie Stone (Juanita Marie Holland, "Augusta Christine Savage: A Chronology of Her Art and Life, 1892–1962," in *Augusta Savage and the Art Schools of Harlem,* ed. Deirdre L. Bibby [New York: Schomburg Center for Research in Black Culture, 1988], 15).

19. Poston's memoir became *Dark Side of Hopkinsville.* Murray produced *Proud Shoes,* which Poston reviewed, calling it an "extraordinary chronicle" of her American forebears, but he complained that she "tells too little of her own story" (TP, "A Truly American Family," review of *Proud Shoes,* by Pauli Murray, *New York Post,* Oct. 21, 1956). Its sequel, *Song in a Weary Throat,* was more personal but published posthumously, a decade after Poston's death, two years after Murray's own death on July 1, 1985. Murray had been impressed with the bust Stone had sculpted of Poston, for Stone had "caught the essence of his personality, and Ted in clay seemed as alive as Ted in the flesh." Stone also sculpted Murray. Stone's niece says Maysie was usually reticent in talking about herself, except for her childhood, "precious little vignettes about her fears, or her impression of school, and family." When Murray's *Proud Shoes* was republished in 1978, she sent Maysie a couple of reviews with an inscription, "45 years after 'the girl with a thousand faces' told you the first *Proud Shoes* stories" (Pauli Murray, letter to Maysie Stone, July 3, 1978). Murray wrote that her and Stone's "mutual enthusiasm for Ted was an enduring bond" (Murray, *Song in a Weary Throat,* 90).

20. TP, "Retreat to Harlem: Communist Party Purges Ford as Scapegoat for Failure Among Negroes," *New Leader,* Mar. 30, 1940, 4.

21. Moon, "Ted Poston," 12.

22. Locke chaired Howard's Department of Philosophy from 1917 to 1925 and again from 1928 to 1954. Leonard Harris claims that "Langston Hughes was Locke's ideal author" (Harris, ed., *The Philosophy of Alain Locke: Harlem Renaissance and Beyond* [Philadelphia: Temple University Press, 1989] 6, 7). Homer Smith—described as a "clerical worker" in the *Tattler* announcement of the group's departure—wrote, "In mid-ocean the voyagers (tourist class) unexpectedly met and discussed their adventure with Dr. Ralph Bunche and Dr. Alain Locke (first class passengers) on their way to Paris" (Smith, *Black Man in Red Russia,* 24).

23. Moon looked upon Locke as a guru, even though Moon's grade in Locke's course had been "Incomplete." Moon said, "I admire intellect and scholarship. He knew music, art, and literature. His talent was critical, not creative" (interview with author).

24. Locke, letter to Charlotte Mason, June 19, 1932, Locke Papers.

25. Locke, letter to Mason, Aug. 11, 1932, ibid.

26. Locke, letter to Mason, Aug. 25, 1932, ibid.

27. Hughes, *I Wonder as I Wander,* 69.

28. Arnold Rampersad, *The Life of Langston Hughes,* 2 vols. (New York: Oxford University Press, 1986, 1988), 1:243.

29. Gordon A. Craig, "Be Quiet, Father Is Writing," review of *Reminiscences and Reflections: A Youth in Germany,* by Golo Mann, *New York Times Book Review,* Sept. 16, 1990, 15, 16.

30. Smith, *Black Man in Red Russia,* 24.

31. Hughes, *I Wonder as I Wander,* 71.

32. Ibid., 72.

33. Rampersad, *Life of Hughes,* 1:244; also see Dorothy West, letter (penned on brown toilet paper because writing paper in Russia was hard to come by) to Grace and Marie Turner, July 13, 1932, West Papers, Special Collections, Boston University.

34. Smith, *Black Man in Red Russia,* 25.

35. Michael Boyer, "Negrochanski tovarish!" *Old Birmingham* [Alabama broadside], 1991.

36. Hughes, *I Wonder as I Wander,* 75.

37. Rampersad, *Life of Hughes,* 1:244.

38. Hughes, *I Wonder as I Wander,* 73.

39. Rampersad, *Life of Hughes,* 1:245

40. Moon, interview by Jackson; Smith, *Black Man in Red Russia,* 26.

41. Lucile M. Scott says, "Ted told me that story when he found out that I was the first wife of W. A. Scott [founder of the *Atlanta Daily World*]. Ted's big laugh boomed out when he learned who I was. My husband had married Mildred, not knowing. She was his second wife. She got a lot of clothes out of him, then went on back to New York to live with a white girl at an all-girls' school is what I've heard. The woman taught there and they became infatuated with each other" (telephone interview, Sept. 13, 1992). W. A. Scott did not have much luck after he had divorced both her and Mildred Jones. "He married another girl, named Ella, a lovely person. She was nice to my sons and I respected her for that. Then he married the last girl, Agnes. It was reputed that her brother killed W. A., that he was not going to let W. A. treat his sister the way he had treated the other wives. W. A. lived seven days after the shooting. I was his only wife to have children" (Lucile Scott, personal interview, Sept. 15, 1992). Langston Hughes remembered Mildred Jones for her cooking, and he wrote Dorothy West in 1933, "Wouldn't you like to be back in the Mininskaya eating some of that good old bread and gravy Mildred used to make and listening to the thirty being shot over in the Kremlin?" (Langston Hughes, letter to Dorothy West, Dec. 5, 1933, West Papers).

42. Hughes, *I Wonder as I Wander,* 82–86.

43. Ibid., 80, 76.

44. When the group was sent south to Odessa to sightsee while awaiting a fresh script, Poston resumed the nude bathing he had tested in Moscow. Since Hughes did not name names in *I Wonder as I Wander* (94), Rampersad asked some of the principals still alive and learned that it had been Poston and Thurston Lewis who had "willfully defied custom by stripping off their swim suits" (*Life of Hughes,* 1:249).

45. Moon, interview by Jackson.

46. Rampersad, *Life of Hughes,* 1:246. Also see Hughes, *I Wonder as I Wander,* 73–74.

47. Thompson quoted in Rampersad, *Life of Hughes,* 1:246, 249; Smith, *Black Man in Red Russia.* Poston's widow, Ersa, saw Thurston Lewis at Mollie Moon's funeral in 1990. Even at Lewis's then advanced age, Ersa said, "He's gorgeous. He has fair skin and an air of having lived in Europe, a delight."

48. Stalin knew of the extent of peasant opposition to him and of the "disasters caused by forced collectivization," that if the party "became divided and lost its grip over the country, anarchy would follow, and they would be massacred to a man by the infuriated peasants" (Ian Grey, *Stalin: Man of History* [Garden City, N.Y.: Doubleday, 1979], 250–51); also see Ulam, *Stalin,* 345.

49. Robert Cullen, "Report from Ukraine," *New Yorker,* Jan. 27, 1992, 27.

50. Dmitri Sollertinsky and Ludmilla Sollertinsky, *Pages from the Life of Dmitri Shostakovich* (New York: Harcourt, 1980), 66–71. In 1932, Stalin's wife committed suicide after he addressed her "rudely in front of others at the banquet on the 15th anniversary of the October Revolution" (Ulam, *Stalin,* 354–55). In the winter and spring of 1932–33, the people "were in a mood of savage desperation" (Grey, *Stalin,* 255). The theatrical director Meyerhold had put the play *Semyon Kotko* into production, then he was "arrested in the middle of it. . . . The work went on as though nothing had happened. . . . At first everyone shuddered. Each thought: I'm next. Then they prayed . . . that the next one would be someone else" (Shostakovich, *Testimony,* 100).

51. Hughes, *I Wonder as I Wander,* 81. Eisenstein, distinguished by a noble forehead and delicate hands, had eyes that retained a quizzical expression. Herbert Marshall "could never tell whether he was laughing . . . for he possessed a perpetual Mona Lisa smile." In personality, Eisenstein "seemed like a Russian *matriushka*— the carved wooden doll hiding within it another doll" (Marshall, in Sergei M. Eisenstein, *Immoral Memories: An Autobiography,* trans. Marshall [Boston: Houghton Mifflin, 1983], vii). Eisenstein was more enamored of books than any other material possession and had recently returned from America. Coming through London he had filled trunks with volumes from booksellers on Charing Cross Road (Marie Seton, *Sergei M. Eisenstein* [New York: Wyn, 1952], 317).

52. Seton, *Eisenstein,* 116. Eisenstein had studied Toussaint L'Ouverture while he was in America and "desired to express his admiration of the Negro people" (ibid., 317). "If a race is biologically and psychologically inferior in its roots such a man [as Toussaint] could not appear in its midst," Eisenstein said. He had hoped he could

make arrangements to work with Paul Robeson, whom he had not met but of whom he had heard a great deal, yet he was "shy about approaching Robeson as a stranger" (ibid., 116–17).

53. Kennan described entertaining in Russia that year: "There is a relaxed atmosphere where people don't care if homes, apartments, are shabby. There is endless talk. We ice-skate down the Moscow River from rink to rink." When Stalin's purges began, "Soviet society was being crushed" (Kennan, speech). Eisenstein's apartment at Chistye Prudi 23 had "fallen into decay," a North American visitor, Marie Seton, reported. "The paint on the stairway was chipping off; the shallow stone stairs had many cracks and the bell . . . was broken." A "wizened peasant woman dressed in rusty black with a kerchief over her head opened the door," Tyotya, Eisenstein's former teacher, who had taught him to love simple people. Upon request for "Tovarish Eisenstein, she grunted, moved back and pointed to a door down a narrow passage lighted by a dim and naked electric bulb." The apartment "gave the impression of a medieval cell. . . . Two bare, uncurtained windows faced the street. The other three walls were lined with bookshelves reaching from floor to ceiling. . . . Squeezed in beside the bed . . . was a rickety little table with a reading lamp" (Seton, *Eisenstein*, 251–52).

54. There were exceptions to the rule of poverty in Russia. Sculptor Sergei Dmitrievich Merkurov and his wife, Asta, lived well. In their youth they had cycled through Europe practically penniless, but when Stalin came to power, the old statues of tsars and national heroes were torn down and replaced with new monuments to revolutionaries. Merkurov became "one of Moscow's wealthiest men, owing largely to the great number of Lenin and Stalin statues he had produced which stood in city squares all over the land" (Suzanne Rosenberg, *A Soviet Odyssey* [Toronto: Oxford University Press, 1988], 54–55). Dorothy West wrote a sketch of the evening, "An Adventure in Moscow," in *The Richer, the Poorer* (New York: Doubleday, 1995), 205–10.

55. Tracy B. Strong and Helene Keyssar, *Right in Her Soul: The Life of Anna Louise Strong* (New York: Random House, 1983), 54; Barbara Wilson, introduction to *I Change Worlds: The Remaking of an American*, by Anna Louise Strong (1935; rpt. Seattle: Seal Press, 1979), vii, x. "Simplistic vigor" was a part of Strong's "charm" (Martin B. Duberman, *Paul Robeson* [New York: Knopf, 1988], 541). In Moscow, colleagues described Strong "as full of energy as a young girl. . . . She will raise hell with anyone from the telephone operator to the Central Committee of the Party in order to get what she wants" (Strong and Keyssar, *Right in Her Soul*, 158).

56. Anna Louise Strong, "15 Years of Moscow," *Moscow News*, Nov. 15, 1932, 5.

57. Strong and Keyssar, *Right in Her Soul*, 151. Ed Falkowski, a Kentucky miner turned writer and a member of the *Moscow News* staff, wrote a humorous story on "the difficulties of finding an apartment in Moscow," but it was blue-penciled out as "slander" (ibid., 152; also see Harvey O'Connor, "I Worked on the *Moscow Daily News*," *Soviet Russia Today*, Nov. 1934, 10).

58. Strong and Keyssar, *Right in Her Soul*, 154. TP told of the episode at the

fifteenth Headliner Banquet at Lincoln University, Missouri, when he accepted a human relations citation for the *Post*. His account was republished as "Poston Thrilled by Sell-Out Edition" in *Editor and Publisher,* Apr. 20, 1963, 146. But it could not be determined whether an issue of the *Moscow News* with such a streamer headline actually existed. Some issues of the paper are extant in archives but none has turned up for August or September 1932, around the time of Jimmy Walker's resignation as mayor of New York, when TP and Moon were in the Union of Soviet Socialist Republics.

59. Lawrence D. Hogan, *A Black National News Service: The Associated Negro Press and Claude Barnett, 1919–1945* (Cranbury, N.J.: Associated University Press, 1984), 48. Politicians would pay Barnett well for "the access he could offer to a press that spoke to the voters they wanted to reach" (ibid., 27). Apparently U. S. Poston used money the Democratic party allotted him for public relations and paid Barnett for positive coverage in the black press syndicate. Tall, distinguished-looking Claude Barnett was a protégé of Richard Warren Sears, founder of Sears-Roebuck. Barnett's mother had worked for Sears; she "chose families who had a library" so her son "could read and have access to the library" (Etta Moten Barnett, interview by Ruth Edmonds Hill, Feb. 11, 1985, Black Women Oral History Project, Schlesinger Library, Radcliffe College).

60. Claude A. Barnett, letter to T. R. Poston, Mar. 2, 1932, Barnett Papers.

61. After the film was canceled, the group was moved from the Grand Hotel to the Mininskaya, across the street from the Kremlin, more of a flophouse than a hotel, Homer Smith says. The hotel was probably named for Kuzma Minin, "the butcher who drove out the Poles in 1613" (Nellie M. H. Ohr, personal interview). Dorothy West said, "Henry and another man were in a bar one night when they overheard Hugh Cooper, the American who was building that incredible Dneprostroi Dam, say that if the Russians went ahead and made the movie denigrating the way Americans treated blacks, he would never finish the dam."

62. Moon, personal interview, July 15, 1982; and Moon, interview by Jackson.

63. TP, "One-Man Task Force" [Henry Lee Moon], *New York Post,* June 7, 1948, sec. 2, p. 1.

64. Hughes, *I Wonder as I Wander,* 98; Rampersad, *Life of Hughes,* 1:250; also see "Soviet Abandons Negro Photoplay," *Amsterdam News,* Aug. 17, 1932, 3; "Four Actors Balk at Russian Movie," *Chicago Defender,* Sept. 3, 1932, 7; "Soviet Film Actors Enjoying Stay in Russia," *Amsterdam News,* Sept. 21, 1932, 8; "Amsterdam News Reporters Reveal Why Soviet Russia Dropped Film Project," *Amsterdam News,* Oct. 5, 1932, 1, 2; "Players Denounce Attack on Soviet," *Amsterdam News,* Oct. 26, 1932, 16.

65. West stayed on in Russia and said "that was my very happy year." She got "a little contract with one of the movie studios in Moscow," then she, Hughes, and Jones wanted to go to China. She asked her interpreter "to break my contract . . . 'because Mildred and Langston and I want to fly to China.' The interpreter said, 'Are you a bird?'" (West, interview by Guinier, 70). Mollie Lewis went back to Berlin to

study, according to Himes's autobiography. Thurston Lewis says, "Mollie stayed in Germany for four years. She returned to the U.S. in early 1937 after furthering her pharmaceutical studies at the University of Berlin" (Lewis, telephone interview, 1993; and letter, Feb. 23, 1993).

66. "A few years after we returned, Loren Miller said he had made an error in taking so strong a position on the side of the Communists. . . . He's a bright guy . . . a good judge until his death. . . . He represented us [NAACP] in some of our Supreme Court cases" (Moon, interview by Jackson).

67. "We went to Russia for the adventure of it . . . but we had faith in the USSR. We believed that they were out to aid us in our crusade for equality in America [but] when it comes to the acid test, they dump us" (ibid.). For the *Nation* magazine, Moon explained the trip from a political perspective ("A Negro Looks at Soviet Russia," *Nation*, Feb. 28, 1934, 244–46). Apparently a movie named *Black and White* was made in 1934; *Soviet Russia Today*, Nov. 1934, 16, carried a picture captioned "Arley Teets, American negro radio singer, plays the leading role in the recently finished Soviet film, *Black and White*." In 1936, Lovett Forte-Whiteman "was purged from the Communist party and disappeared in Moscow" (Starr, *Red and Hot*, 105).

68. TP, letter to Gould, Apr. 6, 1942, FBI file.

69. FBI agent W. D. Dunne reported that when Ted had lived with his brother the lease was in Ulysses' name. "The rent was slow in coming in," but "that factor was not applicant's responsibility," for he had "always been a desirable tenant in every sense" (W. D. Dunne, FBI Agent, Special Inquiry, Advisory Committee to the Council of National Defense, Jan. 8, 1941).

CHAPTER 6. NEW DEAL AND NEWSPAPER GUILD: 1932–1935

1. Frank R. Crosswaith, "The Political Future of the Negro," Negro Labor News Service, in Philip S. Foner and Ronald L. Lewis, eds., *The Black Worker*, Vol. 6: *The Era of Post-War Prosperity and the Great Depression, 1920–1936* (Philadelphia: Temple University Press, 1981), 393; O'Connor, *Heywood Broun*, 179. Norman Thomas, like Garvey, was inspired by the Irish freedom movement. Thomas knew Harlem; he, his wife, and six children had been residents there for "seven crowded, happy years" (ibid., 50, 83).

2. Ulysses S. Poston, "An Ideal Ticket," *New York Contender*, Oct. 22, 1932.

3. "Pork" in politics, a concomitant of patronage, led to the coining of the term "pork-chop-ology" by Charlie Payne when he was championing Ferdinand Q. Morton of the United Colored Democracy, the organization U. S. Poston and J. Raymond Jones opposed. In his detailed history of the United Colored Democracy, Poston referred to "Charles (Pork-chop-ology) Payne for spending his own money for a specially-constructed speaking car from which to deliver a speech, 'Politics isn't the science of psychology or etymology—it is the science of pork-chop-ology'" (T. R. Poston, "The Rise of Colored Democracy," *Amsterdam News*, Apr. 6, 1932). He

who gets "pork" for his constituents wins the elections. J. Raymond Jones remembered the phrase as "beef-stew-ology" (Walter, *Harlem Fox,* 58). J. Raymond Jones says that the election of a black judge, James S. Watson, "did not mean that much had changed at the district level. This was illustrated by the case of Sybil Bryant Poston . . . the wife of our acknowledged chief, U. S. Poston." After the election of Judge Watson, "Mrs. Poston indicated her desire to be Watson's secretary, a patronage position, in which the secretary actually served as an administrative aide. The salary was far above that of a secretary, and what with generous vacation time and other little perquisites, it was a job to be desired. My colleagues and I, now that we quickly learned how the system worked, felt it was only fair to U. S. Poston to support his wife for the job, and at the suggestion of Judge Watson, I headed a delegation to see our district leader, Mr. McCormick, about the matter. . . . McCormick's reply was that if he were given the authority to choose the secretary, it would go to someone who had supported him all these years. What he meant was that the position would go to a white person" (ibid., 52).

4. Lash, *Eleanor and Franklin,* 326, 668–69, 470. Eleanor Roosevelt was independent in her activities and opinions. She asked President Roosevelt whether her advocacy of the antilynching bill would hurt his efforts to get southern votes for his rearmament program. He told her, "You go right ahead and stand for whatever you feel is right" (ibid., 599).

5. Walter, *Harlem Fox,* 55.

6. Dykeman and Stokely, *Seeds of Southern Change,* 193.

7. Quoted ibid.

8. Moon, interview by Jackson, 169. *Polk's New York City Directory—Boroughs of Manhattan and the Bronx, 1933–1934* (New York: R. L. Polk, 1933), 2647, shows the address of the three Postons—"Theo," "U. S.," and "Sybil"—as 2588 Seventh Avenue. Sybil's job is "typist, courts," which could be an alternative patronage position to that she sought with Judge Watson. "Theo's" job is "reporter, *New York Amsterdam News*"; and U. S. is "reporter, *Inter-State Tattler,* 224 West 135th." FBI agent Dunne found that Sybil was a "stenographer in the City Courts building at 32 Franklin Street."

9. U. S. Poston, "Relief Ahead for Home Owners," *Amsterdam News,* July 19, 1933, 3, 9, contains an analysis of the new Home Loan Bank bill. This appears to be Ulysses' last published piece, at least with a byline.

10. See Carl Carmer, "From Wyck to O'Dwyer," in *The Greater City: New York, 1898–1948,* ed. Allan Nevins and John A. Krout (1948; rpt. Westport, Conn.: Greenwood, 1981), 98; and "Portrait of Harlem," 148. U. S. Poston's assistant, J. R. Jones, was surprised the first time he saw a political payoff, but "I grew wiser from reading and experience" and "found that what I thought was a random payoff . . . was routine" (Walter, *Harlem Fox,* 45). Corrupt practices in Harlem gave TP front-page stories when he started at the *New York Post.* Unlike white investigative reporters, he could get inside the gaming houses of Harlem because of his protective coloration.

11. The usual gathering place for Harlem politicians was Herbert Bruce's tavern at Seventh Avenue and 137th Street (Connable and Silverfarb, "J. Raymond Jones," 339). In 1935 Bruce was elected the first black Tammany district leader, which Jones called "satisfying" for "he and I had been undergraduates . . . at the Pennsylvania Station Red Cap Political College. His election meant that [our] dreams . . . were not so farfetched" (Walter, *Harlem Fox*, 60–61). Jones recollected long afterward that his move, by 1963, into the leadership of Tammany started with "our little group of U. S. Poston, Captain Gaines, Chick Jones," all "refugees from the UNIA" (ibid., 49–51; also see TP, "Prejudice and Progress in New York: The Negro in Politics, *New York Post*," Apr. 25, 1956.

12. The rest of the story of the ham, according to Moon: "His wife was there to grab it. They caught up with him and the thief's alibi was, 'I don't know what it is but every time I pass, that woman there says shit to me so I pick up the first thing I can find and throw it at her'" (Moon, interview by Jackson).

13. Quoted in Dan T. Carter, *Scottsboro: A Tragedy of the American South* (Baton Rouge: Louisiana State University Press, 1979), 351.

14. Buni, *Robert L. Vann*, 235.

15. Carter, *Scottsboro*, 243, 248–49.

16. TP, "Interracial Reporting"; Moon, "Ted Poston," 12. Cab Calloway, whose band toured the South, said that Negroes were not allowed to stay in the hotels where they played, so "everywhere we went the company had a list of Negro families. . . . These beautiful folks would rent a room and feed us some of the best damned cooking around for $10 a week" (Calloway and Rollins, *Of Minnie the Moocher and Me*, 55).

17. Doris Willens, "Adventures of a Negro Reporter," *Editor and Publisher*, Sept. 24, 1949, rpt. in *Negro Digest*, Dec. 1949, 15; also TP, "Interracial Reporting."

18. TP, "Interracial Reporting."

19. Moon called Leibowitz's defense of the Scottsboro boys "thorough, brilliant, and unanswerable. . . . All this, however, meant nothing to the insensitive Alabama backwoodsmen who composed the jury" (*Balance of Power* [New York: Doubleday, 1948], 124); also see Moon, "Ted Poston"; TP, "Interracial Reporting"; and TP, "The American Negro and Newspaper Myths," in *Race and the News Media*, ed. Paul L. Fisher and Ralph L. Lowenstein (New York: Frederick A. Praeger, 1967), 66.

20. Lydia Braxton Moten and Johnella Braxton Palmer, personal interviews.

21. "New Harlem Press Club Organizes," *Inter-State Tattler*, Feb. 25, 1932, 2.

22. J. B. S. Hardman, introduction to Len Giovannatti, *Sidney Hillman, Labor Statesman* (New York: Amalgamated Clothing, 1948), 22.

23. Matthew Josephson, *Sidney Hillman, Statesman of American Labor* (Garden City, N.Y.: Doubleday, 1952), 52; T. H. Watkins, *Righteous Pilgrim: The Life and Times of Harold L. Ickes, 1874–1952* (New York: Holt, 1990), 142.

24. Georgetta Merritt Campbell, *Extant Collections of Early Black Newspapers: A Research Guide to the Black Press, 1880–1915, with an Index to the Boston Guardian, 1902–1904* (Troy, N.Y.: Whitston, 1981), 1.

25. Scott, *Domination and the Art of Resistance*, 11.

26. "Thelma Berlack Wins Walker Scholarship," *Inter-State Tattler,* Mar. 13, 1925, 10.

27. Theodore R. Poston, CPR.

28. White reporters earned little, but black reporters earned less. White newspeople in 1935 averaged $38 per week. One perquisite they sought was a group health plan. Because of the stresses of the job, they had higher sickness and mortality rates than other professionals. Eye trouble was pervasive, and according to one insurance man, who did not want to be identified, cirrhosis of the liver was a particular hazard. Union proponents argued that newspeople could not afford to go to the doctor, but with a group health plan, they could get care earlier, and with group health, families would not be devastated when ill health did hit (Jean Lyon, "Group Medicine: I. Size of Our Headaches," *Guild Reporter,* Aug. 1, 1936, 7).

29. Wagner's willingness to stand up for the Negro, Moon has pointed out, was noteworthy in 1930, when President Hoover nominated a southern Republican judge, John Johnston Parker, for the Supreme Court: "Although the influence of the Negro protest was generally recognized," only Wagner "deigned" to mention it on the floor of the Senate (Moon, *Balance of Power,* 111).

30. Kluger, *Paper,* 271–72.

31. Broun, ed., *Collected Edition,* 297, column for August 7, 1933, in *World-Telegram;* O'Connor, *Heywood Broun,* 184.

32. Leab, *Union of Individuals,* 58–60.

33. Kluger, *Paper,* 271–72.

34. TP, "Interracial Reporting." Randeau became president of New York Guild.

35. Moon, "Farewell to Heywood Broun," *Crisis,* Feb. 1940, 52.

36. William O'Dwyer, *Beyond the Golden Door,* ed. Paul O'Dwyer (Jamaica, N.Y.: St. John's University, 1987), 131–32.

37. Charles Lionel Franklin, *The Negro Labor Unionist of New York: Problems and Conditions Among Negroes in the Labor Unions in Manhattan with Special Reference to the N.R.A. and Post-N.R.A. Situations* (1936; rpt. New York: AMS Press, 1968), 210. TP picketed for fellow Guild members at the *Newark Ledger.* So did Broun's son Woodie, for one evening. Woodie's moment of glory went awry because the police were so fond of Broun that they refused to arrest his son (Heywood Hale Broun, *Whose Little Boy Are You? A Memoir of the Broun Family* [New York: St. Martin's, 1983], 168). For a contemporaneous discussion of the strike, see "Newspaper Employees Dismissed," *New York Age,* Oct. 12, 1935, 1; "Announcement," *Amsterdam News,* Oct. 19, 1935, 1; and "Famous Columnist Files $250,000 Libel Action for Story in Local Weekly," *New York Age,* Oct. 26, 1935, 1.

38. Percival L. Prattis, letter to Claude Barnett, Oct. 18, 1935, "P. L. Prattis, 1924–1936 file," Box 138, folder 9, Barnett Papers.

39. Leab, *Union of Individuals,* 234.

40. See ibid., 233, and Henry Lewis Suggs, *P. B. Young, Newspaperman: Race, Politics, and Journalism in the New South, 1910–1962* (Charlottesville: University Press of Virginia, 1988), 148–49, for more on blacks and the Guild.

41. TP, "Negro Press," n.d., Record Group 208, Box 40, National Archives.

42. *"Amsterdam News* Strike," editorial, *Crisis,* Mar. 1936, 81.

43. Leab, *Union of Individuals,* 234; Ottley and Weatherby, eds., *Negro in New York,* 284.

44. Twenty years later he recollected the history of that committee in a clear-sighted analysis (Crosswaith, "The Negro Labor Committee," speech, Mar. 6, 1952, in Philip S. Foner and Ronald L. Lewis, eds., *The Black Worker,* Vol. 7: *The Black Worker from the Founding of the CIO to the AFL-CIO Merger, 1936–1955* [Philadelphia: Temple University Press, 1983], 538–539). After World War I, Crosswaith attended the Socialist Rand School of Social Service in lower Manhattan, then taught there for many years (Foner and Lewis, eds., *Black Worker,* 6:598; also see Foner and Lewis, eds., *Black Worker,* 7:541). Crosswaith helped Randolph get the Brotherhood of Sleeping Car Porters recognized, and Randolph paid tribute to Crosswaith for his "instrumental genius, spirit, courage, and fortitude, devotion and loyalty to the cause of the worker." So obdurate was Crosswaith that blacks must pay and be paid a living wage that he came out against Father Divine for "undercutting the average wage standards" (McKay, *Harlem,* 64). Crosswaith laid the groundwork for the *Amsterdam News* reporters to join the American Newspaper Guild (Leab, *Union of Individuals,* 6).

45. TP and Frank Crosswaith, letter to Friends of the Newspaper Guild of New York, Oct. 11, 1935, Spingarn Papers, Moorland-Spingarn Research Center, Howard University.

46. Moon, "Farewell to Heywood Broun"; Leab, *Union of Individuals,* 234.

47. Leab, *Union of Individuals,* 234.

48. Thomas Kessner, *Fiorello H. LaGuardia and the Making of Modern New York* (New York: McGraw-Hill, 1989), 371. Delaney's sisters, Sara and Bessie, as nonagenarians would write a best-selling autobiography, *Having Our Say* (New York: Farrar, 1993).

49. On Thursday, November 14, 1935, Crosswaith said on radio station WEVD, "In one of the few instances when the Citizens Committee was able to talk to Mrs. Davis in the presence of attorney Aiken Pope, it was apparent . . . that Mrs. Davis could be convinced of the justice of her employees' claim to exercising the right of collective bargaining if she was not so dependent upon the advice of her . . . attorney. . . . Attorney Pope not only showed poor taste but became so indignant even to become offensive to the citizens who had volunteered their services in an effort to settle the dispute." See "Newspaper Strike in 6th Week," *New York Age,* Nov. 23, 1935; and "Newspaper Employees Dismissed," *New York Age,* Oct. 12, 1935, 1.

50. Quoted in Ottley and Weatherby, eds., *Negro in New York,* 285.

51. Quoted in Leab, *Union of Individuals,* 236. The day-by-day struggle can be followed in the pages of the *New York Age* and the *Pittsburgh Courier* from October through December 1935.

52. When St. Clair Bourne was chairman of the Guild unit at the *Amsterdam News* for three years, "Powell and I got to be favorite enemies." When Bourne's son set off for Syracuse University to study journalism, his father warned, "Oh, don't go in the newspaper business. You'll starve to death" (Bourne, personal interview).

53. FBI Agent W. D. Dunne, Special Inquiry, Advisory Committee to the Council of National Defense, Jan. 8, 1941.

54. I could not locate Miriam Rivers. Archer Winsten thought that she was living in Arizona in the 1980s, "when I last heard from her younger sister, Cleota 'Dee' Rivers, who used to have an apartment in lower Manhattan and was employed in the welfare organization of the city" (Winsten, letter to author, July 22, 1987).

55. Bourne says that Rouzeau was a competent reporter. He contributed stories to the *New York Daily News* during the strike but was fired once the strike was settled. "Some years later I found him running a small candy store in Brooklyn" (Bourne, personal interview).

CHAPTER 7. FEDERAL WRITERS' PROJECT: 1936–1940

1. Miriam Rivers Poston became less squeamish in time and went into nursing (Moon, personal interview).

2. An unidentified female source for Poston's FBI report in 1941 said that she was "not necessarily prejudiced in his favor" but that she was on "much better terms" with Poston's wife, Miriam. She had overheard that Poston "engaged in a fistfight on Broadway as the result of some comment made by a white man where the term 'nigger' was used; that he was extremely quick-tempered, and that he had been in a number of fistfights" (Dunne, Special Inquiry).

3. Himes, *Lonely Crusade,* 143, 39.

4. TP et al., "Prejudice and Progress: The Negro in New York."

5. FBI agent Dunne wrote: "——— [name deleted] stated that applicant [Poston] and his wife" had resided there for "approximately one year ending sometime in 1936, and that they had shared apartment 11-B with ——— paying a monthly rental of $85, the lease being in the name of ———. Applicant was described as a sober tenant whose business was unknown." The fourteen-story "409," as it was known, was home to such people as Du Bois, Thurgood Marshall, and Walter White (Anderson, *This Was Harlem,* 345).

6. Years later Langston Hughes, recalling rent parties, could "still hear their laughter in my ears, hear the soft slow music, and feel the floor shaking as the dancers danced" (Hughes, *The Big Sea* [1940: rpt. New York: Hill, 1963], 233). Also see TP, "Socialist Uncovers Something New in Harlem—The House Rent Party," *Amsterdam News,* Mar. 16, 1935, 2; Lewis, *When Harlem Was in Vogue,* 107; and Banks, ed., *First-Person America,* 252–54.

7. See TP, "Pickets Fight Rent Boost as House Is Opened for Negroes," *Amsterdam News,* July 13, 1935, 1, 2.

8. FBI agent Dunne (Special Inquiry) said that bank records revealed TP opened a checking account in February 1939, which he maintained until December 1940, when he withdrew all but two dollars from the account, which remained credited to him. Dunne pointed out that "this bank account was opened while the applicant was still on the relief rolls."

9. A dispossess order was served on Poston on April 3, 1940. He and Miriam had

rented apartment 4-H on November 15, 1938, and resided there until April 10, 1940. The informant recalled Poston as being "quiet and businesslike" (ibid.).

10. Moon thought that Ted and Ming were divorced by 1938 but added, "Don't hold me to that date." Tarry calculated 1939 or 1940 because they were still together when Tarry's book *Janie Belle* was published, even though "they may not have been lovin' each other" then.

11. FBI Report 77-1244, Theodore R. Poston, Jan. 31, 1942.

12. "Strike Chairman," photo caption, *Guild Reporter* (American Newspaper Guild) 1, no. 2, Jan. 1, 1936): 2.

13. See Franklin, *Negro Labor Unionist,* 154, for the Harlem Labor Committee's six goals.

14. *Dictionary of American Biography,* s.v. "Crosswaith, Frank." Crosswaith was executive secretary of that organization until he joined the Brotherhood of Sleeping Car Porters full-time.

15. Franklin, *Negro Labor Unionist,* 155–57.

16. "Negro Labor Conference, July 20, 1935," in Foner and Lewis, eds., *Black Worker,* 6:551–52.

17. Himes, *Lonely Crusade,* 138–39.

18. FBI Report 77-1244. The Harlem Labor Committee is also called, in the records, the Negro Labor Committee.

19. Du Bois, *Black Reconstruction,* 22.

20. Gilbert Ware, *William Hastie: Grace Under Pressure* (New York: Oxford University Press, 1984), 38.

21. Ed Morrow, telephone interview; also see Ware, *William Hastie,* 38.

22. Ottley and Weatherby, eds., *Negro in New York,* 288–89.

23. Lash, *Eleanor and Franklin,* 460 and 605.

24. Savage established the Harlem Artists Guild in 1935; in 1936 as assistant supervisor on the Federal Arts Project, she organized classes in a renovated garage in back of her private brownstone. See Deirdre L. Bibby, *Augusta Savage and the Art Schools of Harlem* (New York: Schomburg Center for Research in Black Culture, 1988), 8; Ellen Tarry, *The Third Door: The Autobiography of an American Negro Woman* (1955; rpt. Tuscaloosa: University of Alabama Press, 1992), 133. Romare Bearden said Savage "poured out her warmth and enthusiasm" on the gifted children of Harlem (Anderson, *This Was Harlem,* 273). Also see Holland, "Augusta Christine Savage," 18; Ellen Harkins Wheat, *Jacob Lawrence, American Painter* (Seattle: University of Washington Press, 1986), 44–45, 65; and *Dictionary of American Negro Biography,* s.v. "Augusta Savage."

25. Darlene Clark Hine, Elsa Barkley Brown, and Rosalyn Terborg-Penn, eds., *Black Women in America and Historical Encyclopedia,* Vol. 1 (Bloomington: Indiana University Press, 1993), 124. During its life span, from 1935 to 1944, the National Youth Administration offered young people, ages sixteen to twenty-four, job placement services and work relief. When defense became the country's preoccupation, NYA trained youth for war production jobs. During its final year, it transported trained youth to areas of labor shortages, then housed them temporarily in regional

induction centers while they learned the ways of a new community. It established the concept of direct federal assistance to youth.

26. Banks, ed., *First Person America,* xiii.

27. See Tarry, *Third Door,* 106–7. Roi Ottley and Adam Clayton Powell, Jr., set up an Emergency Relief Bureau at the Abyssinian Baptist Church to "care for the thousands of Harlemites who were out of work."

28. Orrick Johns, *Time of Our Lives: The Story of My Father and Myself* (1937; rpt. New York: Octagon, 1973), 342–43.

29. Jerre Mangione, *The Dream and the Deal: The Federal Writers' Project, 1935–1943* (Boston: Little, Brown, 1972), 158, 138.

30. Johns, *Time of Our Lives,* 347. Hopkins was not sensitive to the implications of racial discrimination. See Jane Motz, "The Black Cabinet: The Negroes in the Administration of FDR" (M.A. thesis, University of Delaware, 1964), 65; Lash, *Eleanor and Franklin,* 661; and Jonathan Daniels, *White House Witness, 1942–1945* (New York: Doubleday, 1975), 39, 197.

31. See Wheat, *Jacob Lawrence,* 59, for Lawrence on McKay. Cafe Society, a political cabaret, was started as a money-raising vehicle for the American Communist party (Buckley, *The Hornes,* 141).

32. Moon, TP, Philip Rahv, Harry Roskolenkier, et al., letter "To the Workers on the Federal Writers Project," n.d., Moon Papers.

33. Mangione, *Dream and the Deal,* 184–85.

34. Tarry, *Third Door,* 150.

35. Tarry said: "Ted was unique inasmuch as after the *Post* hired him, instead of staying downtown, he brought his downtown friends uptown—people like Archer Winsten and John Woodburn—and introduced them" (personal interview).

36. See *DSOH,* 18, 92.

37. Suggs, *P. B. Young,* 81.

38. While on the Florida Writers' Project, Zora Neale Hurston published three books. McKay based part of *Harlem, Negro Metropolis* on his Federal Writers' Project materials (Mangione, *Dream and the Deal,* 257). In 1991 columnist Marilyn Geewax recollected her playground created by the WPA: "To those smart-aleck politicians who belittle the idea of a public-works program . . . think again. So many adults need jobs and so many children deserve a childhood" (Geewax, "Emulate WPA to Give Children and the Jobless a Chance," *Atlanta Journal and Constitution,* June 28, 1991, sec. A, p. 13).

39. Thomas A. Johnson, "A Graduate of the Black Press Looks Back," in Henry G. LaBrie III, ed., *Perspectives of the Black Press, 1974* (Kennebunkport, Me.: Mercer House Press, 1974), 183.

40. The color bar had already been broken in some cities. When TP was city editor of the *Amsterdam News,* he printed an article on the *Newark Ledger*'s African American feature editor Hunter Maxwell, who had first frequently contributed to its "Letters to the Editor" column ("Hunter Maxwell, Feature Editor of Newark Ledger, Won Post by Writing to the Paper," *Amsterdam News,* July 26, 1933, sec. 2, p. 1).

41. Moon interview by Jackson, 10, 26.

42. On May 12, 1937, exactly a year from his first supplication, Moon reminded Sulzberger that since he first applied, "the Sunday *Times* has published five" of his stories "and has accepted three others. Mr. Joseph has given me a number of city assignments at space rates." Moon wanted to go on the *Times* full-time. Sulzberger again replied, "I regret to advise you that I do not think it will be possible at this time to extend the work" (Moon, "New York Times" portion of memoir, typescript, Moon Papers). In 1945, the *Times* employed its first African American, George Streator, whose degree was in math. "He was of the George Schuyler ilk, biased," says Moon (interview by Jackson, 94).

43. Gerard Chapman, *William Cullen Bryant: The Cummington Years* (Milton, Mass.: Trustees of Reservations, 1980), 16. Bryant's education resembled Ted's in that he loved nature and reading in his father's library. Bryant was excited about the prospect of going to Yale, but his father could not afford it. So Bryant read law in an attorney's office, then became an editorial assistant at the *New York Evening Post,* which Alexander Hamilton had founded in 1801 to "propagate his Federalist doctrines." Under Bryant, the paper espoused the Democratic party's liberal attitudes. That party was "riven by the issue of slavery," and when Abraham Lincoln launched his campaign for the presidency, Bryant introduced him at Cooper Union. It was Bryant who persuaded the city to set aside a large tract of land for Central Park. Richard Kluger, a historian of New York newspapers, claims that "editors tended to be lazy, uncultivated men—William Cullen Bryant, arriving on the *Evening Post* in 1836, was the only authentic man of letters among them" (*The Paper,* 30). Walt Whitman, who edited the *Brooklyn Eagle,* recalled of Bryant, "We were both walkers. . . . He several times came over, middle of afternoons, and we took rambles, miles long, till dark." Whitman said Bryant had "a dry, spare visage" and "a huge white beard of ragged appearance," and he strode along "regardlessly and rapidly, a book in his hand, a thought—and more too—inside his head, a rustical straw hat . . . turned sharp up behind and down before, like a country boy's" (quoted in Chapman, *Bryant,* 18). Back home in Massachusetts, Bryant daily walked ten or fifteen miles. "He never went through [a] gate. He would walk up to it, put his hand on it, and vault over it." At eighty years he could vault over a four-foot gate (ibid., 24). A guest in his household was "awakened in the morning by a series of thumps." Bryant was taking his " 'Daily Dozen'. . . . The thumps, which shook the house, were caused by the use of a vaulting pole, he jumping back and forth over the bed with it" (ibid., 20–21). When Bryant died, New York City flags were lowered to half-staff and he was mourned across America as a poet and editor. Probably Ted Poston did not know these colorful aspects of Bryant's history, but by joining the *Post,* he joined Bryant's tradition.

44. Bryant's son-in-law broadened the editorial view from antislavery (Jeffrey Potter, *Men, Money and Magic: The Story of Dorothy Schiff* [New York: Coward, 1976], 161).

45. "We couldn't afford office space, until Ozzie gave us two rooms free in the old *New York Evening Post* building down at 20 Vesey St." (TP, "Two Score and Ten

Years Ago," *New York Post,* Feb. 8, 1959, sec. M, p. 4); also see Oswald Garrison Villard, *Fighting Years: Memoirs of a Liberal Editor* (New York: Harcourt, 1939), 9–12, 346.

46. J. David Stern, *Memoirs of a Maverick Publisher* (New York: Simon and Schuster, 1962), 183, 33–34.

47. George Seldes, *Lords of the Press* (New York: Messner, 1946), 156.

48. Stern, *Memoirs,* 215–18.

49. Ibid., 10.

50. O'Connor, *Heywood Broun,* 189; also see Seldes, *Lords of the Press,* 159, 170.

51. Stern, *Memoirs,* 237.

52. "Portrait of Harlem," 308.

53. Willens, "Adventures," 14. Some informant at the *Post* with a blanked-out name, probably Walter Lister, told FBI agent Dunne in 1941 that a "working arrangement" had been devised with TP "whereby he was to be paid twelve dollars per column for material submitted, and five dollars per assignment if non-productive of a story." "———— was of the opinion that Poston averaged approximately fifty dollars monthly, and that he may have, on a few occasions, earned as much as one hundred dollars a month, but he was definitely of the opinion that he could never have earned more than seven or eight hundred dollars per annum." Poston's Civilian Personnel Record says that he worked for the *New York Post* from July 1936 to 1940 as "Harlem correspondent" and "feature writer" and was paid forty dollars a week. This record does not mention the Federal Writers' Project. In another version of his start, Poston said that when he obtained a two-hour interview with the notorious Huey Long of Louisiana, "That settled it. My city editor figured that if I could handle Huey Long, I could handle anyone" (TP, "Interracial Reporting"). Curiosity such as TP had was a journalistic requirement. Stanley Walker says: "Of the four who wrote of Jesus, John was the only one who showed signs of being a lively, inquisitive reporter. He wanted to know things, and he asked about them." A modern reporter is "too easily content with a collection of perfunctory statements" (Walker, *City Editor,* 46–47). Although Poston pioneered in the transition from black press to white, he considered the black press essential "for Negro Americans have learned that only in their own weekly newspapers can they find a record of their achievements (often overemphasized), a mirror of their emotions, and an expression of their yearnings for full citizenship and dignity. . . . The best chance an ordinary Negro has to get into a white newspaper is by committing a crime" (TP, "Negro Press," n.d., Record Group 208, Box 40, National Archives).

54. TP, "Interracial Reporting."

55. Someone preparing Ted's copy for the printer mistakenly put the byline "Ed Poston" on "Fast on Again for Harry Wills," *New York Post,* Apr. 1, 1937, 16.

56. Stern, *Memoirs,* 286, 483.

57. TP, memo to Paul Sann, July 17, 1962, Box 6, Wechsler Papers.

58. Eleanor Roosevelt knew that the day of aristocrats' estates was ending. When

her neighbor had to sell Krum Elbow and Father Divine bought it, she commented that it was "pleasant to feel that in the future this place will be heaven to some people, even if it cannot be to its former owner" (quoted in Lash, *Eleanor and Franklin*, 633).

59. TP, "Sorry, Father, But It's Not Wonderful," review of *Fr. Divine, Holy Husband*, by Sara Harris, *New York Post*, Nov. 1, 1953, sec. M, p. 12. In a 1965 *Post* column, Hughes recalled Father Divine and a teacher who, when she was first struggling in New York, did not know what she would have done without Divine's "plate of pigs' feet, rice and greens, and bread free" ("Father Divine," *New York Post*, Sept. 17, 1965).

60. TP, "Interracial Reporting."

61. TP, interview by Richard Kluger, July 22, 1971, notes in Beinecke Rare Book and Manuscript Library, Yale University, New Haven, Connecticut.

62. Moon, "Farewell to Heywood Broun."

63. Stern and Broun agreed on the need for a union "to raise the status of the reporter" but parted company over the necessity of raising it at management's expense (Stern, *Memoirs*, 288–89).

64. In 1923 Dorothy Schiff, born in 1903—the same year as Poston's sister Lillian—had married Richard B. W. Hall and had two children, Mortimer and Adele. Her marriage to George Backer produced Sarah Ann in 1934.

65. Lash, *Eleanor and Franklin*, 582. David Brinkley says that much of Roosevelt's "almost magical talent for persuading and manipulating the American people" was owing to his ability to state his thoughts in simple, homely phrases (*Washington Goes to War* [New York: Ballantine, 1988], 47).

66. Lash, *Eleanor and Franklin*, 583. Doggerel of this campaign mocked the Roosevelts: "You kiss the Negroes / I'll kiss the Jews / We'll stay in the White House / As long as we choose" (ibid., 585).

67. Geoffrey T. Hellman, "Profiles: Publisher Dorothy Schiff," *New Yorker*, Aug. 10, 1968, 40. New York City had no library of the highest distinction until 1895. Then "such special gifts as the Jacob Schiff library of Jewish materials" made it "one of the principal fortresses of learning and research in the land" (Nevins, "Past, Present, and Future," 28).

68. Potter, *Men, Money and Magic*, 143–47.

69. TP, "A Book on Harlem," review of *Harlem: Negro Metropolis*, by Claude McKay, *New Republic*, Nov. 25, 1940, 732.

70. Hill et al., eds., Garvey Papers, 4:826.

71. TP, "Harlem Shadows," *Pittsburgh Courier*, Jan. 10, 1931.

72. Himes wrote that Negroes "think Jews control all the money in the world," therefore they "have the power to do more for us than anyone else." Himes believed, "like other Negroes, that Jews fight, and underhandedly, our struggle for equality" (*Lonely Crusade*, 155, 159). Nazi propaganda chief Joseph Goebbels thought that America was ripe for demise because of its racial discord. Asked about that at a news conference, FDR replied, "Justice will be done for all concerned . . . but the Federal

Government does not intend to be hampered either by brown shirts or night shirts" (Statement with Goebbels quotes, n.d., ca. 1942, Record Group 208, Box 40, National Archives).

73. Robert L. Poston, "The 'Why' of It," editorial, *Negro World*, Oct. 8, 1921, 4.

74. Ottley and Weatherby, eds., *Negro in New York*, 283.

75. O'Dwyer, *Beyond the Golden Door*, 150.

76. Potter, *Men, Money and Magic*, 35.

77. Quoted in Stern, *Memoirs*, 254.

78. Quoted in Hellman, "Profiles," 60.

79. Peter Benjaminson, *Death in the Afternoon* (Kansas City: Andrews, 1984), 1.

80. TP, "Negroes Assail Nazis, Ask Fight on U.S. Fascism: Urge Americans to End Race Discrimination in Own Country," *New York Post*, Nov. 25, 1938.

81. Broun, *Whose Little Boy Are You?*, 207.

82. Wambly Bald, "This Was Heywood Broun: He Died 10 Years Ago Today," *New York Post*, Dec. 19, 1949, 49. "What differentiated [Broun] from most of his newspaper colleagues was that he cared. . . . His deepest instinct was kindliness and a devout sense that we are all brothers" (James A. Wechsler, "Heywood Broun," editorial, *New York Post*, Dec. 18, 1962, sec. M, p. 32).

83. TP, "Social Security Act Bars Most of Us," *Pittsburgh Courier*, Dec. 23, 1939, 24.

84. In the 1940s Rowe founded the Louis-Rowe Enterprises public relations agency in conjunction with Joe Louis, and later he co-founded 100 Black Men.

85. Billy Rowe, "Out of Billy Rowe's Harlem Notebook," *Pittsburgh Courier*, Apr. 20, 1940, 7.

86. John Kenneth Galbraith, "Sunday Morning," CBS, WAGA, Atlanta, July 17, 1990.

87. Moon, interview by Jackson. See Ware, *William Hastie*, 34, for Weaver and Hastie at Harvard. Robinson had also been employed on the Federal Writers' Project. Moon did not marry until age thirty-seven. He recalled that when "my friends were getting married, I would say, 'What are you doing that for? All these lovely ladies out here and you're tying yourself down.'"

88. TP, "You Go South," *New Republic*, Sept. 9, 1940, 348–50. Poston's complaint may have helped change the law if not the practice. Langston Hughes wrote Arna Bontemps three years later: "This week's *Amsterdam News* [has] swell spread with laws that inter-state passengers DO NOT and NEED NOT change to Jim Crow cars when going South as Supreme Court has ruled that such state laws do not apply to interstate travelers and they can sit anywhere they wish all over the train!!! Here's hoping they do. The Jim Crow car seems to me the most antiquated and barbarous thing on this continent" (quoted in Nichols, ed., *Bontemps-Hughes Letters*, 142).

89. Ottley, *New World A-Coming*, 22.

90. Why Marie and her mother changed the spelling of their last name from Bird to Byrd is not known. Perhaps Marie's mother's unwed status caused it; her alliance with a tall white man, which produced Marie, may have been considered a blot on

the Bird family escutcheon. Crystal Bird had married Arthur Huff Fauset in 1931. He was half-brother to Jessie Redmon Fauset, who describes in *Plum Bun* and *There Is Confusion* the milieu in which Marie Byrd grew up. Fauset's protagonists belong to "a third world of beauty, breeding, and dignity. . . . Equal to whites in every respect (save money), these brown aristocrats are really superior because of the tremendous handicaps surmounted" (quoted in Lewis, *When Harlem Was in Vogue,* 235). Fauset, *Chinaberry Tree,* 20.

91. Ed Morrow, telephone interview; and Daniels, *White House Witness,* 93–97. The breach-of-promise suit provided Marie's aunt with funds for her education at Boston University and her 1925 trip to Europe. See "Philadelphia," *Inter-State Tattler,* July 26, Sept. 6, Oct. 11, 25, 1929, for mentions of Crystal Bird.

92. TP, "You Go South."

93. Murray, *Song in a Weary Throat,* 146–47. Murray was "convinced that [Mrs. Roosevelt] had little understanding of what it meant to be a Negro in the United States at that time." TP, "Two New Yorkers Ready for Appeal of Conviction in Greyhound Case," *Pittsburgh Courier,* Apr. 13, 1940.

94. Description of Moton in Dykeman and Stokely, *Seeds of Southern Change,* 68–71.

95. William Fowlkes, editor of the black *Atlanta Daily-World,* knew Poston as an aggressive and accomplished writer (telephone interview).

96. Lash, *Eleanor and Franklin,* 799.

97. Poston is relating his own experience ("Interracial Reporting"). Himes expressed the anxiety a black feels in a white milieu in *Lonely Crusade,* 167–68.

98. FBI Report 77-1244.

99. Buni, *Robert L. Vann,* 316.

100. Moon, "Ted Poston."

101. Lewis says TP told her that he had "married Marie by accident," that she took his sending her that cartoon as a proposal. Diana Bonnor Lewis met Marie in 1981, when Marie was seventy, and found her "very attractive. A lot of charm." Lewis says TP was "awfully fond of Marie. They were always friends" (personal interview).

102. Marie's childhood friend Eloise Scott Reed said that Tancil was "a Philadelphia fellow. You'd never have known he wasn't white. Marie's mother had a thing about color. She pushed Marie into that marriage and it didn't work out" (telephone interview). Tancil was in the company that Major Ed Morrow commanded during World War II. He was "tall, like Marie, an artificer who did repair and maintenance of artillery, a damn nice person and a damn fine mechanic," but Tancil was over his head "married to somebody who was super articulate, super-everything, a great big, passionate butterfly" (Morrow, telephone interview). Neither Reed nor Morrow could remember Tancil's first name. Ersa Poston, who had met him socially, recalled that it was Albert.

103. Robert C. Weaver called Alexander "something of a rainmaker seeding the clouds" (quoted in Dykeman and Stokely, *Seeds of Southern Change,* 259).

104. "Ickes," *Current Biography 1941,* 426. Ickes spoke from his crusty, cur-

mudgeonly heart when he told the NAACP in 1936 that it was among his lifelong interests (Harold Ickes, "The Negro as a Citizen," *Crisis,* Sept. 1936, 230+).

105. Dykeman and Stokely, *Seeds of Southern Change,* 186. The *Atlanta Constitution*'s Ralph McGill received a Rosenwald grant in 1937 and went to Europe. In 1939 and 1940, two young women in the mountains of Georgia, Lillian Smith and Paula Snelling, who edited *South Today,* won fellowships (ibid., 270–71). Barnett thought that his Associated Negro Press needed a Washington representative, so he applied and in December 1935, the ANP received from the Rosenwald Fund $1,500 "to be used in reporting activities in Washington as they relate to the status of Negroes" (Hogan, *Black National News Service,* 95).

106. Buni, *Robert L. Vann,* 208.

107. Ickes, whose forebears immigrated with William Penn, worked his way through the University of Chicago, took civil liberties cases without pay, taught Americanization classes at Jane Addams's Hull House, and was a reporter for Chicago newspapers from 1897 to 1900. After leaving government, he wrote a syndicated newspaper column carried by the *New York Post* ("Ickes," *Current Biography 1952,* 285; also see Naomi Bliven, "Books: Say Not the Struggle Naught Availeth," review of *Righteous Pilgrim,* by T. H. Watkins, *New Yorker,* Jan. 28, 1991, 90).

108. Ickes had also been labeled "Harold the Meddler" and a "common scold" (William H. Hastie, interview by Jerry N. Hess, Jan. 5, 1972, 8, draft 1 in William H. Hastie Papers, Truman Library, Independence, Missouri).

109. Quoted in "Ickes," *Current Biography 1941,* 426.

110. Motz, "Black Cabinet," 14.

111. Dykeman and Stokely, *Seeds of Southern Change,* 195.

112. Buni, *Robert L. Vann,* 209.

113. Quoted in Dykeman and Stokely, *Seeds of Southern Change,* 249.

114. Carey McWilliams, *Brothers Under the Skin* (1942; Boston: Little, Brown, 1964) 5.

115. Alexander made "better homes for the rural poor his first priority" (Suggs, *P. B. Young,* 79). A regional director told him that "those families ought to have, first of all, a wagon and a mule and a cook stove. . . . Anybody in this age who didn't have a wheel under him was going to fall behind in the progress of civilization." Dykeman and Stokely, *Seeds of Southern Change,* 235; also see 205.

116. Lash, *Eleanor and Franklin,* 549.

117. "A Newspaper Pro," in Fisher and Lowenstein, *Race and the News Media,* 67.

118. Josephson, *Sidney Hillman,* 463.

119. TP, CPR.

120. See R. E. Kehres, FBI agent, New York City, report on T. R. Poston, May 22, 1941, for TP's residences; in 1940 he no longer had a permanent apartment in Harlem but stayed at the Theresa Hotel when he was in town. The Theresa was managed by the father of Ron Brown, secretary of commerce in the administration of President William Jefferson Clinton until Brown's death in an air crash in 1996.

121. Regarding "additional experience" in support of his application, Poston

gave his background up to then as "charter member of Newspaper Guild of New York and organized first Negro unit of that union on *New York Amsterdam News*. Served as chairman of that unit from 1934 to 1937. Was member of city executive committee of New York Guild from 1935 to 1937. Served as negotiator in contract sessions with publishers of several New York weeklies and dailies. Was also member of strike committees in labor disputes on the *Amsterdam News, Long Island Daily Star* and *North Shore Journal*. . . . Member of the executive committee of the Negro Labor Committee, a federation of CIO and A.F. of L. unions with Negro membership, involved in organizational drives and contract negotiations for various groups of workers, including barbers, butchers, clerks, taxicab drivers, pharmacists, newspaper workers and others. Committee maintains headquarters at 312 West 125th St. Frank R. Crosswaith is chairman. Applicant has done extensive research and publicity work for a number of social and welfare organizations, including the NAACP, 69 Fifth Avenue, New York City. Directed similar work for the New York State Temporary Commission on the Condition of the Urban Colored Population (a legislative committee) from October 1938 to April 1939. . . . Also directed publicity work for commission and assisted in community organization. More than 300 separate clippings attest to effectiveness of press relations work for group. Applicant took special courses in journalism, short story and editorial writing at New York University in 1928 and 1929. No credits were sought for this work which was undertaken only as a means of improving applicant's training in his craft. Applicant believes that continuous employment in the weekly and daily newspaper field since 1929 and extensive work in publicity and community organization work, as well as in the field of labor relations, will enhance his value to Advisory Committee in its Race Relations Division" (TP, CPR).

CHAPTER 8. BLACK CABINET, WORLD WAR II: 1940–1945

1. Brinkley, *Washington Goes to War*, 193.
2. Jonathan Daniels, "I Am a Bureaucrat," *Atlantic Monthly*, Apr. 1944, 96–97.
3. Chester Himes, *The Primitive* (New York: Signet, 1955), 100.
4. Daniels, *White House Witness*, 27.
5. Quoted in Dykeman and Stokely, *Seeds of Southern Change*, 261.
6. Tokyo Radio, n.d. [Apr. 16, 1943?], Record Group 208, Box 40, National Archives.
7. Office of War Information, release, "Justice Department," Feb. 12, 1943, Record Group 208, Box 52, National Archives; also see Daniels, *White House Witness*, 165–66, for Roosevelt's racial humor.
8. Kessner, *Fiorello H. LaGuardia*, 529.
9. Ware, *William Hastie*, 104.
10. Ploski and Williams, eds., *Negro Almanac*, 846. Dorie Miller was lost at sea on November 12, 1943. Not until March 7, 1942, were a few black pilots allowed to complete training and become commissioned in the air corps. A year later, Execu-

tive Order 9279 required all services to accept Negro recruits through the Selective Service System (ibid., 861).

11. For example, "If a regimental commander of a colored unit is white, the regimental surgeon, we believe, should be white," Brig. Gen. Larry B. McAfee, assistant to the surgeon general, wrote in a memo to Lt. Col. C. J. Gridley, G-3, Jan. 30, 1942, copy in Hastie Papers, Harvard Law Library.

12. In 1904 Bethune founded Bethune-Cookman College in Florida; in 1935 she founded the National Council of Negro Women" (Motz, "Black Cabinet," 15–16). She undertook the "role of spokesman for all the Negroes in the United States" (ibid., 67–68).

13. See Nichols, ed., *Bontemps-Hughes Letters,* 6, 41, 407, for the influence of Bethune on Hughes.

14. Jane Motz did valuable and basic research on the Black Cabinet for her 1964 thesis at the University of Delaware. I am indebted to her for the otherwise unattributed information in this chapter.

15. Motz, "Black Cabinet," 22, and Lash, *Eleanor and Franklin,* 681.

16. William A. H. Birnie, "Black Brain Trust," *American Magazine,* Jan. 1943, 95.

17. Motz, "Black Cabinet," 74, 69–70. The Black Cabinet received useful information from friendly sources such as "lowly Negro messengers . . . who occasionally risked their jobs by conveying to a Black Cabineteer a bit of information, such as word of a proposal which might be considered dangerous to Negroes."

18. Ottley, *New World A-Coming,* 260.

19. *Who's Who Among Black Americans, 1990–91,* 466; Franklin, *Negro Labor Unionist,* 532–33.

20. Weaver's wife, Ella, holder of a Ph.D. degree, had taught speech at Brooklyn College. TP bragged that when someone telephoned the Weavers and asked for "Dr. Weaver," the maid habitually responded, "Which one?" (Ersa Hines Poston, telephone interview; TP, "It's a Tough Job—He Likes It," *New York Post,* Mar. 4, 1956, 2).

21. TP, "It's a Tough Job."

22. Public relations consultant (racial problems) in the office of Robert C. Weaver, Division of Labor Supply, War Manpower Commission, CPR.

23. Dates for Poston's employment record given here are from his Civilian Personnel Record file rather than from the FBI. The CPR seems more reliable; the FBI "informants" are unnamed, and their information is unoffical, often mere rumor and gossip.

24. TP told cronies of his "arduous tasks and brilliant performance" in Washington as "assistant President" (Moon, "Ted Poston").

25. TP, CPR.

26. Successful black employees "developed certain psychological skills" to help them handle abusive passengers so as to defuse explosive situations before they escalated into threats of violence, even though in doing so, they were "forced to swal-

low their pride for the sake of their job" (Perata, *Those Pullman Blues,* xviii; also see xxviii, 132, 133).

27. He held P-4 rank at an annual salary of $3,800.

28. Josephson, *Sidney Hillman,* 10, 11.

29. Quoted in Ware, *William Hastie,* 82.

30. Dykeman and Stokely, *Seeds of Southern Change,* 257.

31. Quoted in Ottley, *New World A-Coming,* 262. It became "evident that War Manpower Commission chairman Paul V. McNutt had no intention of encouraging a serious effort to fight racial inequities" (August Meier and Elliott Rudwick, *Black Detroit and the Rise of the UAW* [New York: Oxford University Press, 1979], 112).

32. Robert C. Weaver, *Negro Labor: A National Problem* (New York: Harcourt, 1946), 17.

33. TP, CPR, Employee No. 17-08850. FBI Report 77-1244, January 31, 1942, said "Poston was 24 or 25 at the time he made the trip [to Russia] and was the type of person who could not be bossed and he did his own thinking." Poston was friendly with communists, but the informant could "definitely say that Poston is not interested in Communism. . . .The Communist element considered him an excellent prospect and wanted to convert him to Communism so that he could be taken into the Harlem Branch of the Communist Party as a leader. . . . Since his return and after the report of his interview with newspaper men of the New York *Herald Tribune,* the Communists have actually hated [Ted Poston] and he in turn now hates the Communists." Someone else whom the FBI interviewed said TP spoke "disparagingly of the Communists and often stated that certain meetings which he covered as a reporter were 'pinkish' or 'C. P.-dominated' or 'Party-sponsored,' but he always referred to these meetings in a sarcastic way. . . . Informant further stated that Poston often talks to known Communists or Communist sympathizers and makes such remarks as 'You and your C. P.' or 'You and your Party Line.'" Another "informant" said, "Any person who labels Poston a Communist would be the type of person who has a grudge against him." He was "positive Poston made the trip when the opportunity presented itself. As Negroes generally do not often get a chance to go abroad or beyond the confines of the United States, Poston took advantage of the chance."

34. Hughes says black skin alone convinces some people that one is communist (Nichols, ed., *Bontemps-Hughes Letters,* 233).

35. J. R. Jones, Agent, Theodore R. Poston FBI File, Mar. 22, 1941.

36. "I am represented as having told an FBI Investigator that Poston was a Communist. . . . a completely wrong and unforgivable construction of my remarks. . . . I was surprised at the FBI man's persistence. He did not seem to be satisfied with my answers . . . and kept going over and over Poston's entire life, as if determined to wring from me something discreditable about him. . . . Poston's entire outlook was too sane and wholesome to be encompassed by the narrow confines of Communistic doctrine. I ended the interview by strongly reiterating what I had said at its beginning; that I recommended Poston 100% as an able, loyal candidate for any post in the service of the government. If this interview has been in some way tortured or

twisted to represent me as accusing Poston of being a Communist . . . I feel that I am entitled to an explanation. . . . I find it hard to believe that an FBI man could have so completely perverted the sense of my remarks in regard to Poston. . . . [Name deleted]" (Anonymous, letter to George J. Gould, Chief Investigator, U.S. Civil Service Commission, Apr. 4, 1942, TP FBI file).

37. TP wrote to someone on April 13, 1942, with a return address of War Production Board, 5054 Just St., NE, Washington, D.C.: "Everything went cockeyed" and he "just about folded up under it. . . . This FBI business came as a climax to a single week in which I had been working from 12 to 16 hours a day assisting in the preparation of articles for the following publications: *Time, Life, Fortune, Supervision, Reader's Digest, Mill and Factory,* and *Newsweek.* Each one of these sheets decided to discover the Negro problem the *same* week." Poston was disturbed by the FBI's conclusion. He was "glad to learn, from my own investigation, however, that these misstatements were not usually made by the FBI agents who personally interviewed many persons, but were written into a summary on which the charges were based. . . . Dr. Weaver says that Dr. Powell told the field investigator: 'I do not like Poston; he is headstrong and a trouble-maker. He is not a Communist, though, and I would never call him one. He's much too headstrong to bow to Communist Party discipline or any other kind.' An even more stupid and deliberate misquote was taken from Claude McKay's book, *Harlem: Negro Metropolis.* The summary states, 'According to McKay's book, the Communist party supported and financed the *Amsterdam News* strike, expecting in return that Theodore Poston and Henry Lee Moon would become, at least, good "fellow travelers" after having been out of the Communist party for some time.' What McKay's book actually said was this: 'The Communists, active in supporting and financing Harlem's *Amsterdam News* strike, had expected that Moon and Poston would show gratitude at least and become good "fellow travelers." For these two Harlemites had been chalked up on the Communist blacklist for over five years—ever since their part in exposing the ruthless opportunism of the red apostles of idealism!' Further, McKay's book devotes at least 10 pages to Moon and Poston's continued fight against the Communists. . . . This nice smear job seems to have been done by one man—the person who prepared the 'summary'. . . . (Signed) Ted." The letter is in TP's FBI file.

38. Poston explained exactly how his participation in the journey came about: "I am accused of being a Communist apparently because in 1932 (and not 1930) I made a trip to Russia with 21 other persons who apparently are accused of being Communists for the same reason. . . . The group which made this trip was organized by Miss Louise Thompson, a Negro woman who was then employed in the Race Relations Division of the Congregational Church in New York. Miss Thompson began organizing this project in the winter of 1931, after she stated that she had received an invitation from the Meschrabpom Film Company to bring a group of Negroes to Russia to make a proposed film called *Black and White.* It is believed that this offer was transmitted to Miss Thompson by James Ford, who later became the Communist Party's candidate for Vice-President of the United States. Ford had been to Rus-

sia prior to this time but had not attained his present prominence as a Communist. Efforts were made to secure funds for this project through a series of public benefits to pay the fares of 26 Negroes. These benefits failed and then efforts were made to raise money through gifts from well-known Negro artists and others. This effort also failed. During this period, I was not connected with the group in any way.

"Soon after this second failure, Miss Thompson appealed to any 26 Negroes who could pay their fare to Russia. The project was pictured as a glorified tour and vacation, and all announcements stressed the fact that Communist affiliation was not desirable since the group was expected to bring back an unprejudiced report on the Soviet Union. Such an offer appealed to me as a newspaper man, and it was then that I made Miss Thompson's acquaintance. I regarded it as an excellent opportunity to see for myself the much publicized Soviet Union and possibly to write stories about it. My fellow workers on the New York *Amsterdam News,* where I served as a reporter and at times as Assistant City Editor, gave a 'Send Poston to Russia' party and helped me raise the $110 boat fare required. I also made arrangements with the Associated Negro Press, the *New York Sunday Times,* and the *Amsterdam News* to write stories about a Negro's views of the Soviet Union, and arranged leave from the last named paper to make the trip. I was the last member to join the group. Of the 22 Negroes who raised money for the trip, only two were known or admitted Communists. Subsequent developments indicated that at least three others were then Communists or became Communists during the course of the trip. . . . Upon our return to America, we were vilified in the Communist press and handbills were distributed on the streets of Harlem denouncing us for expressing our opinions of the Communist Party and the Soviet Union" (TP, letter to Gould, Apr. 6, 1942; a copy of the letter is in his FBI file).

39. "Powell called me and said Henry Moon was a Communist and demanded that I fire him. I told him to go to hell" (Robert C. Weaver, personal interview, Aug. 18, 1986). Jonathan Daniels, too, "carefully examined for subversiveness," passed his inquisition, then regarded the matter lightly, "glad that . . . not being a menace, I have been allowed to remain to contribute my mite" ("I Am a Bureaucrat," 100).

40. Henry Ford felt he was doing right by employees ever since he shocked the world by raising industrial wages to five dollars a day in 1914. He was one of the first industrialists to hire Negroes. He groomed black University of Michigan football standout of the 1930s Willis F. Ward to act as ombudsman in dealing with his black employees. As Ford's emissary, Ward authorized blacks that the one occasion when they could fight was if they were called "nigger," but even then there were rules: "The word was such that there was no better way to get into a fight with a colored fellow than to call him a nigger. If he didn't fight, the general consensus was that he wasn't a man. . . . That was the chip that they all carried on their shoulder, myself included. Your manhood depended upon what you would do if a white fellow called you a nigger. Our policy was not to discharge colored fellows for fighting if they had been called that name, and if they fought fair. If they picked up steel or pulled a knife that was a different proposition" (Willis F. Ward, "The Reminiscences of Willis F. Ward," interview by Owen Bombard, 1954, Ford Motor Company Archives, Detroit, 98; see

also 57–58). After World War II, Ward went to law school and became an assistant U.S. attorney.

41. Meier and Rudwick, *Black Detroit,* 112. Jim Daniels, "Time, Temperature," in *M-80* (Pittsburgh: University of Pittsburgh Press, 1994), 32–33.

42. Meier and Rudwick, *Black Detroit,* 127–30.

43. The article has no byline. Authorship was ascertained by August Meier and Elliott Rudwick in an interview with Louis Martin (ibid., 264). Louis Martin lived a generation longer than Ted. At his death in 1997, *Time* magazine hailed Martin as an "influential presidential confidante responsible for bringing black and minority concerns into the corridors of power." It capsulized Martin's career: "Dubbed 'the godfather of black politics,' he helped clinch black votes for Kennedy in 1960; persuade Johnson to appoint Thurgood Marshall to the Supreme Court; advise Carter on minority affairs; and propel the career of Bill Clinton advisor Vernon Jordan" ("Milestones," *Time,* Feb. 10, 1997, 25).

44. [TP and Louis Martin], "Detroit Is Dynamite," *Life,* Aug. 17, 1942, 16.

45. Ibid., 17.

46. Weaver, "Eulogy for Theodore R. Poston," Benta's Funeral Home, New York, Jan. 14, 1974, Moon Papers.

47. Mary said that another Chopin Etude—Opus 10, No. 12—"expresses all the turmoil in our lives at that time." Despite their separation, Ted inspired Mary to "reach her potential." She wanted to finish school; her husband said she did not need to. She contacted a former employee of her father's and asked the person to cash in an insurance policy Dr. Duncan had bought, then split the money with Mary. They did that, Mary went to school, and finished her B.A. at age thirty-nine in 1950. She says, "I felt I was doing it for my father, for Ted, and for me. Their respect was something that I never wanted to lose" (personal interview).

48. Many times throughout his life, Poston told the "Evil Fairies" story with body movements to show how he slashed at his unfortunate light-skinned rival Leonardius. Edith Rosenfels Nash surmised, "Ted was really in love with that dainty little girl. That story represents Ted's version of how he saw himself—as a very black person, first; and second, as a person who was always being discriminated against. But it did not influence his own behavior or make him feel in any way servile or diminished" (telephone interview, Oct. 24, 1992).

49. Parents wanted their children to marry well and, in the Negro community, that meant "marry light."

50. Marie's mother would have fit Du Bois's findings in *Philadelphia Negro* that Philadelphia domestics provided "brownskin service." One employer told Du Bois, "If you get a good class of colored people they are the most faithful, honest and biddable servants in the world." But Du Bois also found that "there is a point beyond which docility and a respectful bearing cease to be virtues" (*Philadelphia Negro,* 480–82).

51. Even Herbert Bayard Swope, at just short of age sixty, wanted to participate (Kahn, *World of Swope,* 443).

52. "Talk of the Town," *New Yorker,* Mar. 14, 1942; Scott Donaldson, *Archibald*

MacLeish: An American Life (Boston: Houghton Mifflin, 1992), 362. "A Job for Elmer Davis," *New Republic,* June 22, 1942, 847. Davis "often typed his own letters in the uneven, x'ed out style, the mark of a working newsman" ("The Administration: Truth and Trouble," *Time,* Mar. 15, 1943, 15).

53. The Office of Facts and Figures was called pejoratively Office of Fuss and Feathers ("Man of Sense," *Time,* June 22, 1942, 21). MacLeish directed the OFF for eight months of "living hell" before the agency was dissolved. The OWI was inaugurated with "an executive order that had teeth." That gave Elmer Davis "the kind of clout at OWI that MacLeish had yearned for at OFF" (Donaldson, *Archibald MacLeish,* 351, 363).

54. "A Job for Elmer Davis," 847.

55. Walter White, letter to Elmer Davis, Dec. 8, 1942, Record Group 208, Box 8, National Archives.

56. Theodore M. Berry, Liaison Officer, Group Morale, letter to Crystal B. Fausett [*sic*], Office of Civilian Defense, Mar. 14, 1942, Record Group 208, Box 3, National Archives.

57. Milton Starr, memo to Ulric Bell, Office for Emergency Management, Executive Office of the President, Feb. 12, 1942, Record Group 208, Box 40, National Archives.

58. Malcolm Cowley, Office for Emergency Management, memo to Archibald MacLeish, Jan. 26, 1942, Record Group 208, Box 40, National Archives. The grievances of which Poston and Moon told Cowley included "1) . . . John M. Carmody, Clark Foreman and Percy Straus were forced to resign because Congress—or a certain bloc in Congress—thought they had shown partiality to Negroes in housing projects; 2) . . . the Red Cross's refusing to accept Negro blood donors; 3) Joe Louis's donation [of fight proceeds] to the Navy has revived the issue over the refusal of the Navy to accept Negroes as fighting men, and has been the subject of cartoons in the Negro press; 4) . . . trouble is sure to result whenever Negroes from the North are sent to training camps in the Deep South."

59. See "Challenge Statements Made by ANP: Office of War Information Falsely Hit of Charge," *Michigan Chronicle,* Nov. 14, 1942, 5.

60. Charles A. Siepmann, memo to W. B. Lewis, Aug. 6, 1942, Record Group 208, Box 8, National Archives.

61. Reginald Foster and Robert Huse, memo to Elmer Davis, Sept. 12, 1942, Record Group 208, Box 8, National Archives.

62. "The Administration," 14.

63. "ABC of OWI," *Newsweek,* July 20, 1942, 71.

64. Margaret Proctor, telephone interview.

65. Ottley, *New World A-Coming,* 269.

66. Personal interview; shortly, Tarry was summoned to Chicago by Bishop Sheil to open and co-direct a branch of Baroness Catherine de Hueck's Harlem-based Friendship House. Tarry remembers that TP was in town and "came to Penn Station and gave me one rose and wished me well. I thought that was a beautiful gesture." Also see Tarry, *Third Door,* 188–90.

67. TP, "Negro Press," *Reporter,* Dec. 6, 1949, 14–16.

68. The OWI received a multitude of requests for *Negroes and the War,* and Black Cabinet members were asked for copies. Poston sent them out saying, "At the request of Mr. W. J. Trent, Jr., I am sending you six copies," for example, to E. L. McKinstry (Mar. 18, 1943, Record Group 205, National Archives).

69. W. C. Hodges, letter to Senator John H. Bankhead, Mar. 16, 1943, Record Group 208, Box 8, National Archives.

70. Senator John H. Bankhead, Alabama, Committee on Appropriations, letter to Elmer Davis, Mar. 18, 1943, ibid.

71. Ralph E. Shikes, memo to James Allen, Deputy, Mar. 20, 1943, ibid.

72. C. F. Hach, letter to Senator Harry F. Byrd, June 19, 1943, ibid.

73. Elmer Davis, letter to Senator Harry F. Byrd, June 30, 1943, ibid.

74. John Haynes Holmes, letter to Elmer Davis, Apr. 15, 1943; Davis, letter to Holmes, May 1, 1943, ibid.

75. Holmes letter to Davis, May 5, 1943; Davis, letter to Holmes, May 1, 1943, ibid.

76. O. W. Connor, letter to President F. D. Roosevelt, Feb. 13, 1943; TP, letter to Connor, Mar. 1943, ibid.

77. Luther R. White, letter to Ted Poston, Apr. 9, 1943, Office of War Information Papers, Record Group 205, National Archives.

78. TP, letter to Luther R. White, Apr. 20, 1943, ibid.

79. Margaret Proctor, letter to Francis J. Price, May 18, 1943, Record Group 205, National Archives.

80. A letter from Perry B. Jackson shows the sacrifices of unrecognized citizens. Jackson sent a check from the Elks of Dayton made out to the Treasurer of the United States for the purchase of an ambulance. Could the OWI take pictures? (letter to Ted Poston, May 18, 1943, ibid.). Margaret Proctor wrote Jackson, "Your organization is to be commended on the fine work and patriotism shown in purchasing an ambulance for the United States Army," even though "our limited staff makes it impossible for us to cover such an event" (May 21, 1943, ibid.).

81. A North Carolina private misspelled words (e.g. *veiw; effect* for *affect*) yet sought a position in government public relations. TP responded as cordially as had Crystal Bird Fauset to ungrammatical letters: "I agree with you that a competent Negro might be a great aid in the Washington office, but I am not in a position to give you any assistance in this direction. I would suggest . . . that you write frankly . . . to Mr. Truman K. Gibson, Civilian Aide to the Secretary of War" (TP, letter to Walter J. McLean, Mar. 31, 1943, Record Group 205, National Archives).

82. Gordon Parks, *To Smile in Autumn: A Memoir* (New York: Norton, 1979), 20–23.

83. TP, letter to Emory A. James, Principal, Booker T. Washington Junior High School, Indianapolis, Sept. 11, 1943, Record Group 208, Box 8, National Archives.

84. Eustace Gay of the *Philadelphia Tribune* asked TP where the popular cartoon "Color Guard" was for August (May 26, 1943, Office of War Information Papers, National Archives), and Ted had to write: "Necessitated by the recent cut in the ap-

propriations of the Domestic Branch of the OWI. . . . in the immediate future the Negro News Section will be able to send only one cartoon weekly" (Aug. 24, 1943, ibid.). E. P. Thompson, a teacher at Reynolds School, Philadelphia, on November 24, 1943, asked for "pamphlets on Negro activities in the war effort" (Record Group 205, National Archives). Poston had to reply, "I am sorry to inform you that we are unable to fill your request. . . . Under new Congressional regulations placed on the OWI, we are no longer permitted to distribute such material. I would suggest that you write to the National Urban League, 1133 Broadway, New York, and the NAACP, 69 Fifth Avenue, New York. These organizations should be able to furnish you with a certain amount of material and to suggest other private agencies which may assist you." For most requests, by the end of 1943, Poston had to reply in euphemisms meaning "Sorry, no pictures, no pamphlets, no films" (TP, letter to E. P. Thompson, Dec. 27, 1943, Office of War Information Papers).

85. Nash's Ph.D. dissertation, "The Place of Religious Revivalism in the Formation of the Intercultural Community on the Klamath Reservation," dealt with the Klamath Indian ghost dance of 1870. See "Nash, Philleo," *Current Biography 1962*; Bart Barnes, "Philleo Nash Dies at 77," *Washington Post*, Oct. 13, 1987, sec. B, p. 6; and Ralph J. Bishop, Introduction to Ruth H. Landman and Katherine Spencer Halpern, eds., *Applied Anthropologist and Public Servant: The Life and Work of Philleo Nash*, NAPA Bulletin 7 (Washington, D.C.: National Association for the Practice of Anthropolgy, 1989), 1–2.

86. *Dictionary of American Biography*, s.v. "Niles, David K."

87. Peggy Lamson, *Roger Baldwin: Founder of the American Civil Liberties Union* (Boston: Houghton Mifflin, 1976), 254–55.

88. Moon says that the Negro community in Detroit "affords greater contrasts than any similar group in an American city. During the boom years of full employment and high wages, the upper crust of business and professional men, battening on the income of the black workers, attained a glittering affluence. Their ranks were augmented by the sportsmen-racketeers, whose take from the policy game ran into the millions. Like the white robber barons of the nineteenth century who ruthlessly fleeced the people, the policy kings of Detroit turned to legitimate business and moved into respectable circles. Their comfortable, and sometimes palatial, homes and living standards contrast sharply with the ancient and dilapidated slums of the ghetto, incongruously known as Paradise Valley, in which the great bulk of Negroes are compelled to live, even in a period of good wages. These are among the worst slums in the country" (Moon, *Balance of Power*, 149).

89. Lash, *Eleanor and Franklin*, 868. To a woman in Philadelphia who complained that Negroes were ruining the neighborhood, Eleanor Roosevelt wrote that "we are largely to blame. We brought them here as slaves and we have never given them equal chances for education, even after we emancipated them. . . . I often marvel that they are as good as they are in view of the treatment which they have received" (ibid., 683). The southern image of Mrs. Roosevelt "as a racial firebrand had little relation to reality"; she was criticized in the Negro community for counseling

"patience and moderation" (ibid., 869). James Roosevelt has written of his mother's repeated rebuffs in her advocacy of blacks in James Roosevelt, with Bill Liddy, *My Parents: A Differing View* (Chicago: Playboy, 1976), 155.

90. Philleo Nash, "Science, Politics, and Human Values: A Memoir," *Human Organization: Journal of the Society for Applied Anthropology* 45 (Fall 1986): 191.

91. Ibid., 192.

92. Theodore R. Poston, Celebration of National Negro Newspaper Week, station WINX, Washington, D.C., Feb. 25, 1944, Record Group 208, Box 52, National Archives.

93. A. E. Kehres, FBI Agent, New York City, report on T. R. Poston, May 22, 1941.

94. Daniels, *White House Witness*, 247.

95. Bertram D. Hulen, "Shivering Thousands Stamp in the Snow at Inauguration," *New York Times*, Jan. 21, 1945, 1, 27.

96. Black newsmen had "deluged" Ted with requests for admission to the inauguration. He could not get passes for all of them (TP, memo to Dowsley Clark, Jan. 19, 1945, Record Group 208, Box 965, National Archives).

97. A Harlem "character" of the 1930s, Hubert Fauntleroy Julian, M.D. "(for Mechanical Designer)," was born in Port of Spain, Trinidad, in 1897. He descended on New York in 1922. An "erratic pilot," his exploits were "more interesting in print than in the cockpit" (Lewis, *When Harlem Was in Vogue*, 111).

98. Ted Poston, interview by Robert D. Graff, Dec. 20, 1961, Small Collections, Papers of Robert D. Graff, ABC producer, transcripts of interview with Ted Poston for the Roosevelt story, no. 519, take 2, Franklin D. Roosevelt Library, Hyde Park, New York.

99. Paul Sann, *Trial in the Upper Room* (New York: Crown, 1981), 167–68.

100. C. Vann Woodward, "Made in USA," review of *Truman*, by David McCullough, *New York Times Book Review*, July 16, 1992, 27.

101. C. A. Scott, publisher of the *Atlanta Daily World*, remembered that TP "belonged to the NNPA even before 1940" (personal interview).

102. "Presidential Appointments File," Truman Library.

103. Hastie, Interview by Hess, 34.

104. Dowsley Clark, Chief, News Bureau, memo to Louis Priscilla, Oct. 5, 1945, Record Group 208, Box 965, National Archives. Poston's final salary, $6,440, contrasted with his entering $3,800 (TP, CPR). It reflected wartime inflation as well as his rise in stature.

105. TP described the scenario: "You're doing all right in the Fair Deal government. But one night you come back home and tell your Philadelphia-born wife that you're going back to New York. 'I can't take it anymore,' you say, recalling a near-fist fight with a white bus driver that morning and a donnybrook that night with a Negro cab driver who preferred white customers in Washington. 'Maybe New York spoiled me,' you admit, 'but I'm tired of Jim Crow theaters, Jim Crow restaurants, Jim Crow hotels and this whole Jim Crow town.' (That was wartime Washington.)

"'But aren't you thinking of making your White House work official?' your wife protests. 'Wouldn't that make you the first Negro to serve officially as an Administrative Assistant to the President of the United States?'

"'Sure,' you concede. 'But suppose I took the job. And suppose President Truman passed on Walter White or Lester Granger or some other Negro leader and asked me to take him to lunch? What could I do? Grab a cab and take them two miles up to 14th and U St. Northwest? There's no nearer place to the White House that a Negro can eat in dignity, if at all.'

"You win the argument, and a few days later you are back in New York and at the *Post*" (TP, "Prejudice and Progress: The Negro in New York," II, *New York Post,* Apr. 17, 1956).

106. Paul A. Tierney, letter to Ted O. Thakrey, Aug. 20, 1945; Thackrey, confidential memo to Tierney, Aug. 24, 1945, Box 82, Dorothy Schiff Papers, Manuscripts and Archives Division, New York Public Library; Paul Sann, memo to Blair Clark, Oct. 13, 1965, Box 57, ibid.

107. Grant Lucas, M. D., Resolution for Ted Poston, Sept. 27, 1945, Ted Poston Album, Manuscripts, Archives, and Rare Books, Schomburg Center for Research in Black Culture, New York Public Library.

108. Also see Frederick D. Patterson, *Chronicles of Faith: The Autobiography of Frederick D. Patterson,* ed. Martia Graham Goodson (Tuscaloosa: University of Alabama Press, 1991), 129.

109. Clarence M. Mitchell, director of field operations for the President's Fair Employment Practice Committee, wrote: "Your will to get things done and the incisive judgment you brought from the newspaper field have meant far more in accomplishment than the public will ever know. The solution to a number of problems was as near as my telephone because I could dial your number."

J. Hugo Warren, of the Washington office of the *Pittsburgh Courier,* wrote: "As Mrs. Mary McLeod Bethune told you at the Roosevelt plaque ceremonies last week, your passing makes us realize that times are changing before our very eyes; that time, the imperceptible thief, has taken away from us a gem. May God bless you and keep you, Ted."

Alfred Edgar Smith, chief of the Washington Bureau of the *Chicago Defender* and chairman of the Capital Press Club, said, "Where will the club now get its dash and color? We'll look for you back by election time. Meanwhile, we'll limp along as best we can."

Ernest E. Johnson, Washington correspondent for the Associated Negro Press, said: "The first bum steer I got when I came . . . was to keep away from the OWI. . . . [But] I found cues for and tips to many a good story on and around your desk at OWI—not to mention those into which I bumped while a guest in your home. . . . The pity of it is that I have never been able to tell any of the story of Ted Poston in Washington, to add to the saga of a boy from Hopkinsville. . . . [and] a man who works and loves his job."

The "silent, graying veteran of the last war who hardly speaks above a whisper," Col. Campbell C. Johnson of the Selective Service System, said: "I hope when a report is made of the work of Negro officials in government agencies during World War II the writers of the report will try in some measure to give due credit to your services."

George L-P Weaver wrote: "As [one] of those taken under your broad and generous wing during my first days in Washington, and having profited from your sage advice and help during those years . . . we will miss you."

Philleo Nash wrote Ted: "It is hard to see a team break up. You and I worked in OWI from its beginning. . . . I have a feeling that we have interrupted, not ended our partnership." All the letters are in Ted Poston Album, Manuscript, Archives, and Rare Books, Schomburg.

110. McKay, *Harlem*, 16–17. U. S. Poston's realty office was listed in the telephone directory from 1943 to 1946 as at 1728 Fulton. While Ulysses bowed out of the political fray, J. Raymond Jones began his moves to head Tammany in 1963 (Edwin R. Lewinson, *Black Politics in New York City* [New York: Twayne, 1974], 146–47).

111. Fern Eckman wrote: "As reporters, we had photographers with cars to drive us wherever we needed to go; out of town, we had expense accounts to hire cars and drivers. Also, living in New York with all forms of mass transportation makes a car a burden, not a necessity" (letter to author).

112. See Moon, *Balance of Power*, 134–35, 139–40. The CIO-PAC, formed in 1943, was a model for later political action committees. "It was Sidney Hillman's conviction that the basic interests of organized workers and the Negro masses were essentially the same" (ibid., 142). "When CIO came in, it was a new technique where they would unionize the entire shop, not on a skill or craft level. . . . They believed that one should unionize even the janitor, which meant that you had to unionize the Negroes too." See Ward, "Reminiscences," 58; also see Himes's autobiography, *Quality of Hurt*, 6–7; and Josephson, *Sidney Hillman*, 596–99.

113. TP, "A 'Clumsily-Great Government' in Action," review of *Frontier on the Potomac*, by Jonathan Daniels, *New York Post*, Oct. 31, 1946.

CHAPTER 9. POSTWAR *NEW YORK POST:* 1945–1954

1. TP, "Prejudice and Progress in New York: The Negro in Politics," IX, Apr. 25, 1956, 4, 71.

2. O'Dwyer, *Beyond the Golden Door*, 228–29; Nevins, "Past, Present, and Future," 33.

3. O'Dwyer, *Beyond the Golden Door*, 80, 87, 217, 318. O'Dwyer established the precursor to the city's Human Rights Commission when he set up a committee to help Puerto Ricans in employment, housing, and other essential services. Educated for the priesthood in Spain, O'Dwyer learned that "having a Spanish-speaking Mayor

in City Hall tended to make the new arrivals feel more at home, but that was a far cry from solving their psychological, social and economic difficulties" (ibid., 324; also see Carmer, "From Wyck to O'Dwyer," 113).

4. Walter, *Harlem Fox,* 8; Lewinson, *Black Politics,* 147.

5. TP, "Interracial Reporting."

6. "Dorothy Schiff, 86, Ex-Post Owner, Dies," *New York Times,* Aug. 31, 1989, sec. B, p. 11; Jack Newfield, "Goodbye, Dolly!" *Harper's,* Sept. 1969, 92–98; Nora Ephron, *Scribble, Scribble* (New York: Knopf, 1978), 3–11; Gail Sheehy, "The Life of the Most Powerful Woman in New York," *New York,* Dec. 10, 1973, 51–69.

7. Schiff sold the paper to Rupert Murdoch in 1976, but Poston was gone by then. He retired in 1972.

8. Potter, *Men, Money and Magic,* 175. Alicia Patterson, editor of *Newsday,* thought Backer was so sexy that just looking at him enter a room aroused her (ibid., 180). For the Swopes and Backer see Kahn, *World of Swope,* 26, 337.

9. Potter, *Men, Money and Magic,* 182.

10. Ibid., 176, 220–21.

11. Ibid., 198, 176, 231.

12. Ibid., 195.

13. Niles, born Neyhus, of Russian Jewish immigrants, was reared in a poor section of North Boston. He crusaded unsuccessfully to save Sacco and Vanzetti from execution, then in 1928 directed the National Committee of Independent Voters for Al Smith, where he met Roosevelt and Hopkins (Robert J. Donovan, *Conflict and Crisis: The Presidency of Harry S. Truman, 1945–1948* [New York: Norton, 1977], 315–16). Nash's work was with black groups and organizations and "writing Truman's speeches (a famous one at Howard University, and another in Harlem, in the 1948 election) and helping create the President's Commission on Civil Rights" (Edith Rosenfels Nash, "Philleo Nash and Georgetown Day School," in Landman and Halpern, eds., *Applied Anthropologist,* 34).

14. "This is the White House calling" was a standard form of telephone identification in Truman's day (Donovan, *Conflict and Crisis,* 7).

15. Philleo Nash, "Anthropologist in the White House," in Landman and Halpern, eds., *Applied Anthropologist,* 4.

16. See Woodward, "Made in USA," 26–28, 59; Nash, "Anthropologist," 5; and Nash, "Science," 193–95.

17. Woodward, "Made in USA," 28. Loyalty oaths "put fear in thousands of government employees. . . . for a wholesale inquisition. Faithful government workers, many among the lowest paid, were brought in for questioning about such things as their social life. . . . 'Do you now or did you ever entertain Negroes in your home?'" (O'Dwyer, *Beyond the Golden Door,* 415).

18. Brinkley, *Washington Goes to War,* 260.

19. Donovan, *Conflict and Crisis,* 316.

20. Potter, *Men, Money and Magic,* 201–2.

21. Shedding Thackrey was not painful for Schiff (ibid., 181).

22. See ibid., 283, and Hellman, "Profiles," 65, on lunches with Schiff.

23. The way Ruth Banks got the story, embellished by Poston, was that the "*New York Post* owner refused TRAMP's proposal to seduce her" (letter to author, Mar. 15, 1991). The rumors of the "affair" occurred after the mid-1960s, when both Schiff and TP were what was at that time considered old. "I do not think Ted would have had an affair with Dolly Schiff. Dolly was fascinated by a lot of men. Ted would have hinted to me and he never did" (Fern Marja Eckman, personal interview). Perhaps the rumors were started by people who saw Poston in the mid-1960s with Diana Bonnor Lewis, who was similar in age and appearance to Schiff. Lewis and Poston met when they were both sixty and were friendly until his death.

24. Eckman said: "Dolly is tall, slim and elegant." In 1984, George Trow said, "She doesn't believe in dying, in cancer, or anything like that." In 1989, Schiff died of cancer, having refused treatment.

25. Ersa Hines Poston and Diana Bonnor Lewis, interviews and letters.

26. Poston was reusing a line from his *Dark Side of Hopkinsville,* 19.

27. Himes expressed the love-hate relationship of some Negroes for Jews. Negroes "think Jews control all the money in the world," therefore they "have the power to do more for us than anyone else." Himes believed, "like other Negroes, that Jews fight, and underhandedly, our struggle for equality" (*Lonely Crusade,* 155, 159).

28. Sann's sensitivity about being Jewish is expressed in *Trial in the Upper Room,* 41.

29. Also see "The Werewolf of Woolworth's," *DSOH,* 47.

30. Hellman, "Profiles," 53–54.

31. Churchill told Schiff, "If I were a liberal newspaper publisher, God forbid, I would make Jimmy Wechsler my editor" (ibid., 44); Potter, *Men, Money and Magic,* 210–11; also see Lash, *Eleanor and Franklin,* 906–7. James A. Wechsler, *Age of Suspicion* (New York: Random House, 1953), 202.

32. "The *Post* was known to have the best rewrite bank in New York, and Ted was part of that" (George Arzt, telephone interview).

33. Walker, *City Editor,* 57.

34. The prevailing top minimum for reporters in 1949 was $110 per week. But the director of research and information for the Newspaper Guild adds, "Since there was no differential for rewrite and copy-desk work, the top for those jobs was no different" (David J. Eisen, letter to author, Jan. 28, 1994). Unions in some quarters were becoming non grata in the 1950s although Poston and most of his generation who had lived through the preunion days remained loyal to the Newspaper Guild. See Stern, *Memoirs,* 293–98; and Robert F. Keeler, *Newsday: A Candid History of the Respectable Tabloid* (New York: Arbor, 1990), 530–31.

35. "When I called in a story, Ted was quick to grasp what I was telling him. Also, whereas I rewrote a story God knows how many times, Ted did one draft, with lightning speed" (Eckman, letter to author).

36. When Ezzard Charles challenged Joe Louis for the heavyweight championship in 1950, Charles's mother allowed Poston into her home to witness the family's reaction (TP, [name of story missing], *New York Post,* Sept. 27, 1950).

37. Moon, not getting support at the NAACP, appreciated a gesture made by Ralph Bunche. Wilkins and Bunche wrote most of their own speeches, but "one time when Bunche was to address an NAACP group," he "sent a draft over to me," Moon says, "and I sent it back with two or three paragraphs on a matter that Bunche hadn't covered. To my utter surprise, [Bunche] delivered the speech and indicated, when he got to my section, that Henry Lee Moon had contributed this" (Moon, interview by Jackson).

38. TP, "Throngs View Bojangles Bier, Taps for Great Dancer Monday," *New York Post,* Nov. 23, 1949, 5, 28; TP, "Bojangles Takes His Last Curtain Call," *New York Post,* Nov. 28, 1949, 2. The title "Mayor" was an honorific. On how Robinson managed his mayoralty, see Calloway and Rollins, *Of Minnie the Moocher and Me,* 134–35.

39. Lewinson, *Black Politics,* 76. Walter, *Harlem Fox,* 8. J. Raymond Jones's first full-time political job had been as deputy U.S. marshal, his duty to escort prisoners from one jail to another (Lewinson, *Black Politics,* 145).

40. The founding of the Federal Housing Authority in 1934 made it possible for the first time for many people to own private homes with 10 percent down. But the government kept mortgages from Negroes (Keeler, *Newsday,* 136).

41. James A. Wechsler, *Reflections of an Angry Middle-Aged Editor* (New York: Random House, 1960), 124, 234–39.

42. "A Newspaper Pro: Ted Poston," in *Careers for Negroes on Newspapers,* brochure, American Newspaper Guild, Aug. 1964, 16.

43. TP, "American Negro," 66–67.

44. TP, "Interracial Reporting."

45. James A. Wechsler, memo to Don Hollenbeck, CBS, Dec. 19, 1949, Wechsler Papers.

46. TP, "American Negro," 66–67; TP, "Interracial Reporting." Poston put his awards and plaques on the wall by his basement bar. Hanging there at the time of his death were the Geist Foundation Award, 1949; Heywood Broun Award, 1949; Long Island University Award, 1950; NAACP Award, 1951; Beta Delta Nu Award, 1951; New York City Service Award, 1954; Lincoln University [Missouri] Citation, 1956; Brotherhood Council of Queens Award, 1957; Defiant Ones Award, 1958; Omega Psi Phi Award, 1958; Morningside Community Citation, 1961; Tennessee A. & I. Citation, 1962; Journalism Department, Lincoln University Citation, 1963; ARA Sorority Citation, 1964; Heywood Broun Award, 1966; and New York Urban League Award, 1967. The list is in Moon Papers, Schomburg.

47. TP, "A Novel from Africa," review of *Mine Boy,* by Peter Abrahams, *New York Post,* June 12, 1955.

48. Some people thought "Poston of the *Post*" was a made-up name, a "house by-

line," like "Godfrey Gloom," an Elmer Davis nom de plume (George Trow, personal interview).

49. Potter, *Men, Money and Magic,* 197. Schiff purchased the *Bronx Home News* in 1946.

50. Benjaminson, *Death in the Afternoon,* 194.

51. Hellman, "Profiles," 37.

52. Benjaminson, *Death in the Afternoon,* 1–2.

53. This may have been the Willie Reid stories, e.g. TP, " 'They'll Shoot Me in the Back of the Head,' " *New York Post,* Aug. 26, 1959, 5+, even though Reid was ultimately executed.

54. Tom Teepen of the *Atlanta Journal and Constitution* says that even today, "It is the dirty little secret of good journalists that they go into this business hoping to make the world better" ("Strout Wore Well the Hats of Both Reporter, Opiner," Aug. 28, 1990, sec. A, p. 15).

55. Trow said: "It could not be compared with Turner Catledge's *Times.* He was one of the greatest newspapermen in the history of the whole world. The *Times* was the mother of us all. We wouldn't have been able to get out our paper without the *Times.* The *World-Telegram* had in executives three-to-one what Dolly had—picture editors, assistant picture editors, a feature editor, assistant feature editor, every kind of a goddamn editor you ever heard of. Down at the *Post* we had about three guys" (personal interview). Also see Ephron, *Scribble, Scribble;* Newfield, "Goodbye, Dolly!"; and Sheehy, "Life of the Most Powerful Woman."

56. Bert Cochran, *Harry Truman and the Crisis Presidency* (New York: Funk and Wagnalls, 1973), 397.

57. See Buckley, *The Hornes,* 209; O'Dwyer, *Beyond the Golden Door,* 416, 423; Rampersad, *Life of Hughes,* 2:209–221; Barnes, "Philleo Nash"; Nash, "Anthropologist," 6; Donaldson, *Archibald MacLeish,* 398.

58. When McCarthy "discovered gold in the hills of anti-communism, he mined it diligently" but extracted "mainly fool's gold" (Harry Fleischman, *Norman Thomas, a Biography* [New York: Norton, 1964], 270); also see O'Dwyer, *Beyond the Golden Door,* 415.

59. Wechsler, *Age of Suspicion,* 34. Fern and Irving Eckman call Broun the hero of every liberal journalist. When Irving was at City College, "we had blacks who were graduating and attending the prom." When the hotel found that out, it tried to cancel. "We contacted Broun. He came and sat in the lobby all evening. Didn't say a word." And with Broun there, the hotel did not dare protest (interview with author). Wechsler remembers covering a meeting for the Columbia *Spectator* at which Broun spoke and Wechsler's "ineradicable recollection is the huge slug of gin [Broun] zestfully downed before mounting the narrow base of the Sun Dial across the street from the library steps" (*Age of Suspicion,* 54–55); also see Fleischman, *Norman Thomas,* 70.

60. Wechsler, *Age of Suspicion,* 56.

61. Wechsler, *Age of Suspicion,* 72–73. McCarthy's committee learned that in 1937 the Wechslers had led the Columbia Student Union's annual European summer tour, which included ten days in the Soviet Union. Wechsler had never been abroad; his wife had gone as a child. At the preembarkation party, the students' parents "expressed concern at the visible youthfulness" of the leaders. "They were reassured to learn that Nancy had been there before" (ibid., 110). Once in Europe, the Wechslers' charges were more interested in the opposite sex than politics. But it was "hard to explain all this to Senator McCarthy who seemed convinced that the group I had led was composed of hardened communist operatives conducting a large-scale espionage junket through Europe" (ibid., 112, 115–18).

62. As a senior in high school, Wechsler had "gone down to meetings at the Rand School where the Socialists held forth" and "found something fundamentally right and just about the view that no man should exploit his brother" (ibid., 34, 71, 300).

63. Wechsler's family endured further trauma. Every day at work he had been comforted by the photo on his desk circa 1948 of his son Michael, then six, and daughter Holly, two. The picture attained added poignancy when Michael, sometime before entering Harvard, asked to see a psychiatrist, then in 1969 died from a drug overdose (James A. Wechsler with Nancy F. Wechsler and Holly W. Karpf, *In a Darkness* [New York: Norton, 1972], 27).

64. David Remnick, "Profile: Prince of the City" [Murray Kempton], *New Yorker,* Mar. 1, 1993, 49. Kempton's career path resembled Poston's, based in 1930s labor organizing. He was hired by the *Post* in 1942 while Ted was in Washington but was then drafted into the army, where "I read an awful lot" because "there wasn't much to do" (ibid.). Kempton admired Norman Thomas, "conscience of the American people," for, among other things, his accomplishments in the fields of civil liberties and of better race relations (Fleischman, *Norman Thomas,* 298).

65. Quoted in Remnick, "Profile," 49–50. In 1949, Kempton succeeded Riesel and "expanded his beat from labor to whatever it was that struck him as a good story on a given day" (Wechsler, *Age of Suspicion,* 256–57).

66. Wechsler, *Age of Suspicion,* 281, 295. The notoriety caused Wechsler to be banned from a weekly television show *Starring the Editors* on which he had appeared with the editor of the Long Island paper *Newsday,* Alicia Patterson. Patterson was so incensed that she condemned the advertisers for removing him (Keeler, *Newsday,* 187–88).

67. Potter, *Men, Money and Magic,* 229–30, shows "the tensions and ugliness" of that period.

68. Quoted in TP, "Negro's Vivid Report on Jim Crow Land," review of *South of Freedom,* by Carl T. Rowan, *New York Post,* Aug. 3, 1952, sec. M, p. 12; also see Richard Bardolph, *The Negro Vanguard* (New York: Vintage, 1961), 250, for discriminatory techniques used on Rowan.

69. TP, letter to Philleo Nash and enclosure, Feb. 19, 1952, Truman Library.

70. Philleo Nash, memo to William D. Hassett, Feb. 26, 1952, Truman Library.

71. TP, "News (Good News) About the Negro in the Armed Forces," review of

Breakthrough on the Color Front, by Lee Nichols, *New York Post,* Feb. 7, 1954, sec. M, p. 12.

72. TP, "JFK and the Negro," *New York Post,* Nov. 24, 1963.

73. "Ted was a newsman, first; a raconteur at home, in good company, telling stories with the best, he could hold his liquor like the rest of us, but he never did a lot of woman-chasing that I knew about, or that, I think, anybody else knew about" (St. Clair Bourne, letter to author).

74. Inklings of the idea for the Urban League Guild's Beaux-Arts Ball, which joined her social consciousness to social life, were coming together for Mollie Lewis through the 1930s as she, Dr. Myra Logan, Lucile Armistead, Louise Logan, and a few others tried to raise money through "soliciting sponsors" and the "giving of entertainments" for the NAACP's *Crisis* magazine ("Some of the Officers and Members of the New York Crisis Committee," *Crisis,* n.d. [ca. 1938]). Before the Beaux-Arts Ball, black society had been stratified into the cafe group, "which earns a livelihood by competing in the white world," and the Negro upper class, which "moves smoothly and complacently within its own segregated orbit, content to live upon the Negro market as doctors, lawyers, dentists, and merchants" (Ottley, *New World A-Coming,* 167, 176–80). Lena Horne regarded much of black society as "just black Babbittry" (Buckley, *The Hornes,* 227).

75. "Negro Society's Biggest Ball: Urban League's Beaux Arts Brings Park Avenue to Harlem," *Ebony,* May 1954, 17–22.

76. Winthrop Rockefeller, on the Urban League board since 1940, after the army toured the United States checking on black veterans in housing and employment, the two main areas of concern of the board (Joe Alex Morris, *Those Rockefeller Brothers* [New York: Harper, 1953], 107–20; and John Ward, *The Arkansas Rockefeller* [Baton Rouge: Louisiana State University Press, 1978], 80–82).

77. At the 1949 Beaux-Arts Ball, Rockefeller was "star of the evening," the "most photographed and stared-at guest." For a time, with the blessing of Rockefeller, Mollie and Marilyn Kaemmerle ran a Fifth Avenue public relations firm (Marguerite Cartwright, "Useful People: Mollie Moon," *Negro History Bulletin,* Feb. 1957, 110). Perhaps the firm was Winthrop Products, O.T.C. Marketing, underwritten by Rockefeller. Henry Lee and Mollie Moon's papers at the Schomburg Center contain writings by Moon on this letterhead.

78. Previously blacks had not been welcome downtown. Miscegenation was a crime in some states; in California, for example, it was illegal for Lena Horne to marry bandleader Lennie Hayton. Eventually Horne sang at the Waldorf and made sure TP was given a table at ringside (TP, "Prejudice and Progress: Jim Crow in New York"); also see Arnold Rampersad, ed., *The Collected Poems of Langston Hughes* (New York: Knopf, 1994), 143. Hughes's parody, "Advertisement for the Waldorf-Astoria," *New Masses,* Dec. 1931, mocked such a luxury hotel when the streets were full of homeless people.

79. Nichols, ed., *Bontemps-Hughes Letters,* 244.

80. TP, "One-Man Task Force."

81. In 1947 the CIO-PAC sent Moon, essentially as a lobbyist, to Washington and on the road. He did not like the travel and seized the opportunity to get back to New York (Moon, letter to Julian Steele, 1947, Special Collections, Boston University Library); also see Moon, *Balance of Power,* 34 and 134, for Moon's explication of the work of the CIO-PAC and Negroes in conjunction with the Democratic National Committee.

82. Moon, though "quiet and unassuming," was a diplomatic "everybody's man Friday, a pal," Jackson says. "I've seen young women come up to him on the street and tell him 'I love you.'"

83. Henry Lee Moon, letter to Walter White, June 12, 1951, Moon Papers.

84. TP, confidential memo to James A. Wechsler, Mar. 25, 1955, Wechsler Papers.

85. Moon, interview by Jackson.

86. Thurgood Marshall wrote the charter for the Girl Friends, of which his wife, Vivian, and Marie Poston were original members (Michael D. Davis and Hunter R. Clark, *Thurgood Marshall* [New York: Birch Lane, 1993]). Rosemary Reed says that the Continentals were "friends who came together and did fund raising" for the NAACP or the Children's Hospital. "The women were high professionals, or wives of. They enjoyed entertaining, but they would put a social purpose to it so they wouldn't feel too guilty about having luncheons." TP used black women's clubs as a theme in his short story "Knee Baby Watkins," *DSOH,* 18.

87. "Mollie's parties" were a topic of correspondence between Hughes and Arna Bontemps; see Nichols, ed., *Bontemps-Hughes Letters,* 150, 159, 223.

88. Marie handled unpleasant incidents of discrimination briskly and assertively, according to Margaret Proctor, who remembers when she and Marie, in a New York restaurant, were taken to a table near the servants' door. "Marie said, 'We won't sit there!' She turned on her heel, and the *maitre d'* sat us elsewhere. That's how Marie was" (telephone interview, Sept. 3, 1985).

89. TP, "New York, New York," *New York Post,* Dec. 9, 1952, 4, 52.

90. TP, memo to John Bott, Sept. 22, 1966, Box 57, Schiff Papers.

91. "Ted Poston Wins American Newspaper Guild Award for 1949," *Bulletin,* Tennessee Agricultural and Industrial State College, Mar. 1950, 6.

92. *The Stage Is Set,* yearbook (Nashville: Tennessee Agricultural and Industrial State College, 1953), n.p.

93. In Hopkinsville, Fleming taught elementary school for forty-four years and Sunday school for thirty. Her mother and a sister Ione lived with her. "Ione was sweet and lovely, but no mental giant. She maintained the home, did the cooking. The family was protective of her" (Ersa Hines Poston, telephone interview).

94. Instead Bernice Bell Torian became a teacher like her female forebears and taught first grade at Belmont Elementary (Torian, telephone interview, Feb. 1, 1985).

95. TP, "Town Finally Honors Ignored Negro PWs," *New York Post,* Sept. 11, 1953.

96. TP, "Dixie's Fight for Freedom—IV," *New York Post,* June 27, 1954, 4, 23. Jennie Knight Baker says that because of segregation, she had not been permitted to

matriculate at the state university to get her master's degree in library science; she had to earn it out of state (personal interview).

97. Davis's son Mike co-wrote the biography of Thurgood Marshall.

98. Freda DeKnight, "Date with a Dish: Barbecued Squab; Succulent Birds Are Ted Poston's Favorite Dish," *Ebony*, Aug. 1955, 96.

99. TP and Roi Ottley, "New York vs. Chicago: Which City Is Better Place for Negroes?" *Ebony*, Dec. 1952, 16–24; see Bardolph on Ottley's eccentricity (*Negro Vanguard*, 250).

100. Roland E. Wolseley, *The Black Press, U.S.A.* (Ames: Iowa State University Press, 1972), quoted Poston on the sparsity of skilled workmanship in the black press (312).

101. TP, "Negro Press."

102. TP, "On Appeal in the Supreme Court" [profile of Thurgood Marshall], *Survey*, Jan. 1949.

103. See Ware, *William Hastie,* 170, for how Marshall started a case; also Moon, interview by Jackson.

104. For Truman's reaction to the eye-gouging, see Donovan, *Conflict and Crisis,* 242–44, and David McCullough, *Truman* (New York: Simon and Schuster, 1992), 589.

105. On NBC in 1959, Waring's nephew disputed with Roy Wilkins on school desegregation. Thomas Waring said that the "overwhelming majority of Southern people are unalterably opposed to mixing races in public schools. . . . [Most colored people] are happy and satisfied" ("Mr. Wilkins vs. Mr. Waring: The Battle of the South," *New York Post*, Feb. 15, 1959, sec. M, p. 10).

106. J. Waties Waring, "Reminiscences," 1972, Columbia University Oral History Project.

107. TP, interview by Kluger; Waring, letter to TP, Apr. 4, 1950, Waring Papers; also see Richard Kluger, *Simple Justice: The History of Brown vs. Board of Education and Black America's Struggle for Equality* (New York: Vintage, 1977), 306.

108. TP, letter to Waring, Apr. 13, 1950, Waring Papers; Elizabeth A. Waring, letter to TP, Oct. 18, 1950, ibid.

109. "An inner joyousness affecting everyone" permeated the house that a doctor had turned over to NAACP counsel use. "A lot of our skull sessions were in this attached garage because it was cooler out there and the breeze came through" (TP, interview by Kluger).

110. Waring, "Reminiscences."

111. Quoted in TP, interview by Kluger.

112. TP, "Hits Wagner Snub of Delany, Quits as Adviser," *New York Post*, Sept. 17, 1955, 5, 42.

113. Kluger, *Simple Justice,* 705.

114. TP, interview by Kluger.

115. TP, "Prejudice Is a Two-Way Street, Negro Learns," review of *The Seekers,* by Will Thomas, *New York Post*, July 5, 1953, sec. M, p. 12.

116. TP, "Timeworn Rusty Chain Binds Novelist's Miss. Negroes," review of *Chain in the Heart,* by Hubert Creekmore, *New York Post,* July 26, 1953, sec. M, p. 12.

117. TP, "Wright's Terrible Reality in a Violent, Explosive Novel," review of *The Outsider,* by Richard Wright, *New York Post,* Mar. 22, 1953.

118. TP, "Himes Writes of Prison Life: Novel Highlights Unconventional Love Story," review of *Cast the First Stone,* by Chester Himes, *New York Post,* Feb. 8, 1953.

119. TP, "Love and Vigilance in the South: The Case of Ruby McCollum," *New York Post,* Aug. 29, 1954, sec. M, p. 10.

120. TP, "How It Feels to Be Negro in America," review of *On Being Negro in America,* by J. Saunders Redding, *New York Post,* Oct. 21, 1951.

121. TP, "Fighting Editor: Fights for the Same Old South," review of *Where Main Street Meets the River,* by Hodding Carter, *New York Post,* May 24, 1953.

122. TP, "The Negro and His War: He Didn't Sit It Out in 1860–65," review of *The Negro in the Civil War,* by Benjamin Quarles, *New York Post,* Aug. 9, 1953, sec. M, p. 12.

123. TP, "Hailing a New Talent from Barbadoes," review of *In the Castle of My Skin,* by George Lamming, *New York Post,* Aug. 30, 1953.

124. TP, "Sorry, Father, But It's Not Wonderful."

125. "Portrait of Harlem," 149.

126. See William H. Hastie, "No Royal Road," in *Many Shades of Black,* ed. Stanton L. Wormley (New York: Morrow, 1969), 233.

127. Scott, *Domination and the Art of Resistance,* 202.

128. TP, interview by Kluger. Poston seemed undismayed by the pessimistic prediction: "One teacher told us it may cost her her job . . . but she said it may also make it possible for others to get a better one long after we have forgotten her" (TP, "South Takes School Bias Ban Calmly, Negro Leaders Move to Widen Fight," *New York Post,* May 18, 1954, 5, 40).

CHAPTER 10. INTEGRATION BY LAW: 1954–1957

1. TP, "Dixie's Fight for Freedom," *New York Post,* June 25, 27, 1954. Also see Dunnigan, *Fascinating Story of Black Kentuckians,* 196.

2. TP, "The Post's Reporter Gets to See Gov. Talmadge—by the Back Door," *New York Post,* May 25, 1954, 5, 32. The editor of the *Atlanta Daily World* "was convinced" that there would be "potential violence" in any attempt to implement the decision in Georgia immediately. C. A. Scott feared "widespread bloodshed when we first got the right to vote down here while old Gene Talmadge was governor." See TP, "Dixie's Fight for Freedom," June 25, 27, 1954.

3. "Our schools were integrated with no trouble whatsoever," TP's cousin Johnella Braxton Palmer says, because "the persons in the leadership positions in the black community were intelligent enough to help bring it about smoothly."

4. TP, "Dixie's Fight for Freedom," June 27, 1954. Talmadge, in his 1987 auto-

biography, says he has "since changed my views about the wisdom of segregated education" (Herman E. Talmadge, with Mark Royden Winchell, *Talmadge, a Political Legacy, a Politician's Life: A Memoir* [Atlanta: Peachtree, 1987], 155). His story resembles Poston's except regarding race (14–15, for example).

5. Claude Sitton, who covered the South for the *New York Times* during the civil rights era, thought he had "the greatest job in the world. So many great stories to choose from" (Gary Pomerantz, "Just the Facts," *Atlanta Journal and Constitution,* Dec. 2, 1990, sec. M, pp. 1, 4).

6. Such a reception undergirds a Himes character's pleasure at solitude, out from under white hegemony (*Primitive,* 72–73).

7. Ted told Ersa that Marie was born out of wedlock. Her mother changed the spelling of their last name and took Marie to New Jersey where Mae worked as a domestic (Ersa Hines Poston, telephone interview). Lea Adams says that although Marie and her mother were equally committed to the church, Mae Byrd was "different in virtually every other respect. Aunt Marie was elegant and vivacious; her mother was a plain, short woman who did not laugh easily. I recall only one conversation with her, when she taught me to say the 'Hail Mary.'" Regarding Marie on religion, her godchild Lea Adams says, "When I started going to Sunday School regularly, I attended St. Luke's Episcopal Church in Washington, at the insistence of my Aunt Elinor, who was a devout Episcopalian. Aunt Marie encouraged me to take my new faith seriously, despite her expression of mild disapproval that we 'renegade Catholics' did not accept the infallibility of the Pope. . . . On birthdays, Aunt Marie's card came without fail, until I was in my early 30s, and always arrived on time. She explained, after the first year of lapse, that she had lost her birthday book. She was clearly distressed at no longer being able to remember her many friends on their birthdays each year" (letter to author).

8. *Life* magazine claimed that Till was a "young man whose father had died a hero's death in Europe," then it discovered that Till's father was hanged in Italy under Dwight D. Eisenhower "for the crime of double murder and rape" (Howell Raines, *My Soul Is Rested: The Story of the Civil Rights Movement in the Deep South* [New York: Penguin, 1983], 299).

9. Remnick, "Profile," 50. See Raines, *My Soul Is Rested,* 132, on the circuslike atmosphere at the Till trial.

10. TP, "Interracial Reporting"; and interview by Kluger.

11. Ann Allen Shockley, *Afro-American Writers, 1746–1933: An Anthology and Critical Guide* (New York: NAL, 1989), 421. Walker delineates the erratic quality of a reporter's life in *City Editor,* 47–48. Apparently Marie was prepared to be jealous of Ted's women friends. Jennie Knight Baker remembers going to New York one summer and telephoning him. "He said, 'Meet me at the Hotel Theresa.' He brought Marie with him. She might have thought—a lady calling her husband—there was romance, but Marie said, 'Oh, you're just a country girl. I expected a sophisticated lady.' There was no malice. I was down-to-earth and she had no reason to fear my seeing Ted. We went to the hotel bar and chatted" (Baker, personal interview).

12. Poston's last wife, Ersa, studied a photocopy of the handwritten note and said that it was not from her.

13. The end of the second marriage was hard on Marie. She had felt committed to marriage as a sacrament and later told Lea Adams that she had "remained single for many years . . . while waiting for a Papal dispensation to remarry. She even showed me the petition which the Archbishop of New York had submitted on her behalf to the Vatican" (Adams, letter to author). Following the divorce, Marie visited the Reeds in Philadelphia and was incensed, Rosemary says, when her father "told Marie he would like to keep a friendship with Uncle Ted. For Marie, it was like, 'You either love me or him!' She seemed to feel that my parents should share her point of view. Marie could have been warmer. I did expect and get more warmth from Uncle Ted. Marie was a *grande dame,* an Auntie Mame. I don't consider that terrible. When I knew her as an adult, it was like admiring a tycoon." When Reed looked for work in Puerto Rico, she asked Marie for contacts. "When I was job hunting or traveling she gave me a lot of names, a good career person and resource. I thought, 'This is her gift to me.' She didn't relate well, but I appreciated what she offered" (Reed, telephone interview).

14. See "Jet Profile: First Woman Director of EEOC Regional Office" [Marie Byrd Poston], *Jet,* July 20, 1967, 10, for the range of jobs Marie held.

15. TP, "Bus Boycott Leader Hailed as Symbol of Hope in Bias Fight," *New York Post,* Mar. 26, 1956, 5, 37.

16. Hall got the idea for "Tell It Not in Gath" from the Bible: "David's lament over Saul and Jonathan, in which, in a flight of poetic imagination, he voiced the wish that the misfortunes of his friends and nation be not made known to their heathen enemies" ("'. . . Lest the Daughters of the Philistines Rejoice,'" *Montgomery Advertiser,* Apr. 7, 1956, sec. A, p. 4).

17. "Casting the First Stone," editorial, *Hartford Courant,* reprinted in *Montgomery Advertiser,* Apr. 17, 1956, sec. A, p. 4.

18. "Invasion of the South," *Newsweek,* Apr. 2, 1956, 86. Also see Remnick, "Profile," on Kempton. Hall was a "writer with pungency," the *Christian Science Monitor* said, whose editorial page was judged "every bit as interesting" as when his father edited it (quoted in "It's Published in Askelon—I," *Montgomery Advertiser,* Apr. 17, 1956, sec. A, p. 4). Hall was "anything but" a conventional white citizen. "Scorning piety and most social orthodoxy, he cultivated his own eccentricity. . . . [He was] a dandy," says Taylor Branch in *Parting the Waters: America in the King Years, 1954–63* (New York: Simon and Schuster, 1988), 152. *Time* credited Hall for "blasting Alabama's Governor James ('Kissin' Jim') Folsom" by saying, "This untaught knave . . . lacks the grace and prudence to keep zippered his flapping mandible to conceal his void" ("Southern Hospitality," *Time,* June 25, 1956, 76).

19. TP, "Jim Crow in New York," *New York Post,* Apr. 22, 1956, 4, 5.

20. One writer addressed the *Advertiser* testily, "I have read the *Newsweek* accounts of your exchange of letters with *New York Post* editor Pinkie Wechsler relative to your working with their bleeding heart reporter Murray Kempton, and am in accord with your principles" (Tom Johnson, "Tell It Not in Gath, Publish It Not in the Streets of Askelon, VIII," *Montgomery Advertiser,* Apr. 3, 1956).

21. "Southern Hospitality."

22. TP, "American Negro," 65. The *Advertiser* won awards for typography, makeup, and printing. See "Typography Award Won by Advertiser," *Montgomery Advertiser,* Apr. 20, 1956, 1.

23. "The Education of a Negro Reporter," *Montgomery Advertiser,* June 22, 1956, sec. A, p. 4.

24. TP, "Interracial Reporting."

25. "The Negroes of Montgomery: How They Work," X, *New York Post,* June 21, 1956, 4, 48.

26. Wechsler, *Reflections,* 130.

27. TP, "The Negroes of Montgomery: Letter to an Alabama Editor," XII, June 24, 1956, 5, 16.

28. "Dear Editor: He Might Even Let Them Play with White Boys," *New York Post,* June 20, 1956, 41.

29. N. G. Sherouse, "Poston Is Not Reliable." See "Tell It to Old Grandma," *Montgomery Advertiser,* Apr. 4, 1956, sec. A, p. 4.

30. "Dear Editor: Never Better," *New York Post,* June 15, 1956.

31. TP, "'Back to Ol' Virginny . . . First Class,'" *New York Post,* Sept. 7, 1956, 1, 47.

32. "Poston, Ted," *Who's Who in Colored America,* 7th ed. (Yonkers-on-Hudson, N.Y.: Burckel, 1950), 423. Also see Patterson, *Chronicles,* 162, for more on Poston's former facetiously named "Capahosic Country Club" becoming the site for United Negro College Fund planning sessions.

33. TP, "Dinner for 4 Was OK, But Not for 5," *New York Post,* Oct. 7, 1956, 4, 25. His "Filipino" friends were Albert W. Dent, president of Dillard University; Rufus E. Clement, president of Atlanta University; William J. Trent, executive director of the United Negro College Fund; and F. D. Patterson, executive director of the Phelps-Stokes Fund.

34. TP, "Mama's Whammy Runs into Poston's Jinx," *New York Post,* Oct. 11, 1956, 3, 81.

35. TP, "Mahalia Jackson Sings and Montgomery Rocks," *New York Post,* Dec. 7, 1956, 10.

CHAPTER 11. DEAN OF BLACK JOURNALISTS: 1957–1964

1. "Ms. Dorothy Schiff, 86, Owned New York *Post,*" *Atlanta Journal and Constitution,* Aug. 31, 1989. Of the 1949 Geist Foundation Awards for the most distinguished contributions to interfaith and interracial understanding, the $500 first prize went to Eleanor Roosevelt for her newspaper columns opposing discrimination in all forms. TP and Oliver Pilat of the *Post* shared the $400 second place award for "outstanding reporting on the subject of group friction" ("Mrs. FDR, Poston, Pilat Win Awards for Fighting Bias," *New York Post,* Jan. 23, 1950).

2. Ted Poston, interview by Robert D. Graff, Dec. 20, 1961, Small Collections, Papers of Robert D. Graff, ABC producer, transcripts of interviews with Ted Poston

for the Roosevelt story, No. 521, take 1, Franklin D. Roosevelt Library. Another time, after a meeting, Poston hailed a cab for Mrs. Roosevelt. "The cabbie was surprised when we got in and said 'White House!' but after a double take, he carried us there and she reached for her purse to pay for it." Poston told her, "Never mind! I'll pay for this," but the cabbie piped up, "Nobody's gonna pay anything for this! *I* carried Mrs. Roosevelt!" (ibid.).

3. "Post Honored by AJC, Called 'Spokesman for Liberalism,'" *New York Post,* Mar. 6, 1957, 59.

4. TP, "She Prepared for Norfolk for a Lifetime," *New York Post,* Feb. 5, 1959.

5. TP, "Martin Luther King: Where Does He Go from Here?" VI, *New York Post,* Apr. 14, 1957, sec. M, p. 5; TP, "Graduation Ceremony—for a Class and an Era," *New York Post,* June 3, 1957, 7.

6. Also see Stephen B. Oates, *Let the Trumpet Sound: The Life of Martin Luther King, Jr.* (New York: Harper, 1982), 139; and TP, "For Rev. King, Get-Well Wishes—and a Trickle of Hate Mail," *New York Post,* Sept. 25, 1958; TP, "Rev. King Continues to Gain: Takes First Steps Since Stabbing," *New York Post,* Sept. 23, 1958, 4, 17; TP, "Rev. King Wants to Go Back to Work," *New York Post,* Sept. 24, 1958, 4, 30. In his review of *Stride,* TP praised King's writing style as "prose the most experienced newspaper rewrite man might envy" ("Epic of Our Time," review of *Stride Toward Freedom,* by Martin Luther King, Jr., *New York Post,* Sept. 28, 1958).

7. TP, "Althea Gibson," *New York Post* series, Aug. 25, 1957, to Sept. 1, 1957; also see TP, "Althea Would Love All the Acclaim—If She Could Only Get Some Sleep," *New York Post,* July 10, 1957, 2; and TP, "Exalted, Exhausted, Althea Hides Away," *New York Post,* July 10, 1957, 2.

8. Quoted in Helen Dudar, "Woman in the News: Mrs. Ersa Poston," *New York Post,* Dec. 13, 1964, 25. For Dudar, see Keeler, *Newsday,* 197.

9. "500,000," in *Famous Blacks Give Secrets of Success* (Chicago: Johnson, 1973).

10. Quoted in Dudar, "Woman in the News."

11. "I would say Marie was insecure. She was vicious towards me, and I had nothing to do with their separation or divorce. Marie was able to keep good jobs, but she'd kill folks in the way on her critical path to achievement" (Ersa H. Poston, telephone interview).

12. "He used a little stubby cigarette holder with a filter in it, before cigarettes had all those built-in filters. He thought that would discourage him from smoking so much. I kidded him that he looked old-fashioned" (ibid.).

13. Quoted in Wechsler, *Reflections,* 113.

14. Daisy Bates, *The Long Shadow of Little Rock* (1962; rpt. Fayetteville: University of Arkansas Press, 1987), 165.

15. "On 2 Sept., [1957] Governor Orval E. Faubus ordered the Arkansas National Guard and State Police to surround Central High School . . . to 'prevent disorder.' . . . In a speech delivered that evening, Governor Faubus declared that 'blood will run in the streets,' if Negro students tried to enter" ("Bates, Daisy," Biography, State Historical Society of Wisconsin).

16. TP, "Nine Kids Who Dared: Gloria Ray," VII, *New York Post,* Oct. 28, 1957,

sec. M, p. 2. Gloria Ray Karlmark became a lawyer. See Peter Baker, "40 Years Later, 9 Are Welcomed: Little Rock Marks Civil Rights Milestone," *Washington Post*, Sept. 26, 1997, sec. A-1, pp. 8, 9.

17. TP, "Nine Kids."

18. Bates, *Long Shadow of Little Rock*, 111.

19. TP, "Nine Kids."

20. TP, "7 Kids Who Tried," XI, *New York Post*, Nov. 1, 1957, sec. M, p. 2.

21. TP, "Little Rock, Four Months After . . . ," *New York Post*, Jan. 27, 1958, 2.

22. TP, "Little Rock—Where Minnie Jean Fights Back," *New York Post*, Feb. 7, 1958, 4, 10.

23. See also TP, "The 19-Day Ordeal of Minnie Jean Brown," *New York Post*, Feb. 9, 1958, 3; TP, "Minnie Jean Will Attend School Here," *New York Post*, Feb. 18, 1958; TP, "Minnijean Wants to Be 'Just a Teen-Ager,'" *New York Post*, Feb. 24, 1958, 5, 21; TP, "NAACP to Little Rock: Don't Expect Minnie Jean," *New York Post*, Feb. 14, 1958, 7.

24. TP explained, "Brown's own background . . . would only lend support to Superintendent Blossom's and other racists' proclamations . . . that 'The nigger kids ain't nothing and they came from nothing.'. . . An unlettered man, Brown is known for his violent temper, and—of all the parents—he hangs out with a tough bunch" (TP, memos to James A. Wechsler, May 27, Sept. 9, Nov. 20, 1958; July 24, 25, 1959, Mar. 7, [no year], Box 6, Wechsler Papers).

25. Bates, *Long Shadow of Little Rock,* 150–61, 164.

26. Ibid., 184.

27. TP, "Little Rock High Schools Reopening; Gang Fires on Home of Daisy Bates," *New York Post*, Aug. 12, 1959, 3.

28. "It Reads Like a Thriller," review of *The Long Shadow of Little Rock,* by Daisy Bates, *New York Post*, Oct. 28, 1962.

29. TP, "Suicide in the CHA: Feared Loss of Job over Race Issue," *New York Post*, Jan. 13, 1958.

30. TP, "Fresh Air in Dixie," review of *An Epitaph for Dixie,* by Harry S. Ashmore, *New York Post*, Jan. 26, 1958.

31. "'We Have So Much to Say'" [Lorraine Hansberry], *New York Post*, Mar. 22, 1959, sec. M, p. 2; Langston Hughes, "Harlem," in *Selected Poems* (New York: Vintage, 1974), 268.

32. TP, "The Simple World of Langston Hughes," *New York Post*, Nov. 24, 1957, sec. M, p. 2; TP, "A Hughes Omnibus," review of *The Langston Hughes Reader: The Selected Writings of Langston Hughes, New York Post*, Apr. 6, 1958.

33. TP, "Two Score and Ten Years Ago," *New York Post*, Feb. 8, 1959, sec. M, p. 4. The Spingarn Medal, awarded annually for Negro achievement, was instigated in 1914 by Arthur's brother, Joel Spingarn, who headed the NAACP until his death in 1939.

34. Hughes, letter to Poston, Sept. 20, 1961, Beinecke Rare Book and Manuscript Library, Yale University. Hughes continually pressed Poston to write a book. "I like your Hopkinsville stories enormously, and if it was me (and they were mine) while

the iron is hot (current interest in things Negro) I'd put them all together and make a book out of them" (Hughes, letter to Poston, July 2, 1964, ibid.).

35. TP, "At Home with the Poet" [Langston Hughes], *New York Post,* June 11, 1962.

36. "We had a policy on the *Post,* that if there was an arrest or murder, you didn't identify the culprit by race. That suddenly changed" (Fern Marja Eckman, personal interview).

37. TP, "Three Flights Up to the Fourth Estate," *New York Post,* June 11, 1959, 5.

38. TP, "'There Are No Seats in the Colored Section,'" *New York Post,* June 12, 1959, 5, 17.

39. Wechsler's dismay at southern "justice" is recorded in *Reflections,* 127–28.

40. James A. Wechsler, "A Reporter in Florida," editorial, *New York Post,* June 12, 1959. Because of the *Post*'s desire to emphasize more good news about Negroes than crime stories, in a July 25 memo, Poston explained to Wechsler how Police Commissioner Steve Kennedy's own dealings with blacks had contributed to another near riot in Harlem (Box 6, Wechsler Papers).

41. TP, "'They'll Shoot Me in the Back of the Head,'" *New York Post,* Aug. 26, 1959, 5+; "Rockefeller Orders Willie Reid Sent Back to Florida Prison," *New York Post,* Nov. 23, 1959.

42. Muriel I. Symington, "Dear Editor: Unselfish Words," *New York Post,* May 28, 1959, 41.

43. TP, "The Strength of Non-Violence" [Z. K. Matthews], *New York Post,* Sept. 28, 1952; TP, "The Man from Ghana" [Kwame Nkrumah], *New York Post,* July 27, 1958, sec. M, p. 4.

44. TP, "Powell's Harlem Threat to Tiger Grows," *New York Post,* Aug. 6, 1958.

45. TP, "Randolph for Powell, Cites Seniority," *New York Post,* May 28, 1958; also see TP, "The Bell Rings in Powell's School," *New York Post,* May 20, 1958, 5, 31; Arthur Massolo and Ted Poston, "Jack Says Powell Stirs Hooliganism in Effort to Scare Off Political Foes," *New York Post,* May 19, 1958, 5+; Alfred D. Hendricks and Ted Poston, "Survey Reveals Heavy Support for Powell in Harlem," *New York Post,* May 23, 1958, 4+.

46. Pete Hamill, *A Drinking Life: A Memoir* (Boston: Little, 1994), 217–22.

47. Hellman, "Profiles," 40.

48. *Gamin* may have represented the Ted she first knew in 1923, a "saucy Negro boy . . . quizzical and scornful as he looks askance at a world he has come to know too early and too intimately" (*Dictionary of American Biography,* s.v. "Savage, Augusta"). Neither Savage nor Maysie Stone had been able to earn a living wage through sculpture. A 1994 television documentary said that Savage "with a pickax . . . destroyed all her unsold sculptures" (*Against the Odds,* documentary [Augusta Savage], prod. Nila Arnow, dir. Amber Edwards, PBS, WPBA, Atlanta, Feb. 16, 1994).

49. TP, "Negro Voters Feeling the Squeeze in Tennessee," *New York Post,* June 29, 1960, 8; TP, "Oil Firms: Can't Stop Squeeze on Tenn. Negroes," *New York Post,* June 30, 1960; TP, "FBI Investigating Squeeze on Tenn. Negro Voters," *New*

York Post, July 1, 1960; "N.Y. Group Plans Aid to Negroes in Tenn. Boycott," *New York Post,* July 7, 1960.

50. Theodore H. White, *In Search of History* (New York: Harper & Row, 1979), 472; also see 321–23; and TP, "CORE Warns Sit-Ins Will Go on in South," *New York Post,* Oct. 18, 1960.

51. "The Rev. King Hails Kennedy for His 'Courageous Stand,'" *New York Post,* Nov. 1, 1960.

52. Arthur M. Schlesinger, Jr., *Robert Kennedy and His Times* (New York: Ballantine, 1978), 334.

53. TP, "Weaver Set for Top U.S. Housing Job," *New York Post,* Dec. 30, 1960.

54. TP, "It's a Tough Job"; also see Arthur M. Schlesinger, Jr., *A Thousand Days: John F. Kennedy in the White House* (New York: Fawcett, 1965), 606, 851, 857.

55. The archivist at the Kennedy Library perused several collections of papers, including Salinger's, but could not find evidence of the Kennedy administration's feeler to Ted. Salinger says, "The name Ted Poston rings a bell but I do not recall asking him to come work in the press office of the White House. . . . Unfortunately, 26 years after the events, it is difficult to remember everything" (Pierre Salinger, letter to author, Sept. 1, 1987).

56. Wechsler acknowledged Davis and TP for helping him on *Reflections,* published that year.

57. Potter, *Men, Money and Magic,* 266.

58. Sann's wife, Birdye, played poker also and between her and TP "there was a real closeness that persisted through the years" (Paul Sann, telephone interview; also see Sann, *Trial in the Upper Room,* 20, 71–72).

59. On the hobbling of a reporter's spirit, see Walker, *City Editor,* 47.

60. TP, "Interracial Reporting."

61. Was Poston an alcoholic? "He probably drank too much occasionally. We all did. I look at an alcoholic as someone who not only drinks more than is good for his health, but also someone who drinks until it is debilitating, that he can't run his life effectively. That was not true of Ted" (Robert C. Weaver, personal interview).

62. "Noted Newspaper Reporter Ted Poston and Wife," Smirnoff ad, *Jet,* Mar. 28, 1962, 42; *Ebony,* May 1963, 127.

63. See Joseph Osborne, "Arts and Entertainment: Reminiscing over Mollie Moon's Brainchild 'Beaux Arts Ball,'" *Amsterdam News,* Feb. 9, 1991, 23, on the Beaux-Arts. Published in Paris in 1963 as *Mamie Mason,* Himes's book "took Paris by storm." See Gilbert H. Muller, *Chester Himes* (Boston: Twayne, 1989), 18, 75; also see Gerri Major, with Doris E. Saunders, *Black Society* (Chicago: Johnson, 1976), 366–67. Himes mentions the Moons and the Russian trip, although some details are inaccurate, in *Quality of Hurt,* 75.

64. Chester Himes, *Pinktoes* (1961; rpt. Chatham, N.J.: Chatham Bookseller, 1975), 28.

65. Stephen F. Milliken, *Chester Himes: A Critical Appraisal* (Columbia: University of Missouri Press, 1976), 259, 265.

66. Himes, *Pinktoes*, 121. *Pinktoes* is part of Himes's "persistent effort to explore unpleasant truths and basic absurdities in American culture" (Muller, *Chester Himes*, x; also see James Lundquist, *Chester Himes* [New York: Ungar, 1976], 139–40).

67. Poston was "best known," but other black journalists were now infiltrating white papers (Bardolph, *Negro Vanguard*, 338–39).

68. TP, "Muslims."

69. The Horne family biography, by Lena's daughter Gail Buckley, which often cites the *New York Post* as a source for information, supports Poston's contention that Negroes looked to the *Post* for race news. Langston Hughes told Arna Bontemps, "If your Library doesn't get the *New York Post,* I'd say subscribe to it . . . as it has the best coverage of any papers of the Negro in sports—good feature pieces almost daily" (quoted in Nichols, ed., *Bontemps-Hughes Letters,* 419).

70. Also see Tom Johnson in LaBrie, ed., *Perspectives of the Black Press,* 188, and Keeler, *Newsday,* 369.

71. TP, memo to Paul Sann, July 3, 1962, Box 6, Wechsler Papers.

72. A. J. Liebling, *The Wayward Pressman* (Garden City, N.Y.: Doubleday, 1948), 134–39.

73. Kluger, *Paper,* 650; also see Ellis Cose, *The Press* (New York: Morrow, 1989), 188–89, 208; and Liebling, *Wayward Pressman,* 289–91.

74. *Editor and Publisher* says that Poston "did special work for the City's Rent and Rehabilitation Administration" during the shutdown ("New York Post Resumes with 600,000 Daily Run," *Editor and Publisher,* Mar. 9, 1963, 9+).

75. By the 1960s, "fewer and fewer workers could remember the heroic strikes of the 1930s" (William Manchester, *The Glory and the Dream: A Narrative History of America, 1932–1972* [New York: Bantam, 1974], 1000–1001).

76. Hamill, *Drinking Life,* 235.

77. Moon, interview by Jackson.

78. Connable and Silverfarb, "J. Raymond Jones," 351.

79. James Roosevelt, a member of the House Education Committee, says that Powell "truly cared about progressive government and the cause of the inadequately educated and poorly paid workingman. . . . But he was not interested in hard work" (*My Parents,* 335–37).

80. Lewinson, *Black Politics,* 129.

81. James A. Wechsler, "Powell's Folly," *New York Post,* Mar. 27, 1963, 46.

82. Quoted in James M. Washington, ed., *A Testament of Hope: The Essential Writings and Speeches of Martin Luther King, Jr.* (New York: HarperSanFrancisco, 1991), 295.

83. Branch, *Parting the Waters,* 804.

84. TP, "Mail to Help Evers Family Irks Barnett," *New York Post,* Jan. 10, 1964.

85. TP, "Beckwith Goes on Trial for Murder of Evers," *New York Post,* Jan. 27, 1964; and TP, "Beckwith's Day in Court."

86. TP, "Mrs. Medgar Evers Waits to Confront the Accused," *New York Post,* Jan. 29, 1964.

87. TP, "A Statement on Racism—By Beckwith," *New York Post,* Jan. 31, 1964, 11.

88. TP, "Mrs. Evers on Stand: 'Loud Blast, Silence . . . ,'" *New York Post,* Jan. 31, 1964.

89. TP, "Closeup: The Evers Judge," *New York Post,* Jan. 31, 1964.

90. Bertram Wyatt-Brown discusses this technique in his introduction to W. J. Cash's *The Mind of the South* (1941; rpt. New York: Vintage, 1991).

91. TP, "Interracial Reporting."

92. Byron de la Beckwith was not found guilty by his "peers" for thirty-one years. Not until 1994 did "peers" include other than middle-aged white Mississippi males; see Raines, *My Soul Is Rested,* 272.

93. TP, "Harlem Reacts to the Explosion," *New York Post,* Sept. 18, 1963.

94. King said, "The aftermath of nonviolence is the creation of the beloved community, while the aftermath of violence is tragic bitterness" (Washington, ed., *Testament of Hope,* 18).

95. TP, "JFK and the Negro," *New York Post,* Nov. 24, 1963.

96. "If you are a professional newspaperman or woman, you do not refuse assignments" (George Trow, personal interview).

97. Poston's colleague Helen Dudar remembers that Wechsler wanted to hire Jack Newfield because of his liberal leanings, but Al Davis did not. When Schiff asked Davis why he did not hire Newfield, Davis said, "He had another job offer," which Schiff found out was not true. This contributed to Schiff's decision that Davis was finished. Dudar says, "It is interesting that with Al's departure, the paper almost immediately renewed its concerns with black issues with particular attention to a new, emerging leadership" (Dudar, letter to author).

98. Dudar, "Woman in the News."

99. See Nichols, ed., *Bontemps-Hughes Letters,* 407, on the enterprising Rowan.

100. TP, "Closeup: Carl Rowan."

CHAPTER 12. THE TORCH PASSES TO A NEW GENERATION: 1964–1972

1. TP, "Scholarships for Negroes: A Program That Works," *New York Post,* Apr. 19, 1964.

2. TP, "Plain Talk for Both Sides," review of *Crisis in Black and White,* by Charles Silberman, *New York Post,* May 17, 1964, 47.

3. TP, "American Negro," 69.

4. TP, "Interracial Reporting."

5. The *Post* got a telephone tip of a "race riot" on a Harlem River excursion boat, and "hundreds of white parents [were] frightened that their children on a school outing were being slashed by rampaging Negroes," when the incident "was only a fistfight between two tawny Italian youths" (TP, "American Negro," 70).

6. Ted Poston and Joseph Kahn, "Negro Boy, 15, Killed by Cop; Students Riot," *New York Post,* July 16, 1964.

7. TP, "Violence Flares for Third Night: 50 Injured in Harlem," *New York Post,*

July 21, 1964, 2, 53; TP, "Rioting Ebbs in Harlem," *New York Post,* July 22, 1964, 2, 30; also see Bruce Perry, *Malcolm: The Life of a Man Who Changed Black America* (Barrytown, N.Y.: Station Hill, 1991), 308–11, for a discussion of the James Powell case. See Connable and Silverfarb, "J. Raymond Jones," 352–53. Historian William Manchester has recorded the riot's spread in *Glory and the Dream,* 1020–21.

8. Manchester, *Glory and the Dream,* 1022. The Klansman who shot Chaney gloated, "At least I killed me a nigger" (ibid., 1024).

9. TP, "Mississippi: Tragic Anniversary," *New York Post,* June 20, 1965; also see Raines, *My Soul Is Rested,* 178, 278, 282–83.

10. Susie Poston had told Ted about "Nathaniel," "the sweetest kid you'd ever know. All he cared about was that piano." Ted telephoned Susie in Paducah when "Nathaniel" died at age forty-five. She said, "He smoked, son" (TP, "Nat King Cole: As They Remember Him," *New York Post,* Feb. 16, 1965).

11. TP, "Malcolm and the Muslims," *New York Post,* Feb. 22, 1965.

12. Ibid.

13. Journalists who did not see interracial marriages as anathema regarded with amusement those who did. See Wechsler, *Reflections,* 125.

14. Hughes, letter to TP, Mar. 9, 1967, Beinecke Rare Book and Manuscript Library; TP, "Man in the News: Thurgood Marshall, LBJ's Choice for Solicitor General of the U.S.," *New York Post,* July 18, 1965. Also see Carl T. Rowan, *Dream Makers, Dream Breakers: The World of Justice Thurgood Marshall* (Boston: Little, Brown, 1993), 297; Davis and Clark, *Thurgood Marshall,* 248.

15. TP, "Robert C. Weaver, Sec. of Housing," *New York Post,* Jan. 23, 1966.

16. Lady Bird Johnson, *A White House Diary* (New York: Dell, 1970), 387.

17. Benjaminson, *Death in the Afternoon,* 2–3.

18. Moon, interview by Jackson.

19. TP, "Closeup: Unseated Legislator," 24.

20. Ersa Hines Poston, Paul Sann, and Margaret Proctor interviews.

21. *The MARC Experiment,* brochure, Metropolitan Applied Research Center, n.d., 2; and Clayton Knowles, "Group Formed Here to Influence Government Decisions on Aid to Urban Poor," *New York Times,* Mar. 9, 1967.

22. Fraser says, "The *Times* had a black photographer in 1966. I have been here since 1967. Ted was significant because he worked longer in New York than any other black journalist. Poston was the one" (C. Gerald Fraser, telephone interview, Mar. 20, 1982). Paul Sann tendered the accolade: "Ted set a standard for the black newspaperman that, to my *per*sonal knowledge, has not ever been equaled. I had experience with a small army of *dread*ful black reporters, just as I had with dreadful white reporters. They come in all colors, but we never had a black who came within miles of Ted's talent, except Earl Caldwell, who was only on the paper about five minutes before the *Times* discovered him" (Sann, telephone interview).

23. Hellman, "Profiles," 62, and Potter, *Men, Money and Magic,* 188.

24. Charles Kaiser, "Salim L. Lewis, Wall St. Pioneer in Stock Block Trading, Dies at 69," *New York Times,* May 1, 1978, sec. 4, p. 8. Salim Lewis was known as "a fierce fund raiser," garnering $100 million for three hundred building projects while

he was chairman of the City of Life Building Fund of the Federation of Jewish Philanthropies. He was named to the Board of Education by Mayor John V. Lindsay.

25. TP, "Hughes Tribute: 'He Knew Us,'" *New York Post,* May 25, 1967.

26. Ruth Banks, a psychologist, says that if a man who lacks self-esteem gets a desirable woman, he begins to think that maybe she is not that precious because *he* got her: "That does things to men in their patterning years, and this has implications for the adult years" (interview with author).

27. Earl Caldwell and TP, "Harlem Reaction Worries City," *New York Post,* Jan. 10, 1967; "CORE Sets Separate Harlem School Board," *New York Post,* Mar. 1, 1967; "Harlem Vows to Vote Him Back," *New York Post,* Mar. 2, 1967.

28. Dorothy West substantiates the notion of the black militants of the 1960s. "They hated the [black] doctors. In my novel [*The Living Is Easy,* 1948, afterword by Adelaide M. Cromwell (Old Westbury, N.Y.: Feminist, 1982)], I was trying to show they do not spring full-blown as doctors. You would be surprised at the number of doctors who [got] through school by working on the steamers, on the Bangor-Maine Line" (Jane Knowles, "Dorothy West Describes the Harlem Renaissance," *Radcliffe News,* Apr. 1982, 8). Ruth Edmonds Hill, when interviewing Etta Moten Barnett for the Black Women Oral History Project at Radcliffe's Schlesinger Library, commented, "I think there were young people in the 1950s and sixties who almost thought they had discovered civil rights" (Barnett, interview with Ruth Edmonds Hill, 91).

29. TP, "Closeup: Black, White, and Brown," *New York Post,* July 26, 1967.

30. Manchester, *Glory and the Dream,* 1076.

31. Moon told Luther P. Jackson that Rosenthal was "angry as hell at Ted Poston's caustic remark about the shoddy coverage the *Times* was giving the Harlem area" (interview by Jackson, 354).

32. TP, "American Negro," 64, 67, 71.

33. Nancy Hicks and Ted Poston, "Train Negro Vets or Risk Peril: Sutton," *New York Post,* Feb. 22, 1968.

34. TP, "Interracial Reporting."

35. Kerner Commission, *Report of the National Advisory Commission on Civil Disorders* (New York: Bantam, 1968), xv.

36. Quoted in Cose, *The Press,* 246.

37. Kerner Commission, *Report,* 387.

38. George Arzt and Ted Poston, "He's a Pusher at Age 12," *New York Post,* Feb. 26, 1970, 1, 4.

39. Sann remembered the fatigue of the period—no second wind or adrenaline rush came as relief, "like one of those around-the-clock grinds on the paper with a Kennedy or King assassination or an election night or Watergate" (Sann, *Trial in the Upper Room,* 58). Eckman remembers that Ted was disappointed to discover that the stories of King's infidelities were apparently true. When Schiff met with the attorney general, they discussed King. Robert Kennedy was hesitant about bringing up rumors of King's infidelity until she said they already knew about the matter from other sources. Kennedy credited King, however, with keeping violence down.

40. TP, "Interracial Reporting."

41. Manchester, *Glory and the Dream,* 1416.

42. Ed [*sic*] Poston and William Greaves, "Tells Why City OKd Nude Fair," *New York Post,* Dec. 14, 1970.

43. TP, "Interracial Reporting."

44. Scott, *Domination and the Art of Resistance,* 215.

45. Ernie Johnston says, "All of us on the *Post* testified on Artis's behalf—Milne, Ted, and myself. Ted wasn't the aloof type to say, 'Hey, look, I've got mine. You get yours.' In his own way, he was fighting" (personal interview, June 29, 1984). "Everybody [black] testified in Bill's support, that he was a good reporter and was getting shafted. I don't think I was qualified to judge. I just knew he was a good guy. I would have supported *any* black person" (Emile Milne, telephone interview, June 21, 1991).

46. Alan Sverdlik, "Morris Abram Assesses," *Atlanta Journal and Constitution,* June 27, 1988, sec. B, pp. 1, 4.

47. Morris B. Abram, *The Day Is Short* (New York: Harcourt, 1982), 16.

48. Scott, *Domination and the Art of Resistance,* 208.

49. "The *Post* to Appeal Order on Hiring Bias," *New York Times,* Sept. 3, 1971, 24, 6.

50. See "Rights Unit Clears *Post* of Bias Charge," *New York Times,* Aug. 9, 1972, 40. Artis says press coverage of the case was "mostly in the black press. The other papers ran away from it. They knew their day was coming" (telephone interview, July 16, 1987).

51. "The very same week that I fired him, I fired a white kid who got too emotionally involved. On a welfare story, he took his whole paycheck and bought the kids food. I told him, 'You have to have the ability in this business, even if you're a liberal and soft-hearted, to stand off and be detached. Otherwise you're going to destroy yourself'" (George Trow, personal interview).

52. Ron Smothers, hired by the *Washington Post* during the Newark riots and eventually Atlanta bureau chief for the *New York Times,* says, "There were certainly a lot of mediocre white reporters who were being dealt with, so even if Bill Artis was mediocre, there was a double standard" (personal interview, Nov. 15, 1990).

53. "The *Post* Foresees Fiscal 'Problems,'" *New York Times,* Oct. 8, 1971, 38, 5.

54. Kleinman says, "Every once in a while someone was put on rewrite because he was old. I think Ted fell into that category at the end. In a funny way, it was almost a gesture of respect" (telephone interview, Aug. 20, 1987).

CHAPTER 13. RETIREMENT, DEATH: 1972–1974

1. When he retired twenty-seven years after his return from Washington, his weekly salary was $356.72 and his severance pay, based on length of service and including unused vacation pay, was $22,116 before taxes (Leonard Arnold to TP, Mar. 7, 1972; Arnold, memo to Dorothy Schiff, Mar. 8, 1972, Box 57, Schiff Papers). Fern Marja Eckman and Roberta Brandes Gratz, "Ted Poston Dies at 67; A

Legendary Reporter," *New York Post,* Jan. 10, 1974, 2, 58. Poston's own mentor, Broun, closed his last column for the *World* with the words from *Pilgrim's Progress* that open this chapter (quoted in Morris Watson and Ernest L. Meyer, eds., *Heywood Broun: As He Seemed to Us* [New York: Random House, 1940], 46).

2. "Veteran Black Journalist Retires From N.Y. *Post,*" *Louisville Courier-Journal,* Mar. 30, 1972.

3. Moon, "Ted Poston," 11.

4. Scott, *Domination and the Art of Resistance,* 7.

5. "Guild Honors Poston," *New York Post* [Retirement Parody Issue], Apr. 14, 1972, 1. Poston was also given an award by the borough of Brooklyn for his having brought, "during nearly fifty years . . . distinction, discretion and dignity to his chosen profession as a pioneer in the continuing struggle for black representation and perspective in the American press" ("Brooklyn Hails Reporter—Citation," ibid., 1).

6. Fern Marja Eckman, "Ted Poston—Newspaperman," ibid., 1.

7. Moon, interview by Jackson; guest list in Moon Papers.

8. Adriawa Evans, letter to Kenneth B. Clark, Apr. 6, 1972, Hastie Papers.

9. Kenneth B. Clark, letter to Adriawa Evans, Apr. 17, 1972, copy in Hastie Papers.

10. A Silurian meeting would feature "a once-brilliant senior mumbling through the reading of interminable memoirs, and more than a hundred Silurians—wearied, sturdy, and sympathetic," who "kept their seats as politely as if in church" (George Britt and Peter Kihss, "The Silurians' Story, 1924–1984," *Silurian News,* Apr. 1984).

11. Hughes, *Selected Poems,* 38.

12. "Building Corp. President Dies in Chicago at Age 82," *Jet,* Oct. 1973, 84.

13. Marie Byrd Poston Jackson died on June 24, 1994, in a nursing home in Florida after a long illness (Rosemary Reed, note to author, Aug. 16, 1994).

14. "Ted Poston Victim of Amnesia," *New York Post,* Jan. 5, 1974.

15. "My picture *was* in the *Amsterdam News,* but that had nothing to do with Ted. I was at a party at the Museum of Modern Art for black artists, talking with Charles Alston and Coretta King, and a photographer thought I was Charles Alston's wife, Myra Logan. The Logans were so light, they could easily 'pass.' Myra was lovely, [Ted's doctor] Arthur Logan's sister. The photographer put the picture in the *Amsterdam News* with the caption 'Mr. and Mrs. Charles Alston and Coretta King.' Myra called me up the next day and said, 'Honey, I just didn't know I was so good-looking'" (Diana Bonnor Lewis, personal interview).

16. Robert D. McFadden, "Snowstorm, Rain and Drizzle Leave City Awash with Slush," *New York Times,* Jan. 11, 1974, 12.

17. Eckman and Gratz, "Ted Poston."

18. Bill Powell, "Yesteryear with Bill Powell," *Louisville Courier-Journal,* n.d.

19. "Ted and I *never* had a conference on separation and even unto his death we had never been legally separated. That was proved conclusively in Probate Court where my attorneys presented the numbers of checks issued by me to pay for his numerous hospital, rehabilitation, et al. involvements. No separation papers had been filed or sought. . . . I moved out while Ted was at work, but he got word from a neigh-

bor and came home. The police permitted me to take what was on the van" (Ersa Hines Poston, letter to author, June 6, 1993). Ersa also wondered why Ted's fast friends were suddenly absent when the moment came to assume responsibility for his funeral and burial (letter to author, Mar. 10, 1994).

20. A local man, Dee Laster, wanted to buy the Paducah house but explained that "I am a disable man only get disability once a month I woulden be able to give only eight hundre [*sic*] dollar for it and I would haft to pay it by the month" (Dee Laster, letter to Robert A. Lewis, June 3, 1974, Moon Papers). Laster was not in luck. Curlee Brown, Sr., president of the Paducah branch of the NAACP, advised Moon that "$3 500 would be a good price for the above-captioned premises" and suggested they "offer the property at $4000 with leeway to reduce the price to $3 500?"

21. Moon told Luther P. Jackson, Jr., that Roy Wilkins's putting him at the bottom in salary of top NAACP executives hastened his exit. "It affected my pension to the extent that I don't get enough money to live on. . . . I ended my career with $25,000 a year. The next group of people got $35,000" (Moon, interview by Jackson).

22. Ellison, "World and the Jug," 111.

23. Murray, *Song in a Weary Throat*, 89.

24. "Although we found it impossible to live together as husband and wife, we adored each other in such a way that many of our friends found almost mysterious. We remained loyal friends and companions for as long as he was mentally able to comprehend what was happening around him. As life began to slip away and the illness became incurable, there was little one could do but see that he was comfortable" (Ersa Hines Poston, letter to author).

25. In 1994, the institute was renamed the Robert C. Maynard Institute for Journalism Education. It is located in Oakland, California. Bob Maynard, a forward-looking risk taker, was considered by many as America's foremost black journalist of his era when he died (of prostate cancer) in 1993.

Bibliography

MANUSCRIPT COLLECTIONS

Claude Barnett Papers, Chicago Historical Society.
Daisy Bates Papers, State Historical Society of Wisconsin, Madison.
Blazer Library, Kentucky State University, Frankfort.
Civilian Personnel Records, National Personnel Record Center, St. Louis, Missouri.
Columbia University Oral History Project, New York City.
William H. Hastie Papers, Manuscript Division, Harvard Law School Library, Cambridge, Massachusetts.
Kathleen A. Hauke Papers, Auburn Avenue Research Library on African American History and Culture, Atlanta-Fulton County Public Library, Atlanta, Georgia.
Kentucky Department for Libraries and Archives, Frankfort.
Alain Locke Papers, Moorland-Spingarn Research Center, Howard University, Washington, D.C.
Henry Lee and Mollie Moon Papers, Schomburg Center for Research in Black Culture, New York Public Library, New York City.
Moorland-Spingarn Research Center, Howard University, Washington, D.C.
Record Group 205, Negro Press Section, News Bureau, Office of War Information, National Archives, Suitland, Maryland.
Record Group 208. Civil Defense, National Archives, Suitland, Maryland.
Franklin D. Roosevelt Library, Hyde Park, New York.
Dorothy Schiff Papers, Manuscript, Archives, and Rare Books Division, New York Public Library.
Schomburg Center for Research in Black Culture, Astor, Lenox, and Tilden Foundations, New York Public Library.
Spingarn Papers, Moorland-Spingarn Research Center, Howard University, Washington, D.C.
Harry S. Truman Library, Independence, Missouri.
J. Waties Waring Papers, Moorland-Spingarn Research Center, Howard University, Washington, D.C.
James A. Wechsler Papers, State Historical Society of Wisconsin, Madison.
Dorothy West Papers, Special Collections, Boston University, Boston, Massachusetts.

BOOKS

Abram, Morris B. *The Day Is Short.* New York: Harcourt, 1982.

Anderson, Jervis. *A. Philip Randolph.* New York: Harcourt, 1973.

———. *This Was Harlem: A Cultural Portrait, 1900–1950.* New York: Farrar, 1982.

Annual Catalogue, Kentucky Normal and Industrial Institute, 1912–13, 1913–14, 1914–15, 1916–17, 1921. Frankfort: Institute Press.

Banks, Ann, ed. *First-Person America.* New York: Knopf, 1980.

Barbeau, Arthur E., and Florette Henri. *The Unknown Soldier: Black American Troops in World War I.* Philadelphia: Temple University Press, 1974.

Bardolph, Richard. *The Negro Vanguard.* New York: Vintage, 1961.

"Basketball Review of the 1925–26 Season." *The Radio,* 81. Nashville: Tennessee Agricultural and Industrial Institute Yearbook, 1926.

Bates, Daisy. *The Long Shadow of Little Rock.* 1962. Reprint. Fayetteville: University of Arkansas Press, 1987.

Beasley, Maurine H. "T. Thomas Fortune." In *American Newspaper Journalists, 1873–1900, Dictionary of Literary Biography.* Vol. 23. Edited by Perry J. Ashley. Detroit: Gale, 1983.

Benjaminson, Peter. *Death in the Afternoon.* Kansas City: Andrews, 1984.

Berry, Faith. *Langston Hughes: Before and Beyond Harlem.* Westport, Conn.: Lawrence Hill, 1983.

Bibby, Deirdre L. *Augusta Savage and the Art Schools of Harlem.* New York: Schomburg Center for Research in Black Culture, 1988.

Bishop, Ralph J. Introduction to Ruth H. Landman and Katherine Spencer Halpern, eds. *Applied Anthropologist and Public Servant: The Life and Work of Philleo Nash.* NAPA Bulletin 7. Washington, D.C.: National Association for the Practice of Anthropology, 1989.

Branch, Taylor. *Parting the Waters: America in the King Years, 1954–63.* New York: Simon and Schuster, 1988.

Brinkley, David. *Washington Goes to War.* New York: Ballantine, 1988.

Brooks, W. T. "Editorial, The End of Education." *Kentucky Normal and Industrial Institute Students' Bulletin,* Vol. 3. Frankfort: Institute Press, 1916.

Broun, Heywood Hale, ed. *Collected Edition of Heywood Broun.* Freeport, N.Y.: Books for Libraries Press, 1941.

———. *Whose Little Boy Are You? A Memoir of the Broun Family.* New York: St. Martin's, 1983.

Buckley, Gail Lumet. *The Hornes: An American Family.* New York: NAL, 1986.

Buni, Andrew. *Robert L. Vann of the Pittsburgh Courier.* Pittsburgh: University of Pittsburgh Press, 1974.

Caldwell, Earl. *Black American Witness: Reports from the Front.* Washington, D.C.: Lion House, 1994.

Calloway, Cab, and Bryant Rollins. *Of Minnie the Moocher and Me.* New York: Crowell, 1976.

Campbell, Georgetta Merritt. *Extant Collections of Early Black Newspapers: A Research Guide to the Black Press, 1880–1915, with an Index to the Boston Guardian, 1902–1904.* Troy, N.Y.: Whitston, 1981.

"Candidates for Graduation, 1928." *Tennessee Agricultural and Industrial State College Catalogue, 1927–30*, p. 80.

Caron's Hopkinsville Directory, 1907, 1910–11, 1912–13, 1914–16, 1916–18, 1922–24, 1924–25, 1928–29.

Carmer, Carl. "From Wyck to O'Dwyer." In *The Greater City: New York, 1898–1948*, edited by Allan Nevins and John A. Krout. 1948. Reprint. Westport, Conn.: Greenwood, 1981.

Carter, Dan T. *Scottsboro: A Tragedy of the American South.* Baton Rouge: Louisiana State University Press, 1979.

Cash, W. J. *The Mind of the South.* 1941. Reprint. Introduction by Bertram Wyatt-Brown. New York: Vintage, 1991.

Castle Clues. Bensalem, Pa.: Sisters of the Blessed Sacrament, n.d.

Catalogue, Walden College, 1921–22. Nashville, Tenn.

Chapman, Gerard. *William Cullen Bryant: The Cummington Years.* Milton, Mass.: Trustees of Reservations, 1980.

"Classification of Regular Students for 1927–28." *Tennessee Agricultural and Industrial State College Catalogue,* Vol. 15, No. 12, August 1927.

Cochran, Bert. *Harry Truman and the Crisis Presidency.* New York: Funk and Wagnalls, 1973.

Connable, Alfred, and Edward Silverfarb. "J. Raymond Jones." In *Tigers of Tammany,* 334–64. New York: Holt, 1967.

Cose, Ellis. *The Press.* New York: Morrow, 1989.

Couture, Richard T. *Powhatan: A Bicentennial History.* Goochland, Va.: Powhatan Historical Society, 1980.

"Crosswaith, Frank Rudolph." *Who's Who in Colored America, 1950.* 7th ed. Yonkers-on-Hudson, N.Y.: Burckel, 1950.

Daniels, Jim. "Time, Temperature." In *M-80,* 29–47. Pittsburgh: University of Pittsburgh Press, 1994.

Daniels, Jonathan. *White House Witness, 1942–1945.* New York: Doubleday, 1975.

Davis, Michael D., and Hunter R. Clark. *Thurgood Marshall.* New York: Birch Lane, 1993.

Delaney, Sara, and Bessie Delaney. *Having Our Say.* New York: Farrar, 1993.

Donaldson, Scott. *Archibald MacLeish: An American Life.* Boston: Houghton Mifflin, 1992.

Donovan, Robert J. *Conflict and Crisis: The Presidency of Harry S. Truman, 1945–1948.* New York: Norton, 1977.

Drake, St. Clair, and Horace R. Cayton. *Black Metropolis: A Study of Negro Life in a Northern City.* New York: Harcourt, 1945.

Duberman, Martin B. *Paul Robeson.* New York: Knopf, 1988.

Du Bois, W. E. B. *Black Reconstruction in America, 1860–1880.* 1935. Reprint. Introduction by David Levering Lewis. New York: Atheneum, 1992.

————. *The Philadelphia Negro: A Sociological Study.* 1899. Reprint. Philadelphia: University of Pennsylvania Press, 1967.

————. *The Souls of Black Folk.* 1903. Reprint. New York: Fawcett, 1961.

Dunbar, Paul Laurence. *The Complete Poems of Paul Laurence Dunbar.* 1895. Reprint. New York: Dodd, 1980.

Dunnigan, Alice Allison. *A Black Woman's Experience—From Schoolhouse to White House.* Philadelphia: Dorrance, 1974.

————. *The Fascinating Story of Black Kentuckians.* Washington, D.C.: Associated, 1982.

Dykeman, Wilma, and James Stokely. *Seeds of Southern Change: The Life of Will Alexander.* New York: Norton, 1962.

Eckman, Fern Marja. *The Furious Passage of James Baldwin.* New York: Evans, 1966.

Egerton, John. *Speak Now Against the Day: The Generation Before the Civil Rights Movement in the South.* Chapel Hill: University of North Carolina Press, 1995.

"Eight Links Club." *The Radio,* 66. Nashville: Tennessee Agricultural and Industrial Institute Yearbook, 1926.

Eisenstein, Sergei M. *Immoral Memories: An Autobiography.* Translated by Herbert Marshall. Boston: Houghton Mifflin, 1983.

Elledge, Scott. *E. B. White.* New York: Norton, 1984.

Ellison, Ralph. "The World and the Jug." In *Shadow and Act.* New York: Random House, 1964.

Ephron, Nora. *Scribble, Scribble.* New York: Knopf, 1978.

Evers, Charles. *Have No Fear.* New York: Wiley, 1997.

Fairbairn, Ann. *Five Smooth Stones.* New York: Crown, 1966.

Famous Blacks Give Secrets of Success. Chicago: Johnson, 1973.

Fauset, Jessie. *The Chinaberry Tree: A Novel of American Life.* 1931. Reprint. College Park, Md.: McGrath, 1969.

————. *Plum Bun.* New York: Stokes, 1929.

————. *There Is Confusion.* 1924. Reprint. New York: AMS Press, 1974.

Federal Writers' Project. *These Are Our Lives.* Chapel Hill: University of North Carolina Press, 1939.

Ferguson, Mary D., and William T. Turner. *A History of Newspapers of Christian County.* Hopkinsville: Southern Printing, 1980.

Fisher, Paul L., and Ralph L. Lowenstein. *Race and the News Media.* New York: Praeger, 1967.

Fleischman, Harry. *Norman Thomas, a Biography.* New York: Norton, 1964.

Foner, Philip S., and Ronald L. Lewis, eds. *The Black Worker,* Vol. 6: *The Era of Post-War Prosperity and the Great Depression, 1920–1936.* Philadelphia: Temple University Press, 1981.

————. *The Black Worker,* Vol. 7: *The Black Worker from the Founding of the CIO to the AFL-CIO Merger, 1936–1955.* Philadelphia: Temple University Press, 1983.

Franklin, Charles Lionel. *The Negro Labor Unionist of New York: Problems and Conditions Among Negroes in the Labor Unions in Manhattan with Special*

Reference to the N.R.A. and Post-N.R.A. Situations. 1936. Reprint. New York: AMS Press, 1968.

Giovannitti, Len. *Sidney Hillman, Labor Statesman.* New York: Amalgamated Clothing, 1948.

Grey, Ian. *Stalin: Man of History.* Garden City, N.Y.: Doubleday, 1979.

Hamill, Pete. *A Drinking Life: A Memoir.* Boston: Little, Brown, 1994.

Hardin, John A. *Onward and Upward: A Centennial History of Kentucky State University, 1886–1986.* Frankfort: Kentucky State University, 1987.

———. *Fifty Years of Segregation: Black Higher Education in Kentucky, 1904–1954.* Lexington: University Press of Kentucky, 1977.

Harris, Leonard, ed. *The Philosophy of Alain Locke: Harlem Renaissance and Beyond.* Philadelphia: Temple University Press, 1989.

Hastie, William H. "No Royal Road." In *Many Shades of Black,* edited by Stanton L. Wormley. New York: Morrow, 1969.

Hill, Robert A., et al., eds. *The Marcus Garvey and Universal Negro Improvement Association Papers.* Vols. 1, 2, 4, 5. Berkeley: University of California Press, 1980–86.

Himes, Chester. *Cotton Comes to Harlem.* 1965. Reprint. New York: Vintage, 1988.

———. *Lonely Crusade.* 1947. Reprint. New York: Thunder's Mouth, 1989.

———. *Pinktoes.* 1961. Reprint. Chatham, N.J.: Chatham Bookseller, 1975.

———. *The Primitive.* New York: Signet, 1955.

———. *The Quality of Hurt: The Autobiography of Chester Himes.* Vol. 1. New York: Doubleday, 1972.

Hine, Darlene Clark, Elsa Barkley Brown, and Rosalyn Terborg-Penn, eds. *Black Women in America and Historical Encyclopedia.* Vol. 1. Bloomington: Indiana University Press, 1993.

Hogan, Lawrence D. *A Black National News Service: The Associated Negro Press and Claude Barnett, 1919–1945.* Cranbury, N.J.: Associated University Press, 1984.

Holland, Juanita Marie. "Augusta Christine Savage: A Chronology of Her Art and Life, 1892–1962." In *Augusta Savage and the Art Schools of Harlem,* edited by Deirdre L. Bibby. New York: Schomburg Center for Research in Black Culture, 1988.

hooks, bell. *Talking Back: Thinking Feminist, Thinking Black.* Boston: South End Press, 1989.

Hughes, Langston. *The Big Sea.* 1940. Reprint. New York: Hill and Wang, 1963.

———. *The Dream Keeper.* New York: Knopf, 1932.

———. *I Wonder as I Wander.* New York: Hill and Wang, 1956.

———. *Selected Poems.* New York: Vintage, 1974.

———, ed. *The Book of Negro Humor.* New York: Dodd, 1967.

Hutchens, John K., and George Oppenheimer, eds. *The Best in the World.* New York: Viking, 1973.

"Jackson, A. L." *Class of 1914—Sexennial Report.* Records of the Class. Cambridge, Mass.: Harvard University. 143.

Jackson, Luther P., Jr. "Popular Media: Part I, The Mission of the Black Newsman." In *Black American Reference Book,* edited by Mabel Smythe. New York: Prentice-Hall, 1976.

Jeanes Supervision in Georgia Schools: A History of the Program from 1908–1975. Atlanta: Southern Education Foundation, 1975.

Johns, Orrick. *Time of Our Lives: The Story of My Father and Myself.* 1937. Reprint. New York: Octagon, 1973.

Johnson, Lady Bird. *A White House Diary.* New York: Dell, 1970.

Johnson, Thomas A. "A Graduate of the Black Press Looks Back." In Henry G. LaBrie III, ed. *Perspectives of the Black Press, 1974.* Kennebunkport, Me.: Mercer House Press, 1974.

Josephson, Matthew. *Sidney Hillman, Statesman of American Labor.* Garden City, N.Y.: Doubleday, 1952.

Kahn, E. J. *The World of Swope.* New York: Simon and Schuster, 1965.

Keeler, Robert F. *Newsday: A Candid History of the Respectable Tabloid.* New York: Arbor, 1990.

Kenez, Peter. *Cinema and Soviet Society.* New York: Cambridge University Press, 1992.

Kerner Commission. *Report of the National Advisory Commission on Civil Disorders.* New York: Bantam, 1968.

Kessner, Thomas. *Fiorello H. LaGuardia and the Making of Modern New York.* New York: McGraw-Hill, 1989.

Kluger, Richard. *The Paper: The Life and Death of the New York Herald Tribune.* New York: Vintage, 1986.

———. *Simple Justice: The History of Brown vs. Board of Education and Black America's Struggle for Equality.* New York: Vintage, 1977.

KNII Students' Bulletin. Vol. 3. Frankfort, Ky.: Institute Press, 1917.

Kolchin, Peter. *Unfree Labor: American Slavery and Russian Serfdom.* Cambridge, Mass.: Harvard University Press, 1987.

Krock, Arthur. *Memoirs: Sixty Years on the Firing Line.* New York: Funk, 1968.

LaBrie, Henry G., III, ed. *Perspectives of the Black Press, 1974.* Kennebunkport, Me.: Mercer House Press, 1974.

Lamson, Peggy. *Roger Baldwin: Founder of the American Civil Liberties Union.* Boston: Houghton Mifflin, 1976.

Landman, Ruth H., and Katherine Spencer Halpern, eds. *Applied Anthropologist and Public Servant: The Life and Work of Philleo Nash.* NAPA Bulletin 7. Washington, D.C.: National Association for the Practice of Anthropology, 1989.

Lash, Joseph P. *Eleanor and Franklin.* New York: Signet, 1971.

Leab, Daniel J. *A Union of Individuals: The Formation of the American Newspaper Guild, 1933–1936.* New York: Columbia University Press, 1970.

Lewinson, Edwin R. *Black Politics in New York City.* New York: Twayne, 1974.

Lewis, David Levering. *When Harlem Was in Vogue.* New York: Knopf, 1981.

Liebling, A. J. *The Wayward Pressman.* Garden City, N.Y.: Doubleday, 1948.

Lundquist, James. *Chester Himes.* New York: Ungar, 1976.

Maguire, Jane. *On Shares: Ed Brown's Story.* New York: Norton, 1975.

Major, Gerri, with Doris E. Saunders. *Black Society.* Chicago: Johnson, 1976.

Manchester, William. *The Glory and the Dream: A Narrative History of America, 1932–1972.* New York: Bantam, 1974.

Mangione, Jerre. *The Dream and the Deal: The Federal Writers' Project, 1935–1943.* Boston: Little, Brown, 1972.

The MARC Experiment. Brochure. Metropolitan Applied Research Center, n.d.

Martin, Tony. *Literary Garveyism.* Dover, Mass.: Majority, 1983.

Mather, Frank Lincoln, ed. *Who's Who of the Colored Race, 1915.* 1915. Reprint. Detroit: Gale, 1976.

Maynard, Robert C., with Dori J. Maynard. *Letters to My Children.* Kansas City, Mo.: Andrews, 1995.

"Maynard, Robert C." Interview by Peter Benjaminson. In *Contemporary Authors.* Vol. 115, 295–98. Detroit: Gale, 1985.

McCullough, David. *Truman.* New York: Simon and Schuster, 1992.

McKay, Claude. *Harlem: Negro Metropolis.* New York: Dutton, 1940.

———. *Home to Harlem.* 1928. Reprint. Chatham, N.J.: Chatham, 1973.

McWilliams, Carey. *Brothers Under the Skin.* 1942. Reprint. Boston: Little, Brown, 1964.

Meacham, Charles Mayfield. *A History of Christian County, Kentucky, from Oxcart to Airplane.* Nashville: Marshall, 1930.

Meier, August, and Elliott Rudwick. *Black Detroit and the Rise of the UAW.* New York: Oxford University Press, 1979.

Merriweather, Claybron W. *Goober Peas.* Boston: Christopher, 1932.

———. *The Voice of the Soul.* N.p.: n.d.

Milliken, Stephen F. *Chester Himes: A Critical Appraisal.* Columbia: University of Missouri Press, 1976.

Moon, Henry Lee. *Balance of Power.* Garden City, N.Y.: Doubleday, 1948.

Morris, Joe Alex. *Those Rockefeller Brothers.* New York: Harper, 1953.

Motz, Jane. "The Black Cabinet: The Negroes in the Administration of FDR." M.A. thesis, University of Delaware, 1964.

Muller, Gilbert H. *Chester Himes.* Boston: Twayne, 1989.

Murray, Pauli. *Proud Shoes.* 1956. New York: Harper & Row, 1978.

———. *Song in a Weary Throat: An American Pilgrimage.* New York: Harper, 1987.

Nash, Edith Rosenfels. "Philleo Nash and Georgetown Day School." In Ruth H. Landman and Katherine Spencer Halpern, eds., *Applied Anthropologist and Public Servant: The Life and Work of Philleo Nash.* NAPA Bulletin 7. Washington, D.C.: National Association for the Practice of Anthropology, 1989.

"Nash, Philleo." *Current Biography 1962,* 315–17.

Nash, Philleo. "Anthropologist in the White House." In Ruth H. Landman and Katherine Spencer Halpern, eds., *Applied Anthropologist and Public Servant: The Life and Work of Philleo Nash.* NAPA Bulletin 7. Washington, D.C.: National Association for the Practice of Anthropology, 1989.

————. "Science, Politics, and Human Values: A Memoir." *Human Organization: Journal of the Society for Applied Anthropology* (Fall 1986): 189–201.

Nevins, Allan. "Past, Present, and Future." In *The Greater City: New York, 1898–1949,* edited by Allan Nevins and John A. Krout. 1948. Reprint. Westport, Conn.: Greenwood, 1981.

Newman, Debra L., ed. *Black History: A Guide to Civilian Records in the National Archives.* Washington, D.C.: National Archives Trust Fund Board, 1984.

"A Newspaper Pro: Ted Poston." In *Careers for Negroes on Newspapers.* New York: American Newspaper Guild, Aug. 1964.

Nichols, Charles H., ed. *Arna Bontemps–Langston Hughes Letters, 1925–1967.* New York: Dodd, 1980.

Oates, Stephen B. *Let the Trumpet Sound: The Life of Martin Luther King, Jr.* New York: Harper, 1982.

O'Connor, Richard. *Heywood Broun: A Biography.* New York: Putnam, 1975.

O'Dwyer, William, *Beyond the Golden Door.* Edited by Paul O'Dwyer. Jamaica, N.Y.: St. John's University, 1987.

Ottley, Roi. *New World A-Coming.* Boston: Houghton Mifflin, 1943.

Ottley, Roi, and William J. Weatherby, eds. *The Negro in New York: An Informal Social History.* New York: New York Public Library and Oceana, 1967.

Parks, Gordon. *To Smile in Autumn: A Memoir.* New York: Norton, 1979.

Patterson, Frederick D. *Chronicles of Faith: The Autobiography of Frederick D. Patterson.* Edited by Martia Graham Goodson. Tuscaloosa: University of Alabama Press, 1991.

Payne, Ethel L. "Loneliness in the Capital: The Black National Correspondent." In Henry G. LaBrie III, ed., *Perspectives of the Black Press, 1974.* Kennebunkport, Me.: Mercer House Press, 1974.

Perata, David D. *Those Pullman Blues: An Oral History of the African American Railroad Attendant.* New York: Twayne, 1996.

Perry, Bruce. *Malcolm: The Life of a Man Who Changed Black America.* Barrytown, N.Y.: Station Hill Press, 1991.

Picturesque Clarksville, Past and Present: A History of the City of Hills. Clarksville, Tenn.: Titus, 1887.

Ploski, Harry A., and James Williams, eds. *The Negro Almanac: A Reference Work on the Afro-American.* New York: Wiley, 1982 and 1983.

Polk's New York City Directory: Boroughs of Manhattan and the Bronx, 1933–34. New York: R. L. Polk, 1933.

"Portrait of Harlem." In *New York Panorama: A Comprehensive View of the Metropolis, Presented in a Series of Articles Prepared by the Federal Writers' Project of the Works Progress Administration in New York City.* St. Clair Shores, Michigan: Scholarly Press, 1976.

Poston, Ted. "The American Negro and Newspaper Myths." In *Race and the News Media,* edited by Paul L. Fisher and Ralph L. Lowenstein. New York: Frederick A. Praeger, 1967.

————. *The Dark Side of Hopkinsville.* Edited by Kathleen A. Hauke. Athens: University of Georgia Press, 1991.

Potter, Jeffrey. *Men, Money and Magic: The Story of Dorothy Schiff.* New York: Coward, 1976.

Raines, Howell. *My Soul Is Rested: The Story of the Civil Rights Movement in the Deep South.* New York: Penguin, 1983.

Rampersad, Arnold. *The Life of Langston Hughes.* 2 vols. New York: Oxford University Press, 1986, 1988.

————, ed. *The Collected Poems of Langston Hughes.* New York: Knopf, 1994.

R. L. Polk & Co.'s Trow General Directory of New York City, Boroughs of Manhattan and the Bronx, 1922–23. New York: R. L. Polk, 1922.

Roosevelt, James, with Bill Liddy. *My Parents: A Differing View.* Chicago: Playboy, 1976.

Rosenberg, Suzanne. *A Soviet Odyssey.* Toronto: Oxford University Press, 1988.

Rowan, Carl T. *Dream Makers, Dream Breakers: The World of Justice Thurgood Marshall.* Boston: Little, Brown, 1993.

Sann, Paul. *Trial in the Upper Room.* New York: Crown, 1981.

Schlesinger, Arthur M., Jr. *Robert Kennedy and His Times.* New York: Ballantine, 1978.

————. *A Thousand Days: John F. Kennedy in the White House.* New York: Fawcett, 1965.

Scott, James. *Domination and the Art of Resistance: Hidden Transcripts.* New Haven: Yale University Press, 1990.

Seldes, George. *Lords of the Press.* New York: Messner, 1946.

Seton, Marie. *Sergei M. Eisenstein.* New York: Wyn, 1952.

Shockley, Ann Allen. *Afro-American Writers, 1746–1933: An Anthology and Critical Guide.* New York: NAL, 1989.

Shostakovich, Dmitri. *Testimony: Memoirs of Dmitri Shostakovich.* Edited by Solomon Volkov. London: Hamilton, 1979.

Smith, Homer. *Black Man in Red Russia.* Chicago: Johnson, 1964.

Sollertinsky, Dmitri, and Ludmilla Sollertinsky. *Pages from the Life of Dmitri Shostakovich.* New York: Harcourt, 1980.

The Stage Is Set. Yearbook. Nashville: Tennessee State University, 1953.

Starr, S. Frederick. *Red and Hot: The Fate of Jazz in the Soviet Union, 1917–1980.* New York: Oxford University Press, 1983.

Stern, J. David. *Memoirs of a Maverick Publisher.* New York: Simon and Schuster, 1962.

Strong, Tracy B., and Helene Keyssar. *Right in Her Soul: The Life of Anna Louise Strong.* New York: Random House, 1983.

Suggs, Henry Lewis. *P. B. Young, Newspaperman: Race, Politics, and Journalism in the New South, 1910–1962.* Charlottesville: University Press of Virginia, 1988.

Sugrue, Thomas. *There Is a River: The Story of Edgar Cayce.* Virginia Beach, Va.: Association for Research and Enlightenment, 1973.

Talmadge, Herman E., with Mark Royden Winchell. *Talmadge, a Political Legacy, a Politician's Life: A Memoir.* Atlanta: Peachtree, 1987.

Tarry, Ellen. *Katharine Drexel: Friend of the Oppressed.* Nashville, Tenn.: Winston-Derek, 1990.

———. *The Third Door: The Autobiography of an American Negro Woman.* 1955. Reprint. Tuscaloosa: University of Alabama Press, 1992.

Taylor, Alrutheus Ambush. *The Negro in Tennessee, 1865–1880.* Washington, D.C.: Associated, 1941.

Thornbrough, Emma Lou. *T. Thomas Fortune: Militant Journalist.* Chicago: University of Chicago Press, 1972.

Turner, William T. *Gateway to the Past.* Vol. 2. Hopkinsville, Ky.: Pennyroyal, 1981.

Ulam, Adam B. *Stalin: The Man and His Era.* New York: Viking, 1973.

Villard, Oswald Garrison. *Fighting Years: Memoirs of a Liberal Editor.* New York: Harcourt, 1939.

Walker, Stanley. *City Editor.* New York: Stokes, 1934.

Walter, John C. *The Harlem Fox: J. Raymond Jones and Tammany, 1920–1970.* Albany: State University of New York Press, 1989.

Ward, John. *The Arkansas Rockefeller.* Baton Rouge: Louisiana State University Press, 1978.

Ware, Gilbert. *William Hastie: Grace Under Pressure.* New York: Oxford University Press, 1984.

Washington, James M., ed. *A Testament of Hope: The Essential Writings and Speeches of Martin Luther King, Jr.* New York: HarperSanFrancisco, 1991.

Watkins, T. H. *Righteous Pilgrim: The Life and Times of Harold L. Ickes, 1874–1952.* New York: Holt, 1990.

Watson, Morris, and Ernest L. Meyer, eds. *Heywood Broun: As He Seemed To Us.* New York: Random House, 1940.

Weaver, Robert C. *Negro Labor: A National Problem.* New York: Harcourt, 1946.

Wechsler, James A. *The Age of Suspicion.* New York: Random House, 1953.

———. *Reflections of an Angry Middle-Aged Editor.* New York: Random House, 1960.

Wechsler, James A., with Nancy F. Wechsler and Holly W. Karpf. *In a Darkness.* New York: Norton, 1972.

West, Dorothy. *The Living Is Easy.* 1948. Reprint. Old Westbury, N.Y.: Feminist, 1982.

———. *The Richer, the Poorer.* New York: Doubleday, 1995.

Wheat, Ellen Harkins. *Jacob Lawrence, American Painter.* Seattle: University of Washington Press, 1986.

White, Theodore H. *In Search of History.* New York: Harper, 1979.

Who's Who in Colored America, 7th ed., 182–83, 423. Yonkers-on-Hudson, N.Y.: Burckel, 1950.

Wilson, Barbara. Introduction to *I Change Worlds: The Remaking of an American,* by Anna Louise Strong. 1935. Reprint. Seattle: Seal Press, 1979.

Wilson, Emma Parke. *Under One Roof.* New York: Funk, 1955.

Wilson, George C. "Footprints in the Sand." Unpublished manuscript. 1982. Blazer Library, Kentucky State University.

Wolseley, Roland E. *The Black Press, U.S.A.* Ames: Iowa State University Press, 1972.

The WPA Guide to New York City: The Federal Writers' Project Guide to 1930s New York. New York: Pantheon, 1982.

Wright, George C. *Life Behind a Veil: Blacks in Louisville, Kentucky, 1865–1930.* Baton Rouge: Louisiana State University Press, 1985.

Yarbrough, Tinsley E. *A Passion for Justice: J. Waties Waring and Civil Rights.* New York: Oxford University Press, 1987.

ARTICLES

"ABC of OWI." *Newsweek,* July 20, 1942, 70–71.

"The Administration: Truth and Trouble." *Time,* Mar. 15, 1943, 13+.

"*Amsterdam News* Strike." Editorial. *Crisis,* Mar. 1936, 81.

"And Yet We Smile." *Detroit Contender,* Nov. 13, 1920.

"Announcement." *Amsterdam News,* Oct. 19, 1935, 1.

Arzt, George, and Ted Poston. "He's a Pusher at Age 12." *New York Post,* Feb. 26, 1970, 1, 4.

Baker, Peter. "40 Years Later 9 Are Welcomed: Little Rock Marks Civil Rights Milestone." *Washington Post,* Sept. 26, 1997, sec. A, pp. 1, 8, 9.

Bald, Wambly. "This Was Heywood Broun: He Died 10 Years Ago Today." *New York Post,* Dec. 19, 1949, 49.

Barnes, Bart. "Philleo Nash Dies at 77." *Washington Post,* Oct. 13, 1987, sec. B, p. 6.

Bisphan, A. H. "His Loss a Bitter Affliction, Says Member of Cambridge." *Negro World,* Apr. 5, 1924, 2.

Bliven, Naomi. "Books: Say Not the Struggle Naught Availeth." Review of *Righteous Pilgrim,* by T. H. Watkins. *New Yorker,* Jan. 28, 1991, 89+.

Boyer, Michael. "Negrochanski tovarish!" *Old Birmingham* [Alabama broadside], 1991.

Britt, George, and Peter Kihss. "The Silurians' Story, 1924–1984." *Silurian News,* Apr. 1984.

"Brooklyn Hails Reporter—Citation." *New York Post,* Apr. 14, 1972, 1.

"Broun to Address Hospital Meeting." *Amsterdam News,* Feb. 22, 1933, 1.

"Broun Urges Negro to Become Radical." *Amsterdam News,* Aug. 17, 1932, 9.

"Building Corp. President Dies in Chicago at Age 82." *Jet,* Oct. 1973, 84.

"The Business League's Inconsistency." Editorial. *Inter-State Tattler,* June 23, 1932, 4.

Butler, Bennie. "The Harlem Urge, II." *Inter-State Tattler,* Mar. 17, 1932, 9.

———. "This Harlem Urge, I." *Inter-State Tattler,* Mar. 10, 1932, 12.

Caldwell, Earl, and Ted Poston. "CORE Sets Separate Harlem School Board." *New York Post,* Mar. 1, 1967.

———. "Harlem Reaction Worries City." *New York Post,* Jan. 10, 1967.

———. "Harlem Vows to Vote Him Back." *New York Post,* Mar. 2, 1967.

Calvin, Floyd. "As Able a Young Man as the Race Has Produced." *Negro World,* Apr. 5, 1924, 2.

Cartwright, Marguerite. "Useful People: Mollie Moon." *Negro History Bulletin,* Feb. 1957, 110.

"Casting the First Stone." Editorial. *Hartford Courant.* Reprinted in *Montgomery Advertiser,* Apr. 17, 1956, sec. A, p. 4.

"Challenge Statements Made by ANP: Office of War Information Falsely Hit of Charge." *Michigan Chronicle,* Nov. 14, 1942, 5.

Craig, Gordon A. "Be Quiet, Father Is Writing." Review of *Reminiscences and Reflections: A Youth in Germany,* by Golo Mann. *New York Times Book Review,* Sept. 16, 1990, 15, 16.

Crosswaith, Frank R. "Crusading for the Brotherhood." In Philip S. Foner and Ronald L. Lewis, eds., *The Black Worker,* Vol. 6: *The Era of Post-War Prosperity and the Great Depression, 1920–1936.* Philadelphia: Temple University Press, 1981.

———. "The Political Future of the Negro." Negro Labor News Service. In Philip S. Foner and Ronald L. Lewis, eds., *The Black Worker,* Vol. 6: *The Era of Post-War Prosperity and the Great Depression, 1920–1936.* Philadelphia: Temple University Press, 1981.

———. "The Porter Asserts His Manhood." In Philip S. Foner and Ronald L. Lewis, eds., *The Black Worker,* Vol. 6: *The Era of Post-War Prosperity and the Great Depression, 1920–1936.* Philadelphia: Temple University Press, 1981.

———. "Toward the Home Stretch." In Philip S. Foner and Ronald L. Lewis, eds., *The Black Worker,* Vol. 6: *The Era of Post-War Prosperity and the Great Depression, 1920–1936.* Philadelphia: Temple University Press, 1981.

———. "The Trade Union Committee for Organizing Negroes." *Messenger,* Aug. 1925, 296–97.

Cullen, Robert. "Report from Ukraine." *New Yorker,* Jan. 27, 1992, 27.

Daniels, Jonathan. "I Am a Bureaucrat." *Atlantic Monthly,* Apr. 1944, 96–101.

"Dear Editor: He Might Even Let Them Play with White Boys." *New York Post,* June 20, 1956, 41.

"Dear Editor: Never Better." *New York Post,* June 15, 1956.

DeKnight, Freda. "Date with a Dish: Barbecued Squab; Succulent Birds Are Ted Poston's Favorite Dish." *Ebony,* Aug. 1955, 96, 99.

"Distinguished Workers Whose Names Will Adorn Our Honor Roll, No. 6. Robert L. Poston." *Negro World,* Oct. 23, 1923, 4.

"Dorothy Schiff, 86, Ex-Post Owner, Dies." *New York Times,* Aug. 31, 1989, sec. B, p. 11.

Dougherty, Romeo L. "My Observations." *Amsterdam News,* Aug. 10, 1932, 8.

———. "Observations." *Amsterdam News,* Aug. 17, 1932, 8.

Dudar, Helen. "Woman in the News: Mrs. Ersa Poston." *New York Post,* Dec. 13, 1964, 25.

Eckman, Fern Marja. "Ted Poston—Newspaperman." *New York Post* [retirement parody issue], Apr. 14, 1972, 1.

Eckman, Fern Marja, and Roberta B. Gratz. "Ted Poston Dies at 67; A Legendary Reporter." *New York Post,* Jan. 10, 1974, 2, 58.

"The Education of a Negro Reporter." *Montgomery Advertiser,* June 22, 1956, sec. A, p. 4.

"Eulogies and Resolutions: Bishop McGuire's Sermon." *Negro World,* Mar. 29, 1924, 2.

"Eulogies and Resolutions: Hon. Marcus Garvey's Eulogy." *Negro World,* Mar. 29, 1924, 2.

"Eulogies and Resolutions: Sir William Sherrill's Tribute." *Negro World,* Mar. 29, 1924, 2.

"Ex-Newsman Services Held at Concord" [U. S. Poston]. *Amsterdam News,* May 21, 1955, 9.

"Famous Columnist Files $250,000 Libel Action for Story in Local Weekly." *New York Age,* Oct. 26, 1935, 1.

Ferris, William H. "Tallaboo." *Negro World,* Jan. 21, 1922, 9.

"Forrest-Poston." *Hopkinsville New Age,* Apr. 25, 1924, 1.

Fraser, C. Gerald. "Ted Poston Dies." *New York Times,* Jan. 12, 1974, 1.

Frederick, William G. "Radcliffe to Be in Charge." *Louisville Courier-Journal,* July 25, 1918, 12.

Geewax, Marilyn. "Emulate WPA to Give Children and the Jobless a Chance." *Atlanta Journal and Constitution,* June 28, 1991, sec. A, p. 13.

Grove, Gene, and Ted Poston. "CCNY's Hello and Goodbye to Gov. Ross Barnett." *New York Post,* May 21, 1964.

"Guild Honors Poston." *New York Post,* Apr. 14, 1972, 1.

"Harlem Agog over Newspaper 'War.'" *Pittsburgh Courier,* Apr. 25, 1931, 3.

Hellman, Geoffrey T. "Profiles: Publisher Dorothy Schiff." *New Yorker,* Aug. 10, 1968, 37–65.

Hendricks, Alfred D., and Ted Poston. "Survey Reveals Heavy Support for Powell in Harlem." *New York Post,* May 23, 1958, 4+.

Hicks, Nancy. "Harlem's Mood: The Gunman Aimed at Us." *New York Post,* June 5, 1968, 6.

Hicks, Nancy, and Ted Poston. "Train Negro Vets or Risk Peril: Sutton." *New York Post,* Feb. 22, 1968.

Hiss, Anthony. "Boss [J. R.] Jones of Tammany Hall." *New York Times Magazine,* Feb. 19, 1967, 32–33, 40–46.

Hogan, Lawrence D. "The Gift of Alvin White: Sharing a World That Jim Crow Kept Apart." *Commonweal,* Feb. 10, 1984, 84.

"Hopkinsville in Brief." *New Age,* Apr. 25, 1924, 1.

Howe, Irving. "From Rebel to Bureaucrat." Review of *Labor Will Rule: Sidney Hillman and the Rise of American Labor,* by Steven Fraser. *New York Times Book Review,* Oct. 24, 1991, 54.

Hughes, Langston. "Advertisement for the Waldorf-Astoria." *New Masses,* Dec. 1931.

———. "Dream." In Hughes, *The Dream Keeper.* New York: Knopf, 1932.

———. "Father Divine." *New York Post,* Sept. 17, 1965.

———. "More on Booker T." *New York Post,* Apr. 23, 1965.

———. "Mother to Son." In Hughes, *Selected Poems.* New York: Vintage, 1974.

———. "Sylvester's Dying Bed." In Hughes, *Selected Poems.* New York: Vintage, 1974.

Hulen, Bertram D. "Shivering Thousands Stamp in the Snow at Inauguration." *New York Times,* Jan. 21, 1945, 1, 27.

Hunter, Charlayne. "Many Blacks Say Beame Uses a Double Standard." *New York Times,* Jan. 11, 1974, 1.

"Hunter Maxwell, Feature Editor of Newark Ledger, Won Post by Writing to the Paper." *Amsterdam News,* July 26, 1933, sec. 2, p. 1.

"Ickes." *Current Biography 1941,* 426; *Current Biography 1952,* 285.

Ickes, Harold. "The Negro as a Citizen." *Crisis,* Sept. 1936, 230+.

"In the Dining-Car." Advertisement. *Detroit Free Press,* Nov. 24, 1920, 22.

"Insanity and Genius Hailed." *Louisville Courier-Journal,* Nov. 3, 1918, 4.

"Invasion of the South." *Newsweek,* Apr. 2, 1956, 86.

"It's Published in Askelon—I." *Montgomery Advertiser,* Apr. 17, 1956, sec. A, p. 4.

"Jet Profile: First Woman Director of EEOC Regional Office" [Marie Byrd Poston]. *Jet,* July 20, 1967, 10.

"A Job for Elmer Davis." *New Republic,* June 22, 1942, 847–48.

Johnson, Greenleaf. "Thriving Business Enterprises of the Universal Negro Improvement Association" [profile of Ulysses S. Poston]. *Negro World,* July 8, 1922, 3–5.

Johnson, Tom. "Tell It Not in Gath, Publish It Not in the Streets of Askelon." *Montgomery Advertiser,* Apr. 3, 5, 15, 1956, sec. A, p. 4.

———. "Tell It Not in Gath, Publish It Not in the Streets of Askelon." *Montgomery Advertiser,* Apr. 8, 1956, sec. B, p. 2.

Johnston, Ernie, Jr. "Pioneering Black Newsman Writes 30 to a Brave Career." *Editor and Publisher,* Apr. 29, 1972, 34.

"Judge Hastie." *New Yorker,* Nov. 12, 1984, 42–44.

Kaiser, Charles. "Salim L. Lewis, Wall St. Pioneer in Stock Block Trading, Dies at 69." *New York Times,* May 1, 1978, sec. 4, pp. 8, 4.

Knowles, Clayton. "Group Formed Here to Influence Government Decisions on Aid to Urban Poor." *New York Times,* Mar. 9, 1967.

Knowles, Jane. "Dorothy West Describes the Harlem Renaissance." *Radcliffe News,* Apr. 1982, 8.

"'. . . Lest the Daughters of the Philistines Rejoice.'" *Montgomery Advertiser,* Apr. 7, 1956, sec. A, p. 4.

"Lester Walton Joins Herald-Tribune Staff." *Chicago Defender,* Mar. 21, 1931, 3.

Lyon, Jean. "Group Medicine: I. Size of Our Headaches." *Guild Reporter,* Aug. 1, 1936, 7.

Massolo, Arthur, and Ted Poston. "Jack Says Powell Stirs Hooliganism in Effort to Scare Off Political Foes." *New York Post,* May 19, 1958, 5+.

McFadden, Robert D. "Snowstorm, Rain and Drizzle Leave City Awash with Slush." *New York Times,* Jan. 11, 1974, 12.

McPherson [first name missing]. "Tallaboo." *Negro World,* Jan. 21, 1922.

"Milestones," *Time,* Feb. 10, 1997, 25.

Milne, Emile, and Ted Poston. "Mayor at the Carey Funeral." *New York Post,* July 7, 1969.

Moon, Henry Lee. "Farewell to Heywood Broun." *Crisis,* Feb. 1940, 52.

———. "IV. The Struggle for Reason: Counted Out—and In." *Survey Graphic,* Jan. 1947, 78–81.

———. "A Negro Looks at Soviet Russia." *Nation,* Feb. 28, 1934, 244–46.

———. "Ted Poston: A Creative Journalist." *Black Perspective,* Spring 1972, 11–12, 40.

Moon, Henry Lee, and T. R. Poston. "Amsterdam News Reporters Tell Why Soviet Russia Dropped . . . : American Prejudice Triumphs over Communism." *Amsterdam News,* Oct. 5, 1932, 1.

"Mr. Wilkins vs. Mr. Waring: The Battle of the South." *New York Post,* Feb. 15, 1959, sec. M, p. 10.

"Mrs. FDR, Poston, Pilat Win Awards for Fighting Bias." *New York Post,* Jan. 23, 1950.

"Ms. Dorothy Schiff, 86, Owned New York *Post.*" *Atlanta Journal and Constitution,* Aug. 31, 1989.

"NAACP Honors Ted Poston." *New York Post,* Dec. 7, 1951, 3.

"Negro Society's Biggest Ball: Urban League's Beaux Arts Brings Park Avenue to Harlem." *Ebony,* May 1954, 17–22.

Newfield, Jack. "Goodbye, Dolly!" *Harper's,* Sept. 1969, 92–98.

"New Harlem Press Club Organizes." *Inter-State Tattler,* Feb. 25, 1932, 2.

"Newspaper Employees Dismissed." *New York Age,* Oct. 12, 1935, 1.

"Newspaper Strike in 6th Week," *New York Age,* Nov. 23, 1935.

"New York Post Resumes with 600,000 Daily Run." *Editor and Publisher,* Mar. 9, 1963, 9+.

"Noted Newspaper Reporter Ted Poston and Wife." Ad for Smirnoff. *Jet,* Mar. 28, 1962, 42; *Ebony,* May 1963, 127.

O'Connor, Harvey. "I Worked on the *Moscow Daily News.*" *Soviet Russia Today,* Nov. 1934, 10.

Osborne, Joseph. "Arts and Entertainment: Reminiscing over Mollie Moon's Brainchild 'Beaux Arts Ball.'" *Amsterdam News,* Feb. 9, 1991, 23.

"The Passing of 'The World.'" Editorial. *Pittsburgh Courier,* Mar. 7, 1931, 10.

Petry, Ann. "Harlem." *Holiday,* Apr. 1949, 110, 116, 163–66, 168.

"The Phantom Press Again." Editorial. *Inter-State Tattler,* Mar. 17, 1932, 4.

"Philadelphia." *Inter-State Tattler,* July 26, Sept. 6, Oct. 11, 25, 1929.

Pomerantz, Gary. "Just the Facts." *Atlanta Journal and Constitution,* Dec. 2, 1990, sec. M, pp. 1, 4.

Porter, A. "The Voice of the Porter." *Messenger,* Sept. 1927, 205.

"The *Post* Foresees Fiscal 'Problems.'" *New York Times,* Oct. 8, 1971, 38, 5.

"Post Honored by AJC, Called 'Spokesman for Liberalism.'" *New York Post,* Mar. 6, 1957, 59.

"The *Post* to Appeal Order on Hiring Bias." *New York Times,* Sept. 3, 1971, 24, 6.

Poston, Ed [*sic*]. "Fast on Again for Harry Wills." *New York Post,* Apr. 1, 1937, 16.

Poston, Ed [*sic*], and William Greaves. "Tells Why City OKd Nude Fair." *New York Post,* Dec. 14, 1970.

Poston, Ephraim. "The KNEA." *Kentucky Negro Education Association Journal,* Jan.–Feb. 1940, 18–19.

"Poston of the Post." *Newsweek,* Apr. 11, 1949, 62.

Poston, Robert L. "Is There a Race Question in America?" *Negro World,* Mar. 31, 1923, 4.

———. "The Negro's Prayer." *Negro World,* Sept. 2, 1922, 4.

———. "The Reason Why I Accepted the Garvey Program." *Negro World,* May 12, 1923, 4.

———. "When You Meet a Member of the Ku Klux Klan." *Negro World,* Oct. 21, 1921.

———. "The 'Why' of It." Editorial. *Negro World,* Oct. 8, 1921, 4.

Poston, T. R. "'I Taught Father Divine' Says St. Bishop the Vine." *Amsterdam News,* Nov. 23, 1932, 1.

———. "The Rise of Colored Democracy: Black GOP Begins New Tammany Hall Organization." *Amsterdam News,* Apr. 6, 1932, 1, 6.

———. "This Columnist Racket." In "Harlem Shadows." *Pittsburgh Courier,* Apr. 25, 1931.

Poston, Ted. "Age Meets Youth." In "Harlem Shadows." *Pittsburgh Courier,* Jan. 24, 1931.

———. "Althea Gibson." *New York Post* series, Aug. 25, 1957, to Sept. 1, 1957.

———. "Althea Would Love All the Acclaim—If She Could Only Get Some Sleep." *New York Post,* July 10, 1957, 2.

———. "At Home with the Poet" [Langston Hughes]. *New York Post,* June 11, 1962.

———. "At Last, A Good Novel from Himes." Review of *The Third Generation,* by Chester Himes. *New York Post,* Mar. 16, 1954.

———. "'Back to Ol' Virginny . . . First Class.'" *New York Post,* Sept. 7, 1956, 1, 47.

———. "Beckwith Goes on Trial for Murder of Evers." *New York Post,* Jan. 27, 1964.

———. "Beckwith's Day in Court: A Smile Suddenly Fades." *New York Post,* Jan. 28, 1964.

———. "Behind the Row on the African Students: The Kennedy Foundation, $100,000 & the GOP." *New York Post,* Aug. 18, 1960, 5, 57.

———. "The Bell Rings in Powell's School." *New York Post,* May 20, 1958, 5, 31.

———. "Bells Toll and Negroes Pray in Montgomery." *New York Post,* Dec. 6, 1956.

———. "Beloved Prophet Martin Makes Last Plea to Harlem." *New York Post,* July 20, 1937.

———. "Big Turnout at Polls by Alabama Negroes." *New York Post,* May 3, 1966, 5.

———. "Bojangles Takes His Last Curtain Call." *New York Post,* Nov. 28, 1949, 2.

———. "A Book on Harlem." Review of *Harlem: Negro Metropolis,* by Claude McKay. *New Republic,* Nov. 25, 1940, 732.

———. "Breathless Reporter Gets His Story as Dodgers Hit Town." *New York Post,* Oct. 3, 1949, 3, 19.

———. "A Brother's Eulogy: The Cause He Died For." *New York Post,* Jan. 27, 1964.

———. "Bus Boycott Leader Hailed as Symbol of Hope in Bias Fight." *New York Post,* Mar. 26, 1956, 5, 37.

———. "Closeup: Black, White, and Brown" [H. Rap Brown]. *New York Post,* July 26, 1967.

———. "Closeup: Carl Rowan, The Next 'Voice of America.'" *New York Post,* Jan. 26, 1964.

———. "Closeup: Embattled Editor, Harry S. Ashmore." *New York Post,* Sept. 21, 1967.

———. "Closeup: 'Equal'" [Clifford L. Alexander]. *New York Post,* Aug. 2, 1967.

———. "Closeup: The Evers Judge." *New York Post,* Jan. 31, 1964.

———. "Closeup: Kenneth Clark, Civil Rights Front-Runner." *New York Post,* Mar. 22, 1964.

———. "Closeup: Mississippi Candidate, Charles Evers." *New York Post,* Feb. 6, 1968.

———. "Closeup: Mrs. Peabody." *New York Post,* Apr. 1, 1964.

———. "Closeup: Unseated Legislator" [Julian Bond]. *New York Post,* Jan. 19, 1966, 24.

———. "A 'Clumsily-Great Government' in Action." Review of *Frontier on the Potomac,* by Jonathan Daniels. *New York Post,* Oct. 31, 1946.

———. "CORE Warns Sit-Ins Will Go on in South." *New York Post,* Oct. 18, 1960.

———. "The Day Mama Put the Whammy on the Yankees." *New York Post,* Oct. 10, 1956, 9, 34.

———. "Depression Brings Harlem Better Food." *Amsterdam News,* Nov. 4, 1931.

———. "A Different Kind of War Novel." Review of *And Then We Heard the Thunder,* by John O. Killens. *New York Post,* Mar. 31, 1963.

———. "Dinner for 4 Was OK, but Not for 5." *New York Post,* Oct. 7, 1956, 4, 25.

———. "Dixie's Fight for Freedom—III." *New York Post,* June 25, 1954, 4, 34.

———. "Dixie's Fight for Freedom—IV." *New York Post,* June 27, 1954, 4, 23.

———. "Epic of Our Time." Review of *Stride Toward Freedom,* by Martin Luther King, Jr. *New York Post,* Sept. 28, 1958.

———. "Exalted, Exhausted, Althea Hides Away." *New York Post,* July 10, 1957, 82.

———. "Fake Robin Hood Also Posed as a Russian Count." *New York Post*, April 1, 1949.

———. "FBI Investigating Squeeze on Tenn. Negro Voters." *New York Post*, July 1, 1960.

———. "Fighting Editor: Fights for the Same Old South." Review of *Where Main Street Meets the River*, by Hodding Carter. *New York Post*, May 24, 1953.

———. "Fighting Pastor: Martin Luther King." III. *New York Post*, Apr. 10, 1957, 4, 65.

———. "Fighting Pastor: Martin Luther King." IV. *New York Post*, Apr. 11, 1957, 4, 46.

———. "For Rev. King, Get-Well Wishes—and a Trickle of Hate Mail." *New York Post*, Sept. 25, 1958.

———. "Fresh Air in Dixie." Review of *An Epitaph for Dixie*, by Harry S. Ashmore. *New York Post*, Jan. 26, 1958.

———. "Garland Patton, Gigolo." *Amsterdam News*, Aug. 5, 1931, Nov. 4, 1931, Apr. 6, 13, 1932.

———. "Graduation Ceremony—for a Class and an Era." *New York Post*, June 3, 1957, 7.

———. "Grandma and Little Boy Lost All Night." *New York Post*, Dec. 23, 1947.

———. "Hailing a New Talent from Barbadoes." Review of *In the Castle of My Skin*, by George Lamming. *New York Post*, Aug. 30, 1953.

———. "Harlem." *New York Post*, July 26, 1964.

———. "Harlem Gasps for Cool Breath of Air." *Amsterdam News*, Aug. 5, 1931.

———. "Harlem Limps on Bunions After Battle of Ballrooms." *New York Post*, Oct. 29, 1939.

———. "Harlem Reacts to the Explosion." *New York Post*, Sept. 18, 1963.

———. "Harlem Shadows." *Pittsburgh Courier*, Jan. 10, 24, Feb. 7, 14, 28, Mar. 28, Apr. 4, 11, 1931.

———. "Harlem Shadows." Review of *Battle of the Bloods*, by John Louis Hill. *Pittsburgh Courier*, Mar. 21, 1931, sec. 1, p. 1.

———. "He'd Outlaw His Own Good Job." *New York Post*, Nov. 12, 1948, 55.

———. "Here's a Primer on Desegregation." Review of *Now Is the Time*, by Lillian Smith. *New York Post*, Feb. 13, 1955.

———. "Himes Writes of Prison Life: Novel Highlights Unconventional Love Story." Review of *Cast the First Stone*, by Chester Himes. *New York Post*, Feb. 8, 1953.

———. "His Goal: Jobs for Blacks" [Whitney Young]. *New York Post*, Mar. 11, 1971, 2.

———. "Hits Wagner Snub of Delany, Quits as Adviser." *New York Post*, Sept. 17, 1955, 5, 42.

———. "Horror in the Sunny South." *New York Post*, Sept. 1, 4, 6, 7, 9, 11, 12, 24, 1949.

———. "How It Feels to Be Negro in America." Review of *On Being Negro in America*, by J. Saunders Redding. *New York Post*, Oct. 21, 1951.

———. "A Hughes Omnibus." Review of *The Langston Hughes Reader: The Selected Writings of Langston Hughes. New York Post,* Apr. 6, 1958.

———. "Hughes Tribute: 'He Knew Us.'" *New York Post,* May 25, 1967.

———. "Inside Story: Newspaper Is Mirror of People It Served 25 Years." *Amsterdam News,* Dec. 22, 1934, 3.

———. "Island of Nassau Now Woos Negro Tourists." *New York Post,* Sept. 2, 1955.

———. "It Reads Like a Thriller." Review of *The Long Shadow of Little Rock,* by Daisy Bates. *New York Post,* Oct. 28, 1962.

———. "It's a Tough Job—He Likes It" [Robert C. Weaver]. *New York Post,* Mar. 4, 1956, 2.

———. "I Witness My First Lynching (Nashville—1926)." *Pittsburgh Courier,* Mar. 7, 1931.

———. "JFK and the Negro." *New York Post,* Nov. 24, 1963.

———. "Jim Crow in New York." *New York Post,* Apr. 22, 1956, 4, 5.

———. "Judge Lynch Presides." *Amsterdam News,* Mar. 9, 1935, 9; Mar. 23, 1935, 9.

———. "The Kennedys and the Lodges Pay a Visit to East Harlem." *New York Post,* Oct. 13, 1960, 3.

———. "Langston Hughes: A Poetic Farewell." *New York Post,* May 26, 1967.

———. "Leading Harlem's War on Poverty: Livingstone Wingate, Arthur C. Logan." *New York Post,* July 12, 1964, 24.

———. "The Legacy of Langston Hughes." *New York Post,* May 27, 1967.

———. "A Letter from a Miss. Jail: The Fight Goes On." *New York Post,* June 16, 1961, 11.

———. "Letter to an Alabama Editor." *New York Post,* June 24, 1956, 5, 16.

———. "Little Rock, Four Months After . . ." *New York Post,* Jan. 27, 1958, 2, 22.

———. "Little Rock High Schools Reopening; Gang Fires on Home of Daisy Bates." *New York Post,* Aug. 12, 1959, 3.

———. "Little Rock—Where Minnie Jean Fights Back." *New York Post,* Feb. 7, 1958, 4, 10.

———. "Love and Vigilance in the South: The Case of Ruby McCollum." *New York Post,* Aug. 29, 1954, sec. M, p. 10.

———. "Mahalia Jackson Sings and Montgomery Rocks." *New York Post,* Dec. 7, 1956, 10.

———. "Mail to Help Evers Family Irks Barnett." *New York Post,* Jan. 10, 1964.

———. "Malcolm and the Muslims." *New York Post,* Feb. 22, 1965.

———. "Mama's Whammy Runs into Poston's Jinx." *New York Post,* Oct. 11, 1956, 3, 81.

———. "The Man from Ghana" [Kwame Nkrumah]. *New York Post,* July 27, 1958, sec. M, p. 4.

———. "Man in the News: Thurgood Marshall, LBJ's Choice for Solicitor General of the U.S." *New York Post,* July 18, 1965.

———. "The Many Sides of Walter Reuther." *New York Post,* Dec. 7, 1952, sec. M, p. 2.

———. "Martin Luther King: Where Does He Go from Here?" VI. *New York Post,* Apr. 14, 1957, sec. M, p. 5.

———. "Minnie Jean Will Attend School Here." *New York Post,* Feb. 18, 1958.

———. "Minnijean Wants to Be 'Just a Teen-Ager.'" *New York Post,* Feb. 24, 1958, 5, 21.

———. "The Mississippi Still Flows Downstream" [Gardner C. Taylor]. *New York Post,* Feb. 16, 1958, sec. M, p. 2.

———. "Mississippi: Tragic Anniversary." *New York Post,* June 20, 1965.

———. "Mrs. Evers on Stand: 'Loud Blast, Silence . . .'" *New York Post,* Jan. 31, 1964.

———. "Mrs. Medgar Evers Waits to Confront the Accused." *New York Post,* Jan. 29, 1964.

———. "Muslims—Myth or Menace?" Review of *The Black Muslims in America,* by C. Eric Lincoln. *New York Post,* Apr. 30, 1961.

———. "NAACP to Little Rock: Don't Expect Minnie Jean." *New York Post,* Feb. 14, 1958, 7.

———. "Nat King Cole: As They Remember Him." *New York Post,* Feb. 16, 1965.

———. "The Negro and His War: He Didn't Sit It Out in 1860–65." Review of *The Negro in the Civil War,* by Benjamin Quarles. *New York Post,* Aug. 9, 1953, sec. M, p. 12.

———. "Negroes Assail Nazis, Ask Fight on U.S. Fascism: Urge Americans to End Race Discrimination in Own Country." *New York Post,* Nov. 25, 1938.

———. "The Negroes of Montgomery." IV. *New York Post,* June 14, 1956, 4.

———. "The Negroes of Montgomery." V. *New York Post,* June 15, 1956, 4, 48.

———. "The Negroes of Montgomery: Books and Ballots." XI. *New York Post,* June 22, 1956, 4, 52.

———. "The Negroes of Montgomery: How They Live." IX. *New York Post,* June 20, 1956, 4, 56.

———. "The Negroes of Montgomery: How They Work." X. *New York Post,* June 21, 1956, 4, 48.

———. "The Negroes of Montgomery: Letter to an Alabama Editor." XII. *New York Post,* June 24, 1956, 5, 16.

———. "The Negroes of Montgomery: 'Rebel with a Cause.'" VII. *New York Post,* June 18, 1956, 4, 38.

———. "The Negroes of Montgomery: They Are No Longer Afraid." VIII. *New York Post,* June 19, 1956, 4, 52.

———. "The Negro Press." *Reporter,* Dec. 6, 1949, 14–16.

———. "A Negro's Vivid Report on Jim Crow Land." Review of *South of Freedom,* by Carl T. Rowan. *New York Post,* Aug. 3, 1952, sec. M, p. 12.

———. "Negro Voters Feeling the Squeeze in Tennessee." *New York Post,* June 29, 1960, 8.

————. "New Man on the Bench" [Thurgood Marshall]. *New York Post,* Oct. 7, 1962.

————. "News (Good News) About the Negro in the Armed Forces." Review of *Breakthrough on the Color Front,* by Lee Nichols. *New York Post,* Feb. 7, 1954, sec. M, p. 12.

————. "New York, New York." *New York Post,* Dec. 10, 1952, 4; Dec. 8, 1952, 4, 38; Dec. 9, 1952, 4, 52.

————. "Nine Kids Who Dared." *New York Post,* series, Oct. 20 to Nov. 1, 1957.

————. "Nine Kids Who Dared: Carlotta Walls." *New York Post,* Oct. 29, 1957, sec. M, p. 2.

————. "Nine Kids Who Dared: Gloria Ray." VII. *New York Post,* Oct. 28, 1957, sec. M, p. 2.

————. "The 19-Day Ordeal of Minnie Jean Brown." *New York Post,* Feb. 9, 1958, 3.

————. "A Novel from Africa." Review of *Mine Boy,* by Peter Abrahams. *New York Post,* June 12, 1955.

————. "N.Y. Group Plans Aid to Negroes in Tenn. Boycott." *New York Post,* July 7, 1960.

————. "Oil Firms: Can't Stop Squeeze on Tenn. Negroes." *New York Post,* June 30, 1960.

————. "On Appeal in the Supreme Court." [Profile of Thurgood Marshall] *Survey,* Jan. 1949.

————. "One-Man Task Force" [Henry Lee Moon]. *New York Post,* June 7, 1948, sec. 2, p. 1.

————. "Out of Billy Rowe's Harlem Notebook." *Pittsburgh Courier,* Apr. 6, 1940.

————. "Pickets Fight Rent Boost as House Is Opened for Negroes." *Amsterdam News,* July 13, 1935, 1, 2.

————. "Plain Talk for Both Sides." Review of *Crisis in Black and White,* by Charles Silberman. *New York Post,* May 17, 1964, 47.

————. "Poston Thrilled by Sell-Out Edition." *Editor and Publisher,* Apr. 20, 1963, 146.

————. "The Post's Reporter Gets to See Gov. Talmadge—by the Back Door." *New York Post,* May 25, 1954, 5, 32.

————. "Powell Cuts His Tour, Heads for P. R. Home." *New York Post,* Sept. 6, 1962.

————. "Powell's Harlem Threat to Tiger Grows." *New York Post,* Aug. 6, 1958.

———— (with Henry Beckett, Peter J. McElroy, Marcy Elias, Joseph Kahn, Irving Lieberman, and Edward Katcher). "Prejudice and Progress: The Negro in New York." I. *New York Post,* Apr. 16, 1956, 4.

————. "Prejudice and Progress: Jim Crow in New York." IV. *New York Post,* April 19, 1956, 4, 18.

————. "Prejudice and Progress: The Negro in New York." II. *New York Post,* April 17, 1956, 4, 40.

————. "Prejudice and Progress in New York: Jobs for Negroes." *New York Post,* Apr. 26, 1956, 4, 40.

———. "Prejudice and Progress in New York: The Negro in Politics." IX. *New York Post,* Apr. 25, 1956, 4, 71.

———. "Prejudice Is a Two-Way Street, Negro Learns." Review of *The Seekers,* by Will Thomas. *New York Post,* July 5, 1953, sec. M, p. 12.

———. "Randolph for Powell, Cites Seniority." *New York Post,* May 28, 1958.

———. "Retreat to Harlem: Communist Party Purges Ford as Scapegoat for Failure Among Negroes." *New Leader,* Mar. 30, 1940, 4.

———. "Rev. King Continues to Gain: Takes First Steps Since Stabbing." *New York Post,* Sept. 23, 1958, 4, 17.

———. "The Rev. King Hails Kennedy for His 'Courageous Stand.'" *New York Post,* Nov. 1, 1960.

———. "Rev. King Wants to Go Back to Work." *New York Post,* Sept. 24, 1958, 4, 30.

———. "The Revolt of the Evil Fairies." *New Republic,* Apr. 6, 1942, 458–59.

———. "Rioting Ebbs in Harlem." *New York Post,* July 22, 1964, 2, 30.

———. "Robert C. Weaver, Sec. of Housing." *New York Post,* Jan. 23, 1966.

———. "'Robin Hood of Soviet Zone' Just Imposter from Minnesota." *New York Post,* Mar. 30, 1949, 54.

———. "Rockefeller Orders Willie Reid Sent Back to Florida Prison." *New York Post,* Nov. 23, 1959.

———. "Scholarships for Negroes: A Program That Works." *New York Post,* Apr. 19, 1964.

———. "7 Kids Who Tried." XI. *New York Post,* Nov. 1, 1957, sec. M, p. 2.

———. "Seventh Ave. Finance: Harlem Shadows." *Pittsburgh Courier,* Jan. 10, 1931.

———. "She Prepared for Norfolk for a Lifetime." *New York Post,* Feb. 5, 1959.

———. "The Simple World of Langston Hughes." *New York Post,* Nov. 24, 1957, sec. M, p. 2.

———. "Socialist Uncovers Something New in Harlem—The House Rent Party." *Amsterdam News,* Mar. 16, 1935, 2.

———. "Social Security Act Bars Most of Us." *Pittsburgh Courier,* Dec. 23, 1939, 24.

———. "Sorry, Father, But It's Not Wonderful." Review of *Fr. Divine, Holy Husband,* by Sara Harris. *New York Post,* Nov. 1, 1953, sec. M, p. 12.

———. "South Takes School Bias Ban Calmly, Negro Leaders Move to Widen Fight." *New York Post,* May 18, 1954, 5, 40.

———. "A Statement on Racism—By Beckwith." *New York Post,* Jan. 31, 1964, 11.

———. "The Strength of Non-Violence" [Closeup of Z. K. Matthews]. *New York Post,* Sept. 28, 1952.

———. "Suicide in the CHA: Feared Loss of Job over Race Issue." *New York Post,* Jan. 13, 1958.

———. "Ted Poston From Alabama: A First-Time Voter at 77, 'Good, So Good.'" *New York Post,* May 4, 1966, 5, 74.

———. "Ted Poston in Alabama: The Negroes of Montgomery." I. *New York Post,* June 11, 1956, 4, 42.

————. "Ted Poston in Alabama: The Negroes of Montgomery." III. *New York Post,* June 13, 1956, 4, 66.

————. "Ted Poston in Alabama: The Negroes of Montgomery." IV. *New York Post,* June 14, 1956, 4, 49.

————. "Ted Poston in Alabama: The Negroes of Montgomery." VI. *New York Post,* June 17, 1956, 5, 28.

————. "Ted Poston in Montgomery: The Negroes of Alabama." II. *New York Post,* June 12, 1956, 4, 24.

————. " 'There Are No Seats in the Colored Section.' " *New York Post,* June 12, 1959, 5, 17.

————. " 'They'll Shoot Me in the Back of the Head.' " *New York Post,* Aug. 26, 1959, 5+.

————. "Three Flights Up to the Fourth Estate." *New York Post,* June 11, 1959, 5.

————. "Throngs View Bojangles Bier, Taps for Great Dancer Monday." *New York Post,* Nov. 23, 1949, 5, 28.

————. "Timeworn Rusty Chain Binds Novelist's Miss. Negroes." Review of *Chain in the Heart,* by Hubert Creekmore. *New York Post,* July 26, 1953, sec. M, p. 12.

————. "The Tolling Bells and the Prayers." *New York Post,* Nov. 25, 1963.

————. "Town Finally Honors Ignored Negro PWs." *New York Post,* Sept. 11, 1953.

————. "A Truly American Family." Review of *Proud Shoes,* by Pauli Murray. *New York Post,* Oct. 21, 1956.

————. "Two New Yorkers Ready for Appeal of Conviction in Greyhound Case." *Pittsburgh Courier,* Apr. 13, 1940.

————. "Two Score and Ten Years Ago." *New York Post,* Feb. 8, 1959, sec. M, p. 4.

————. "Violence Flares for Third Night: 50 Injured in Harlem." *New York Post,* July 21, 1964, 2, 53.

————. "Weaver Set for Top U.S. Housing Job." *New York Post,* Dec. 30, 1960.

————. " 'We Have So Much to Say' " [Lorraine Hansberry]. *New York Post,* Mar. 22, 1959, sec. M, p. 2.

————. "Widow Leads King March." *New York Post,* Apr. 8, 1968, 1+.

————. "Widow Talks of Her Life With Malcolm." *New York Post,* Feb. 23, 1965.

————. "Wright's Terrible Reality in a Violent, Explosive Novel." Review of *The Outsider,* by Richard Wright. *New York Post,* Mar. 22, 1953.

————. "You Go South." *New Republic,* Sept. 9, 1940, 348–50.

Poston, Ted, and Joseph Kahn. "Negro Boy, 15, Killed by Cop; Students Riot." *New York Post,* July 16, 1964.

[Poston, Ted, and Louis Martin.] "Detroit Is Dynamite." *Life,* Aug. 17, 1942, 15–23.

Poston, Ted, and Roi Ottley. "New York vs. Chicago: Which City Is Better Place for Negroes?" *Ebony,* Dec. 1952, 16–24.

Poston, Theodore. "Mother's Day Reflections." *Blue and Gold,* 7. Nashville: Tennessee Agricultural and Industrial Institute, June 1927.

Poston, Ulysses S. "Harlem Economist Tells Needs of Community." *Pittsburgh Courier,* Oct. 15, 1927, sec. 1, p. 4.

———. "How Some Presidents Expressed Their Attitude Toward the Colored Man." *Inter-State Tattler,* Mar. 13, 1925, 4.

———. "An Ideal Ticket." *New York Contender,* Oct. 22, 1932.

———. "Political Buzz-Saw." *Inter-State Tattler,* Apr. 28, 1932.

———. "The Political Buzz-Saw: Communism and the Negro." *Inter-State Tattler,* May 19, 1932, 4.

———. "The Political Buzz-Saw: The Democratic Party." *Inter-State Tattler,* June 16, 1932, 4.

———. "The Political Buzz-Saw: Georgia Goes Lily-White." *Inter-State Tattler,* Mar. 31, 1932, 4.

———. "The Political Buzz-Saw: Herbert Clarke Hoover." *Inter-State Tattler,* Jan. 21, 1932, 4.

———. "The Political Buzz-Saw: Mayor James J. Walker, Whole Life and Works Symbolize the Spirit of New York." *Inter-State Tattler,* Feb. 11, 1932, 4.

———. "The Political Buzz-Saw: An Open Letter to Negro Voters." *Inter-State Tattler,* June 9, 1932, 4.

———. "The Political Buzz-Saw: Silhouette, Abraham Lincoln." *Inter-State Tattler,* Feb. 18, 1932, 4.

———. "Relief Ahead for Home Owners." *Amsterdam News,* July 19, 1933, 3, 9.

Powell, Bill. "Yesteryear with Bill Powell." *Louisville Courier-Journal,* n.d. [Jan. 1974].

"Published in Askelon—IV: The North's Hypocrisy on Negroes." *Montgomery Advertiser,* May 12, 1956, sec. A, p. 4.

"Quit Singing the Blues." Editorial. *Detroit Contender,* May 7, 1921, 2.

Remnick, David. "Profile: Prince of the City" [Murray Kempton]. *New Yorker,* Mar. 1, 1993, 41–54.

"Rights Unit Clears *Post* of Bias Charge." *New York Times,* Aug. 9, 1972, 40.

"Robert C. Maynard." *Editor and Publisher,* Mar. 2, 1985, 42.

"Robert L. Poston." Obituary. *Negro World,* Mar. 29, 1924, 7.

Rowe, Billy. "Out of Billy Rowe's Harlem Notebook." *Pittsburgh Courier,* Apr. 6, 20, Oct. 5, 1940, 7.

Savage, Augusta. "An Autobiography." *Crisis,* Aug. 1929, 269.

———. "The Old Homestead." *Negro World,* Dec. 26, 1922, 3.

———. "Supplication." *Negro World,* Nov. 18, 1922.

"Savage, Augusta." Obituary. *New York Times,* Mar. 27, 1962, 37.

Sheehy, Gail. "The Life of the Most Powerful Woman in New York." *New York,* Dec. 10, 1973, 51–69.

Sherouse, N. G. "Poston Is Not Reliable." See "Tell It to Old Grandma." *Montgomery Advertiser,* Apr. 4, 1956, sec. A, p. 4.

"Some of the Officers and Members of the New York Crisis Committee." *Crisis,* ca. 1938.

"Southern Hospitality." *Time,* June 25, 1956, 76.

"Strike Chairman." Photo caption. *Guild Reporter* (American Newspaper Guild). Jan. 1, 1936, 2.

Striking Employees. "Striking Employees and Publishers of *Amsterdam News* Issue Statements." *New York Age,* Oct. 19, 1935, 1.

Strong, Anna Louise. "15 Years of Moscow." *Moscow News,* Nov. 15, 1932, 5.

———. "A New World in the Caucasus." *Soviet Russia Today,* Nov. 1934, 7.

Sverdlik, Alan. "Morris Abram Assesses." *Atlanta Journal and Constitution,* June 27, 1988, sec. B, pp. 1, 4.

Symington, Muriel I. "Dear Editor: Unselfish Words." *New York Post,* May 28, 1959, 41.

"Tallaboo Cast Consists of Good Array of Amateur Talent." *Negro World,* Jan. 7, 1922, 11.

"Tallaboo Once More: In Answer to a Request from Prominent White People," *Kentucky New Era,* May 22, 1920, 7.

"Tallaboo Tonight at Tabernacle." *Kentucky New Era,* May 17, 1920, 5.

Tallmer, Jerry, and Roberta Brandes. "Mixed Marriages." *New York Post,* May 3, 1965.

"Tattler Platform." *Inter-State Tattler,* Jan 14, 1932, 4.

"Ted Poston Dies; Organized Guild at Black Paper, Held Mellett Post." *Guild Reporter,* Jan. 25, 1974, 4.

"Ted Poston Named to Important Post by Sidney Hillman." *New York Post,* Oct. 12, 1940, 12.

"Ted Poston Victim of Amnesia." *New York Post,* Jan. 5, 1974.

"Ted Poston Wins American Newspaper Guild Award for 1949." *Bulletin,* Tennessee Agricultural and Industrial State College, Mar. 1950, 6.

Teepen, Tom. "Strout Wore Well the Hats of Both Reporter, Opiner." *Atlanta Journal and Constitution,* Aug. 28, 1990, sec. A, p. 15.

"Thelma Berlack Wins Walker Scholarship." *Inter-State Tattler,* Mar. 13, 1925, 10.

"They're Off! Group Sails to Moscow to Make Black and White Film." *Inter-State Tattler,* June 16, 1932, 2.

"Typography Award Won by Advertiser." *Montgomery Advertiser,* Apr. 20, 1956, 1.

"Urban League to Present News Media Awards to 8." *New York Times,* Mar. 20, 1968, 6.

"U. S. Poston, Writer, Editor, and Political Analyst, Joins the *ITS* Staff Beginning Next Week." *Inter-State Tattler,* Aug. 6, 1931.

"Ulysses S. Poston, Real Estate Man." *New York Times,* May 16, 1955, 23.

"Veteran Black Journalist Retires from N.Y. *Post.*" *Louisville Courier-Journal,* Mar. 30, 1972.

"Walton Gets No By-Line in N.Y. Herald Tribune." *Pittsburgh Courier,* Apr. 18, 1931, 4.

"Wanted." *New Age,* Apr. 25, 1924, 2.

Wechsler, James A. "Heywood Broun." Editorial. *New York Post,* Dec. 18, 1962, sec. M, p. 32.

———. "Powell's Folly." *New York Post,* Mar. 27, 1963, 46.

———. "A Reporter in Florida." Editorial. *New York Post,* June 12, 1959.

"What Colored Ministers Say about 'Tallaboo.'" *Kentucky New Era,* May 24, 1920, 5.

White, E. B. "Here Is New York." *Holiday,* Apr. 1949.

Willens, Doris. "Adventures of a Negro Reporter." *Editor and Publisher,* Sept. 24, 1949, reprinted in *Negro Digest,* Dec. 1949, 13–15.

Woodward, C. Vann. "Made in USA." Review of *Truman,* by David McCullough. *New York Times Book Review,* July 16, 1992, 26–30.

INTERVIEWS

Artis, Bill. Telephone interview, July 16, 1987.

Arzt, George. Telephone interview, Aug. 15, 1987.

Bacon, Clara Emma. Personal interview, Feb. 7, 1984.

Baker, Jennie Knight. Personal interviews, Jan. 7, 8, 9, 10, 14, 15, 18, 19, 21, 1984, Jan. 18, 1985.

Banks, Ruth. Personal interviews, Aug. 22, 1983, June 29, 1984; telephone interviews, Oct. 23, 1983, July 17, 1991.

Barnett, Etta Moten. Interview with Ruth Edmonds Hill, Feb. 11, 1985. Black Women Oral History Project. Schlesinger Library, Radcliffe College.

Bates, Daisy. Telephone interview, Mar. 2, 1991.

Bourne, St. Clair T. Telephone interview, Dec. 5, 1990; personal interviews, Jan. 6, July 16, 22, 1993.

Brooks, Sarah. Telephone interview, May 16, 1984.

Clark, Kenneth B. Personal interview, July 18, 1984.

Clark, Rebecca Quarles. Personal interviews, Oct. 10, 1983, Mar. 24, Apr. 9, 1984.

Cumberbatch-Lavender, Georgianna. Personal interview, Oct. 14, 1983; telephone interview, July 7, 1991.

Cunningham, Evelyn. Personal interview, Aug. 8, 1992.

Daniels, Jonathan. Interview conducted by James R. Fuchs, 1964. Truman Library, Independence, Missouri.

Davis, Griffith J. Telephone interview, Apr. 22, 1987; personal interviews, Apr. 23, June 13, 1987.

Davis, Mike. Telephone interview, Aug. 4, 1992.

Delfiner, Rita. Telephone interview, Aug. 24, 1987.

Duncan, James, Jr. Personal interview, Feb. 11, 1985.

Duncan, James, III, and Doris Duncan. Personal interview, Feb. 11, 1985.

Eckman, Fern Marja. Personal interview, Oct. 13, 1984; telephone interview, Sept. 24, 1984.

Eckman, Irving. Personal interview, Oct. 13, 1984.

Elliot, Mollie Lee Moon. Telephone interview, Nov. 2, 1982.

Evers, Charles. Personal interview, Jan. 15, 1997.

Fowlkes, William. Telephone interview, Apr. 30, 1987.

Francis, Holly B. Personal interview, June 28, 1984.

Fraser, C. Gerald. Telephone interview, Mar. 20, 1982.

Galbraith, John Kenneth. *Sunday Morning*. CBS. WAGA, Atlanta. July 17, 1990.

Gratz, Roberta. Telephone interview, Oct. 7, 1990.

Hastie, William H. Interview by Jerry N. Hess, Jan. 5, 1972. Draft 1 in William H. Hastie Papers, Truman Library, Independence, Missouri.

Hicks, Nancy. Personal interview, June 4, 1984.

Hogan, Lawrence. Personal interview, Jan. 6, 1993.

Howard, Mrs. Harriet, Records clerk. Western State Hospital, Hopkinsville, Kentucky. Personal interview, Mar. 1984.

Jackson, Barbara Loomis. Telephone interviews, Aug. 25, 1983, Mar. 15, 1994.

Jackson, Esther Joiner. Personal interview, Feb. 2, 1985.

Jackson, Luther P., Jr. Telephone interviews, Oct. 15, 20, 1982.

Johnston, Ernie, Jr. Personal interviews, June 29, 1984, June 20, 1991.

Joiner, Philip. Personal interviews, Mar. 12, 1984, Feb. 2, 1985.

Joiner, Theodore Roosevelt "Rat." Personal interview, Oct. 8, 1983.

Kahn, Joe. Personal interview, July 5, 1984.

Kleinman, Larry. Telephone interview, Aug. 20, 1987.

Knight, Frances Wagner. Personal interviews, Feb. 15, 18, 28, Apr. 10, 1984.

Lasley, A. R. Personal interview, Oct. 10, 1983.

Leavell, Rozelle. Personal interview, July 3, 1983.

Ledford, Martha, Director, Pupil Personnel, Christian County Public Schools, Hopkinsville, Ky. Personal interview, Mar. 1984.

Lewis, Diana Bonnor. Personal interview, Dec. 29, 1984; telephone interviews, Sept. 16, Nov. 29, 1983.

Lewis, John. Personal interview, Feb. 26, 1993.

Lewis, Hylan. Personal interview, July 18, 1984.

Lewis, Thurston. Telephone interview, 1992.

Lynch, J. T. Personal interviews, Mar. 24, 29, 1984.

Major, Brooks. Personal interview, Feb. 22, 1984.

Mancini, Tony. Telephone interview, May 18, 1991.

McHarry, Elizabeth Poston. Telephone interview, Mar. 25, 1992.

Milne, Emile. Telephone interview, June 21, 1991.

Moon, Henry Lee. Interviews by Luther P. Jackson, Jr., Jan. 11, July 12, 1979; Jan. 16, 1980. Columbia University Oral History Project.

———. Personal interviews, July 15, Aug. 4, Sept. 16, 30, 1982, Aug. 14, Sept. 28, Nov. 28, 1983, June 29, 1984; telephone interviews, July 13, 1982, May 27, 1983.

Morrow, Ed. Telephone interviews, Feb. 6, May 7, 1993.

Moten, Lydia Braxton. Personal interview, July 3, 1983.

Nash, Edith Rosenfels. Telephone interview, Oct. 24, 1992.

Ohr, Nellie M. H. Personal interview, Jan. 17, 1992.

Palmer, Johnella Braxton. Personal interview, July 3, 1983.

Patton, Elizabeth Tarry. Personal interview, June 12, 1991.

Poston, Ersa H. Personal interview, July 5, 1983; telephone interviews, Mar. 3, 1985, May 1, Oct. 27, Nov. 16, 1991.

Poston, Ted. Interview by Robert D. Graff, Dec. 20, 1961. Small Collections, Papers of Robert D. Graff, ABC Producer. Transcripts of interviews with Ted Poston for the Roosevelt story, no. 519, take 2, and no. 521, take 1. Franklin D. Roosevelt Library, Hyde Park, New York.

———. Interview by Richard Kluger, July 22, 1971. Notes in Beinecke Rare Book and Manuscript Library, Yale University, New Haven, Connecticut.

Proctor, Margaret J. Telephone interview, Sept. 3, 1985.

Proctor, William H. Telephone interview, Feb. 3, 1991.

Quarles, Marcus. Telephone interview, July 9, 1983.

Reed, Eloise Scott. Telephone interview, Nov. 9, 1991.

Reed, Rosemary. Telephone interview, Nov. 5, 1991.

Sann, Paul. Telephone interview, Oct. 24, 1984.

Scott, C. A. Personal interview, Oct. 1994.

Scott, Lucile M. Telephone interview, Sept. 13, 1992; personal interview, Sept. 15, 1992.

Sitton, Claude. Telephone interview, Jan. 6, 1991.

Smothers, Ron. Personal interview, Nov. 15, 1990.

Smyth, Olga. Personal interview, May 11, 1992.

Stone, Deborah. Personal interview, May 11, 1992.

Tarry, Ellen. Personal Interview, June 12, 1991; telephone interviews, Mar. 9, 16, Oct. 5, 17, 1991.

Torian, Bernice Bell. Personal interview, July 3, 1983; telephone interview, Feb. 1, 1985.

Trent, William J. Telephone interview, July 12, 1991.

Trent, William J., and Viola Trent. Personal interview, Sept. 4, 1991.

Trow, George. Personal interview, Oct. 13, 1984.

Turner, William T. Personal interviews, Mar. 15, 19, 22, 1984.

Ward, Willis F. "The Reminiscences of Willis F. Ward." Interview by Owen Bombard, 1954. Ford Motor Company Archives, Detroit.

Weaver, Robert C. Personal interview, Aug. 18, 1986.

West, Dorothy. Interview by Genii Guinier, May 6, 1978. Black Women Oral History Project, Schlesinger Library, Radcliffe College.

———. Telephone interview, June 1, 1984.

Whitney, Francis Eugene. Personal interview, Feb. 15, 1984.

Williams, Allison. Personal interviews, July 3, Oct. 3, 8, 9, 10, 11, 12, 13, 14, 1983, Jan. 4, 7, 13, 14, 18, 19, 20, 24, Feb. 7, 18, Mar. 29, Apr. 27, May 1, July 3, Nov. 17, 25, 1984, Jan. 22, 1985; telephone interviews, Sept. 3, 10, 1983.

Wilson, Mary Duncan. Personal interviews, Oct. 9, 1983, Feb. 10, 11, 1985; telephone interviews, Sept. 10, 28, 1983, Jan. 29, 1985.

Wooldridge, Roberta. Personal interview, Apr. 21, 1984; telephone interview, Dec. 15, 1984.

LETTERS

Abram, Morris B. Letter to author. June 19, 1987.

Adams, Lea and Ruth. Letter to author, Feb. 26, 1992.

Arnold, Leonard. Memo to Ted Poston, Mar. 7, 1972, Box 57, Schiff Papers.

———. Memo to Dorothy Schiff, Mar. 8, 1972, Box 57, Schiff Papers.

Bacon, Clara Emma. Letters to author, Jan. 26, 1991, Jan. 22, 1992.

Baker, Jennie Knight. Letters to author, July 13, Aug. 24, 1984, Apr. 25, 1986, Aug. 6, 1991.

Bankhead, Senator John H., Alabama, Committee on Appropriations. Letter to Elmer Davis, Mar. 18, 1943. Record Group 208, Box 8, National Archives.

Banks, Ruth. Letters to author, Sept. 13, Oct. 17, Dec. 7, 1983, Jan. 2, Feb. 3, 21, Mar. 10, 15, Apr. 16, May 18, Aug. 5, 21, Sept. 15, 1984, Jan. 23, 31, Feb. 20, Apr. 2, 1985, Mar. 1, 10, 15, 23, 25, May 15, 1991.

———. Letters to Henry Lee Moon, Oct. 31, 1972, Oct. 28, 1973. Moon Papers.

Barnes, George A., Office of War Information. Memo to Milton S. Eisenhower, Sept. 28, 1942. Memo to Ted Poston, n.d. (ca. 1943), Record Group 208, Box 8, National Archives.

Barnett, Claude A. Letter to Alvin E. White, Feb. 20, 1942, Record Group 208, Box 40, National Archives.

———. Letters to T. R. Poston, Mar. 2, June 6, July 3, Aug. 3, 1932. "Russia (USSR), 1932–1964" file, Box 202, Folder 4, Claude Barnett Papers.

Bell, Ulric. Memo to Archibald MacLeish, Jan. 24, 1942, Record Group 208, Box 40, National Archives.

Berry, Theodore M., Liaison Officer, Group Morale. Letter to Crystal B. Fausett [*sic*], Office of Civilian Defense, Mar. 14, 1942, Record Group 208, Box 3, National Archives.

Bourne, St. Clair. Letters to author, May 6, July 5, 1991, July 16, 22, 1993.

Brennan, Edward J. Letter to Director, Bureau of Investigation, June 30, 1923, Marcus Garvey file, FBI, microfilm.

Cayce, Delbert D., III. Letters to author, June 7, 25, 1991.

Clark, Dowlsey, Chief, News Bureau. Memo to Louis Priscilla, Oct. 5, 1945, Record Group 208, Box 965, National Archives.

Clark, Kenneth B. Letter to Adriawa Evans, Apr. 17, 1972, copy in Hastie Papers.

———. Letter to Ford Foundation, Oct. 9, 1974, copy in Moon Papers.

———. Letter to William H. Hastie, June 13, 1972, Hastie Papers.

Connor, Rev. O. W. Letter to FDR, Feb. 13, 1943, Record Group 208, National Archives.

Conover, Mrs. Jerry H., Princeton University Alumni Office. Letters to author, Nov. 9, 1982, Oct. 11, 1983.

Costikyan, Edward. Letter to author, Feb. 21, 1991.

Cowley, Malcolm. Office for Emergency Management. Memo to Archibald Mac-Leish, Jan. 26, 1942, Record Group 208, Box 40, National Archives.

Davis, Elmer. Letter to Senator John H. Bankhead, Mar. 30, 1943, Letter to Senator Harry F. Byrd, June 30, 1943; Letter to Laurence Foster (drafted by TP), Oct. 27, 1943; Letter to Rev. John Haynes Holmes, May 1, 1943; Letter to Emory A. James, Principal, Booker T. Washington Junior High School, Indianapolis, Sept. 11, 1943, Record Group 208, Box 8, National Archives.

Dawkins, Maurice A. Letter to Henry Lee Moon, Apr. 1974; "An Ode to Ted Poston," enclosed in letter to HLM, Apr. 5, 1974, Moon Papers.

Dudar, Helen. Letters to author, June 6, 1987, May 1, 1994.

Duncan, James R., M.D. Letter to Sina Duncan, June 28, 1925, in possession of Mary Duncan Wilson.

Eckman, Fern Marja. Letters to author, Sept. 24, Oct. 31, Nov. 8, 1984, June 16, 1985, Apr. 10, 18, 1986, Feb. 20, 1988, Mar. 5, 18, May 7, July 11, Aug. 1, Oct. 22, 29, 1991.

Eisen, David J. Letters to author, Feb. 10, 1992, Jan. 28, 1994.

Embree, Edwin. Letter to William H. Hastie, July 1, 1930, Box 107-11, Hastie Papers.

Ephron, Nora. Letter to author, July 20, 1987.

Evans, Adriawa. Letter to Kenneth B. Clark, Apr. 6, 1972, Hastie Papers.

Fauset, Crystal B. Letter to Carrie Raymond Dodson, Oct. 16, 1941, Record Group 171, Box 27; Letter to Emma L. McCall, Oct. 15, 1941, Record Group 171, Box 35, National Archives.

Foster, Reginald, and Robert Huse. Memo to Elmer Davis, Sept. 12, 1942, Record Group 208, Box 8, National Archives.

Franklin, Charles L. Letter to Ted Poston, Sept. 27, 1945, Moon Papers.

Gavin, Lania Davis. Letter to Ted Poston, Jan. 17, 1943, Office of War Information Papers, National Archives.

Gay, Eustace. Letter to Ted Poston, May 26, 1943, Office of War Information Papers, National Archives.

Gillette, Jean. Memo to James Wechsler, Dec. 11, 1962, Box 6, Wechsler Papers.

Graves, Lem. Wire to Charles Ross, Mar. 13, 1949, Truman Library.

Griffin, Edna K. Letters to Ted Poston, Jan. 24, 1943, May 1, 7, 1943, Record Group 205, National Archives.

Hach, C. F. Letter to Senator Harry F. Byrd, June 19, 1943, Record Group 208, Box 8, National Archives.

Hardin, John A. Letters to author, Sept. 4, 1992, Sept. 4, 1997.

Hastie, William H. Letter to Judge Julian W. Mack, June 17, 1930, Box 107-11, Hastie Papers.

Herrick, R. G. Confidential memo to Ulric Bell, May 4, 1942, Record Group 208, Box 40, Entry 7, National Archives.

Hodges, W. C. Letter to Senator John H. Bankhead, Mar. 16, 1943, Record Group 208, Box 8, National Archives.

Hogan, Lawrence D. Letter to author, Sept. 5, 1990.

Holmes, John Haynes, Community Church of New York. Letters to Elmer Davis, Apr. 15, May 5, 1943, Record Group 208, Box 8, National Archives.

Hughes, Langston. Letter to Will Alexander, Jan. 31, 1942, Record Group 171, Box 17, National Archives.

———. Letter to Dorothy West, Dec. 5, 1933, West Papers.

———. Letters to Ted Poston, Sept. 20, 1961, July 2, 1964, Sept. 30, 1966, Mar. 9, 1967, Beinecke Rare Book and Manuscript Library, Yale University.

Hurston, Zora Neale. Letter to Dorothy West, Mar. 24, 1927, West Papers.

Huse, Robert. Memo to Gardner Cowles, Feb. 4, 1943, Record Group 208, Box 8, National Archives.

Jackson, Marie B. Letter to author, Sept. 27, 1983.

Jackson, Perry B. Letter to Ted Poston, May 21, 1943, Record Group 205, National Archives.

Johnson, Campbell C. Letter to Ted Poston, Sept. 27, 1945, Ted Poston Album, Manuscripts, Schomburg Center for Research in Black Culture, New York Public Library.

Johnson, Ernest E. Letter to Ted Poston, Sept. 27, 1945, Ted Poston Album, Manuscripts, Schomburg Center for Research in Black Culture.

Johnston, Ernie, Jr. Letters to author, July 25, 1984, Jan. 12, 1985.

Kempton, Murray. Letter to author, July 20, 1987.

Kluger, Richard. Letter to author, Aug. 20, 1990.

LaNier, Carlotta Walls. Letter to author, Mar. 1, 1994.

Laster, Dee. Letter to Robert A. Lewis, June 3, 1974, Moon Papers.

Lawrence, Jacob. Letter to author, June 22, 1987.

Lewis, Diana Bonnor. Letters to author, Sept. 9, 19, Nov. 29, Dec. 5, 1983, Jan. 21, 30, 1984, Feb. 2, 4, Mar. 4, Sept. 18, 1985, Jan. 18, 1987.

Lewis, Robert A. Letter to Arthur J. Harvey, Oct. 17, 1975, Moon Papers.

———. Letter to L. Bruce Hopewell, Jan. 15, 1976, Moon Papers.

———. Letter to Henry Lee Moon, June 10, 1974, Moon Papers.

Lewis, Thurston. Letter to author, Feb. 23, 1993.

Locke, Alain. Letters to Charlotte (Mrs. R. Osgood) Mason, June 17, 19, Aug. 11, 25, 1932, Locke Papers.

Lucas, Grant. Letter to Ted Poston, Sept. 27, 1945, Ted Poston Album, Manuscripts, Schomburg Center for Research in Black Culture.

Mack, Julian W. Letter to William H. Hastie, June 11, 1930, Box 107-11, Hastie Papers.

MacLeish, Archibald. Letter to Paul V. McNutt, Administrator, Federal Security

Agency, May 20, 1942; Letter to Richard Wright, Dec. 1941, Record Group 208, Box 3, National Archives.

Major, Brooks. Letters to author, Nov. 1984, June 11, 1991.

Mancini, Tony. Letter to author, Aug. 24, 1987.

Martin, Thelma J., Chief, Records Reconstruction Branch, National Personnel Records Center, Military Personnel Records, St. Louis, Missouri. Letter to author, Dec. 3, 1991.

Mason, Mrs. Rufus Osgood (Charlotte). Letter to Alain Locke, June 25, 1932, Locke Papers.

Maynard, Robert C. Letter to author, June 25, 1987.

McAfee, Larry B. Brig. Gen., Asst. to the Surgeon General. Memo for Lt. Col. C. J. Gridley, G-3, Jan. 30, 1942, copy in Hastie Papers.

McCall, Emma L. Letter to Eleanor Roosevelt, Oct. 8, 1941, Record Group 208, National Archives.

McGraw, B. T. Letter to Ted Poston, Sept. 27, 1945, Ted Poston Album, Manuscripts, Schomburg Center for Research in Black Culture.

McLean, Walter J. Letter to Ted Poston, May 21, 1943, Office of War Information Papers, National Archives.

McMillan, George E., Office for Emergency Management. Memo to Gardner Cowles, Jr., Feb. 27, 1943. Record Group 208, Box 3, National Archives.

Mitchell, Clarence M. Letter to Ted Poston, Sept. 27, 1945, Ted Poston Album, Manuscripts, Schomburg Center for Research in Black Culture.

Moon, Henry Lee. Draft of letter to National Endowment for the Humanities, Dec. 1, 1983; Letter to Ersa Hines Poston, Dec. 11, 1972; Letter to Roy Wilkins, July 30, 1959, Moon Papers.

———. Letter to author, Jan. 11, 1984.

———. Letter to Julian Steele, 1947, Special Collections, Boston University.

Moon, Henry Lee, Ted Poston, Philip Rahv, Harry Roskolenkier, et al. Letter "To the Workers on the Federal Writers Project," n.d., Moon Papers.

Moon, Mollie. Notes re: Ted Poston estate, to HLM, n.d., Moon Papers.

Murray, Pauli. Letter to Maysie Stone, July 3, 1978, in possession of Deborah Stone.

Nash, Philleo, Assistant to Deputy Director, Office of War Information. Memo to Jonathan Daniels, Administrative Assistant to the President, Aug. 19, 1943, Record Group 208, Box 8, National Archives.

———. Memo to "Mr. Connelly" for Truman, Dec. 5, 1952; Memo to William D. Hassett, Feb. 26, 1952, Truman Library.

———. Letter to Ted Poston, Sept. 27, 1945, Ted Poston Album, Manuscripts, Schomburg Center for Research in Black Culture.

Nunn, William G. Letter to Ted Poston, Jan. 21, 1943, Office of War Information Papers, National Archives.

O'Rourke, Sister Margaret M., Archivist, Sisters of the Blessed Sacrament. Letter to author, Oct. 25, 1991.

Poston, Ersa H. Letters to author, Apr. 21, May 4, Aug. 26, 1982, June 27, Aug. 30, Dec. 1, 1983, Mar. 1, Nov. 19, 1984, May 28, 1985, June 16, 1989, Dec. 31, 1990, Nov. 4, 1991, Feb. 25, 1994, Nov. 7, 1997.

———. Letter to Ted Poston, Jan. 15, no year [1973?], Moon Papers.

[Poston, Marie.] Note to Ted, n.d., Moon Papers.

Poston, T. R. Cable to Claude Barnett, June 3, 1932; Letters to Claude Barnett, Aug. 12, Sept. 21, n.d., 1932, "Russia (USSR), 1932–1964" file, Box 202, Folder 4, Barnett Papers.

———. Letter to Eustace Gay, Aug. 24, 1943, Office of War Information Papers, National Archives.

Poston, T. R., and Frank Crosswaith. Letter to Friends of the Newspaper Guild of New York, Oct. 11, 1935, Spingarn Papers.

Poston, Ted. Letter to "Garner," May 5, 1971, carbon in Moon Papers.

———. Memo to John Bott, Sept. 22, 1966, Box 57, Schiff Papers.

———. Memo to Dowsley Clark, Jan. 19, 1945, Record Group 208, Box 965, National Archives.

———. Letter to O. W. Connor, Mar. 19, 1943, Record Group 208, Box 8, National Archives.

———. Letters to Edna W. Griffin, Jan. 27, Mar. 15, 1943, Record Group 205, National Archives.

———. Letter to Langston Hughes, Nov. 14, 1957, Beinecke Rare Book and Manuscript Library, Yale University.

———. Letter to Emory A. James, Sept. 11, 1943, Record Group 208, Box 8, National Archives.

———. Letter to Ira Lewis, Jan. 2, 1943, Record Group 208, Box 8, National Archives.

———. Letter to E. L. McKinstry, Mar. 18, 1943, Record Group 205, National Archives.

———. Letter to Walter J. McLean, Mar. 31, 1943, Office of War Information Papers, National Archives.

———. Letters to Philleo Nash, Mar. 1, 1949, Feb. 19, 1952, Truman Library.

———. Letter to William G. Nunn, Jan. 27, 1943, Record Group 208, National Archives.

———. Letter to Francis J. Price, May 11, 1943, Record Group 208, National Archives.

———. Letter to E. P. Thompson, Dec. 27, 1943, Office of War Information Papers, Record Group 205, National Archives.

———. Letter to J. Waties Waring, Apr. 13, 1950, Waring Papers.

———. Memos to Herbert Plummer, Jan. 27, Feb. 10, 17, 24, Mar. 10, 31, Apr. 21, 28, May 12, 26, 1945, Record Group 208, Box 965, National Archives.

———. Memos to Paul Sann. July 3, 17, 1962, May 18, 1964, Box 6, Wechsler Papers.

———. Memos to James A. Wechsler, Mar. 25, 1995, May 27, Sept. 9, Nov. 20, 1958, July 24, 25, 1959, Mar. 7 [no year], Box 6, Wechsler Papers.

———. Letter to War Production Board, Apr. 13, 1942, FBI, Record Group 208, National Archives.

———. Letter to Luther R. White, Apr. 20, 1943, Office of War Information Papers, National Archives.

Poston, Theodore R. Letter to Robert A. Hubbard, Harrisburg, Pennsylvania, Aug. 14, 1944, Record Group 208, Box 972, National Archives.

———. Memo to Merle Colby, Mar. 22, 1945, Record Group 208, Box 965, National Archives.

Prattis, Percival L. Letters to Claude Barnett. Oct. 18, 1935, Jan. 7, 1936, "P. L. Prattis, 1924–1936" file, Box 138, folder 9, Barnett Papers.

———. Letters to Ted Poston, Apr. 14, 27, 1943, Office of War Information Papers, National Archives.

Proctor, Margaret. Letter to Francis J. Price, May 18, 1943; Letter to Perry B. Jackson, May 21, 1943, Record Group 205, National Archives.

Reed, Rosemary. Note to author, Aug. 16, 1994.

Rothman, Marcy Elias. Letters to author, Nov. 17, 27, 1984.

Salinger, Pierre. Letter to author, Sept. 1, 1987.

Sann, Paul. Memo to Blair Clark, Oct. 13, 1965, Box 57, Schiff Papers.

Shepard, Marshall L. Letter to Ted Poston, Sept. 27, 1945, Ted Poston Album, Manuscripts, Schomburg Center for Research in Black Culture.

Shikes, Ralph E. Memo to James Allen, Deputy, Mar. 20, 1943, Record Group 208, Box 8, National Archives.

Siepmann, Charles A. Memo to W. B. Lewis, Aug. 6, 1942, Record Group 208, Box 8, National Archives.

Smith, Alfred Edgar. Letter to Ted Poston, Sept. 27, 1945, Ted Poston Album, Manuscripts, Schomburg Center for Research in Black Culture.

Starr, Milton. Memo to George Barnes, Jan. 22, 1943, Record Group 208, Box 8, National Archives.

———. Memo to Ulric Bell, Office for Emergency Management, Executive Office of the President, Feb. 12, 1942, Record Group 208, Box 40, National Archives.

Stevens, Justice Harold A., Supreme Court of State of New York. Letter to James Wechsler, Aug. 15, 1955, Box 6, Wechsler Papers.

Stone, Deborah. Letter to author, Feb. 23, 1992.

Tallmer, Jerry. Letter to author, Sept. 3, 1987.

Talmadge, H. E. Letter to author, Mar. 4, 1991.

Tarry, Ellen. Letter to author, Mar. 4, 1991.

Thackrey, Ted O. Confidential memo to Paul A. Tierney, Aug. 24, 1945, Box 82, Schiff Papers.

Thompson, E. P. Letter to Ted Poston, Nov. 24, 1943, Record Group 205, National Archives.

Tierney, Paul A. Letter to Ted O. Thackrey, Aug. 20, 1945, Box 82, Schiff Papers.

Trent, W. J. Invitation to Dinner for Robert C. Weaver, on United Negro College Fund letterhead, Jan. 14, 1961, Moon Papers.

———. Letter to author, Oct. 15, 1984.

———. Letter to Ted Poston, Sept. 27, 1945, Ted Poston Album, Manuscripts, Schomburg Center for Research in Black Culture.

Truman, Harry S. Letters to Ted and Marie Poston, Nov. 5, 1948, Dec. 16, 1952, Truman Library.

Turner, William T. Letter to author, Nov. 20, 1991.

Vann, Jessie. Letter to Ted Poston, Oct. 19, 1943, Record Group 205, National Archives.

Wagner, Willie. Letters to author, Nov. 24, Dec. 7, 1984.

Waring, Elizabeth Avery. Letter to Ted Poston, Oct. 18, 1950, Waring Papers.

Waring, J. Waties. Letters to Ted Poston, Apr. 4, Oct. 12, Nov. 20, 1950, Waring Papers.

Warren, J. Hugo. Letter to Ted Poston, Sept. 27, 1945, Ted Poston Album, Manuscripts, Schomburg Center for Research in Black Culture.

Weaver, George L-P. Letter to Ted Poston, Sept. 27, 1945, Ted Poston Album, Manuscripts, Schomburg Center for Research in Black Culture.

Weaver, Robert C., Chief, Negro Employment and Training Branch, War Production Board. Letter to Archibald MacLeish, Director, Office of Facts and Figures, Mar. 12, 1942, Record Group 208, Box 3, National Archives.

Weaver, Robert C., and Ernie Johnston, Jr. Memo to "Very Good Friends of Ted Poston," n.d. [1972], Box 6, Wechsler Papers.

Wechsler, James A. Memo to Don Hollenbeck, CBS, Dec. 19, 1949; Memo to Mrs. Schiff, Dec. 11, 1963; Telegram to Ted Poston, Sept. 2, 1949, Box 6, Wechsler Papers.

Wechsler, Nancy F. Letter to author, Nov. 9, 1990.

West, Dorothy. Letter to Grace and Marie Turner, July 13, 1932, West Papers.

White, Luther R. Letter to Ted Poston, Office of War Information, Apr. 9, 1943, Office of War Information Papers, National Archives.

White, Walter, NAACP. Letters to Elmer Davis, Director, Office of War Information, Dec. 8, 1942, Jan. 15, Feb. 2, 1943, Record Group 208, Box 8, National Archives.

Wilkins, Roy. Letter to Henry Lee Moon, July 23, 1959; Memorandum to Henry Lee Moon, July 20, 1951, Moon Papers.

Wilkinson, G. C. Letter to Crystal Byrd Faucett [*sic*], Mar. 10, 1942, Record Group 171, Box 23, National Archives.

Williams, Allison. Letters to author, July 3, 1983, to Feb. 11, 1985.

Wilson, Mary Duncan. Letters to author, Sept. 28, Oct. 14, 24, Dec. 15, 1983, Jan. 12, Feb. 15, Apr. 30, 1985.

Winsten, Archer. Letters to author, June 26, July 8, 22, 1987.

Wright, Richard. Letter to Archibald MacLeish, Office of Facts and Figures, Dec. 21, 1941, Record Group 208, Box 40, National Archives.

Zobrist, Benedict, Director, Truman Library. Letter to author, Aug. 25, 1987.

DOCUMENTS

Against the Odds. Documentary [Augusta Savage]. Prod. Nila Arnow. Dir. Amber Edwards. PBS. WPBA, Atlanta. Feb. 16, 1994.

Bartlett, O. H., FBI Agent, Nashville and Hopkinsville. Report on Theodore R. Poston, Dec. 30, 1940, File No. 77-102.

Bates, Daisy. Biography. State Historical Society of Wisconsin.

Berry, Theodore M. "Blue Print of Program for Strengthening Negro Morale in War Effort." Mar. 15, [1942?]. Record Group 208, Box 40, National Archives.

———. "Proposed Organization Chart of Division Relating to Negro Activities in OWI." June 23, 1942, Record Group 208, Box 8, National Archives.

———. "War Information and Social Planning." July 20, 1942, Record Group 208, Box 6, National Archives.

Braxton, John and Fannie, to Ephraim Poston. Property on Hayes St. Register of Deeds. Deed Book 137, p. 432. Christian County Court, Hopkinsville, Kentucky.

Cox, Joseph, and Hettie Pea. Marriage Bonds: Negroes and Mulattoes, Book No. 6, Aug. 1873 to Dec. 1874. Hopkinsville, Christian County, Kentucky.

Deaths and Fetal Deaths Reported in 1955. City of New York.

Deaths and Stillbirths Reported in 1951. City of New York.

Dunne, W. D., FBI Agent. Special Inquiry, Advisory Committee to the Council of National Defense. Jan. 8, 1941.

Elledge, F. R., FBI Special Agent, Pittsburgh. Report on T. R. Poston. Apr. 22, 1941.

Fauset, Crystal Bird. Autobiography, typescript. Moorland-Spingarn.

———. Employment Record of former federal employee. Office of Personnel Management, St. Louis, Missouri.

FBI Report 77-1244 on Theodore R. Poston. Jan. 31, 1942.

Foster to Barnes, Deed Book 157, p. 376, Christian County Court, Hopkinsville, Kentucky.

Goebbels, Paul Joseph. Statement, ca. 1942. Record Group 208, Box 40, National Archives.

Gunn, John A. and Annie, conveyed to E. and Mollie Poston, property on South side of Hayes St. 1 Jan. 1902. Register of Deeds. Deed Book 108, pp. 1, 2. Christian County Court, Hopkinsville, Kentucky.

Hamlett, Barksdale, LL.D. *Biennial Report of the Superintendent of Public Instruction of Kentucky for the Two Years ending June 30, 1915.* Frankfort: State Journal, 1915. Kentucky Department for Libraries and Archives, Frankfort.

Harris, Sam. Certificate of Death, No. 31915. By execution. Commonwealth of Kentucky. Filed Dec. 17, 1926.

Jones, J. R., FBI Agent. Theodore R. Poston FBI File. Mar. 22, 1941.

Jones, Thomas H. "Christian Co., Ky., 1850 Federal Census." Hopkinsville: Christian County Genealogical Society, 1968.

Jordan, Vernon. "A Parting Word for Mrs. Mary Duncan Wilson." Eulogy. Jan. 12, 1991.

Kehres, R. E., FBI agent, New York City. Report on T. R. Poston. May 22, 1941.

Kennan, George. Speech at Brown University, Providence, Rhode Island, Nov. 18, 1983.

Kentucky. State Board of Charities and Corrections. *Report of the State Board of Charities and Corrections of the Commonwealth of Kentucky for the Biennial Period Ending June 30, 1925.*

Kentucky Superintendent of Public Instruction. *Biennial Report of the Superintendent of Public Instruction, July 1, 1905 to June 30, 1907.* Louisville: Globe, 1907.

Lovett, Bobby L. "Leaders of Afro-American Nashville. Roger Williams University." Nashville: Conference on Afro-American Culture and History, 1984.

Marriage Certificates, Colored, 1873. Christian County Court, Hopkinsville, Kentucky.

McKee, S. R., FBI Special Agent. Report on T. R. Poston. Oct. 15, 1941.

Moon, Henry Lee. "Autobiography, 23 March 1914." Moon Papers.

———. "New York Times." Portion of memoir, typescript. Moon Papers.

———. Report to the Ford Foundation, Section I, "Inside the NAACP, Beginning of the End." Moon Papers.

———. "Tuskegee Revisited," typescript. Moon Papers.

"Negro Press." N.d. Record Group 208, Box 40, National Archives.

New Deal Agencies and Black America. Microfilm A482. Pusey Library, Harvard University.

Obsequies for Theodore "Rat" Joiner. Dec. 11, 1984. First Street Baptist Church, Hopkinsville, Kentucky.

Office of War Information. Release. "Justice Department." Feb. 12, 1943, Record Group 208, Box 52, National Archives.

Party for Ted Poston by His Many Friends. Invitation. Box 6, Wechsler Papers.

Perrin, C. E., FBI Special Agent. Report on T. R. Poston. Apr. 11, 1941.

Polk's New York City Directory—Boroughs of Manhattan and the Bronx, 1933–34. New York: R. L. Polk.

Poston, Ephraim, and Mollie Cox. Christian Co. Marriage Bonds and Licenses, Book 10, p. 364, December 22, 1887. Christian County Court, Kentucky.

Poston, Ephraim, Jr., age 22, of sarcoma on the neck. Bureau of Vital Statistics, Commonwealth of Kentucky. Mar. 22, 1914.

Poston, Lillian, age 24, of pulmonary tuberculosis. Death Certificate No. 22289. Bureau of Vital Statistics, Commonwealth of Kentucky. Oct. 12, 1927.

———. Hopkinsville Colored School Census Records. Christian County Board of Education, Hopkinsville, Kentucky.

Poston, Mollie, age 43, of acute nephritis. Death Certificate No. 13362, June 2, 1917. Bureau of Vital Statistics, Commonwealth of Kentucky.

Poston, Robert L., 3,104,018. World War Historical Record, Kentucky Council of Defense. National Personnel Records Center, Military Records, St. Louis, Missouri.

Poston, Robert, and Augusta Savage. Marriage Certificate 36790, 1923. City of New

York, State of New York, NYC Dept. of Records and Information Services, Municipal Archives.

Poston, Roberta, age 20, of acute peritonitis. Death Certificate, File No. 12966. Bureau of Vital Statistics, Commonwealth of Kentucky. Apr. 15, 1919.

Poston, Ted. "Interracial Reporting." Speech. Oct. 16, 1968. Cassette audiotape by Luther P. Jackson, Jr.

————. Will. Dec. 13, 1973. Kings County Surrogate Court, Brooklyn, New York.

Poston, Theodore R. Civilian Personnel Records. National Personnel Records Center, St. Louis, Missouri.

————. News Bureau, Office of War Information. Speech Receipt and Clearance Record. Feb. 23, 1944. Celebration of National Negro Newspaper Week, Station WINX, Washington, D.C. Feb. 25, 1944, 8:05 P.M. Record Group 208, Box 52, National Archives.

Poston, Theodore R., and Miriam Rivers. Marriage License. Nov. 13, 1935. Department of Records and Information Services, Municipal Archives, New York City.

Poston, Ulysses S., 3,104,058. World War Historical Record. Kentucky Council of Defense. National Personnel Records Center, Military Records. National Archives and Records Administration, St. Louis, Missouri.

————. Death Certificate no. 9715, 5/14/55. Brooklyn. Deaths and Fetal Deaths Reported in the City of New York, 1955.

"Presidential Appointments File." Truman Library.

Radford, Hettie Cox. Death Certificate. Department of Vital Statistics, State of Kentucky.

Report of C. E. Russell, President of the School, 1912: 669. Kentucky Department of Libraries and Archives.

Speed Defense Production: Open the Gates! Pamphlet. National Urban League. N.d. Record Group 171, Box 17, National Archives.

State of Tennessee. *Annual Report of the Department of Education for the Scholastic Year Ending June 30, 1929.* Nashville: Department of Education, 1929.

Stone, Maysie. *Bust of Ted Poston.* Artifacts, Schomburg Center, New York Public Library.

"Strange Fruit," by Louis Allen, sung by Billie Holiday. *Jazz at the Philharmonic.* Verve VE-2-2504, 1976.

The Summer Program for Minority Journalists. Graduate School of Journalism, University of California, Berkeley, 1987.

To the Workers on the Federal Writers' Project. N.d. Moon Papers.

Tokyo Radio. N.d. [Apr. 16, 1943?]. Record Group 208, Box 40, National Archives.

Tucker, Joseph J. [F]BI Report on Universal Negro Improvement Association. Mar. 15, 1924.

Tunks, F. F. Deed Book 76. Christian County Court, Hopkinsville, Kentucky.

U.S. Census. Christian County, Kentucky. 1900.

————. Clarksville, Montgomery County, Tennessee. 1860.

————. *1860 Census—Tennessee, McKeehan, Sexton.* Vol. 4, p. 268.

————. *1900 Census—Kentucky, Christian County, Hopkinsville.* Sheet B, no. 8, Ward 5, 0723, Twelfth Census of the United States, Supervisor's District no. 2, Enumeration District no. 3; Magisterial District no. 1.

————. Thirteenth Census of the United States, 1910. City of Hopkinsville, File P-235, T-266-129, Drawer 518, Kentucky State Archives, Frankfort.

U.S. FBI. Negro Radical Activities in New York: U.S. vs. Marcus Garvey. Jan. 23, 1923, File R-218-E, Mar. 1, 8, Apr. 5, 1923.

U.S. Senate. Subcommittee of the Committee on Territories and Insular Affairs. *Hearings on the Nomination of William H. Hastie for Appointment as Governor of the Virgin Islands.* Apr. 1, 1946. Washington: Ward and Paul, 1946. Hastie Papers.

————. Work Projects Administration File. Agent J. R. Jones. Mar. 22, 1941, 12.

Waring, J. Waties. "Reminiscences." 1972. Columbia University Oral History Project.

Weaver, Robert C. "Eulogy for Theodore R. Poston." Benta's Funeral Home, New York, New York. Jan. 14, 1974. Moon Papers.

Wilson, Reginald. "Ancestor Interview with Theodore Roosevelt Joiner." Hopkinsville Community College, Kentucky. Spring 1984.

Wright, N. B., FBI Agent, New York City. Report on Theodore R. Poston, Special Inquiry for Advisory Commission to Council of National Defense. Nov. 14, 1940.

Index